D1274007

A HUMANIST'S "TREW IMITATION": THOMAS WATSON'S *ABSALOM*

A Critical Edition and Translation

A HUMANIST'S "TREW IMITATION": THOMAS WATSON'S *ABSALOM*

A Critical Edition and Translation

JOHN HAZEL SMITH

ILLINOIS STUDIES IN LANGUAGE AND LITERATURE

52

UNIVERSITY OF ILLINOIS PRESS, URBANA, 1964

 Manufactured in the United States of America. Library of Congress Catalog Card No. 63-17049.

For Mary Jean

ACKNOWLEDGMENTS

I cannot hope to acknowledge all the assistance which I received during the several years which I devoted to this work, but my indebtedness to some people is so profound that they must be named. My parents were a source of continuous encouragement. The Frederick M. Roa Fund under its executor, A. C. Boeker, President of the Edwardsville, Illinois, National Bank and Trust Company, was more than generous in its support. Besides undertaking the publication of this work, the University of Illinois provided me with teachers and with financial assistance of various kinds, including a Non-Resident Fellowship under which I spent the year 1956-57 in England.

Professor T. W. Baldwin was the director of the work in its original form as a doctoral dissertation. There still are giants in the earth. His inspiration, his friendship, and his scholarship have permeated these pages so completely that to credit him with specific contributions would belittle the magnitude of his influence. I must also mention the kind encouragement and assistance rendered by Professors G. Blakemore Evans, Roland M. Smith, and Burton A. Milligan. Professor Leicester Bradner, who read this work in one stage of its development, disabused me of a number of errors in text, translation, and commentary and suggested several improvements in organization: his learning makes me very humble. Finally, Professor Robert H. Ball receives my thanks for several helpful criticisms. Whatever faults exist in this work are my own; if there are any merits in it, I must share the responsibility for them with these fine scholars.

Librarians have been my constant benefactors. I must mention especially Eva Faye Benton and Isabelle Grant, of the University of Illinois Library, whose generous helpfulness to me extended over many years. I do not name the knowledgeable librarians in the British Museum only because I do not know their names, for they were ever eager to assist me. For help with particular problems I am grateful to Clare Talbot, Archivist of Hatfield House, Herts., England, and to J. Conway Davies, Reader at The Prior's Kitchen, The College, University of Durham.

For permission to publish editions or photographs of manuscripts in their possession I am grateful to the Trustees of the British Museum (the *Absalom* manuscript), to The Most Honourable The Marquis of Salisbury (Watson's letter to William Cecil, Lord Burghley), and to the authorities of the University of Durham (Watson's Durham voucher). I am grateful to these sources and to the following for making available to me microfilms and books needed for my research: the University of Zurich, the University of Illinois, the University of Cincinnati, Wayne State University, and Marquette University.

I must acknowledge the careful efforts of Mrs. Elizabeth G. Dulany, Assistant Editor of the University Press. She made sense out of a very difficult manuscript.

Whatever I might say in gratitude to my wife would be grossly inadequate, for my debt to her is largest. I shall say nothing, therefore, but she knows what I shall always think.

CONTENTS

INTRODUCTION 1

Chapter One

THE MANUSCRIPT 3

Chapter Two

THE AUTHOR 12

Chapter Three

THE DATE OF THE PLAY 31

Chapter Four

THE "IMITATION" OF SOURCE ACCORDING TO CLASSICAL PRECEPTS AND EXAMPLES 41

Chapter Five

THE METHOD OF THIS EDITION 82

ABSALOM: LATIN TEXT AND TRANSLATION 87

APPENDICES 271

LIST OF WORKS USED 283

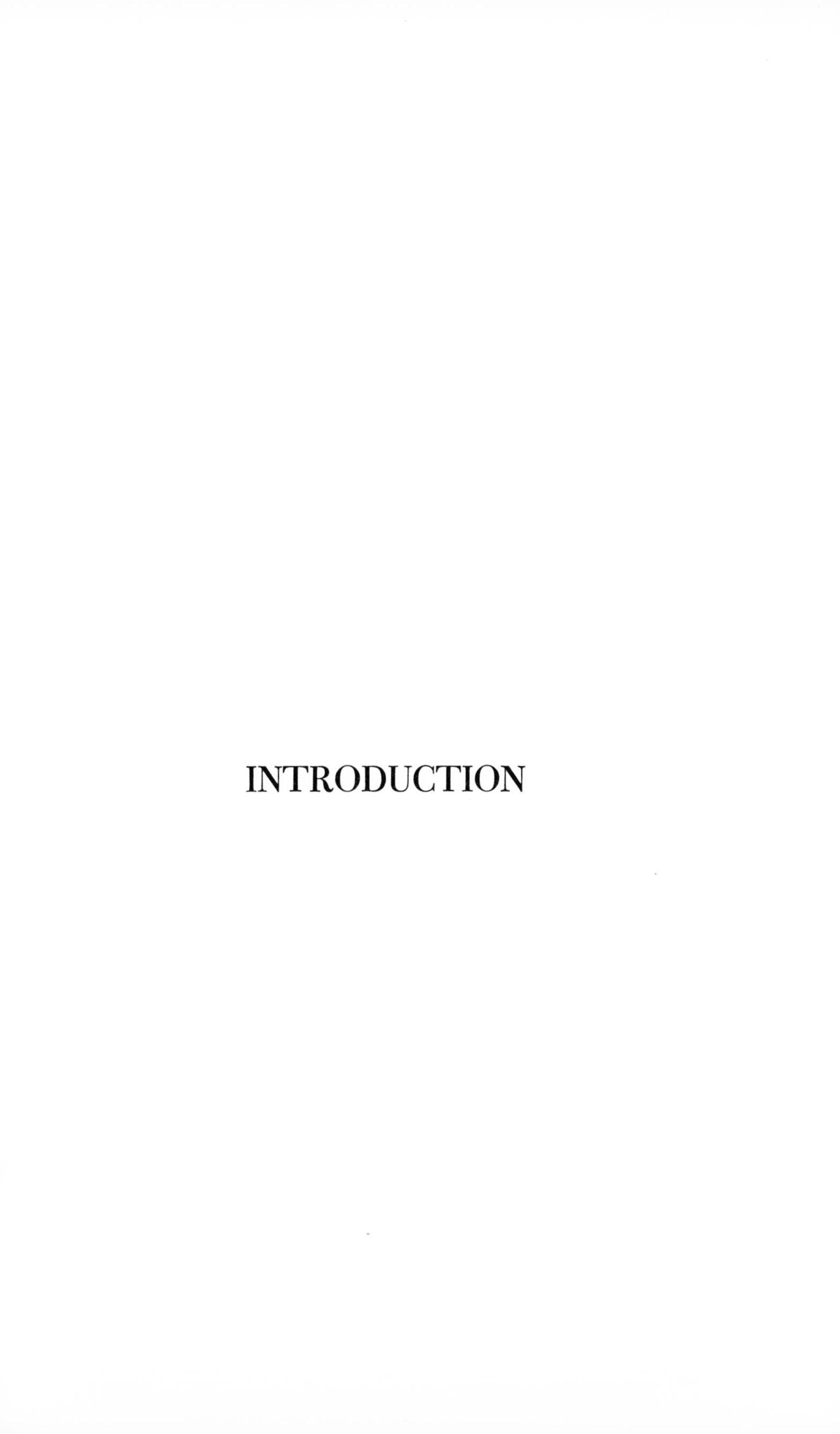

INTRODUCTION

CHAPTER ONE

THE MANUSCRIPT

PHYSICAL DESCRIPTION

Absalom occupies the whole of Stowe MS. 957 in the British Museum; no other copy is known. The scores of textual changes in the manuscript, most of them revisions rather than scribal corrections and all in the original hand, prove that it is a holograph. There was probably an earlier draft, for there are several indications of recopying. For example, at the ends of I.3.1, IV.2.148, IV.3.88, and especially II.3.84 (among other places) occur canceled readings identical with the ends of lines immediately following; some of these probably occurred because the author's eye dropped to a later line as he copied the play.

The leaves of the manuscript now measure approximately 7¾ inches high by 5½ inches wide. They have been trimmed, apparently on all four sides, for binding, and on a few pages the very tips of some long letters and small portions of the watermarks have been cut off. That the manuscript is a quarto is evident from the position and number of its watermarks. Part or all of eight specimens of the same watermark are found; that is, one for each of the eight sheets which would make up a thirty-leaf quarto. Furthermore, each watermark is divided between two leaves at the spine of the book, the tops and bottoms of the watermarks pointing toward the outer margin; this is the normal position in quarto folding. Apparently, however, the sheets were cut into single leaves before the manuscript was written. As nearly as I can determine, the watermarks are divided between leaves 5 and 8, 6 and 7, 11 and 18, 12 and 17, 19 and 20, and 25 and 26; in addition, the upper portions only of two watermarks are seen on leaves 27 and 28. Thus, the two halves of individual watermarks are not on contiguous leaves, as they would be if the manuscript had been written on folded but uncut sheets.

The volume has a modern Russia leather binding, but it must have remained unbound for a considerable time, for the leaves show evidence of exposure. The first few leaves are rather badly frayed, though the text is unimpaired. The last leaf is slightly torn at the top of the spine, and about half of its blank verso is badly soiled. Further indication of exposure is the heavy staining of many leaves, mostly along the outer edges; perhaps because of this exposure the pages are quite flimsy. Fol. 11 has had a piece torn from its outer edge and skillfully repaired. Two or three minute worm holes extend through the first few leaves.

The binder inserted protective sheets at the beginning and end of the volume and also interleaved such sheets. On one of the initial sheets are the words "Press 2 N° 103" in ink; this was the shelfmark of the book when it was a part of the Stowe library. On another initial sheet is the penciled note "Russia," describing or prescribing the binding. The first recto of the manuscript, originally blank, contains two modern notations: one, inked in an early nineteenth-century hand, reads "Press 2. N°. 103"; the other, penciled in a cursive, possibly late nineteenth-century hand,[1] reads "David and Absalom./ by Johan Bale." The first and each succeeding recto is numbered (1-30) in pencil in the upper right-hand corner. On the manuscript itself are no other markings except those made by the author. On one of the protective leaves at the end of the volume is the penciled note "30. Folios Oct 1890. TR." Beneath it, in a different hand, is penciled "Exam[d] G.C.T."

The text of the play begins — with no further preliminary than a scene heading, the names of the speakers in the first scene, and identification of the meter — on the first verso. It continues without a break through a small part of the recto of fol. 30. The hand is a small sixteenth-century pure secretary which, except for the revisions and a few hastily written words, is quite neat. In addition to his revisions, the author made many critical markings in the margins, indicating commonplaces, metrically exceptional lines, line numberings, and the like. On the first five pages the author averaged about fifteen verses per page; near the top of the fourth recto he began to economize on space and for the remainder of the play averaged more than forty verses per page. Shortly thereafter he began checking off the number

[1] E. K. Chambers thought the hand was of the eighteenth century (*The Mediaeval Stage* [Oxford, 1903], II, 458). The British Museum *Catalogue of the Stowe Manuscripts in the British Museum* (London, 1895), I, 639, described the note on fol. 1*r* only as "a modern note," perhaps indicating that it was there before the museum purchased the book.

of lines per page with small marginal scorings; soon he was numbering the lines per act rather than per page.

As indicated above, the manuscript contains thirty leaves, all but the first recto and the final verso containing text; it had the same number when T. R. examined the book in October, 1890. But the earliest known cataloguer of the manuscript, Dr. Charles O'Conor, expressly stated in 1818 that the "written pages of this MS. are 62."[2] Dr. O'Conor may have miscounted, or he may have assumed that he had a full eight sheets (sixty-four quarto pages, two being blank). But if Dr. O'Conor merely counted the leaves — including the blank sides — and multiplied by two to get sixty-two pages, then there was in 1818 one more leaf than there is now. And if he actually counted the "written pages" as sixty-two, then the fifty-eight "written pages" now surviving represent a loss of two leaves since 1818. Nothing, however, is missing from the body of the play.

HISTORY OF THE MANUSCRIPT

The earliest reference which I have found to the *Absalom* manuscript is that of Dr. Charles O'Conor, librarian of the collection of the second Marquis of Buckingham at Stowe. In 1818 he listed the manuscript among his charges as follows:

> "David and Absalom." — *quarto, paper.* The written pages of this MS. are 62. The author was Bale. The handwriting appears to be original, and is certainly of that age. It is a Tragedy, in five acts. . . . A list of Bale's Comedies, Tragedies, and other works, may be seen in Kippis's Biographia, in which the Tragedy now before [us] is not mentioned. He gives a catalogue of his own works in his Catalogus Scriptorum . . . where it is omitted in like manner [I, 386-387].

The subsequent history of the manuscript is of course that of the Stowe collection, which can be traced in several other sources.[3] We may note here only the highlights of its movements. The collection, with

[2] *Bibliotheca MS. Stowensis. A Descriptive Catalogue of the Manuscripts in the Stowe Library* (Buckingham, 1818-19), I, 386.

[3] See the B.M. *Catalogue of the Stowe Manuscripts,* I. For information about the various owners and sales see *The Athenaeum,* No. 1120 (April 14, 1849), pp. 380-381; No. 1121 (April 21, 1849), pp. 407-408; No. 1122 (April 28, 1849), p. 437; No. 1123 (May 5, 1849), p. 463; Bernard Quaritch *et al.,* eds., *Contributions Towards a Dictionary of English Book-Collectors,* Part VII (London, 1895), p. 1; Part X (London, 1897), p. 1; [Edward A. Bond], *Description of the Ashburnham Manuscripts, and Account of Offers of Purchase* [London, 1883], p. 5; Seymour DeRicci, *English Collectors of Books and Manuscripts (1530-1930) and Their Marks of Ownership* (Cambridge, 1930); and standard biographical sources such as *D.N.B.* and *The Complete Peerage.*

Absalom a probably inconspicuous member, remained at Stowe until 1849 under the careful watch (one commentator called it "jealous seclusion"[4]) of O'Conor and his successor, William J. Smith. Because of the profligacy of the Buckinghams, the collection, along with all the other possessions of the family, was scheduled for a forced public auction; instead, the manuscripts were sold to Bertram, fourth Earl of Ashburnham, though it appeared for a time that the British Museum would obtain them. When the fifth Earl succeeded to his father's title and possessions in 1878, he immediately began negotiations for the sale of the collection to the British Museum — a sale which was finally consummated in July, 1883. The trustees of the museum split the collection and took some time to process it; as we have seen, *Absalom* was apparently completely processed by the time T. R. counted the folios and G. C. T. examined the book in October, 1890.

During this period, the *Absalom* manuscript had been listed in three more library catalogues, but all the listings were closely related to O'Conor's.[5] All ascribe "David and Absalom" to John Bale, and two say that the manuscript contained sixty-two "written pages." The British Museum catalogue listing of 1895 was the first to avoid the influence of Dr. O'Conor: it seems to imply greater doubt of Bale's authorship than did O'Conor, and it gives the first correct count (as of now) of the number of leaves:

> David and Absalom. A *Latin* tragedy, in five acts, written in iambic trimeters and various choric meters. The characters are Joab, Absalom, Ahitophel, Messenger, David, Abishai, Cushai, Zadok, Abiathar, Watchman, and Ahimaaz. A modern note on the first page attributes it to John Bale, Bishop of Ossory [1495-1563]; but it is not included in his own list of his works, nor in any other list, and it appears never to have been printed. From the numerous corrections it is apparently in the author's autograph.
> Paper; ff. 30. XVIth cent. Octavo. [I, 639-640]

There are at least two errors in the description: the list of characters (several of whose names are spelled differently from the manuscript spellings) fails to distinguish two personages in Chusai and Chusi; and

[4] *The Athenaeum,* No. 1121 (April 21, 1849), p. 407.

[5] [William James Smith], *Catalogue of the Important Collection of Manuscripts, from Stowe* [London, 1849], p. 153, listed "David and Absalom" under the lot number, S. 665, under which it would have been auctioned; Smith confessed his obligation to O'Conor's catalogue. The *Catalogue of the Manuscripts at Ashburnham Place* (London, 1853), sig. [E2]*r*, which gave an alphabetical tabular listing, used for "David and Absalom" the lot number from Smith's sale catalogue. The *Eighth Report of the Royal Commission on Historical Manuscripts* (London, 1881), Appendix (Part III), p. 30, listed "David and Absalom" as No. 16 of a very small group of "Miscellaneous MSS.; Old English Poetry, &c." in the Ashburnham library.

the manuscript is wrongly described as an octavo (perhaps because the word "Press" on fol. 1*r* looks a little like "8voss").

The earlier history of the *Absalom* manuscript is shrouded from us, and the nature of the manuscript contributes to the darkness. It is something of a misfit in the Stowe collection, which is comprised mainly of religious, historical, or antiquarian items. As the collection is now classified, there are only forty-four manuscripts in the class "Poetry, and Prose Drama," to which the verse *Absalom* loosely belongs; *Absalom* is the only Latin work in the class; and it is one of only three plays in the group, the other two being from the seventeenth and eighteenth centuries. Thus why, when, or how the *Absalom* manuscript came into the Stowe collection may be only conjectured. The collection as such dates from 1804, when the first Marquis of Buckingham bought it from the estate of Thomas Astle, famous antiquary. Both the first Marquis (who died in 1813) and the second were eager spenders on art and literature, and both added to their library, "at various times, several collections, and single volumes of considerable value" (Smith, *Catalogue,* p. v). One of them could have picked up *Absalom* sometime between 1804 and 1818, although I doubt that they would have bought it as a deliberate single purchase. Or it could have come into Stowe along with the Astle collection; if so, there is no way of knowing where Astle got it.[6] I have found no mention of the manuscript in any of a number of sales catalogues which I have examined (see List of Works Used, s.v. "Catalogues").

One basis for conjecture about the early history of the *Absalom* manuscript exists in the tradition that a Latin tragedy called *Absalon* was once in the possession of the Sidney family at Penshurst Place, Kent. James O. Halliwell in the mid–nineteenth century referred to two supposedly distinct *Absalom* plays. One is obviously the play before us now, and the wording is as obviously based ultimately upon Dr. O'Conor's catalogue description:

[6] Astle's close association with John Brand (1744-1806) presents an intriguing possibility. Brand gave to Astle MSS. CI and CII of Stowe's Press II, in 1796 and 1788 respectively (O'Conor, I, 385-386). *Absalom,* as we have seen, was right next to these books at Stowe, No. CIII in Press II. It is just conceivable that, as the former two manuscripts, though acquired eight years apart, were placed together by reason of their common origin, so *Absalom* might have been placed because it came from the same source. It is interesting that Brand had lifelong ties with Newcastle, in Northumberland across the river from Durham County, which was Thomas Watson's home and where he was Dean for some years. However, the *Absalom* manuscript has no note indicating a donation by Brand or anyone else; nor did O'Conor record such a note in 1818, when there may have been an additional leaf.

David and Absolom. A tragedy, in five acts, by Bishop Bale, not mentioned in the catalogue of his works. A manuscript copy of this play, supposed to be in the author's handwriting, and certainly contemporary, containing 62 pages in quarto, is in the Stowe collection of manuscripts, now in the possession of Lord Ashburnham.[7]

The other entry reads as follows:

Absalon. A Latin tragedy by John Watson, afterwards Bishop of Winchester, a manuscript at Penshurst. It is alluded to in Meres' Palladis Tamia, 1598 [p. 2].

Obviously following Halliwell, Frederick Fleay thirty years later gave the same information in a slightly expanded form. Of the play in Stowe MS. 957, which was outside the scope of Fleay's *Chronicle,* he gave incidental mention as "Bale's *David and Absalom* (extant in MS.)."[8] But he too listed as a separate play the following:

Watson, John. (Latin.). . . .
Absalon, T[ragedy], in MS. at Penshurst, is mentioned by Meres in his *Palladis Tamia* with George Buchanan's *Jephtha* . . . [II, 267].

Now, without any doubt at all the "two" plays are in reality one and the same, Thomas Watson's *Absalom.* In *Palladis Tamia,* Meres was quoting Roger Ascham's eulogy of Thomas Watson's play (quoted below), but he identified it only as *"Bishop Watsons Absalon."*[9] At least as early as 1788 someone interpreted this to mean John Watson, Bishop of Winchester,[10] and the 1812 edition of *Companion to the Playhouse* carried on the confusion — or rather compounded it by shifting the authority for "John" Watson's play from Meres to Ascham himself.[11] By Halliwell's time, John Watson had squatter's rights to a play called *Absalon.* But someone (perhaps Halliwell himself) noticed (perhaps in Smith's sale catalogue of 1849) the existence of a play by "John Bale" — really, as I shall show, Thomas Watson's *Absalom.* And then there were two. And one of them was at Ashburnham Place, the other at Penshurst.

[7] *A Dictionary of Old English Plays* (London, 1860), pp. 70-71.

[8] *A Biographical Chronicle of the English Drama 1559-1642* (London, 1891), II, 293.

[9] Francis Meres, *Palladis Tamia. Wits Treasvry Being the Second Part of Wits Commonwealth* (London, 1598), fol. 285*r.*

[10] [John Egerton], *Egerton's Theatrical Remembrancer* (London, 1788), p. 269: "JOHN WATSON, Bishop of Winchester. 'Absalon.' T[ragedy]. n[ot] p[ublished]."

[11] David Erskine Baker, Isaac Reed, and Stephen Jones, *Biographia Dramatica; or, a Companion to the Playhouse* (London, 1812), I, 739, s.v. "John Watson": "Meres speaks of the play by our author. . . . From a passage in Ascham's *Scolemaster* it appears to have been written in Latin, and not published. It was called *Absalon.* T[ragedy]." The first edition of the book (1764) did not mention the play.

At the time when Halliwell wrote, his placing of our manuscript at Penshurst was certainly wrong, for it had been a part of the Stowe collection for decades.[12] Indeed, for our manuscript the Penshurst collection seems a less likely home even than the Stowe collection, for an overwhelming majority of the manuscripts at Penshurst are deeds, letters, and other documents relating strictly to the family history of the Sidneys. Kingsford and Shaw divided the Penshurst manuscripts into eleven classes. Of these, all but a tiny group of "Miscellaneous Books and Manuscripts" at the the end of the eighth section are nonliterary. In this miscellaneous section is found a Latin comedy by Abraham Fraunce, because it was presented by Fraunce to Sir Philip Sidney; there appears to be no literary work not connected with the Sidneys.[13] In addition, all the Sidneys had connections with Oxford, while our manuscript at least originated at Cambridge. And Sidney did not once mention Watson's play, though he did mention Buchanan's tragedies as worthy of "divine admiration" (in *An Apology for Poetry*). There is, nevertheless, a ring of credibility to the report, so positively stated, that *Absalom* was "at Penshurst." It would be extremely interesting to associate the manuscript with the Sidney family, if not with Sir Philip himself. We could judge its credibility better if we knew Halliwell's source, assuming that he had one. Did he perhaps find such a statement in some document dated before 1818, before which date we have nothing concrete about the Watson manuscript? If so, was the statement ever true?

If our manuscript was in fact once at Penshurst, we have no way of knowing when the Sidneys acquired it. The house itself has been in the exclusive possession of the Sidney family since the crown granted it to Sir William Sidney, grandfather of Sir Philip, in 1552, on the execution of one Sir Ralph Fane, its former owner; and the earlier history of the house shows no likely connection with Watson (Kingsford and Shaw, I, xxiii-xxiv). Thus, we have a 266-year period (1552-1818) when our manuscript could have made its way to Penshurst. Of course, both Sir Philip Sidney and his brother Robert, first Earl of Leicester (a "bookish man"[14]), were passionately interested in literature, but they were apparently not collectors. Their father, Sir Henry

[12] Naturally, therefore, the Historical Manuscripts Commission Reports, which postdate Halliwell's entry, list no *Absalom* at Penshurst.

[13] C. L. Kingsford and William A. Shaw, *Report on the Manuscripts of Lord De L'Isle and Dudley Preserved at Penshurst Place, Kent,* Historical Manuscripts Commission Report No. 77 (London, 1925-42), I, v ff.

[14] G[eorge] E[dward] C[okayne], *The Complete Peerage,* new ed., by Vicary Gibbs *et al.* (London, 1910-53), IV, 555n. (d).

Sidney, also interested in letters, did some collecting, but mostly, as we have seen, of family materials; and, though the Sidney Family Papers for 1539-87 record several book purchases (Kingsford and Shaw, I, xxv), the very full index of the papers has nothing which I can connect with the *Absalom* manuscript.

Two sets of facts, however, give us room for separate conjectures. First, we are told that Sir Henry Sidney once rented a house at Canon Row in Westminster which had formerly been occupied by Sir John Cheke, a close friend and associate of Watson while *Absalom* was being written (Kingsford and Shaw, I, xxv). Second, we might recall again that at least as early as 1818 our manuscript was attributed to John Bale. It is just possible that the ascription indicates that Bale once owned the manuscript: for example, if there once was an extra leaf on the front of the manuscript, it could have contained writing — perhaps a title and the name "Johan Bale" — indicating ownership but interpreted by Dr. O'Conor as meaning authorship.[15] Despite prohibitive odds, Bale could have come up with this manuscript somewhere, for between 1548 and 1551 — not more than a decade after *Absalom* was written — he made extensive travels among various stationers and bookbinders as well as monastic and college libraries searching for materials for his literary history; during his travels he gathered a large personal collection of books and manuscripts.[16] It is noteworthy, too, that during the same years Bale was closely associated with Watson's friend John Cheke (Harris, pp. 37-38, 108). When Bale left for Ireland late in 1552 to become Bishop of Ossory, he took with him two "great wayne loades" of his collected books and manuscripts (Harris, p. 39). Less than a year later, forced to flee Ireland's Catholic wrath, he left his library behind. Subsequently, he tried to recover his books and manuscripts: Queen Elizabeth herself wrote a letter to Ireland in his behalf around 1559, and in July, 1560, Bale sought the intercession of Archbishop Matthew Parker. However, he never did secure his books, which eventually came into the possession of Parker.[17] Now it is interesting that Sir Henry Sidney, owner of Penshurst, was a

[15] In this case, the title and the attribution to Bale now found on fol. 1*r* could have been reproduced, after the loss of the extra page, from Dr. O'Conor's description of the manuscript. Incidentally, the spelling "Johan" Bale may indicate that the name was originally written in the sixteenth century.

[16] Jesse W. Harris, *John Bale: A Study in the Minor Literature of the Reformation,* Illinois Studies in Language and Literature, XXV (Urbana, 1940), pp. 112-113.

[17] *Ibid.,* pp. 58-59 and n. 14. As I was forging this conjectural chain, Professor Roland M. Smith (University of Illinois) called this link to my attention.

prominent official in Ireland during several periods of the mid-sixteenth century: in particular, he was Lord Justice of Ireland in 1558-59, just about the time when Bale was trying to get his books; he was also in Ireland in 1556-57 and as Lord Deputy in 1565-71 and 1575-78.[18] Did Sir Henry get *Absalom* from Cheke's former home? Or perhaps from Bale's former home?

Either conclusion, of course, would hang by the flimsiest of conjectural chains. We do not know that Bale owned the manuscript or that the tradition placing *Absalom* at Penshurst is correct. Even were the conclusion correct, we would not be able to determine when or under what circumstances the manuscript passed from the Sidneys to Astle or to the Buckinghams. Thus, without further evidence than we now have we must despair of tracing the history of the manuscript before 1818.[19]

Neither before the *Absalom* manuscript came into the British Museum nor after have many scholars looked at it seriously. Frederick S. Boas gave the play a rather careful reading in incidental connection with his study of the Tudor university drama and printed extensive quotations from it,[20] and George B. Churchill provided a full summary with brief quotations.[21] The play has never been printed in full.

[18] *D.N.B.*, s.v. "Sir Henry Sidney." We must remember, however, that the *Absalom* supposed to be at Penshurst was thought to be a separate work from the manuscript that became Stowe MS. 957 and that the connection with Bale was given only for the latter manuscript. Moreover, I find nowhere in Bale any mention of Watson's play.

[19] We may note in passing that neither Edward Bernard (*Catalogi Librorum Manuscriptorum Angliae et Hiberniae in Unum Collecti* [Oxford, 1697]) nor Gustav Haenel's supplement (*Catalogi Librorum Manuscriptorum, Qui in Bibliothecis . . . Britanniae M. . . . Asservantur* [Leipzig, 1830]) mentions any manuscript likely to be ours.

[20] *University Drama in the Tudor Age* (Oxford, 1914), pp. 352-363.

[21] George B. Churchill and Wolfgang Keller, "Die lateinischen Universitäts-Dramen Englands in der Zeit der Königin Elisabeth," *Sh.-Jbch.*, XXXIV (1898), 229 ff.

CHAPTER TWO

THE AUTHOR

THOMAS WATSON'S *ABSALOM*

The *Absalom* preserved in Stowe MS. 957 was written by Thomas Watson. As I stated earlier, the manuscript is a holograph, and I have examined two other samples of a hand which is identical, both signed by Watson. I present herewith photographs of a page of the *Absalom* manuscript (Plate I) and of the other two samples. Plate II shows a letter written by Watson to William Cecil, Lord Burghley, on October 6, 1578. F. S. Boas knew of the existence of this letter (p. 64, n. 2), but declined to examine it because he thought a comparison would be misleading. He had some justification for thinking so, for the author of the letter was over sixty years old, was suffering from sciatica, was nearly blind, and was in an uncomfortable confinement, whereas Watson wrote the *Absalom* manuscript during his prime. But if Boas had looked at the Hatfield letter, he would have seen scribal likenesses which, surviving all these difficulties, are the more firm proof of identity. The differences between the two hands — particularly the lack of firmness and control in the hand of the old man as compared with the vigor of the hand of the young Cambridge fellow — are in superficialities and are readily explained by the forty-year lapse.[1] Plate III shows a voucher from Durham, where Watson was Dean from 1553 through 1556, and thus presents Watson's hand as it appeared only about fifteen years after the play. The voucher is much less carefully written than the letter or even than the play, but the identity of the handwriting of all three manuscripts is nonetheless unmistakable.[2]

[1] The letter is found in the Cecil Papers, vol. 161, art. 68, among the collection of The Most Honourable the Marquis of Salisbury at Hatfield House, Herts. I am indebted to Lord Salisbury for permitting me to view the manuscript and to reproduce it, and to Miss Clare Talbot, Archivist of Hatfield House, for her assistance.

[2] I am grateful to Dr. J. Conway Davies, Reader at The Prior's Kitchen,

This evidence clears the air of a mass of confusion and error which has accumulated over the years concerning the author of *Absalom*. As early as 1598, Francis Meres apparently failed to distinguish between Thomas Watson the poet, author of *Hecatompathia,* and Thomas Watson the bishop, author of our play, for he juxtaposed the two as though they were one:

As *Georgius Buckananus Iephthe,* amongst all moderne Tragedies is able to abide the touch of *Aristotles* precepts, and *Euripides* examples: so is *Bishop Watsons Absalon.*

As *Terence* for his translations . . . and *Aquilius* for his translation . . . and *Watson* for his *Antigone* out of *Sophocles,* haue got good commendations: so these versifiers for their learned translations are of good note among vs . . . [fol. 285*r*-*v*].

That the first sentence refers to our Watson is evident from the title "Bishop" and from the attribution to him of an *Absalon.* But Meres had no firsthand knowledge: even his simile and his spelling of Buchanan's name are based upon a famous passage in Roger Ascham:

Some in England, moe in France, Germanie, and Italie, also haue written Tragedies in our tyme: of the which, not one I am sure is able to abyde the trew touch of Aristotles preceptes, and Euripides examples, saue onely two, that ever I saw, M. Watsons Absalon, and Georgius Buckananus Iephthe.[3]

In the remainder of his statement Meres was referring to Thomas Watson the poet: there is no evidence that Bishop Watson translated Sophocles, and we have the testimony of Thomas Nashe that the poet Watson, a friend of Nashe, did translate *Antigone.*[4] Meres probably did not know that he was speaking of two men. Even today we are not sure whether another reference of Meres, listing Thomas Watson among "our best for Tragedie," meant the poet or the bishop, but the consensus is toward the former.[5]

The College, University of Durham, for making at my request the search which turned up this document. The voucher has become separated from its annual file and contains no internal evidence of date. Though Watson was selected for the deanery at Durham in November, 1553, he did not resign his mastership at St. John's College, Cambridge, until May, 1554; though elected Bishop of Lincoln in December, 1556, he was not consecrated until August, 1557. Hence, the manuscript probably dates between 1554 and 1557. I wish to thank the authorities of the University of Durham for permission to publish a photograph of the manuscript.

[3] *The Scholemaster* (London, 1570), fol. 57*r*. See Don C. Allen, *Francis Meres's Treatise "Poetrie": A Critical Edition,* Illinois Studies in Language and Literature, XVI (Urbana, 1933), p. 51.

[4] *The Works of Thomas Nashe,* ed. R. B. McKerrow (London, 1910), III, 320. The translation appeared in 1581 as *Sophoclis Antigone, Interprete Thoma VVatsono.*

[5] Meres, fol. 283*r*. See E. K. Chambers, *The Elizabethan Stage* (Oxford, 1923), III, 506.

Some of those who followed Meres certainly confused the two. For example, Anthony à Wood interpreted Meres's statement as follows:

In his younger years [Bishop Watson] was given much to Poetry and making of Plays and gained great commendations for his *Antigone* out of *Sophocles* by the learned Men of his time; who have farther avowed that as *George Buchannans* Tragedy called *Jephthe* have among all Tragedies of that time, been able to abide the touch of *Aristotles* precepts, and *Euripides* Examples: So haue also the Tragedy of this *Tho. Watson* called *Absalon.*[6]

Again, it will be noted that Ascham referred to Watson by the prefix "M." or "Bishop" without a given name; and we have already seen a series of eighteenth- and nineteenth-century writers who associated one or both of these identifications with another Watson. Even in the twentieth century at least two writers have carried on this confusion: W. Davenport Adams spoke of an *Absalom* by "John Watson, Bishop successively of Lincoln and Winchester [*sic!*], referred to by Ascham . . . and Meres";[7] and Gertrude Sibley did not know whether to ascribe *Absalom* to John or Thomas Watson.[8]

On the other hand, some early writers recognized that a confusion had sometimes existed: Edward Phillips, in a work which first appeared in 1675, said, "Wood . . . (confounding the poet with the divine as Meres had done before) . . . has given much credit to Watson, Bishop of Lincoln, for translating the 'Antigone' of Sophocles," and "Thomas Watson . . . afterwards Bishop of Lincoln, had composed a tragedy in Latin, called 'Absolon,' whence the origin of Wood's mistake."[9] And also in the seventeenth century Thomas Baker correctly associated Ascham's statement with Thomas Watson the bishop.[10] But all of these writers (except Ascham) were speaking of a play which they knew only at second or third hand and which they were sure was lost. James Upton may be considered typical: in 1743 he wrote that Watson *"has left nothing behind him, that I know of, but a Copy of Latin Verses to recommend Mr.* Seton's *Logic to the publick"*;[11] but

[6] "Fasti Oxonienses," *Athenae Oxonienses* (London, 1691-92), I, col. 710.

[7] *A Dictionary of the Drama* (London, 1904), I, 6. Of course, John Watson was never Bishop of Lincoln; the only person who was successively Bishop of Lincoln and Winchester during this period was John White, whom Thomas Watson succeeded at Lincoln.

[8] *The Lost Plays and Masques 1500-1642,* Cornell Studies in English, XIX (Ithaca, N.Y., 1933), pp. 1-2; see a review by T. W. Baldwin in *MLN,* XLIX (December, 1934), 552-553.

[9] *Theatrum Poetarum Anglicanorum,* ed. S. E. Brydges (Canterbury, 1800), p. 210 and n.

[10] *History of the College of St. John the Evangelist, Cambridge,* ed. John E. B. Mayor (Cambridge, 1869), I, 139.

[11] In an edition of Ascham's *The Scholemaster* (London, 1743), p. 76n. Thus, he apparently did not know of Watson's sermons.

at least he did know that Watson had written an *Absalom,* for in 1711 he had identified the Watson who had written a "lost" *Absalom* as *"one of the ejected Bishops."*[12] The play before us, Stowe MS. 957, was regarded from its earliest mention as a thing apart. Hence, we have already noticed the double entries of Halliwell and Fleay, including a "David and Absalom" by John Bale. Nearly all of the writers who mentioned such a play admitted that Bale did not claim an *Absalom* in his list of his own works, but none of them committed himself much beyond a simple statement of Bale's silence.[13] Some twentieth-century writers also did no more. John S. Farmer did not print the *Absalom* in his edition of Bale's plays because it was "so doubtful an attribution"; but he intended to print it in an extra volume, for he could not conclusively deny Bale's authorship.[14] And at least one modern writer, Eduard Eckhardt, credited the play to Bale despite Bale's failure to claim it.[15] Of course the play has nothing in common with Bale's other work, and the handwriting of Stowe MS. 957 is nothing like Bale's.[16]

F. S. Boas, who studied the play more closely than any other writer, at least once changed his mind. In 1910 he stated that the play "preserved in the Stowe MSS. 957" is "probably the Absalom of Thomas Watson."[17] But in 1914, after a lengthy analysis of the play, he

[12] In an earlier edition of Ascham's *The Schoolmaster* (London, 1711), p. 175n. A late contemporary of Upton, Thomas Tanner, did not mention *Absalom* during his discussion of Watson (*Bibliotheca Britannico-Hibernica* [London, 1748], p. 754).

[13] Not all early writers credited Bale with an *Absalom* (or a "David and Absalom"): Robert Watt, *Bibliotheca Britannica; or a General Index to British and Foreign Literature* (Edinburgh, 1824), I, 66m-v; S. Austin Allibone, *A Critical Dictionary of English Literature* (London, 1859-71), I, 106-107. Watt did not credit Watson with the play either (II, 953m); Allibone did (III, 2608), but probably thought of the play as lost.

[14] *The Dramatic Writings of John Bale,* Early English Dramatists (London, 1907), p. 295. We may note here William Carew Hazlitt's listing of a *David and Absalom* by Bale among the Stowe manuscripts (*A Manual for the Collector and Amateur of Old English Plays* [London, 1892], p. 59).

[15] *Das englische Drama im Zeitalter der Reformation und der Hochrenaissance,* Geschichte der englischen Literatur im Grundriss (Berlin, 1928), p. 5, n. 8: "Ein Stück [Bales] *David and Absalom* befindet sich unter den Stowe MSS., wird aber im Katalog seiner Werke nicht erwähnt." Though Adams speaks of Bale's *David and Absalom* "among the Stowe MSS." (I, 381), he says elsewhere that Bale's drama is "no longer existent" (I, 6).

[16] For Bale's hand see the B hand in W. Bang, ed., *Bales Kynge Johan nach der Handschrift in der Chatsworth Collection in Faksimile herausgegeben,* Materialen zur Kunde des älteren englischen Dramas, XXV (Louvain, 1909), as identified by J. H. P. Pafford, ed., *King Johan by John Bale,* Malone Society Reprints (Oxford, 1931), p. xi.

[17] "University Plays Tudor and Early Stuart Periods," *CHEL,* VI, 333, 535-536.

reached a different conclusion. Complaining of the "tasteless rhetoric and monotonous versification," he doubted that Ascham would have praised *Absalom* in the same breath with Buchanan's *Iephthes;* he was especially disturbed by the play's violation of the unities, for he thought that Ascham's praise of Watson's play as a good example of imitation would include observance of the unities; and on less critical grounds he thought it unlikely that "an autograph copy, with the author's own corrections, of Watson's jealously guarded play should have come down in this haphazard fashion, without any outward sign of its origin."[18] I shall discuss Boas' critical judgments later. As for Boas' last objection, manuscript transmissions have almost invariably been haphazard, and we may assume that Watson's play was even less "jealously guarded" than some others were while the traitorous Roman Catholic bishop spent the last twenty-odd years of his life in confinement.

Other modern opinion has been divided, but no one has taken a very definite stand. John W. Cunliffe would say only that the *Absalom* mentioned by Ascham is "perhaps the Latin tragedy preserved in Stowe MS. 957."[19] E. K. Chambers thought the play to be "identical with the *Absolon* preserved" in the British Museum.[20] Alfred Harbage, presumably following Boas, thought the *Absalom* "Probably not the Absolon of MS. Stowe 957."[21] Churchill and Keller said that Stowe MS. 957 is "äusserst wahrscheinlich" Watson's play, though they also reported, noncommittally, the Bale tradition.[22] Wilhelm Creizenach, admitting that he had only secondhand knowledge of the manuscript, relied on Boas for the opinion that our play could be identical with Watson's tragedy were the unity of time not violated.[23] Only T. W. Baldwin has taken specific issue with Boas: "I do not believe that the objections which Professor Boas has raised are valid, and I think it highly probable that the surviving *Absalon* is Bishop Watson's."[24]

[18] *University Drama,* pp. 63-64. All later references to Boas are to this work.

[19] "Early English Tragedy," *CHEL,* V, 438. See also his *Early English Classical Tragedies* (Oxford, 1912), p. lxxx.

[20] *Mediaeval Stage,* II, 458. Citing Chambers, Hardin Craig listed an "*Absalon* possibly by Thomas Watson" as surviving and an "*Absalom*" as lost (*English Religious Drama of the Middle Ages* [Oxford, 1955], p. 376).

[21] *Annals of English Drama 975-1700* (Philadelphia, 1940), pp. 28-29.

[22] *Sh.-Jbch.,* XXXIV (1898), 229-230.

[23] *Geschichte des neueren Dramas* (Halle, 1893-1923), II, 431, n. 2. For another secondhand modern opinion see Stanley J. Kunitz and Howard Haycraft, *British Authors Before 1800: A Biographical Dictionary* (New York, 1952), p. 553.

[24] *William Shakspere's Five-Act Structure* (Urbana, Ill., 1947), p. 364.

THE TITLE OF WATSON'S PLAY

The manuscript of this play has no authoritative title. The title "David and Absalom" appears on the first recto and has usually been used to describe the manuscript; but this title has no authority earlier than Dr. O'Conor's 1818 catalogue. Much more authoritative is Ascham's reference to his friend's play by the one-word title *Absalon.* And this title fits the structure of the play, for the tragedy is, as we shall see, Absalom's, not his father's. Hence, I have chosen the one-word title, but I have rejected Ascham's spelling; this spelling (or its variant *Absolon*) has been used by several modern critics. But the spelling *Absalom* has the greater authority of Watson himself: only three times (in the scene headings to I.1 and I.3 and at I.2.42) does the *-n* spelling occur; from I.3.214 to the end of the play the exclusive spelling is *Absalom.* We may note, too, that the latter spelling has the support of most sixteenth-century Bibles: at least fifty of them spelled the name *Absalom,* and the variant *Absolom* also occurred occasionally. Only four of the Bibles which I have seen used the spelling *Absalon* consistently, though isolated instances of this spelling occurred in a few of the other Bibles.

THOMAS WATSON: SCHOLAR, HUMANIST, CATHOLIC

Thomas Watson was born in the diocese of Durham, perhaps at Nun Stinton, near Sedgefield. Pollard gave his birthdate as 1513, but we should perhaps put it in 1515 or 1516.[25] Nothing is known of his

[25] The facts in the brief life which follows are taken basically from A. F. Pollard's account in *D.N.B.,* supplemented and corrected from other sources named. See also the full but colored biography in T. E. Bridgett and T. F. Knox, *The True Story of the Catholic Hierarchy Deposed by Queen Elizabeth* (London, [1889]), pp. 120-207; it is also available in Bridgett's edition of Watson's *Sermons on the Sacraments* (London, 1876). Pollard probably based his date (1513) for Watson's birth on the letter from Watson to Burghley in 1578, in which Watson spoke of "beyng aged of three score and fyve yeares allready past." The letter had been summarized in the Ninth Report of the Historical Manuscripts Commission, *Calendar of the Manuscripts of the Most Hon. the Marquis of Salisbury,* II (London, 1888), 210-211. But in 1548 Watson testified, at a trial of Stephen Gardiner, that he was thirty-three years old (John Gough Nichols, ed., *Literary Remains of King Edward the Sixth* [London, 1857], I, cviii). In 1551, at another trial of Gardiner, he was said at one point to be thirty-four or thirty-five (John Foxe, *Actes and Monuments,* ed. Stephen Reed Cattley [London, 1837-41], VI, 205) and at another to be thirty-three (*ibid.,* p. 151). Whether Watson actually testified to these contradictory ages is not clear, but it is probable that Foxe simply relied on Watson's testimony of 1548 and estimated his age in 1551 (in one instance forgetting to change his age). It is consistent with the ages of matriculators at the universities to assume that Watson was about fourteen when he went to Cambridge in 1529.

life before he went to Cambridge around 1529. Nor do we know anything about his life as an undergraduate at St. John's College, Cambridge. But we can infer that both in grammar school and in the university he applied himself diligently and ably, for Ascham, a close associate of such brilliant men as Thomas Smith and John Cheke, was able to call Watson "one of the best Scholers, that euer S. Johns Colledge bred" (*Scholemaster,* 1570, fol. 23*v*). The few works which Watson has left behind bear out that reputation, for they are filled with knowledge sacred and profane. *Absalom,* as we shall see, is in large part a composite of phrases and lines from the classics, and Watson's sermons are marked by numerous Scriptural quotations, all of Watson's own translation;[26] for *Absalom* too Watson apparently used only a Latin Bible, and there is every evidence that he used primary sources rather than collections of "flowers" for his classical phraseology.

Watson received his A.B. in 1532-33; very soon thereafter he was elected to one of the fellowships set up for St. John's in 1522 under the will of Hugh Ashton, Archdeacon of York. He proceeded M.A. in 1535-36 and B.D. in 1542-43. For some of these dates there is documentary evidence. That 1532-33 is correct for the A.B. is corroborated by the grace books,[27] and there is little disagreement on this date. The date of the fellowship is uncertain. Thomas Baker, citing the "Registrum Academiae" for authority, at one place (I, 138) dated Watson's A.B. and fellowship both in 1533; at another he was less certain, listing "Thos. Watson, dioc. Durh.," as being "Admitted 'cir. an. 1533' " to one of the Ashton fellowships.[28] C. M. Neale, listing Watson's A.B. under date 1532, also dated his fellowship in that year.[29] T. E. Bridgett and T. F. Knox gave 1533 for the election.[30] The Venns, like Baker, gave 1532-33 for Watson's A.B., but chose 1534 for the fellowship.[31] The Coopers were inexplicit about the fellowship, saying that Watson "proceeded A.B. 1533-4,[32] and was soon afterward

[26] T. E. Bridgett, ed., *Sermons on the Sacraments. By Thomas Watson* (London, 1876), pp. xiii-xiv.

[27] William George Searle, ed., *Grace Book* Γ *Containing the Records of the University of Cambridge for the Years 1501-1542* (Cambridge, 1908), p. 267.

[28] Baker, I, 283, in a "Catalogus Sociorum a Fundatione Collegii . . . Usque ad Annum 1546, Desumptus ex Archivis Collegii," under date 24 Henry VIII (i.e., April 22, 1532, through April 21, 1533).

[29] *The Early Honours Lists (1498-9 to 1746-7) of the University of Cambridge* (Bury St. Edmunds, 1909), p. 37.

[30] *Catholic Hierarchy,* p. 129.

[31] John and J. A. Venn, *Alumni Cantabrigienses,* Part I (Cambridge, 1922-27), IV, 350.

[32] On the authority of Searle, p. 267, a vol. III of *Athenae Cantabrigienses,* ed. Henry Bradshaw *et al.* (Cambridge, 1913), p. 122, corrected this to 1532-33.

admitted a fellow."[33] Apparently on this vague authority A. F. Pollard, giving 1533-34 for the A.B., set the latest date of all for the election to fellowship: "about 1535." The earlier date — either 1533 or 1534 — seems likely. The grace books again confirm the dates for Watson's M.A. and B.D.[34]

Whether Watson was actually present during every term of the years 1529-43 is not clear. Baker said (I, 138) that Watson stayed at St. John's "most part of Henry the Eighth's reign, held such offices as were then most valued, was dean and college preacher several years, and commenced B. D. an. 1543." The grace conferring the A.B. on Watson stated that he had spent ten terms, during the major part of which he heard the ordinary lectures and gave the required responses and disputes; most other bachelors in that year had spent eleven or twelve terms, a few nine, a very few eight. The M.A. grace credited Watson with nine terms (presumably beyond the A.B.); the B.D. grace said that Watson had spent seven years in the study of theology. Though monotonously normal in wording, such graces seem usually rather careful of temporal details, and they therefore provide implicit evidence that Watson must not have been away from Cambridge very often or for very long. Some other graces which refer only to the surname Watson but which probably mean Thomas seem to identify him with some of those high offices which Baker mentioned; and they place Watson at Cambridge during nearly all of the years beyond his A.B.[35] In 1536-37 "Smythe et Watson," both identified as "magistri," were inquisitors for the A.B. examinations of Anthony Smythe (Searle, p. 314). In 1539-40 "doctores Redman Babthrop et Glyn magistros Carter et Watson" are listed as *capita senatus* (Searle, p. 341; see Venn, *Grace Book* Δ, p. 569). In this same year Ascham must have meant Thomas when he listed Watson as the "non rudem praedicatorem" of one Burton who was seeking a fellowship.[36] In 1540-41

[33] Charles Henry and Thompson Cooper, *Athenae Cantabrigienses* (Cambridge, 1858-61), I, 491.

[34] Searle, p. 306; John Venn, ed., *Grace Book* Δ *Containing the Records of the University of Cambridge for the Years 1542-1589* (Cambridge, 1910), pp. 6-7.

[35] The only other Watson whose dates make him an eligible referent was Matthew Watson, of whom we know almost nothing: receiving the A.B. in 1530-31 and the M.A. in 1533-34, he was elected a fellow of Pembroke in 1530, and later was ordained deacon at York (1551-52) and vicar of Helmsley (1551) (Venn, *Alumni Cantabrigienses,* Part I, IV, 349). Venn stated that Matthew, like Thomas, was a native of Durham. His record was certainly not so distinguished as Thomas'.

[36] Letter VII, in *The Whole Works of Roger Ascham,* ed. J. A. Giles, I, Part 1 (London, 1865), 12.

Watson was listed as one of the *examinatores questionistarum* (Venn, *Grace Book* Δ, p. 571), and one of the students whom he examined was John Christopherson (Searle, p. 351). And in 1541-42 Watson was one of the appellants in an attempt to get a master removed, on April 5, 1542 (Baker, I, 116). Thus, the only years for which I have found no record of a Watson at Cambridge are 1537-38 and 1538-39. And during at least the second of these years Watson may well have been away somewhere, for there is a letter from Ascham to one "Domino Watson," obviously written from Cambridge, which describes events there which would be news only to one who had been gone for a time. The events described apparently occurred during the spring of 1539.[37]

In any case, the records indicate that Watson made a distinguished career for himself as a graduate student and fellow. In addition, John Strype named a Thomas Watson who was King's Chaplain in 1537 (one of the blank years noted above), but the reference may be a confusion with someone else.[38] Several of Roger Ascham's statements about Watson in *The Scholemaster* clearly refer to the decade of 1534-44. Watson was a member of the Ascham-Cheke circle and took frequent part in their discussions. Ascham tells us that Watson and Cheke agreed with Ascham's strictures on "our rude beggerly ryming" as against the purer unrhymed verse (fols. 59*v*-60*r*). And Ascham did not hesitate to list Watson with those other "men of worthie memorie, M. Redman, M. Cheke, M. Smith, M. Haddon," who had succeeded in moving the university away from its former fault of "reading the preceptes of Aristotle without the examples of other Authors: But herein, in my tyme thies men . . . put so to their helping handes, as that vniuersitie . . . shall be bounde vnto them" (fol. 53*v*). This reputation was a durable one, probably because of Ascham's words, for at the end of the century Thomas Nashe mentioned "sir *Iohn Cheeke,* a man of men . . . sir *Iohn Mason,* Doctor *Watson, Redman, Ascam, Grindall, Leuer, Pilkinton* . . . [as having] either by their priuate readings or publique workes repurged the errors of Arte, expelled from their purities, and set before our eyes a more perfect

[37] Letter IV (*ibid.,* pp. 5-6). Baker listed Watson among the signatories of a letter to Henry VIII on July 4, 1538 (I, 462). But the original contains no names at all, and Baker probably supplied his name from the known list of "Socii et Scholares" during this general time; the letter, signed "Deditissimi Serui ac Scholastici: Socii et Scholares Collegii D. Ioan. Euang. Cantabrigiae," is found in the Public Record Office (State Papers of Henry VIII, vol. 134, fols. 100-101).

[38] *Ecclesiastical Memorials* (Oxford, 1822), I, Part 1, 487-488.

methode of studie."[39] It was during this same decade and according to this "more perfect methode" (Ascham's "touch of Aristotles preceptes, and Euripides examples") that Watson wrote *Absalom.*

Another of Watson's exercises at this time, apparently, was a translation of at least a part of Homer's *Odyssey* into English quantitative verse. Ascham quoted two lines of crude hexameter:

> *All trauellers do gladly report great prayse of Vlysses,*
> *For that he knew many mens maners, and saw many Cities* [I.3].

And Ascham praised it in *The Scholemaster* (fol. 24*r*) because it was done "both plainlie for the sense, and roundlie for the verse" and because it avoided "barbarous ryming." We see here a beginning of the movement, which Gabriel Harvey tried to urge upon Spenser, toward quantitative meter in English.[40] As further evidence of Watson's prepossession with metrical considerations at this time we may mention Ascham's statements that Watson agreed with his own prejudice against rhyme; that Watson would not publish *Absalom* because it had an anapest "twise or thrise" in the even feet; and that Watson had roundly censured a colleague who put trochaic verse into the protasis of a tragedy.[41]

Watson's personal life and feelings at this time we may only surmise. When he first came down to Cambridge, a conservative and a Romanist out of the reactionary north country, the Chancellor of Cambridge was John Fisher. Fisher's religious views are, of course, well known, and Watson must have found the atmosphere under Fisher favorable. Watson surely approved of the academic atmosphere. Fisher's statutes

[39] *Works,* McKerrow, III, 317. We may note too Gabriel Harvey's allusion to Watson's perfectionist tendency in versification; see below, p. 29, n. 60.

[40] See George Saintsbury, "Elizabethan Criticism," *CHEL,* III, 333. Saintsbury put the date of the translation between 1535 and 1554, more likely late than early. We can surely eliminate the period after 1545, when Watson left Cambridge.

[41] The colleague, according to Ascham (fol. 57*r-v*), was "well liked of many, but best liked of him selfe" and wrote "matters . . . which he called, Tragedies. In one, wherby he looked to wynne his spurres, and whereat many ignorant fellowes fast clapped their handes, he began the *Protasis* with *Trochaijs Octonarijs:* which kinde of verse, as it is but seldome and rare in Tragedies, so is it neuer vsed, saue onelie in *Epitasi.* . . . [And so, incidentally, did Watson use it.] I remember ful well what M. Watson merelie sayd vnto me of his blindnesse and boldnes in that behalfe although otherwise, there passed much frendship betwene them. M. Watson had an other maner care of perfection, with a feare and reuerence of the iudgement of the best learned." Chambers (*Mediaeval Stage,* II, 195, n. 1) thought the colleague was John Christopherson. Watson's metrical prepossession is suggested by many revisions in *Absalom* which were probably inspired by metrical motivations; most correct defects, but one (at V.3.114) seems to have been caused by a desire to avoid rhyme. See Textual Notes.

for St. John's, the most comprehensive yet put into effect,[42] were the law of the college from 1530; that Watson was happy with them is evident from the fact that he reinstated them when he later became Master of St. John's. Perhaps indicative of a personal affection for Fisher is Watson's contribution of information to the earliest biography of that martyr.[43] The Master of St. John's through these early days must also have been a source of pleasure for Watson: he was Nicholas Metcalfe, "every way an excellent master" (Baker, I, 108). Ascham's devotion to this man is evident from a long and glowing encomium included in *The Scholemaster* (fol. 54*r-v*).

But these presumably happy days were numbered. Watson has left no statement of his reaction to the Reformation, but it must have become terrifyingly meaningful in 1535 with the martyrdom of Sir Thomas More and John Fisher for their refusal to sign the oath required under the Act of Supremacy. And it was to become even more personal in that same year with the assumption of the chancellorship by the Protestant zealot Thomas Cromwell and with the Royal Injunctions. The first article of the Injunctions demanded compliance by "the chancellor, vice-chancellor, doctors, masters, bachelors, and all other students and scholars, under pain of loss of their dignities, benefices, and stipends, or expulsion from the university," with the requirement that "they should swear to the king's succession, and to obey the statutes of the realm, made or to be made, for the extirpation of the papal usurpation . . ." (Mullinger [1873], pp. 629-630). And in 1536 was passed an Act of Parliament requiring of every person proceeding toward any degree to swear before the commissary of the university "that he from henceforth shall utterly renounce, refuse, relinquissh or forsake the Bishopp of Rome and his auctorite, power, and jurisdiccion."[44] We can only guess what Watson felt about these oaths, but we can be certain of what he did: he signed the required oath and kept his fellowship. He remained a Catholic; so did Henry VIII. But at least publicly he became an English rather

[42] So thorough that Protestant James Bass Mullinger could cavil at them as picayune (*The University of Cambridge from the Earliest Times to the Royal Injunctions of 1535* [Cambridge, 1873], p. 624).

[43] E. E. Reynolds, *Saint John Fisher* (New York, 1955), pp. x-xi, who refers to *Vie du Bien Heureux Martyr Jean Fisher,* ed. Fr. Van Ortroy (Brussels, 1893). Watson apparently wrote none of the life, which survives in English in eleven manuscripts (EETS, 1921, and ed. Fr. Philip Hughes, 1935) and in Latin in five. Professor William C. McAvoy (St. Louis University) called my attention to Watson's connection with this life.

[44] James Bass Mullinger, *The University of Cambridge from the Royal Injunctions of 1535 to the Accession of Charles the First* (Cambridge, 1884), p. 35.

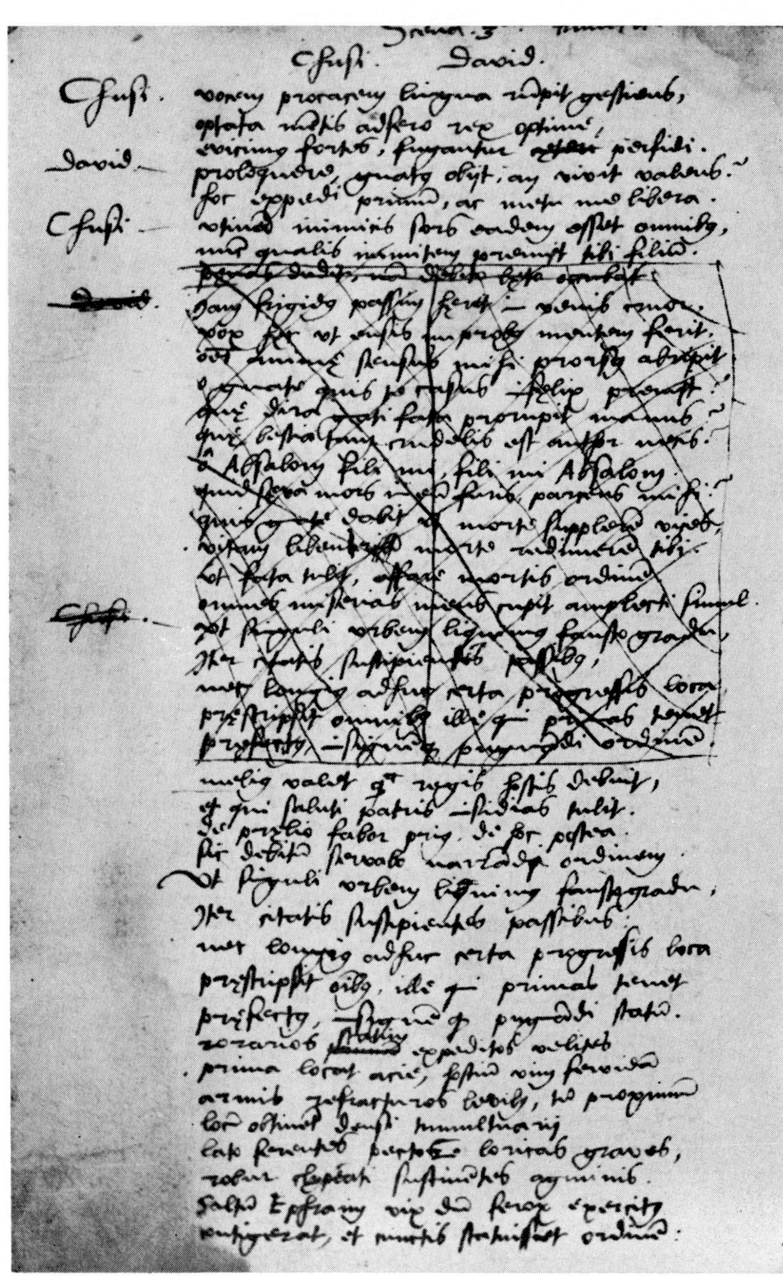

PLATE I. Watson's hand as seen in the *Absalom* manuscript, V.3.1-24 (Stowe MS. 957, fol, 27*v*), reduced

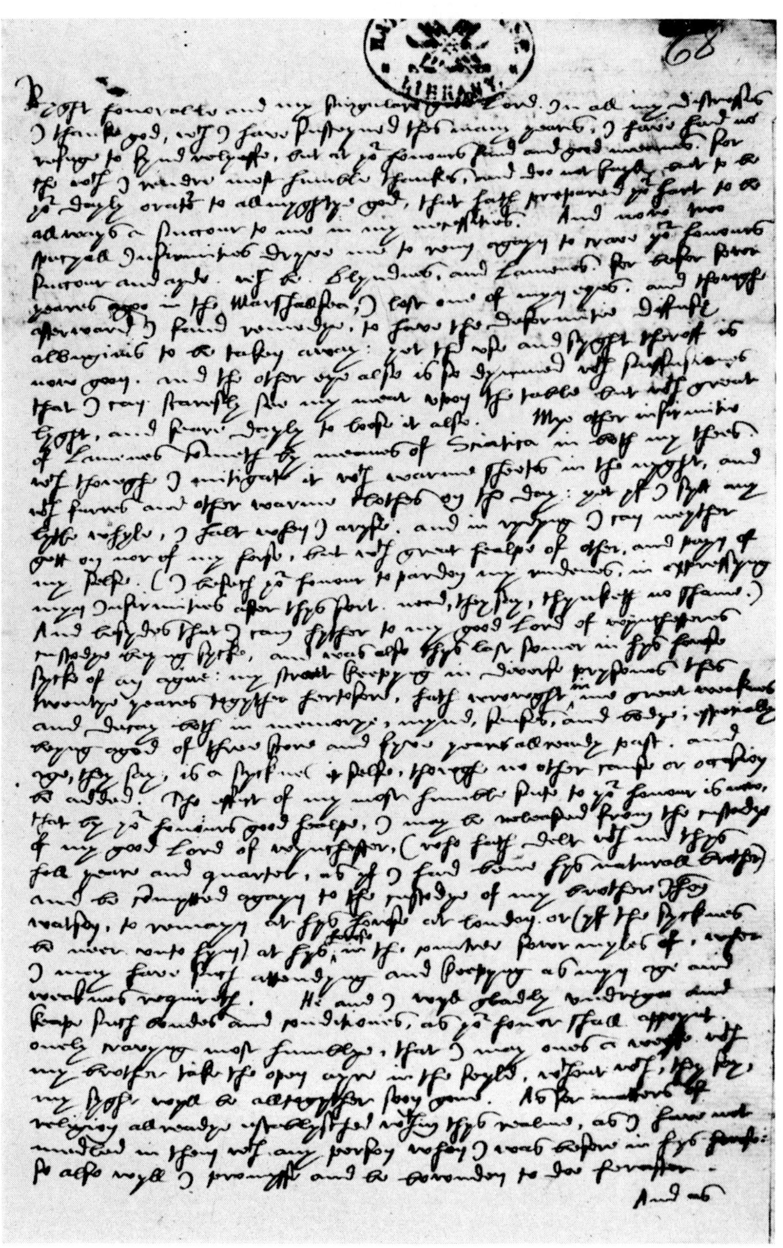

PLATE II. Watson's hand as seen in a letter to Lord Burghley, October 6, 1578 (Cecil Papers, vol. 161, art. 68), reduced. Continued on facing page.

And as for resort of any persons to me, I shall avoyd it may,
onely savyng that the barber, tayler, phisitians and other persons
of a necessitie at some tymes, be not accompted for resorters.
My good Lord of Worcester, I hope, wyll report well of my good
behaviour in this house. what kynd of lyfe I entend to kepe
to my lyfes end. and dayly meditate how I may end it well.
Good my Lord I most humbly desyre your honour, that among
all your good and charitable deeds, this your releasyng of me
in my worship at this tyme, may be one, and I shall
recommend my selfe most devoutly to pray for your honour to my
lyfes end, to almyghty god, who ever preserve the same to
his good wyll. amen. wryten at Farnham this 6. day of
Feb. 1578.

Your honours most humble and
dayly orator. Thom. watson.

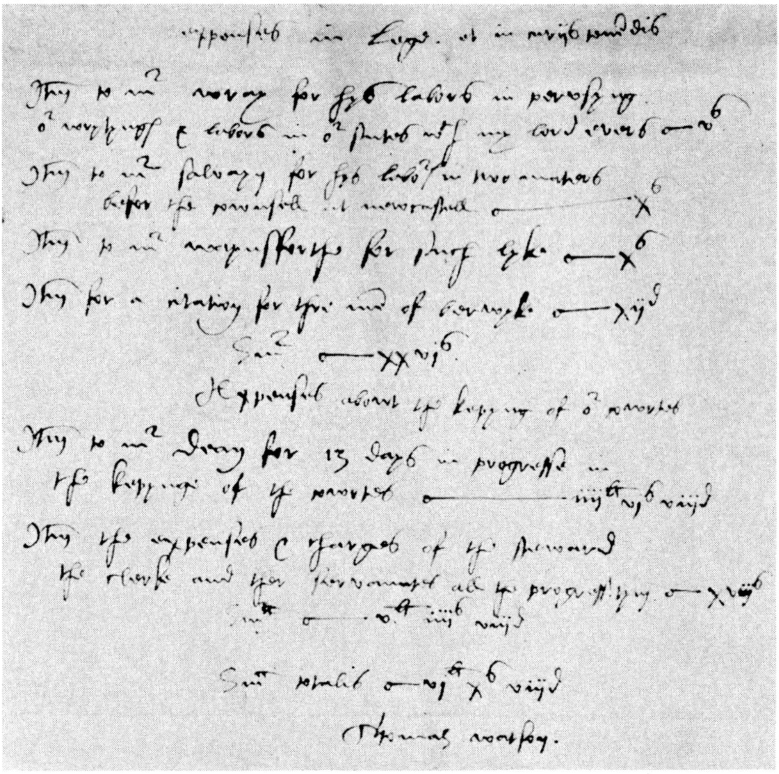

PLATE III. Watson's hand as seen in a voucher from Durham (1553-57), reduced

than a Roman Catholic — as did many other good Catholics, among them Watson's later superior, Stephen Gardiner. Watson's true feelings are to be seen, not only in his actions under Elizabeth, but in his taking part on December 3, 1551, in the second of two disputations against Sir William Cecil, John Cheke, Edmund Grindal, and others: promised immunity from prosecution, Watson upheld the doctrine of transubstantiation so vigorously that he enraged Grindal.[45] And if we are to believe an apocryphal-sounding account by John Strype, he also preached in the north, sometime during Edward's reign, a sermon which was so heretical that he would have been prosecuted for treason but for the intervention in his behalf of John Rough, the Scottish Protestant who was martyred by Queen Mary on December 22, 1557.[46]

Of further concern to many of the fellows of St. John's, and probably to Watson, were the troubles attached to the mastership for several years. Nicholas Metcalfe in 1537 was forced to resign his mastership because he had opposed Henry's divorce and chafed under the Act of Supremacy (Baker, I, 104-105). The fellows, most of whom apparently were conservative, tried to elect Dr. Nicholas Wylson, a friend of Fisher and Metcalfe and a conservative, but they were compelled to name George Day (Baker, I, 110-111). Day, who had worked for Henry's divorce but who later died an ardent Catholic, was apparently not objectionable to the fellows, but within a year he was removed by Henry. The king then forced the fellows to elect John Tayler, an "enthusiastic advocate of the doctrines of the Lutherans."[47] Although the first two years of Tayler's mastership were calm,[48] trouble soon developed which reached a climax in 1542, in the deprivation of three fellows with conservative leanings and the refusal to admit one newly elected fellow, Thomas Leaver. Twenty fellows, including Thomas Watson, appealed to the university visitor, the Bishop of Ely, against Tayler. Nearly all of the signers were, according to Thomas Baker (I, 118), "northern men, or in northern foundations, and most of them men of the old learning"; Baker called them "the greater and sounder part of all the fellows then present." Mullinger (1884) disagreed: ". . . not more than one of the appellants appears to have been distinguished

[45] John Strype, *Memorials of . . . Thomas Cranmer* (Oxford, 1840), I, 385-386, and *The History of the Life and Acts of . . . Edmund Grindal* (Oxford, 1821), p. 10. Watson's argument is preserved in Corpus Christi College, Cambridge (MS. 102, p. 259), and is summarized in John Strype, *Life of the Learned John Cheke* (Oxford, 1821), pp. 69-86.

[46] Strype, *Ecclesiastical Memorials,* III, Part 2, 44-45.

[47] Mullinger (1884), p. 38; see Baker, I, 115.

[48] Roger Ascham, Letter V, to Tayler (Giles, I, Part 1, 7).

in those studies by which St John's was now rising into such honourable pre-eminence. The solitary exception was Thomas Watson. . . . The only other scholar of any note among the appellants was Seton. . . . But the names which mainly justify the proud assertions of Ascham and Grant [e.g., Madew, Redman, and Pember] are to be found in the list of those who probably sympathised with the new master and gave him their moral support" (p. 40). Mullinger severely qualified his statement about Watson: "The impression we obtain of [Watson's] attainments . . . is rather suggestive of the Italian dilettantism than of that more sober enthusiasm which characterises the rising school of classical learning in the Cambridge of this time, — scholars who undoubtedly derived from the masterpieces of antiquity a real and noble inspiration." Certainly the group of appellants as a whole may have been reacting against the deposition of Duns Scotus and the fathers, effected by the Royal Injunctions. But it is wrong, I think, to consider Watson a champion of the old learning or an insincere devotee of the new. He was indeed a Papist, and as such a conservative; in particular, he must have reacted against the Injunctions' prohibition of lessons from the fathers, for his own sermons are particularly rich in references to the fathers.[49] It is also true that, when he returned to St. John's as Master in 1553, he restored the 1530 statutes of John Fisher in preference to the more liberal ones of 1545. And, finally, we hear nothing of Watson's siding with Smith and Cheke in their attempts to revolutionize the pronunciation of Greek, which were so unremittingly opposed by Gardiner in 1542. On the other hand, everything which Ascham tells us of Watson rings of academic liberalism. Particularly significant is Watson's reputation of having "repurged the errors of Arte [from the university] . . . and set before our eyes a more perfect methode of studie." And surely no advocate of the new learning could have quarreled too seriously with Watson's *Absalom,* even if he did not agree with Ascham's high praise of it. As to the innovations in Greek pronunciation, we hear nothing of Watson's opposing them either; but, even if he had, we must remember that Ascham too resisted them at first and was won over only by his awe of Smith and Cheke.[50] With little doubt, Watson

[49] Bridgett (1876), pp. xiii-xiv, calling the sermons "eminently patristic," counted "more than four hundred marginal references to the Fathers and ecclesiastical writers."

[50] Edward Grant, "De Vita & Obitu Rogeri Aschami," *Disertissimi Viri Rogeri Aschami . . . Familiarum Epistolarum Libri Tres* (London, [1576]), sig. Z1. See Alfred Katterfeld, *Roger Ascham. Sein Leben und seine Werke* (Strassburg, 1879), p. 36n.

was a moderate, certainly favoring the old learning in matters theological (as in the use of lessons from the fathers) but as certainly favoring the new in most matters literary and academic. In other words, he was a humanist. Thus, we are to explain Watson's joining the appeal against Tayler on theological or personal grounds: there is no question that in these areas he sympathized with the other northern men. But whatever Watson's motive for joining the appeal, his doing so is another indication that the period 1534-44 was one of some unhappiness for him.

The quarrel with Tayler was compromised when the three fellows whom Tayler had deprived were reinstated and Leaver was promised admission in the following year. But Tayler stayed on, no doubt as a continuing source of distress to the conservatives. It is an indication of the strife which had been caused by the northern men, and accordingly of the discomfort which they had suffered, that the new statutes of 1545, probably formulated by John Cheke and perhaps requested by Tayler, severely restricted the number of fellows from the nine northern counties (Baker, I, 119). Reason enough for Watson to discard those statutes in 1553! Furthermore, Ascham's letters provide ample testimony of the unrest from which the St. John's fellowship was suffering during the early 1540's. In several of those letters Ascham complained of abuse and rumor-mongering at the hands of his colleagues. The most famous of Ascham's troubles resulted from his support of a candidate for a fellowship in opposition to another candidate supported by Redman (and Watson), but the duration and degree of the difficulties suggest that issues transcending the personalities were involved and that the fellowship was badly split by factionalism.[51]

Baker said (I, 138) that Watson left his fellowship "about the second year of" King Edward's reign, i.e., about 1548. This seems too late. In 1545 Watson was appointed rector of Wyke Regis, Dorset, and chaplain to Stephen Gardiner.[52] Now it was not uncommon for men to hold rectorates while maintaining their Cambridge connections: John Redman, a colleague of Watson, and many others did so, and rectorates were often sinecures. But it does seem highly unlikely that

[51] See Ascham's letters (Giles, I, Part 1, 34 ff.). That the national politico-religious strife did affect the scholars' academic moods is indicated by Ascham's complaints, from a point of view opposite that of Watson, of the miseries at St. John's during the reign of Mary (*Scholemaster,* fols. 55 ff.).

[52] Baker (I, 138, n. 2) implied that Watson assumed the chaplaincy in 1546. But Watson testified, at the trial of Gardiner in early 1551, that he had been Gardiner's chaplain "these five years *and more*" (Foxe, VI, 205; italics mine).

Watson could have carried on the duties of both his fellowship and the chaplaincy to Gardiner, as well as his rectorate, at the same time. Two of Gardiner's other chaplains were also Cambridge men — John Seton, who in 1551 said he had been a chaplain "these seven years" (Foxe, VI, 199), and William Medowe (Foxe, VI, 202) — but apparently neither had continued his Cambridge connections after appointment. If we can trust the evidence of Ascham's Letter XXV (Giles, I, Part 1, 60), written about November, 1544, Watson was then still at Cambridge. If we could believe a report that Watson was imprisoned in the Fleet in 1547 for preaching at Winchester against two reformers who complained to Somerset and Sir William Cecil, we could almost certainly rule out Baker's 1548 as the date of Watson's departure from Cambridge; but Pollard stated that there is no record of such imprisonment. Even so, I think it is safe to assume that Watson left at the end of academic year 1544-45 — about July, 1545.

At the end of his Cambridge career Watson wrote a twenty-two line Latin commendatory poem (see Appendix A) for the preface of John Seton's *Dialectica* (1545). It appears with three four-line Latin poems and an eight-line Greek poem, the last by John Cheke.

After leaving Cambridge, Watson was more and more taken up with political and church duties; and he produced no further literary works, unless we include his sermons under that heading. On the third and fifth Fridays of Lent, 1554, Watson preached before Queen Mary on the doctrine of the real presence and on the propriety of private masses; these two sermons were shortly printed in a small quarto volume: *Twoo Notable Sermons . . .* (London, 1554). As Strype put it, the sermons remained unanswered for fifteen years: "such an opinion had [Catholics] of the profound learning of this Doctor, that whatsoever was known of his doing, was thought to be so learnedly done, that none could be found among the Protestants able to answer any part thereof."[53] Eventually, in 1569, Robert Crowley published *A Setting Open of the Subtyle Sophistrie of Thomas Watson . . . Which He Used in Hys Two Sermons . . . upon the Reall Presence,* in which he printed Watson's two sermons side by side with his own strictures upon them. Crowley's publication is sufficient indication of the continuing popularity of Watson's sermons and presumably of Watson's arguments. We know of some of Watson's other sermons, which Pollard said always drew large audiences. For example, on August 20, 1552, he preached at Paul's Cross before the Privy Council, and a

[53] *Ecclesiastical Memorials,* III, Part 1, 114 ff.

heavy guard was stationed to prevent any disturbances; on March 17, 1556/7 he preached again before Mary; on the afternoon of April 4, 1557 — the Sunday before Passion Sunday — he preached at Alhallows the More in Thames Street before a very large audience; on April 21, 1557 — the Wednesday in Easter week — he preached at the Spittle; and on February 20, 1557/8 he preached at Paul's Cross before ten bishops, the Lord Mayor and aldermen, judges and men of law, and a large audience.[54] None of these sermons has survived. In January, 1557/8, a convocation determined to publish a series of expositions of Catholic doctrine similar to the Protestant homilies of 1547, and Watson was called upon to prepare the volume. He revised some sermons which he had preached at court during the previous year and brought out in June, 1558, a volume called *Holsome and Catholyke Doctryne Concerninge the Seuen Sacramentes of Chrystes Church.* The book's popularity is attested by the fact that it was issued ten more times, once (in February, 1558/9) surreptitiously; the only modern edition is T. E. Bridgett's (1876).

The only other writing by Watson of which I know was nonliterary. He helped Stephen Gardiner write an argument against Cranmer: *Confutatio Cavillationum* (printed at Paris in 1552). He left behind a collection of recipes for medicaments called *Certayne Experyments and Approved Medicines Good for Those That Be Any Wayes Diseased;* at least it is attributed to "the famous and renowned Doctor Watson Bishop of Lincoln" by a sixteenth-century hand on the manuscript in the British Museum (Sloan MS. 62, art. 1, fols. 1-15). According to Pollard, a translation of a sermon of St. Cyprian is credited to Watson (Cambridge University MS. KK.1.3, art. 17, and Baker MS. XII, 107) ; I know of no evidence to support the attribution.

Because Watson abandoned literary pursuits after 1545, we need sketch in only briefly the other important events in his life. Baker said (I, 138) that he was uncertain where or how Watson lived in King Edward's time. But at least it is known that Watson was Gardiner's chaplain and that his fortunes fluctuated with Gardiner's: thus, for example, he was an important witness in two of Gardiner's trials and was himself imprisoned two or three times. We hear nothing of Watson from December 3, 1551, when he took part in the disputation mentioned earlier, until Mary's reign. These scattered records do not give a very clear picture of Watson in the period 1545-53, but they seem to indicate that he was only slightly more militant in his religious views than he had been at Cambridge when he signed the oath

[54] *Ibid.*, pp. 2, 3, 108, 513.

upholding the king's supremacy. When he began to hold important offices under Mary, he became more vehement in upholding orthodoxy.

On September 25, 1553, Gardiner, now Chancellor of Cambridge, sent Watson to inquire into the religious conditions of all the colleges there, and on September 28 Watson was admitted Master of St. John's College and made a Doctor of Divinity. Watson was not present at his admission; one Christopher served as his proxy (Baker, I, 137). As stated above, Watson's most significant act as Master was to reinstate Fisher's statutes of 1530 (Baker, I, 138). Gardiner had revoked all the statutes and injunctions put into effect by King Edward; the university had requested their revocation because they "entangled consciences while affording no help to learning" (Mullinger [1884], p. 150), and Gardiner's compliance, as well as Watson's revocation of Cheke's 1545 St. John's statutes, was probably due to politico-religious as much as to academic considerations. In actions not closely connected with his mastership Watson took part in a convocation at St. Paul's on October 23, 1553, and strenuously upheld transubstantiation against James Haddon and others.[55] In April, 1554, Watson was among a party sent to Oxford to dispute with Thomas Cranmer, Nicholas Ridley, and Hugh Latimer a few days before their condemnation; while there Watson was incorporated Doctor of Divinity at Oxford (Strype, *Cranmer,* I, 480 ff.). On November 18, 1553, Watson was named Dean of Durham, and he resigned his mastership of St. John's in May, 1554. In December, 1556, he was elected Bishop of Lincoln; he was confirmed by papal bull on March 24, 1556/7, but not consecrated until August 15, 1557. Meanwhile, on January 26, 1556/7, Watson, Cuthbert Scot, and John Christopherson had been sent by Cardinal Pole to visit Cambridge; while there they presided over the exhumation and burning as heretics of the bodies of Martin Bucer and Paul Fagius (Strype, *Ecclesiastical Memorials,* III, Part 1, 510). Perhaps as much because of circumstances as because of inclination Watson had become the militant Papist he had apparently not been before Mary's reign. Perhaps because those same circumstances had committed him irrevocably, he remained militant under Elizabeth.

With the accession of Elizabeth, Watson's life entered its last phase. In March, 1558/9, he took part in a public dispute between Catholics and Protestants held in Westminster Abbey by order of Elizabeth's Privy Council. The dispute hardly got started before it broke up amid wrangling, and Watson was imprisoned for contempt of Queen Eliza-

[55] Part of the disputation is preserved in the British Museum (Harl. MS. 422, fols. 388 ff.).

beth.[56] He was released in June and given ten days to decide whether to take the new oath of supremacy; refusing, he was deprived of his bishopric on June 26. Less than a year later, in May, 1560, he was again committed to the Tower. He was never again free from confinement, either in the Marshalsea or under the physical supervision of some loyal bishop or in Wisbech Castle, except for three years between 1574 and 1577, when he was released into the custody of his brother John under condition that he not "induce any one to any opinion or act to be done contrary to the laws established in the realm for causes of religion." This freedom he lost because he was accused of having abused it by entertaining subversive persons — a charge which he denied.[57] In April, 1580, he engaged in a mysterious exchange of letters with the King of Portugal and his confessor; the letters were intercepted and were the cause of some rather severe interrogations,[58] suggesting that his denial of subversion may not have been perfectly honest. In October, 1578, he had appealed to Lord Burghley to be released again because his physical condition made further confinement very uncomfortable; the Bishop of Winchester supported his plea in a letter to Burghley dated October 7, 1578.[59] But the appeal was apparently not acted upon, for he lived out his days first under the eye of the Bishop of Winchester and then, after he had entered into correspondence with the Catholics at Douai, at Wisbech Castle with a number of other Roman priests. His name appears periodically in the official correspondence of Cecil and others throughout the years of the confinement as the authorities were ever in doubt as to what to do with the deprived bishops.[60] Watson died September 27, 1584.

Watson has been called "an austere, or rather a sour and churlish

[56] John Strype, *Annals of the Reformation* (Oxford, 1824), I, Part 1, 128 ff.

[57] Note Watson's statement on this subject in the letter to Burghley reproduced herein.

[58] Bridgett (1876), pp. lxiv-lxvi.

[59] *Calendar of the Manuscripts of Salisbury,* II, 212.

[60] One critic argued that Spenser was alluding to Watson in the fable of the briar and the oak (*Shepheardes Calender,* February, 207-213); see Brents Stirling, "Spenser and Thomas Watson, Bishop of Lincoln," *PQ,* X (1931), 321-328. For other suggested Spenserian allusions to Watson, see *The Works of Edmund Spenser: The Minor Poems,* variorum ed., by Edwin Greenlaw *et al.,* I (Baltimore, 1943), 261-262, 361-363. Spenser must have known of Watson in at least a literary context, for Harvey cited Ascham's remarks about him: finding a fault in Spenser's quantitative verse, Harvey chortled, "Lo here . . . *M. Watsons Anapaestus* for all the worlde" ("Tvvo Other Very Commendable Letters," *The Poetical Works of Edmund Spenser,* ed. J. C. Smith and E. de Selincourt [London, 1912], p. 640); see below, pp. 72-80.

man,"[61] and "learned in deep divinity, but surly with an austere gravity."[62] Pollard accepted the austerity, but thought the remainder to be a gloss due to religious antipathy, and what evidence there is supports Pollard's view. Ascham's view of "myne old frend" is well known and has been cited above, but I might call attention particularly to his statement of Watson's having spoken to him "merelie" about his colleague who wrote bad tragedies. Watson apparently had a reputation throughout the century as a wit. Thomas Nashe told "a notable iest I heard long a goe of Doctor *Watson*" concerning a priest who ate meat on a fast day when all other priests present ate the appropriate fish; the guilty priest for excuse "said to his friend that brought him thither, *Profecto, Domine, ego sum malissimus piscator,* meaning by *piscator,* a Fishman. . . . *At tu es bonissimus carnifex,* quoth Doctor *Watson,* retorting very merily his owne licentious figures vpon him" (*Works,* McKerrow, I, 201-202). The work was first published in 1592. These "iests" may have a modicum of bitterness in them, but for merriness of another kind McKerrow thought (IV, 126) that "the witty Tom Watson whose jests are referred to by Harington in his *Ulysses vpon Ajax*" was our bishop.[63]

Whatever his temperament, Watson probably deserved Ascham's praise for his learning and is important for his eminence among Catholics of his century. It is a fortunate accident that this learned English humanist has left us a play by which we may judge the literary temper which guided him and his St. John's colleagues and by which we may evaluate Ascham's judgment of the standards of learning in his age.

[61] By Godwin, as quoted by Strype, *Ecclesiastical Memorials,* III, Part 1, 114.

[62] By Camden, as quoted by Anthony à Wood, I, cols. 710-711.

[63] Harington probably did not write *Ulysses upon Ajax;* see Elizabeth Story Donno, ed., *Sir John Harington's A New Discourse of a Stale Subject, Called the Metamorphosis of Ajax* (London, 1962), pp. 14-17. This reference was called to my attention by Professor Robert H. Ball.

CHAPTER THREE

THE DATE OF THE PLAY

HISTORY OF THE QUESTION

Most critics who have mentioned *Absalom,* often in connection with John Watson rather than Thomas and in ignorance of the survival of the manuscript, gave no date at all. Frederick Fleay was apparently the earliest scholar to say anything about date, but he was speaking not of our play but of a lost *Two Sins of King David,* known from a Stationers' Register entry for 1561-62. Fleay conjectured that the lost play was a revival of "Bale's *David and Absalom* (extant in MS.)" — i.e., of Watson's play.[1] However, this conjecture cannot be seriously entertained. The S.R. entry identifies the play as *"an new interlude of the ij synmes ⟨sins⟩ of kynge DAVYD."*[2] Apart from the fact that even a revival of "David and Absalom" would not be "new" in 1561-62, I cannot see how any amount of revision could make the Senecan tragedy before us now into an "interlude" of any kind, especially one concerned with the sins of David rather than with a result of those sins, the rebellion of Absalom.

Sir Edmund K. Chambers listed "Absolon" under the "Latin Neo-Mysteries" in his monumental work *Mediaeval Stage* (II, 458), and he gave as the limits of composition 1535 and 1545. The former year he probably based upon Pollard's statement (in *D.N.B.*) that Watson was elected a fellow "about 1535," the latter upon Watson's apparently leaving Cambridge to become chaplain to Gardiner in 1545. In his later *Elizabethan Stage* (IV, 409), Chambers, without supplying reasons, gave the date of the play as "*c* 1535." Later writers on the play contributed nothing new. Boas (p. 386), without defining the limits of composition, listed the play as "*c.* 1540," apparently simply

[1] *Biographical Chronicle,* II, 293. See also II, 267.

[2] Edward Arber, ed., *A Transcript of the Registers of the Company of Stationers of London: 1554-1640 A.D.,* I (London, 1875), 181.

choosing a round number midway between the limits set by Chambers. Harbage (pp. 28-29) did not attempt to narrow the limits 1535 and 1544. All other writers apparently followed either Boas or Harbage.[3]

EXTERNAL EVIDENCE

T. W. Baldwin, writing of Foxe's *Christus Triumphans,* said that "at this period in England such plays in Latin were written only or usually for [university audiences]."[4] We would normally assume that *Absalom* was some sort of exercise written by Watson while he was at Cambridge. An oft-quoted passage in Ascham's *Scholemaster* confirms that assumption: "Whan M. Watson in S. Johns College at Cambridge wrote his excellent Tragedie of Absalon, M. Cheke, he and I, for that part of trew Imitation, had many pleasant talkes togither, in comparing the preceptes of Aristotle and Horace *de Arte Poetica,* with the examples of Euripides, Sophocles, and Seneca" (fol. 57*r*). The St. John's bursarial accounts are preserved only after 1555 — too late to help with the dating of *Absalom* (Moore Smith, p. 266). Whether Watson's play was ever performed is problematical. In a continuation of the passage quoted above Ascham said that only *Absalom* and Buchanan's *Iephthes* of the plays "that euer I saw" measured up to Aristotle's precepts and Euripides' examples. Ascham could have "seen" the plays on stage, as Moore Smith thought (p. 268), or in manuscript. We have no independent knowledge of performances of Buchanan's play, which was of course not a St. John's nor even an English product, to assist our interpretation. Boas (p. 21) noted productions at Trinity College, Cambridge, of "*John babtiste* . . . in 1562/3 [which] was probably Buchanan's tragedy, and *Iephthes* in 1566/7 [which was] either his Latin play or the one by Christopherson." Of course these dates are later than the composition of *The Scholemaster* and much later than Ascham's "tyme" in Cambridge. *Iephthes* was a very influential play after it was published in 1554, but whether

[3] Churchill and Keller (p. 299), noting that Cheke left Cambridge in 1544, said only that *Absalom* "scheint . . . vor 1559 geschrieben zu sein." Miss Sibley (p. 1), L. E. Kastner and H. B. Charlton (*The Poetical Works of Sir William Alexander Earl of Stirling,* The Scottish Text Society [Edinburgh, 1921-29], I, cxxxix, n. 1), and G. C. Moore Smith ("Plays Performed in Cambridge Colleges Before 1585," *Fasciculus Ioanni Willis Clark Dicatus* [Cambridge, 1909], p. 268) all gave the date "c. 1540." T. W. Baldwin (*Five-Act Structure,* p. 357) accepted Harbage's limits, "*c.* 1535-44," and added that a "detailed study of the university careers of [Ascham, Cheke, and Watson] would certainly narrow the date very closely."

[4] *Five-Act Structure,* p. 354.

it would have been available in manuscript before then to the English scholars is doubtful. Perhaps Ascham, writing in the 1560's, had "seen" only the 1554 edition of *Iephthes* — and had not seen it at all while he was at Cambridge. However that may be, the very existence of Watson's *Absalom* in a completed form is perhaps presumptive evidence of performance.

Lacking documentary evidence of date, we can do little more than define certain limits of composition. The play was probably written during Watson's fellowship, as indicated by Ascham's remark that he, Cheke, and Watson had "many pleasant talkes *togither*" during its composition. The wording implies some equality of station. As we have seen, Watson's fellowship probably dates from 1533 or 1534, our *terminus a quo*. If Ascham's use of the words "M. Watson," i.e., Master Watson, meant literally that Watson was a master when he wrote the play, we would move up the *terminus a quo* to 1535-36. And in any case we should probably consider the year after each of these *termini* as the first eligible year; for if the play was written for performance, it would have been written for performance during the post-Christmas play "season," which ended before the spring elections to fellowships and the summer awards of degrees. Moreover, I suppose that Watson would not immediately have begun to write a play after being appointed to a fellowship, and I would place the writing at a later period in his college career.

As we have seen, Watson probably left Cambridge in 1545, our *terminus ad quem*. But we can move this back one year too, for Cheke, who was present during the composition of the play, was called to the court in July, 1544, as tutor to Prince Edward (Baker, I, 118), and he apparently did not return to Cambridge until 1548 or 1549 — after Watson had left (Baker, I, 125; *D.N.B.*).

Within these limits we can probably eliminate some years from consideration. As we have seen, Watson may have been absent from Cambridge during at least a part of 1538-39. From all available information Cheke was at Cambridge almost continuously from the time when he received his M.A. (1533) until he departed in 1544, for I have found references to him (in the grace books and in Baker) for every year. But Ascham was not continuously present; and the play was not written while he was gone, for he joined Watson and Cheke in those discussions. Ascham was elected fellow on March 26, 1534 (Baker, I, 283); this date confirms the earlier *terminus a quo* given above, for Ascham would probably not have joined the discussions if he were not an equal of the author. In fact, it moves that *terminus* up to 1535 because of the timing of the play "season" discussed above. After 1534 Ascham was apparently at Cambridge continuously through 1539-40. In Letter II (Giles, I, Part 1, 3-4), Ascham stated that seven years had elapsed between visits to his parents. The letter is undated, but it certainly antedates 1541: that year Ascham spent with his parents because of illness, and his parents died in 1543 or 1544. Thus, it embraces at least some of the years after 1534. Giles dated the letter in 1538 without giving reasons; Katterfeld (p. 21, n. 1) dated it in the fall of 1537 on the guess that the seven-year period began with Ascham's matriculation in the fall of 1530 and ended with his attaining the M.A. on July 3, 1537. Besides this letter, a number of references to Ascham in the Cambridge archives place him in residence during several of these years. Finally, a few of Ascham's other letters were apparently written from Cambridge during the period 1538-40. But he was certainly gone from Cambridge during the 1541-42 academic year, after his quarrels over the election of John Thomson to a fellowship; hence, *Absalom* could not have been written during that year.[5]

Internal circumstances at St. John's give us no sure basis for narrowing the limits further. As we have seen, the late thirties were disturbed by the Royal Injunctions and by the dismissal of Nicholas Metcalfe, by the short mastership of George Day, and by the unpopular one of John Tayler. The early forties were disturbed by a quarrel over Greek pronunciation between Gardiner on the one hand and Thomas Smith and the core of the St. John's fellowship, especially Cheke, on the other; by the continued unhappiness of many fellows with the mastership of Tayler; and by the personal estrangements resulting from Ascham's efforts on behalf of John Thomson in 1540. (Incidentally, though Watson apparently supported Thomson's rival and was thus opposed to Ascham, he apparently did not become estranged from Ascham; for Ascham's glowing references to him would be quite inconsistent with references in the letters to backbiters if Watson had been one of those backbiters.) Katterfeld, after a study of Ascham's personal situation, concluded (pp. 29-30) that the bitterness resulting from the quarrel over Thomson had ended when Ascham returned to Cambridge in 1542 and that the period 1542-44 was the happiest of Ascham's life, when he had no financial worries and when he had time for study, for archery and other recreation, and for conversation with his friends — when, in short, conditions were most nearly like those which Ascham described as prevailing when *Absalom*

[5] I present the evidence for the careers of Ascham and Cheke in Appendix C.

was written. But I think it far more likely that, even during the times of distractions of various sorts, academic routines went along more or less normally just as they do in university circles today, and that the play could have been written and discussed in either the thirties or the forties insofar as the college situation is concerned.

As we shall see in the next chapter, Watson used original sources in the writing of *Absalom.* Those sources were, for the plot, a Latin version of the Bible and, for much of the phrasing, Seneca's tragedies. I have not been able to determine which edition of either he used. Of some forty-four Bibles dating from 1530 to 1544 which I have checked, none matches identically the wording and the spellings of proper names in *Absalom.* Those whose spellings of proper names come closest are two editions of a Paris Bible, one dating from 1531-35,[6] the other from 1531-40.[7] But even these do not have Watson's spellings *Berseba* (accusative, III.3.173); *Mariam* (nominative, III.3.93, altered from *Mariah*); and *Chore* (nominative, I.3.142).[8] In fact, no Bible which I have seen has the first two of these spellings. For the Seneca I am convinced that Watson used original materials rather than collections of "flowers" (of which there were few this early in the century). I have found no commonplace book which could have supplied all the Senecan passages which Watson used (see List of Works Used, s.v. "Commonplaces"); and we might suppose, anyway, that Watson shared his friend Ascham's negative attitude concerning the worth of "Epitomes" like Textor's, Horman's, and Whittinton's. More significantly, as we shall see, Watson quoted Senecan passages not merely because their content was appropriate to his needs but also because they were spoken by characters of types parallel to those in his play; hence, he almost certainly had a thorough knowledge of the whole context of the passages which he quoted.

Even without knowledge of which editions of his sources Watson used in writing *Absalom,* we might gain some helpful information about dating if we knew which edition of Horace or Aristotle formed the basis of the "many pleasant talkes" among Cheke, Ascham, and Watson when the play was written. However, there were many editions of Horace. If the scholars were using a Latin version of Aristotle, it could have been Georgio Valla's translation of 1498, but it would more likely have been Paccius' translation of 1536, which was much

[6] B.M. shelfmark 3015 aa 21: *Pentateuchus Moysi . . . Libri Regum IIII* . . . (Paris: In officina S. Colinaei, 1532, 1531-35).

[7] B.M. shelfmark 3022 b 54: title, city, and publisher identical with that in n. 6 (1539, 1531-40).

[8] See Appendix B.

more influential.[9] More probably, however, they were employing one of several Greek editions. Yet another supplemental book may be useful here: as we shall see in the next chapter, it is possible that Terentianus had some influence on metrical discussions of *Absalom* by the St. John's circle; and this text is said to have come into the hands of John Cheke at Cambridge shortly after 1535 (Mullinger [1884], p. 55).

Other investigations which I have made have not narrowed the date further with any degree of probability. At least, however, some other tests serve a broadly corroborative purpose.

PHYSICAL EVIDENCE

In the *Absalom* manuscript six complete and two half specimens of the same watermark are visible. The "complete" watermarks are in every instance divided between two leaves, but they are easily discernible as the top and bottom halves of one mark. This watermark consists of a shield with two diagonals containing *cotices potencees* and *contre-potencees;* a chef with three fleurs-de-lis; and beneath the shield the initials "I. P." I have found no other record of an identical watermark, and I have not made what might be a fruitful search through Cambridge records of this time for other specimens of this stock of paper. But C. M. Briquet has reproduced several watermarks obviously belonging to the same family.[10] The shield and chef of our watermark constitute the coat of arms of Troyes, in the province of Champagne, France. This city had in the fifteenth century become England's main source of paper and was still an important source in the sixteenth century.[11] Now, those watermarks in Briquet (Plates 1048-55) which show a close relationship to the *Absalom* mark — i.e., which contain the arms of Troyes rather than the similar arms of Champagne — are all from documents dated between 1526 and 1549, with Plate 1054 having as well a lone exemplar from 1561 (Briquet, I, 87-88). Several of these plates (1048-51), from documents dated 1526-47, are especially interesting because, like the *Absalom* mark, they show the initials "I. P." and may therefore have been made by the same papermaker. But all of them are somewhat more complex than

[9] Marvin T. Herrick, *The Fusion of Horatian and Aristotelian Literary Criticism,* Illinois Studies in Language and Literature, XXXII (Urbana, 1946), p. 1.

[10] *Les Filigranes* (Paris, 1907).

[11] Edward Heawood, "Sources of Early English Paper-Supply," *Library,* 2nd ser., X (1929-30), 306-307.

the *Absalom* watermark and could conceivably represent a somewhat later stage in the development of this family. The mark most like ours (Plate 1050) is found in Continental records dated 1530-36. That these papers would have made their way to England is proved by a specimen of Briquet's Plate 1048 (though with indistinct initials) in the State Papers (Domestic) for 1544-46 in the Public Record Office.[12] In general, then, the period of years bracketed by all these closely related marks serves to support the limits already set for the writing of *Absalom*.

INTERNAL EVIDENCE

In the Notes to the Translation I suggest that two passages of *Absalom* (I.2.6-9 and III.1.61) may contain topical allusions. If Watson was in fact alluding to Henry's divorce, to the hard times caused Catholic fellows by the Royal Injunctions of 1535, to the looting of the monasteries, etc., the allusions indicate a *terminus a quo* of about 1535. And because the most definite of these supposed allusions is to the looting of the monasteries, we should assume that enough time had elapsed so that the monasteries were largely despoiled: this would set the composition in or, more likely, later than 1536-37, already suggested as the probable early limit.

T. W. Baldwin's analysis of the structure of the play generally corroborates our previous findings without allowing further narrowing. Arguing that Watson and Ascham would not have interpreted Aristotle as including the minor unities, he pointed out that these unities became "law" only after "Castelvetro promulgated it in 1570." And he associated the act structure of the play with Donatus' theory of the placement of the epitasis rather than the later theory which "became definite with Willichius in 1539, and became 'law' hardly earlier than Scaliger's *Poetics*, 1561." He concluded that "*Absalon* is about what we should expect of an author working in the period 1535-44 on such principles as Ascham describes."[13]

[12] *Ibid.*, p. 430. That this family of watermarks attained fairly wide dissemination is proved by its occurrence in Flanders and Zeeland over a period of almost twenty years, from 1537 to 1554 (J. H. de Stoppelaar, *Het Papier in de Nederlanden gedurende de Middeleeuwen, inzonderheid in Zeeland* [Middelburg, 1869], p. 92). De Stoppelaar found one especially significant example of a watermark, showing the Troyes coat of arms and the initials "I. P.," at Middelburg in a document of 1540; other marks with the same initials occurred in shipping accounts at Sluis between 1547-49 and 1550-54.

[13] *Five-Act Structure*, pp. 362-364.

SIGNIFICANCE

The limits thus defined allow us with little difficulty to fit *Absalom* into the broad trends of the university drama as they were developing in the first half of the sixteenth century. F. S. Boas, by reference to the account books of Magdalen College, Oxford, aptly stated what we know of those trends: ". . . the verbal distinctions in the Magdalen accounts are very suggestive. In 1486, 1487, and 1495 'ludus' (or 'lusores') is used; in 1502, 1512, and 1531 'interludia' is substituted; in 1532 'ludus' reappears in 'ludus baccalaureorum'; in 1535, 1539, 1540, 1541, and 1544 'comedia' and 'tragedia' take the place of the earlier terms. Without unduly pressing the phraseology, it is a fair inference that we see reflected in it the broad lines of transition from the morality to the interlude and thence to the comedy and tragedy of classical origin or inspiration" (pp. 11-12). *Absalom* is a "tragedia," and, assuming roughly parallel development at Oxford and Cambridge, the Magdalen account books at least do not quarrel with our placing Watson's play in the period 1536-44 as a very early example of the trend to true tragedy. However, a closer examination of the drama of the period gives us reason to doubt seriously whether the Magdalen account book intended the word *tragedia* to mean what we infer from it: "Up to 1559 tragedy hardly enters the story of English drama. For the people at large, delight in the rough humour of comic interludes left little demand for 'serious' drama beyond what could be provided by the sermonisings which were the ballast of the moralities and interludes; and for those whose superior learning required a more literary-seeming product, there were the English offshoots of the humanist *tragicomoedia sacra* for performance, generally in Latin, at the universities and, very probably, in English in town and country" (Kastner and Charlton, I, cxxxix). In other words, tragedy was not yet Seneca. No performances of Seneca are recorded earlier than 1551-52, when *Troades* was performed at Trinity College, Cambridge; after that no further performances are recorded until 1559-60, when a *Hecuba* (Seneca's *Troades*?) and an *Oedipus* were put on at Trinity College, Cambridge.[14] Few native tragic productions besides *Absalom* appear in these early years: among the few are Nicholas Grimald's *Christus Rediuiuus* (1540), *Christus Nascens* (1540), and *Archipropheta* (1546-47), all at Oxford; John Christopherson's Ἰεφθάε (Trinity College, Cambridge, *ca.* 1544);[15] and John Foxe's *Christus Triumphans* (?Ox-

[14] Boas, pp. 386-387. Several other performances of Seneca (probably) followed closely after these.

[15] *Ibid.*, p. 386.

ford, 1539-45).[16] But, with the exception of Christopherson's play, these are "not tragedy, but moral plays"[17] — *tragicomoediae sacrae.* Foxe's play especially has no structural or tonal relationship with Seneca, being a "chronicle allegory of the church"[18] without chorus and with no concept of unities. Though Grimald shows "some tincture of the classical tradition," he has written in *Christus Rediuiuus* what his tutor, John Airy, called a tragicomedy,[19] and in *Archipropheta* a play which ends on the victorious note of John the Baptist's being approved by Heaven — not a tragedy, but "a Biblical story in five-act form, with commenting Chorus."[20] Grimald's plays represent, in Kastner and Charlton's words, a drama "created by Northern, and specifically Dutch and German, Humanism. . . . It proceeds not from a tragic but from a comic source, Terence" (I, lix-lx). Only Christopherson's Ἰεφθάε can be called a tragedy in the classical sense, but it is almost unique in the century as being avowedly modeled upon a Euripidean rather than a Senecan model and is thus not comparable to *Absalom.*[21] Not until *Gorboduc* (1561-62) and the small surviving group of plays influenced by it do we find anything comparable in Senecanism to *Absalom.* And then we find it in an altogether different vehicle: in a vernacular play on a native subject having political overtones — in other words, in an entirely different phase of English tragedy. Thus, the "tragedia" of the Magdalen account books in the 1540's does not mean "tragedy" in our sense and, in its own sense, does not apply to *Absalom.* But the Magdalen entries do at least show that *Absalom* reflects the trend of the thirties and forties toward more serious drama in some form; it is in its form, as a more or less strictly Senecan tragedy, that *Absalom* is anomalous in its time in England. But this anomaly should not cause doubt of the early date which we have assigned to the play. *Gorboduc,* of a later stage in the development of English tragedy, is a very early example of that stage because the lawyers who wrote it were literary liberals with tastes advanced beyond those of contemporaries. In the same way *Absalom* is the product of a literary liberal — or rather a group of liberals. The St. John's fellows who originated a new method of pronouncing Greek and nurtured a revolution in educational methods would not, like the rest of English taste, have lagged far behind the Continental view of

[16] Baldwin, *Five-Act Structure,* p. 354.
[17] *Ibid.,* p. 365.
[18] *Ibid.,* p. 355.
[19] *Ibid.,* pp. 349, 353.
[20] *Ibid.,* p. 352.
[21] Kastner and Charlton, I, lxii.

tragedia. And on the Continent at this very time were being produced Senecan plays comparable in structure to *Absalom.* Notable among these, because Ascham paired it with *Absalom* in its following of classical precepts and examples, was Buchanan's *Iephthes.* This play was written "during the time that Buchanan was at Bordeaux, 1539-42,"[22] i.e., at the same general time as we have set for *Absalom.* Even apart from Ascham's tying *Absalom* in with a datable touchstone, his statement gives clear evidence of the St. John's scholars' distaste for contemporary *tragicomoedia;* thus, when Watson as one of that coterie started to write a tragedy, he turned to Seneca himself and turned out a work comparable to that of his Continental contemporaries. And except that the statement ignores Christopherson's play, T. W. Baldwin was quite right in saying that *Absalom* "is really the only possible surviving regular tragedy in England before *Gorboduc.*"[23]

[22] David Murray, "Catalogue of Printed Books, Manuscripts, Charters, and Other Documents Relating to George Buchanan or Illustrative of His Life," *George Buchanan,* Glasgow Quatercentenary Studies 1906 (Glasgow, 1907), pp. 402-403. I should date the play 1541: Buchanan said that he had written four tragedies "in compliance with a custom of the college, which required a tragedy every year," and he named the order as *Baptistes,* the translation of Euripides' *Medea, Iephthes,* and *Alcestis* ("Life of George Buchanan. [Written by Himself Two Years Before His Death]," tr. Alexander Gibb in the appendix to his translation of *The Jephtha and Baptist* [Edinburgh, 1870], p. 214).

[23] *Five-Act Structure,* p. 365.

CHAPTER FOUR

THE "IMITATION" OF SOURCE ACCORDING TO CLASSICAL PRECEPTS AND EXAMPLES

SOURCE

The source of Thomas Watson's *Absalom* was some Latin version of the Bible. I know of no intermediate treatment of the David and Absalom story which Watson might have used to supplement the Bible. In Spain, Vasco Diaz Tanco de Fregenal around 1520 wrote a play which he termed the *Tragedia de Absalon;* but it was apparently never printed and perhaps never acted, and Watson could hardly have known it.[1] Another Continental treatment of the story, by the Swiss writer and minor municipal official Josias Murer, was written later than Watson's play (printed 1565). Watson could not have used Murer, and Murer surely did not use Watson: the Swiss play, a vernacular morality play, covers a much broader scope and gives comic scenes to such characters as sick devils, a fool, a cook, and a simpleton.[2] An English play, George Peele's *The Love of King David and Fair Bethsabe. With the Tragedie of Absalon,* followed Watson's by half a century (printed 1599). Churchill and Keller thought it "nicht unmöglich" that Peele had seen Watson's play (p. 230), but Boas found "not the slightest internal evidence that [Peele's play] was influenced by any academic Latin model" (p. 363). I agree with Boas: not only are the tone and scope of the two works quite different (Peele's play being a romantic treatment of David's whole affair with Bethsabe and of its aftermath, including Absalom's rebellion); Peele's motivations, his arrangement of incidents, and his structure all indicate

[1] Creizenach, III, 127; D. Leandro Fernández de Moratín, *Obras . . . Dadas á Luz por la Real Academia de Historia* (Madrid, 1830-31), I, 150-151.

[2] Josias Murer, *Absolom ein Spyl von einer jungen Burgerschafft . . .* (Zurich, 1565). The play is mentioned by Creizenach, III, 330, and summarized by Emil Weller, *Das alte Volks-Theater der Schweiz* (Frauenfeld, 1863), pp. 193-196. The unique copy of the play is at Zurich University.

direct use of the Bible without reference to or knowledge of Watson's manuscript play.[3] As a classical tragedy directly based upon the Bible, Watson's *Absalom* stands as a unique treatment of the David and Absalom story.

The Biblical account of Absalom's rebellion and its aftermath is given in *2 Samuel* xiii.1-xix.30. (I shall refer to this book as *2 Kings,* for it was so called in the Latin Bibles which Watson would have known and is still so called in many Bibles; unless otherwise indicated, my quotations will be from a modern translation of the Vulgate.) The parts actually dramatized in *Absalom* occur in *2 Kings* between xiv.32 and xix.8. In the background of Absalom's revolt lay David's lust for Bethsabe and consequent murder of her husband, Urias. Because of this act, God had prophesied to David, through Nathan, that the sword would never depart from his house: "Behold, I will raise up evil against thee out of thy own house, and I will take thy wives before thy eyes and give them to thy neighbor, and he shall lie with thy wives in the sight of this sun" (*2 Kings* xii.11). The immediate background of the play was as follows: Amnon, David's oldest son (by Achinoam), had lusted for his half sister Thamar (daughter of David by Maacah) and, with the aid of David's nephew Jonadab, had raped her (*2 Kings* xiii.1-20). Two years later Absalom, full brother of Thamar, contrived to avenge his sister's shame by inviting all of David's sons to a feast and then ambushing and slaying Amnon (*2 Kings* xiii.23-29). Forced to flee David's wrath, Absalom sought refuge in Gessur, Syria, ruled by his maternal grandfather, Tholmai; he remained there three years (*2 Kings* xiii.30-38). After David's anger had abated, Joab, David's nephew and military leader, interceded with the king and gained permission for Absalom to return to Jerusalem (*2 Kings* xiv.1-21); but David's consent was made conditional on Absalom's not being admitted to the king's presence. Two years after his return, Absalom twice besought Joab's further assistance; when Joab refused even to come to see Absalom, the prince ordered his servants to burn Joab's cornfield. Joab then came. With their conversation Watson began his play.

WATSON'S GENERAL METHOD

F. S. Boas (pp. 352 ff.) analyzed in some detail the differences and similarities between Watson's *Absalom* and its source; in the first note

[3] A facsimile of the 1599 edition is available in the Malone Society Reprints, ed. W. W. Greg (Oxford, 1912). Boas (pp. 363-365) compared the two plays critically. For the structure see T. W. Baldwin, *On the Literary Genetics of Shakspere's Plays 1592-1594* (Urbana, Ill., 1959), p. 523.

to each scene of the translation, I have specified the verses which Watson used in that scene. My purpose in the present chapter is to determine the principles by which Watson altered his source to fit his own needs. We get a general impression of these principles from Ascham's encomium of *Absalom,* which must be quoted in full:

. . . who soeuer hath bene diligent to read aduisedlie ouer, Terence, Seneca, Virgil, Horace, or els Aristophanus, Sophocles, Homer, and Pindar, and shall diligently marke the difference they vse, in proprietie of wordes, in forme of sentence, in handlyng of their matter, he shall easelie perceive, what is fitte and *decorum* in euerie one, to the trew vse of perfite Imitation. Whan M. Watson in S. Johns College at Cambrige wrote his excellent Tragedie of Absalon, M. Cheke, he and I, for that part of trew Imitation, had many pleasant talkes togither, in comparing the preceptes of Aristotle and Horace *de Arte Poetica,* with the examples of Euripides, Sophocles, and Seneca. Few men, in writyng of Tragedies in our dayes, haue shot at this marke. Some in England, moe in France, Germanie, and Italie, also haue written Tragedies in our tyme: of the which, not one I am sure is able to abyde the trew touch of Aristotles preceptes, and Euripides examples, saue onely two, that euer I saw, M. Watsons Absalon, and Georgius Buckananus Iephthe [*Scholemaster* (1570), fol. 57*r*].

It has been amply demonstrated that critics in the sixteenth century frequently cited Aristotle as authority at the same time that they "subjugated" Aristotle to Horace in the light of Terentian practice.[4] Much of the reconciliation of the two classical critics occurred after the forties, but no doubt the Cambridge coterie were in one way or another trying to reconcile the two in their "pleasant talkes." In mentioning only Aristotle at the last, Ascham was merely choosing the name with greater prestige (because Greek); in interpreting critical influences on Watson, we must consider both "Aristotle and Horace *de Arte Poetica.*"

Ascham undoubtedly thought "Euripides examples" a more important influence on Watson and Buchanan than he did "Aristotles preceptes": "Surelie, one example," he had said (fol. 20*v*), following Plato, "is more valiable, both to good and ill, than xx. preceptes written in bookes." The key word to consider along with "examples" is "Imitation," both "trew" and "perfite." As Herrick wrote (p. 28), the "sixteenth-century concept of poetic imitation is inherited from Plato and Aristotle by way of Cicero, Horace, and Quintilian." By imitation Aristotle, like Plato, meant representation of life,[5] and many

[4] Herrick, p. 106 *et pass.;* Baldwin, *Five-Act Structure,* pp. 264 ff.

[5] *Poetics* (*On the Art of Fiction: An English Translation* by L. J. Potts [Cambridge, 1953]), Chs. IV, IX, *et pass.*

sixteenth-century commentators on Horace found identical meaning in *Ars Poetica* 317-318:

> respicere exemplar vitae morumque iubebo
> doctum imitatorem et vivas hinc ducere voces.[6]

But this is creative imitation, and Ascham as a teacher of Latin is not concerned with it: "The whole doctrine of Comedies and Tragedies, is a perfite *imitation,* or faire liuelie painted picture of the life of euerie degree of man. Of this *Imitation* writeth *Plato* at large in *3. de Rep.* but doth not moch belong at this time to our purpose" (fol. 47*r*). Nor, we may be sure, did this kind of imitation belong to the purpose of Ascham, Watson, and Cheke as young scholars investigating tragedy. The imitation for which Ascham praised Watson resulted in "proprietie of wordes," in decorous "forme of sentence," in fit "handlyng of . . . matter." Thus, it belongs to the last two of Ascham's kinds of imitation:

> The second kind of *Imitation,* is to folow for learning of tonges and sciences, the best authors. Here riseth, emonges proude and enuious wittes, a great controuersie, whether, one or many are to be followed: and if one, who is that one: *Seneca,* or *Cicero: Salust* or *Caesar,* and so forth in Greeke and Latin.
>
> The third kinde of *Imitation,* belongeth to the second: as when you be determined, whether ye will folow one or mo, to know perfitlie, and which way to folow that one: in what place: by what meane and order: by what tooles and instrumentes ye shall do it, by what skill and iudgement, ye shall trewelie discerne, whether ye folow rightlie or no [fol. 47*r*].

Just so, Ascham recognized, did the Latins imitate the Greeks, and the proper study of their method of imitation would teach us how to imitate. The proper study, or rather the proper teaching, would be to lay a known imitator (say Cicero) and his model (Demosthenes) side by side and "teach plainlie withall, after this sort."

> 1. *Tullie* reteyneth thus moch of the matter, thies sentences, thies wordes:
> 2. This and that he leaueth out, which he doth wittelie to this end and purpose.
> 3. This he addeth here.
> 4. This he diminisheth there.
> 5. This he ordereth thus, with placing that here, not there.
> 6. This he altereth and changeth, either, in propertie of wordes, in forme of sentence, in substance of the matter, or in one, or other conuenient circumstance of the authors present purpose. In thies fewe rude English wordes, are wrapt vp all the necessarie tooles and instrumentes, wherewith trewe *Imitation* is rightlie wrought withall in any tonge [fols. 47*v*-48*r*].

Thus did Tully imitate, and with good effect: "The best booke that

[6] Herrick, pp. 28-29.

euer *Tullie* wrote . . . is his booke *de Orat. ad Q. F.* . . . the whole booke consisteth in . . . good matter, and good handling of the matter. And first, for the matter, it is whole *Aristotles* . . . for the handling of the matter, was *Tullie* so precise and curious rather to follow an other mans Paterne [Plato's], than to inuent some newe shape him selfe" (fol. 48*v*). Thus (after lengthy preparation in double translation, etc.) should we imitate. Then our "proprietie of wordes," our "forme of sentence," and our "handlyng of [our] matter" shall be "fitte and *decorum*." Ascham several times gave credit for his whole system of imitation to Johan Sturm and especially to Sir John Cheke, "my dearest frend, and teacher of all the little poore learning I haue" (fols. 48*r*, 56*v*). No doubt Watson was being converted to the same system (if he was not already one of the faithful) in those "many pleasant talkes" at St. John's. We may recall that Ascham praised Cheke and Watson, among others, for moving Cambridge away from its former fault of "reading the preceptes of Aristotle without the examples of other authors." In any case, Ascham praised Watson's play for its use of the system: i.e., for its judicious retentions of matter, sentences, and words that were fit and decorous in the model; for its "witty," — i.e., purposeful — omissions of indecorous things; for its additions, subtractions, and rearrangements; and (though this is of less importance) for its application of Aristotelian and Horatian principles.

The key to successful imitation, of course, lies in the choice of proper models: "soch Authors, as be fullest of good matter and right iudgement in doctrine . . . [and] most proper in wordes, most apte in sentence, most plaine and pure in vttering the same" (fol. 46*r*). Now Sir John Cheke is quoted as having often said that a student who dwells on "Gods holie Bible" and then joins with it the best Greek and Latin authors "must nedes proue an excellent man" (Ascham, fol. 52*r*). As we have seen, Watson used the matter of "Gods holie Bible." For tragedy, Ascham named as classical models Euripides, Sophocles, and Seneca. The Cambridge circle discussed all three, but Ascham finally associated *Absalom* and *Iephthes* with only Euripides. Yet, as we shall see, Watson's play is shot through with lengthy paraphrases of Seneca and shows no direct similarity to Euripides; and Buchanan's *Iephthes,* while structurally much closer to Greek than to Roman models (in the close organic connection of the choruses with the action and in the division into scenes rather than acts), has been called "completely Senecanised" in all that gives it its tone.[7] In Ascham's

[7] Kastner and Charlton, I, l. See also Boas, pp. 60-61.

eyes, the final naming of the Greek Euripides as example, like the naming of the Greek Aristotle for precepts, was undoubtedly a higher praise of Watson and Buchanan and a more intense implied condemnation of other tragedies. For Ascham, like his colleagues, often expressed admiration for the Greeks: "In Tragedies . . . the *Grecians, Sophocles* and *Euripides* far ouer match our *Seneca* in Latin, namely in οἰκονομία *et Decoro,* although *Senacaes* elocution and verse be verie commendable for his tyme" (fol. 52*v*). It is interesting that of all the Greeks Euripides was Seneca's favorite model.[8] And, though Ascham may have been thinking mainly of matter rather than manner, he recognized Seneca's imitation: in his proposed book on imitation he would include "examples of Imitation . . . out of *Seneca* [compared] with *Sophocles* and *Euripides*" (fol. 53*r*); elsewhere (fol. 52*v*) he named the "matters of *Hercules, Thebes, Hippolytus,* and *Troie*" as imitated by Seneca. Thus, Ascham could compare Watson's and Buchanan's Senecan tragedies with the best model, the Greek Euripides, and actually be correct — indirectly. When Ascham himself translated a Greek tragedy (Sophocles' *Philoctetes*), he did it "ad imitationem quantum potui Senecae."[9] He obviously expected a Latin tragedy to be modeled after the tragedies of Seneca (whose "elocution and verse be verie commendable") — and for *Absalom*'s imitation of Seneca (not Euripides) Ascham praised it highly.

Many years after Ascham's death, Buchanan confirmed Ascham's judgment of *Iephthes* by describing his motives for writing tragedies: "[I] wrote them in compliance with a custom of the college [Bordeaux], which required a tragedy every year; and to the end that, by their representation, [I] might recall the young men, as far as [I] was able, from the allegories, in which France at that time took excessive delight, to the imitation of the ancients" (Gibb, p. 214). Perhaps Watson's motive was similar. But Watson, at least, probably had an additional motive.

THOUGHT AND CHARACTER

Implicit in Cheke's naming of "Gods holie Bible" and of classical authors as examples to be imitated is a belief in a dual function of poetry. Many Renaissance writers (Ascham, in practice, included)

[8] Similarities are great in themes, long speeches, stichomythia, organic detachment of the chorus, and some stock characters. See Clarence W. Mendell, *Our Seneca* (New Haven, Conn., 1941), *pass.;* and Howard Vernon Canter, *Rhetorical Elements in the Tragedies of Seneca,* Illinois Studies in Language and Literature, X (Urbana, 1925), 24-25 *et pass.*

[9] Letter XVI (Giles, I, Part 1, 32).

preferred Seneca to the Greeks, the attraction being Seneca's "stately speeches and well-sounding phrases" and his "notable morality."[10] The moral purpose of literature had theoretical support, too. Horace's statements of a dual poetic function ("prodesse . . . aut delectare," "miscuit utile dulci") are commonplace. And the "commentators have no difficulty finding support for Horace's *delectare* in the *Poetics*" (Herrick, p. 43) — especially in Chapter XIV ("tragic pleasure [comes] from pity and fear [and] has to be produced by imitation").[11] They had more difficulty finding Aristotelian support for Horatian didacticism, since Aristotle's "analysis of character in poetry is . . . controlled by aesthetic rather than moral principles" (Potts, p. 75). But according to Herrick (pp. 42-43), many Horatian commentators found morality in Aristotle's discussion of catharsis (*Poetics,* Ch. VI); and the young Cambridge scholars could have interpreted several other passages as pertaining to morals, or at least to manners: e.g., "if any one strings together moral speeches with the language and thought well worked out, he will be doing what is the business of tragedy" (Potts, p. 25). On whatever basis, Ascham's agreement with Cheke's belief in the *utile et dulce* is implicit in his many references to propriety of matter as well as manner and particularly in his advice, already quoted, that models should be "soch Authors, as be fullest of good matter and right iudgement in doctrine." Watson's agreement is shown by his use in *Absalom* of Biblical matter, by his treatment of character, and by his choric odes.

Horace expressly demanded (*Ars Poetica* 196-201) that the chorus favor the good, counsel well, etc.; and Seneca's choruses are intensely moral. Watson's choruses followed both the precept and the example. In *Absalom* there are, to be sure, relatively few verbal echoes of Seneca's choruses, but there are some rather obvious ones: e.g., the paraphrase (in IV.3) of a Senecan chorus' remarks (*Phaedra* 981-989, 1123 ff.) concerning the virtues of the humble life. More important, there are many tonal and material similarities between Seneca's and Watson's choruses. Canter listed among the moral and philosophic commonplaces of Seneca's choruses the following categories: the universality of death, the inevitability of fate, the fickleness of fortune, and the worries attendant upon exalted position as contrasted with the serenity of the humble life; he noted, too, the frequent recollection of the exploits of famous men of the past for their moral example to the

[10] The phrases are Sidney's in *An Apology for Poetry.* See Kastner and Charlton, I, xxiii ff., and Cunliffe, *Early English Classical Tragedies,* p. viii.
[11] Potts, p. 35.

present.[12] Nearly all of these materials appear in *Absalom*. For example, where Seneca's choruses recount the sinful examples of such mythological transgressors as Tantalus, Tityus, or Sisyphus or the glorious exploits of the gods and heroes of ages past, Watson's recount the experiences of such Biblical personages as Joseph, Isaac, Gedeon, and Miriam (II.3) or review as examples of God's power the ten plagues visited upon Egypt through Moses' agency and other marvelous feats from the Old Testament (IV.2). Again, where Seneca's choruses call apostrophically upon Nature or one of the gods to look with favor upon the suffering people, Watson's often call upon God to halt Absalom's perfidy and to save the people. The choruses of *Absalom,* even more than the choruses of Seneca, are often small sermons addressed to Watson's youthful audience — by a man who later became famous for his sermons. In fact, on two occasions (I.3 and II.3) the chorus in direct address advises the *Iuvenes* to follow good counsel, especially the example of David. The homiletic tone of the choruses is emphasized by an apparent attempt to imitate the words of the Psalms. Several choruses actually weave together scattered phrases from the Bible, but the total resemblance is not more phraseological than tonal: such epithets for God as "iron tower," "hard rock," and "our Life, our Health, our Hope, our Right Way, our Protector" (II.1) were very likely intended to recall similar epithets used in the Psalms, in the songs of Moses, and elsewhere in the Old Testament. Thus, Watson blended Biblical and Senecan sentence and tone: pagan and Christian work together in the interest of morality. In this respect *Absalom* is like the plays of the Christian Terence tradition, except that it uses Biblical rather than classical or pseudo-classical materials.

Structurally Watson's choruses might not satisfy his humanist critics. Implicit in the offices which Horace listed for the chorus (ll. 196-201) is a rather close relationship of the chorus with the characters and with the development of the plot; in fact, he made an explicit requirement that

> actoris partis chorus officiumque virile
> defendat, neu quid medios intercinat actus
> quod non proposito conducat et haereat apte.[13]

Aristotle before him had insisted that the chorus be an integral part of the play, "not as it is in Euripides, but as in Sophocles" (Ch. XVIII; Potts, p. 43). Herrick wrote that Renaissance critics and poets echo this rule, "but very few insist upon a strict obedience to it. The

[12] Canter, pp. 38-51; see also Mendell, pp. 152-168.

[13] *Ars Poetica* 193-195. Some editions, however, printed *auctoris* for *actoris* in l. 193.

chorus, when it is used at all, is used in the Roman rather than in the Sophoclean manner" (pp. 94-95). So it is with Watson. His chorus apparently represents no special group of Israeli citizenry, for it is present wherever the different scenes of the play are set. It is simply a group of men (presumably four, like the chorus of *Gorboduc,* for the choruses are apparently divided into four speaking parts) who are always opposed to Absalom's plot. The choruses occasionally refer to incidents which have occurred shortly before, and they always draw a moral from such incidents; but in many instances their statements are so general that a fourth-act chorus could be removed to the first with little or no loss of continuity. Although the chorus does serve as an actor in II.1, its function is restricted to receiving a message. In all these respects Watson's choruses show a marked resemblance to those of Seneca rather than to the chorus theorized by Aristotle or Horace. Canter noted (p. 33 and n. 9) that in only three cases does Seneca's chorus take a real part in the dialogue of a play; its function is "mechanical, that of announcing persons on entering, questioning messengers, interrupting a lament, in a word that of playing the part of a subordinate confidant." And Mendell agreed (p. 114) that the Senecan chorus "is only on the rarest occasions treated as a reality within the play." No more than half the time are Seneca's choral odes directly concerned with the preceding action (Mendell, pp. 130-134). When the theory and the model were at distinct odds, Watson abandoned the theory; as Ascham said, "one example is more valiable . . . than xx. preceptes." The organic detachment of Watson's choruses emphasizes their moral and homiletic purpose.

Watson's moral central theme, his Thought, was one of singular significance to the young men of his audience. It defined the young man's duties to father, to society, and to God: in general terms, it advised a life of virtue and avoidance of the vices of passion and ambition; in particular, it advocated obedience by the child to his parent and his God. The first-act conversations between Absalom and Joab or Achitophel adequately introduce the theme. Absalom invariably expresses the wrong attitude: "It is right that youth indulge its own pleasure"; "A venerable scepter should grace these hands"; "dare some evil deed about which no son of men may be silent." Joab, and at first Achitophel, always points the right way: "an undutiful son [a father] ought never to suffer"; "it is the role of reason to rule, of pleasure to be ruled"; "To accomplish what you wish by waiting is the part of prudence; to lose it by precipitate haste is the part of madness." The chorus makes sure that the audience knows which is right:

"Absalom rages. . . . He rushes toward the death of his holy parent. Let perish wretchedly whoever violates the pious laws of our mother nature." Early in Act II the chorus repeats the lesson: "What certain protection will fathers find sufficient if sons turn out to be bloody parricides?" Then David is introduced in such a way that the contrast with Absalom emphasizes the moral: David will flee because Absalom "is still my son, esteemed in my heart." Whereas Absalom is rash and impatient, David will endure anything — threatened murder by his son or vilification by Semei — because he places faith in God; and again the chorus emphasizes the contrast. Thereafter the play moves steadily toward Absalom's tragedy, necessary because of his sins (and his foolishness in Act III). The final act dwells in detail on the death of the prince ("Evil always demands an evil end"), but also subjects David to heartbreak. Thus, the play ends as Aristotle thought best, with even the good suffering. And the suffering has its moral purpose too: even the pious David must pay for his sins; and his misfortunes now, we have been told in Acts II and V, are a direct result of his lust for Bethsabe and his murder of Urias.

In these ways Watson's characterization contributes to his Thought, and his interpolations into the characters of David and Absalom are an interesting reflection of his art. David's reason for fleeing from Jerusalem is given in the Bible as preservation of himself and the city (*2 Kings* xv.14); Watson stressed an additional motive — David's desire to spare his son from the sin of parricide. Again in Act V Watson made more of David's solicitous care of Absalom than did the Bible. This emphasis on the gentleness of David makes Absalom's crime the more heinous, and the contrast between the two is heightened by their speeches. Absalom is forever mouthing bloody vows; by contrast, David on at least three occasions incorporates into his speeches lengthy versifications of the holy Psalms. David's first words in the play are a paraphrase of the whole of Psalm iii, which is peculiarly appropriate because the Psalter identifies it as "The psalm of David when he fled from the face of his son Absalom." David closes the same scene with phrases from Psalm xxi, and he opens V.1 with Psalm cxxviii. Boas called this device a "skilful stroke" (p. 355), and it was that. Historically, Watson was plucking from David's own words in the Psalms those which he considered appropriate to his own situation; dramatically, he was emphasizing the contrast between the patient, devout father who repents his sinful past and the rash son who is sinking deeper and deeper into sin.

Despite this obvious contrast, Watson managed to give Absalom a certain complexity of character, and again he did it with interpolations into his source. The Bible gives no reason for Absalom's rebellion, but clearly implies ambition for power.[14] Such too is the motive of Peele's Absolon (ll. 1005-18). Watson, however, clearly made the murder of Amnon the result of Absalom's righteous (though expressly uncondoned) wrath over Thamar's rape; and, more important, he apparently attempted to minimize Absalom's ambition during the early acts. At the very first he passed over completely the Biblical account of Absalom's burning of Joab's cornfield: the prince wins Joab's support by the justice of his cause more than by force — and Joab is a staunch defender of justice. Absalom's opening speech presents a young man deeply troubled by the alienation of his father's affections and by his own guilt. We might note here the interesting revision which the author made at I.1.18: his first adjective to describe David's hatred was *triste;* by making it *pertinax* (which admittedly improves the meter), Watson strengthened Absalom's point of view in rebelling. The ensuing hints at parricide in I.1 of *Absalom* are motivated by desperate indignation more than ambition. The only hint of ambition in this scene comes in the soliloquy (ll. 108-115) while Joab is in the palace, but again Absalom seems more interested in changing his servile status than in gaining the crown ("He makes more of his enemies, while his son he deems unworthy of a gentle look . . . more fitting than servitude would be a diadem").[15] At the end of the scene Absalom is ready to seek revenge if his father is still disdainful, but he also describes himself as willing to be ashamed if his father gives him reason. Achitophel's descriptions, in the next scene, of the injustices in David's court tend to support the righteousness of Absalom's fury because of his unrecognized position. Indeed, the list of injustices is taken from Seneca's *Octavia;* but one of the Senecan crimes which Achitophel omitted was *regni cupido,* probably because the only person who could lust for empire was Absalom and Watson was constructing a less ambitious impression for the prince. It is interesting that at

[14] Some authorities, in fact, have attributed to ambition (rather than to vengeance) even Absalom's slaying of Amnon, since by his eldest brother's death (and the apparent death of another older brother, Chileab, who is not mentioned after *2 Kings* iii.3) he became heir apparent to the throne. These commentators find in Absalom's revolt a desire to gain the throne quickly, before Solomon's star should rise too much. See Samuel Fallows *et al., The Popular and Critical Bible Encyclopaedia and Scriptural Dictionary* (Chicago, 1909), I, 29-30. Cf. Peele's treatment (ll. 1722-1859) (Boas, p. 365).

[15] Peele, on the other hand, did not include David's stipulation that Absolon not look on the king's face. His Absolon smarts only because the "Tribes and Elders, and the mightiest ones" do not honor him (ll. 1008-09).

I.2.13 Watson, speaking of the rape of Absalom's sister, originally called her merely *suae sorori* but then altered *suae* to *piae* and thus implied the righteousness of Absalom's vengeance. Even in the scene (I.3) following Absalom's meeting with David, when the final provocation to vengeance has been given, the prince, far from seeking empire, is shown being tortured by indecision: his passions demand redress, but his filial duty rebukes him. He feels with obvious sincerity that David's reconciliation with him, after the long period of scorn, was hypocritical, and he needs revenge — not power. It should be noted that in I.3 Absalom's thirst for vengeance is only vaguely focused and that such focus as there is seems to be on personal murder of his father; it seems to be Achitophel who guides Absalom's passion into rebellion. As late at II.1, though the messenger speaks of Absalom's "dreams of empire," he also says that Achitophel, not Absalom, has asked the populace to make him "judge over the land" (Boas, p. 354); in the Bible (*2 Kings* xv.4) this speech is made by an excessively ambitious Absalom. Watson made the prince (and perhaps his father) better than he was in life — and thus observed an Aristotelian dictum (*Poetics,* Ch. II; Potts, p. 19). The Biblical Absalom does not appear in Watson's play until Act III; indeed, as we shall see below, much of the early emphasis is on the evil of Achitophel, not Absalom.

Viewed objectively, the motivation which Watson gave Absalom is weak enough reason to plunge all Israel into civil war and, later, to cry again and again for the most dreadful executions of vengeance against his father; and it rings hollower still when we hear Absalom upbraid Chusai (III.3) for treachery to David. But the rebuke had Biblical precedent; and in any case the earlier acts show at least an attempt by Watson to provide motivation where his source showed none and where the commentators (as many as I have seen) gave only brutal ambition as Absalom's motive. It seems almost certain that Watson was trying to make his Absalom suitable according to the Aristotelian attitude that a tragic hero should be a man neither wholly evil nor wholly good (Ch. XIII; Potts, p. 33).

Watson's use of Seneca in the treatment of Absalom is an interesting manifestation of his — and Ascham's — doctrine of imitation. The opening line is quoted from *Hercules Oetaeus;* in fact, the first three lines were rewritten so that the opening would be Senecan. And the opening speech is tonally equivalent to a Senecan prologue: "The prologues of all nine of Seneca's completed plays begin with a monologue, or equivalent . . . the rhetorical basis of these introductory monologues rests largely upon pathos and brooding reflection, as opposed to the dramatic, narrative tone of the Euripidean models. Their content also is of such a kind that the characterization of the prologue speakers discloses the motives for action, the basis for sorrow, anger, jealousy, revenge, guilt, passion, etc. . . ." (Canter, pp. 24-25). Mendell (pp. 64-66) pointed out that a second character is sometimes present but is always mute for many lines; though Joab is presumably present from the beginning of *Absalom,* the prince's speech is monologic in tone. Absalom's motives, too, are similar to those of Seneca's bloodiest villains: though we may shrink from the extremity of the actions of Atreus, Medea, and Clytemnestra, they always have what they consider ample justification for revenge. Significantly, most of Absalom's Senecan quotations are selected from the speeches of these characters: for example, when he repeatedly (but at first indecisively!) spurs himself toward crimes such as no one can ever forget (I.3.20 ff.), his speech contains quotations from speeches by Atreus (*Thyestes* 192-194), Medea (*Medea* 931-932), and others. David speaks the pious verses of the Bible, and the scenes of Act II in which David appears have little Senecan borrowing except when Absalom's actions are described; Absalom, on the other hand, quotes Senecan villains. The contrast makes clear Absalom's villainy, but also shows Absalom's point of view. Watson followed "Aristotles preceptes and [Seneca's] examples"; and it would seem that to the St. John's circle imitation meant not merely choosing well-sounding phrases but taking passages appropriate because of the similarity of character types.

In another respect Watson's treatment of Absalom would seem a violation of critical doctrine. Aristotle made the last of his four requirements of character that "it should be consistent" (Ch. XV; Potts, p. 37); and Horace agreed (ll. 125-127). Buchanan's characters are truly consistent with themselves; Absalom, however, develops. When we see him in III.1, he has undergone a distinct change from what he appeared to be in Act I, for he has now become a thoroughly ambitious seeker after power, and he boasts of founding his empire in Jerusalem. Having satisfied the critical need to make his character a man between the extremes of good and evil, Watson can now let Absalom's evil drag him (such being the nature of evil) to whatever depths it will. Absalom's depths are Senecan, in actual wording as well as tone. When Absalom exults (III.3) that he is now master of all that he surveys, he transcends the Biblical Absalom, who makes no such boast. (Peele's Absolon makes a similar boast [ll. 1211-29].) Absalom's speech is a patchwork of phrases taken from a similarly gloating speech by Atreus in Seneca's *Thyestes* (885-919). Nearly every speech by Absalom from

Act III on is replete with similar horrors. Particularly interesting is the fact that in III.3 Absalom is finally convinced that he should himself take the field by Chusai's suggestion that the son is the person most deserving of the opportunity to slay David. The evil impression is intensified for an audience which knows that in the Bible the debate concerned whether *David* should take the field, and the conclusion was that he should not: as evil was removed from Absalom and given to Achitophel in Act II, now goodness is removed from David and assigned to Absalom in such a distorted fashion that it is evil. In his deterioration Absalom proves what the chorus says several times: that one besmirched with sin becomes more and more filthy. Such a one also loses his judgment, apparently, because it is in III.3 that Absalom commits the two Aristotelian errors that lead to his death: gathering troops from Dan to Bersabe and taking the field himself. The "inconsistency" in Absalom is more apparent than real and represents a change in degree, not in kind: the seed of ambition and of evil was in him in Act I. The Cambridge critics obviously did not consider this development of character a violation of Horatian-Aristotelian precepts.

Watson's treatment of Achitophel also shows his method of imitation. In the Bible Achitophel is relatively colorless, and very little space is devoted to him. We are told (*2 Kings* xvi.23) that "the counsel of Achitophel . . . was as if a man should consult God: so was all the counsel of Achitophel, both when he was with David, and when he was with Absalom." And at *2 Kings* xv.31 there is a distinct implication (but only that) that David is seriously disturbed by the knowledge that Achitophel has joined the conspiracy: "Infatuate, O Lord, I beseech thee," David cries, "the counsel of Achitophel." But Achitophel is given no role at all in the early stages of the conspiracy: Absalom had already raised a band of men before he "sent for Achitophel the Gilonite, David's counsellor, from his city Gilo" (*2 Kings* xv.12). In the later stages his advice (that Absalom defile David's concubines [*2 Kings* xvi.21] and that the prince immediately pursue the fleeing David [*2 Kings* xvii.1-3]) is recounted, but the emphasis throughout is on Absalom. Watson expanded the role greatly — and along Senecan lines. He brought Achitophel into the plot even before Absalom's decision to rebel and gave Achitophel an active role in the early stage of the rebellion. In I.3 his role is negative, for except at the end of the scene he is consistently against the impiety of revolt. He is finally won over to Absalom's cause only by his rationalization that David is doomed anyway and that, by helping Absalom, he may perhaps be able to guide the new government into proper rule; in his appearance in I.2, entirely invented by Watson, Achitophel had already been complaining of the evils of David's court. Thus, Achitophel, like Absalom, was given a reasonably good motivation for treachery. Watson was probably guided again by "Aristotles preceptes" concerning character or by the Horatian-Aristotelian doctrine of verisimilitude. The increased importance of Achitophel in Watson's play is emphasized by the chorus in I.3, which devotes one of its lyrical sections to an attack on this "perfidious adviser." One motive for expanding the role is to be found in Seneca, for Achitophel was to Watson the perfect exemplar of the Senecan *consigliere.* (Interestingly, Peele's play, not a Senecan treatment, follows the Bible in making Achitophel's an insignificant role.) Like the Nurses of Phaedra, Medea, Clytemnestra, and Deianira and the attendant of Atreus, Achitophel at first tries to dissuade the protagonist from his villainous action and, failing that, assists and advises his villainy. And, as Absalom is frequently given speeches containing passages from speeches by Seneca's villains, several of Achitophel's have echoes of speeches by Senecan *consiglieri,* especially the Nurse in *Phaedra.* Aristotle and Seneca are again blended with the Bible.[16]

Perhaps Watson had another motive for expanding Achitophel's role. Once Achitophel is convinced that he should join Absalom's rebellion, he assumes much of the brunt of the opprobrium. Indeed, the chorus in I.3 and David in II.2 seem to stress the evil of the counselor more than that of Absalom. And Achitophel's end in Watson's account has moral significance. In IV.3, Achitophel, in despair that his counsel has been defeated by Chusai, decides to commit suicide because he cannot bear to face David; thus far the Biblical account (*2 Kings* xvii.23) agrees. But Watson motivated his choice of hanging in what Boas called a "noticeably ingenious" way.[17] Achitophel argues that, because his throat was the passageway through which his criminal advice passed to Absalom, his throat should receive the brunt of the punishment. One cannot help feeling that Watson had in mind Aristotle's remarks about the statue of Mitys: "Even when events are accidental the sensation is greater if they appear to have a purpose, as when the statue of Mitys at Argos killed the man who had caused his death, by

[16] Portions of the preceding material were read in a paper (called "A Humanist's 'Trew Imitation' ") presented before the Comparative Literature Group 4 at the Modern Language Association Convention in Philadelphia, December 28, 1960.

[17] Boas, p. 361. Peele's Achitophel may have a hint of a similar motive, but it is not clear: "now thou hellish instrument of heauen [the rope], / Once execute th'arrest of Ioues iust doome, / And stop his breast that curseth Israel" (ll. 1502-04).

falling on him at a public entertainment" (Ch. X; Potts, p. 30). This "purpose" can be taken as a moral one, and so, I suspect, did the St. John's scholars take it: the morality is shown not only by the irony, but by many of Achitophel's words in the scene and by the following chorus, which opens, "Over those who give a king evil counsel hangs a frightful end." We might add that Watson later used similar irony in adopting the old tradition that Absalom's long hair, for which he pleads in Act I, caused his death (see Appendix G).

As Watson made use of two Senecan types, the villain and the *consigliere,* in his construction of Absalom and Achitophel, he made three other characters into Senecan messengers. Only one of them has the title Nuntius, but Achimaas and Chusi (V.2-3) have a Nuntius' function. Achimaas and Chusi were provided with the messenger roles by the Biblical source, but Watson altered their roles. Achimaas' twenty-four lines in V.2 are only a slight expansion of the two verses which Achimaas speaks in the Bible (*2 Kings* xviii.28-29), but Chusi's two verses in the Bible (*2 Kings* xviii.31-32) are inflated to 127 lines in the play. Before each of these messengers arrives, David is allowed to rationalize about the import of their news, and we get a pathetic picture of the divine father clutching at the meager hopes he can find in faulty reasoning, the more pathetic because his son does not deserve his concern. These rationalizations Watson found in the source (*2 Kings* xviii.24-27). When Achimaas arrives first, he subjects David, desperate for word of his son's fate, to a cruel delay by professing ignorance. He does the same thing in the Bible (*2 Kings* xviii.28-29); but in the Bible he has reason, for Joab has ordered him to withhold the news (*2 Kings* xviii.20), and in Watson's play he has no such reason. Chusi's delay is even more cruel: before telling what David longs to hear, he describes at painful length the whole order of the battle, including the exact state of some of the corpses, and the setting in which Absalom died. In the Bible, Chusi reveals his terrible news in two short sentences. Significantly, Chusi's speeches in *Absalom* (unlike Achimaas' shorter ones) are marked by extensive paraphrases from speeches of Senecan messengers, particularly the Messenger in *Phaedra.* Boas complained of the magnification of Chusi's office with "tedious circumlocution" (p. 362), and the result is hardly effective. But Watson was probably trying for suspense; he may also have been trying for an Aristotelian peripeteia. The nature of his material allowed Absalom nothing to discover except that his plans were bad, and this he discovered in action offstage. But David's belief that the messengers were bringing good news allowed a peripeteia when their news eventually proved bad. The undue protraction of his grief was probably intended to heighten the pathos of the discovery — and perhaps also its moral import. Aristotle, however, would probably have called this one of the inartistic sorts of discovery, one "made by the poet" (Ch. XVI; Potts, p. 38).

There may have been a more practical reason for the delay. As soon as David knew the fate of Absalom, there would no longer be good and sufficient reason for the messenger to go on with other details, for David would be in mourning and the audience would be focusing its thoughts on him. (Yet Watson originally conceived the scene in this way, as shown by the canceled lines following V.3.7.) But the audience needs to know what has happened in the whole battle: this is Chusi's essential function in the play, just as it was an important function of the Nuntius in II.1 to tell the audience how Absalom's rebellion was proceeding. One of the "rules" of the sixteenth century was that certain kinds of action must occur offstage (Herrick, pp. 99-104). Aristotle repeatedly stated that the substance and structure of the tragedy are more important than the visual impression (Chs. VI, XIV; Potts, pp. 25, 34-35) and that certain incredible actions, though proper to an epic, are ridiculous if represented onstage (Ch. XXIV; Potts, pp. 53-54). Horace was even more explicit in condemning cruel or fantastic staging: "quodcumque ostendis mihi sic, incredulus odi" (ll. 179-188). Though Seneca has at least one violent action onstage, his characteristic method was to report such actions by messenger; whether according to theoretical dicta or because his plays were read rather than acted (Mendell, p. 92) is unimportant. Watson's "example" and his preceptors agreed, and he followed them. The messenger in II.1 of *Absalom* even reveals some of the rhetorical flavor of his Senecan models: opening with an exclamation about the hardness of the times, he moves on through an ornate description complete with natural similes, hyperbole, and understatement of the movements of Absalom's army. And he has a number of quotations from Senecan messengers; one of his more interesting quotations, however (II.1.28), is from the Bible (*Job* i.15), when Job is informed by a messenger that no one except himself has escaped. Chusi's descriptions of Absalom's tree (a tree which Watson found near Thebes in *Oedipus* 532 ff.) and of the state of the soldiers also parallel purple descriptions by Seneca's messengers. And the description of Absalom's death borrowed significantly from that of Hippolytus in Seneca's *Phaedra*.[18]

[18] See Mendell, pp. 107-111, 170-173. For a list of Watson's Senecan borrowings, see Appendix E.

Of Watson's other characters only Joab is at all distinctive. He has extensive speeches in I.1, II.2, and V.4. The good counselor, he only occasionally quotes Seneca's counselors — and then only their moral advice. He may be summed up as a devoted friend of the right — of Absalom in Act I, of David throughout but seldom of David's policies — and a realistic, unsentimental, shrewd politician and militarist. The treachery for which he is noted in the Bible is only hinted at in *Absalom* (as David recalls Joab's murder of Abner), for the slayer of Absalom is pointedly not identified.

Chusai has an important role in the subversion of Achitophel's advice in Act III; but of his character we can say little beyond a statement of his devotion and obedience to David and of his skill in rhetorical argument. It is highly interesting, though, that in his soliloquy scene (III.2) he echoes Seneca in only three lines at the beginning; thereafter, his quotations are from the Bible, including one apparent paraphrase from the New Testament (III.2.32-33; *Matthew* xi.30). And in the great debate which he conducts against Achitophel in III.3 his Biblical-sounding words are an island of goodness amid the sea of Senecan quotations by Absalom. Similarly, his words — and also those of Sadoc and Abiathar — in IV.1 echo the Bible, specifically sometimes the Psalms.

The other characters are even less well delineated, and only one other need be mentioned: Populus speaks but once in the play (II.2. 149-150), uttering what the Bible (*2 Kings* xv.15) assigns to David's servants. It appears twice with Absalom (III.1 and IV.2) and at those times by its silence seems to favor his cause; it is thus different from the chorus, which invariably opposes the rebellion. Watson apparently meant it to represent the ordinary soldiers following David and Absalom, respectively: but at III.1.130 is a reference to *populo* as the nonmilitary (and uncommitted) people of Jerusalem.

PLOT

To Aristotle, plot rather than character was supreme (Ch. VI; Potts, pp. 25-26). Though Horace ignored plot as such, Horatian commentators found some support for Aristotle's position in *Ars Poetica* 1-13, which advocates unity, and the supremacy of plot became one of the dramatic "rules" of the sixteenth century (Herrick, pp. 69-72). Now Aristotle used two terms — μῦθος (*fabula* or story) and σύνθεσις (*compositio* or structure) — in connection with plot, and his distinction is not always clear, though, as Herrick wrote (p. 69),

"More often than not, perhaps, Aristotle means by plot the combination of incidents . . . that is, the artistic arrangement of action in the drama or narrative." Accordingly, sixteenth-century writers generally used *fabula* to interpret either of Aristotle's terms (Herrick, p. 70). There is no doubt that Ascham accepted the supremacy of plot: in all his discussions of imitation, including his comments on *Iephthes* and *Absalom,* he spoke of matter and manner, not character. And he certainly thought of structure and arrangement of incidents as important parts of "Aristotles preceptes," for when he praised Euripides and Sophocles over "our Seneca," he was thinking expressly of *οἰκονομία* and decorum. And *οἰκονομία* (which meant literally "The guiding and ordering of thinges pertayning to housholde") in sixteenth-century criticism meant "an order in writing or pleading whereby euery thing is set in his due place."[19] Ascham (and no doubt Cheke) would surely have expected Watson to observe classical dicta concerning plot, and particularly concerning *οἰκονομία*.

The most obvious way in which Watson "ordered" his material was in his act divisions. Aristotle, of course, did not speak of act divisions, though writers in the 1550's managed to equate his quantitative divisions of drama (prologue, parodos, episode, stasimon, and exode) with the five-act practice of the Latins.[20] But Horace had commanded (l. 189) that the *fabula* "neve minor neu sit quinto productior actu," and Terentian commentators from Donatus onward had finally worked out a standard formula for the five acts. Watson's act structure apparently stemmed from Donatus' scheme rather than the 1539 modification by Willichius. The first act introduces the characters and the argument, beginning with Absalom's "prologue"; Joab's and Achitophel's injunctions against parricide set the theme. In the third scene a plan of action is decided upon which will develop into the conflict of the tragedy: the plan to rise against David. Under later theory this decision would have been postponed until the end of Act II. The second act "begins the action, as it ought; but it also presents David's perturbation, which, according to the later perfected theory, it really ought not to do." The beginning of the action is Absalom's raising of an army to carry out the plan made in Act I. We meet David in the second act rather than the first, presumably because the tragedy is Absalom's, not his. David's decision, over Joab's objection, to flee from Jerusalem leaves the issue in doubt: it removes the king from Absa-

[19] Thomas Cooper, *Thesavrvs Lingvae Romanae & Britannicae* (London, 1573), s.v. "Oeconomia." Cooper cited Quintilian for the usage.

[20] Baldwin, *Five-Act Structure,* pp. 264-283; the following analysis is based on Baldwin's (pp. 360-362).

lom's path of personal vengeance, but does not actually raise any obstacle to Absalom's rebellion; in fact, it assists Absalom to the extent of leaving the capital city unprotected. In the third act "the issue is irrevocably drawn": Absalom takes Jerusalem and, in order to preclude reconciliation, dishonors David's concubines. The first countermovement also begins in this act, as it should: David sends Chusai to subvert Achitophel's advice. Chusai's success, after a brilliant debate with Achitophel, causes Absalom to commit his fatal error (delaying the pursuit of David until a large army has been raised) and starts him toward defeat and tragedy. David's countermovement is fully developed in Act IV: Sadoc and Abiathar prepare to send their intelligence to David. Conversely, the first movement is in decline: Absalom is chafing under delay, and Achitophel commits suicide because he realizes that Absalom's cause is lost. Thus, in Acts III and IV Absalom's conflict has increased to its most desperate point. The fifth act is the catastrophe: the fall of Absalom's army and, more important, of Absalom himself is related to David by Senecan messengers.[21]

Baldwin suggested a relationship between Watson's turning point in the third act and the *∂έσις* and *λύσις* of Aristotle (Ch. XVIII; Potts, p. 41), and the suggestion is quite reasonable. At least there can be little doubt that the rise and fall of Absalom hinge upon that tragic error in Act III. This turning point comes considerably earlier than it does in many later plays, in which the ending is usually precipitated by an action at the end of Act IV or the beginning of Act V. Watson was apparently avoiding any hint of a *deus ex machina* so that "the untying" of his play would "follow on the circumstances of the fable itself, and not be done *ex machina*." This had been Aristotle's demand (Ch. XV; Potts, p. 37); and Horace too commanded, "nec deus intersit, nisi dignus vindice nodus/ inciderit" (ll. 191-192). There seems again to be an awareness in Watson of classical dicta.

In passing we may note a smaller indication of Watson's awareness of critical precepts. Seneca and the Greeks used no more than three speaking characters per scene, and Aristotle noted without comment that Sophocles had added the third actor (Ch. IV; Potts, p. 22). Horace made it a rule: "nec quarta loqui persona laboret" (l. 192). In few scenes of *Absalom* do as many as three actors speak, but in Act V Watson seems to have had a problem. The speaking roles in V.1-3 are David's, the Watchman's, Achimaas', and Chusi's; only David and

[21] We might note that Buchanan's *Iephthes* is divided into scenes, not acts, and generally reflects Greek rather than Roman structure; its tone, however, remains Senecan.

one other speak in each scene, but the three scenes are a continuous whole, so that the effect is of four speaking characters onstage at once. Watson got around the difficulty by using an unimportant line from the Bible, "Pass, and stand here" (*2 Kings* xviii.30); he altered the meaning by having David order Achimaas to withdraw before Chusi enters (so I interpret a difficult line). No similar instructions are given Chusi before Joab enters in V.4, but I assume that the scene had changed and the other characters had withdrawn.

Certainly connected with the concept of *οἰκονομία* were Watson's striking rearrangements of some of his source material. Boas commented favorably on Watson's skill in thus giving his material clearer, more compact meaning (pp. 357-360). These rearrangements consist primarily of the bringing together into single scenes of the treatment of Chusai's proffer of fealty to Absalom and the treatment of the spies Sadoc and Abiathar; in the Bible these incidents are fragmented among other incidents. But Boas discussed only the aesthetic effect of these changes; I think there were historical and critical reasons for them as well. They secured what Dr. Johnson would have called concatenation of events and they avoided Aristotelian censure of episodic arrangements which fail to show continuity: "Of simple fables, those whose action is episodic are the worse. By an episodic fable I mean one in which scene follows scene without probability or necessity" (*Poetics*, Ch. IX; Potts, p. 30). They also indicate that Watson was following Aristotle's advice to "first reduce [the story] to a significant and unified outline" (Ch. XVII; Potts, p. 40). They reveal a sensitivity to the concept of *οἰκονομία*. And they reflect the five-act formula which Watson was following: Watson's plan, apparently, was to begin to show Absalom's deterioration in Act III with the prince's exultation on entering Jerusalem and with the decision to violate David's concubines. Following the Biblical chronology would have necessitated placing in Act II the commission of Chusai, Sadoc, and Abiathar. But the mission of these men is the beginning of David's counteraction to Absalom's plot, and, as we have seen, such counteraction is postponed under the five-act formula until Act III. Thus, Watson deftly satisfied five-act structure requirements by disturbing Biblical chronology — and achieved greater continuity than the Scriptural historian had.

This unifying of incidents makes more obvious the play's unity of action. Perhaps the "rule" most frequently discussed by Aristotle concerned this important unity, and those discussions are among the most famous today (Chs. VII-IX, XVII, XXIII; Potts, pp. 27-29, 40,

51-52). Similarly, Horace opened the *Ars Poetica* with a lengthy plea for unified presentation, ending "denique sit quodvis, simplex dumtaxat et unum" (l. 23). Some Renaissance critics used these statements to proscribe subplots (Herrick, pp. 76-77) — though it is probably accidental that *Absalom* has no subplot. The basis of this attitude was Horace's "simplex et unum," but the "simplex" was confused with Aristotle's statements concerning simple and complex fables. Aristotle first defined simple fables as those which proceed to their catastrophe "directly and singly, without Irony of events [περιπέτεια] or Disclosure" (Ch. X; Potts, p. 31), and later defined them as admitting "no change from misfortune to good fortune, but only the opposite, from good fortune to misfortune."[22] He used the same word, ἁπλοῖ, for both definitions. He praised the latter kind of single fable, in which even the good suffer — and we have seen the grief of both David and Absalom in Watson's play; the former kind he found less satisfactory than fables moved by peripeteia or disclosure — and we have seen the attempt to achieve peripeteia in Watson's handling of David in Act V and in his means of bringing Achitophel and Absalom to their deaths.

Although there is some question whether Watson deliberately followed these interpretations of Aristotle's "simple" and "complex" fables, there is no question that he deliberately altered his source to achieve unity of action. First, he limited his play to the single action of Absalom's revolt. The background of the rebellion (Amnon's rape of Thamar and murder by Absalom, Absalom's exile in Gessur and long seclusion in Jerusalem), as well as the ultimate cause of it (David's murder of Urias), is merely recalled by characters in the play. And the aftermath (David's political troubles and his eventual disposition of Semei) is all but ignored. *Absalom* (like *Iephthes,* which also begins *in medias res*) has an Aristotelian "beginning" and "end." Watson also ignored certain extraneous incidents described in the Biblical account: the coming of Ethai to David (*2 Kings* xv.18-22); David's conversation with Siba (*2 Kings* xvi.1-4); the bringing of food to David by Sobi, Machir, and Berzellai (*2 Kings* xvii.27-29); and the difficulties of Jonathan and Achimaas in taking news to David (*2 Kings* xvii.17-20). The Scriptural narrator was a historian and therefore had to "present not a single action but a single period and everything that happened in it to one or more persons, with a purely accidental relationship of one event to the others" (*Poetics,* Ch. XXIII; Potts,

[22] Ch. XIII; Potts, p. 33. Potts translated this ἁπλός "single," the other "simple"; the corresponding opposites he rendered "double" and "complex."

p. 51). But Watson recognized that the poet must select his incidents with a careful view to unity. Further evidence of a conscious unifying of the action is the occasional recollection of previous events which are thematically related to present actions (e.g., Achitophel's recollection in IV.3 of Absalom's promise [I.3] to follow his counsel and David's recollection [II.2] of Nathan's prophecy).[23]

Apparently Watson did, however, violate unity of action with one scene, for he included one of the extraneous incidents occurring during David's flight from Jerusalem: in fact, he devoted the whole of II.3 to the cursing of David by Semei. He may have been motivated by a desire for symmetry. Though Seneca's tragedies had been divided by sixteenth-century editors into asymmetrical acts and though Donatus had complained of strict and artificial symmetry,[24] nonetheless some sixteenth-century playwrights seem to have observed general symmetry;[25] and Servius had observed that all poets (i.e., playwrights) compose their books "in consistent and limited divisions, and that the divisions are almost of the same length" (Baldwin, p. 67). Now, the five acts of *Absalom* (all except Act V having three scenes) have, in order, 455, 483, 580, 400, and 335 lines: not equal, but nearly so, and following a pattern of relative brevity when complications are few and of greater prolixity when complications are at their highest. That Watson was consciously aware of the length of his acts is indicated by his counting off of lines per act from Act II on (see Textual Notes); perhaps, indeed, the fact that this counting off begins in the very act which Watson padded with an extraneous scene is significant. Act IV, which has relatively little to do, is similarly padded with two long monologues by Absalom and Achitophel and with two choruses which together contain more lines (139) than do the choruses of any other single act. Perhaps Watson wanted to bring both acts more nearly into proportion with the other three. Act II had accomplished its entire purpose at the end of the second scene, but was much shorter than the acts around it, despite two choruses totaling 137 lines and a very long messenger speech. For several

[23] James Edward Robinson, in his fine unpublished dissertation, "The Dramatic Unities in the Renaissance: A Study of the Principles, with Application to the Development of English Drama," University of Illinois (Urbana, 1959), pp. 134, 191, *et pass.* My Notes to the Translation record some instances of this *oeconomia,* which Robinson defined (p. 134) as "a term applied to the links in the organic unity of the action." Robinson's study of the play was based on his independent analysis of my text and translation while this edition was in preparation.

[24] Baldwin, *Five-Act Structure,* pp. 28-29.

[25] Perhaps most pronounced in the plays of John Lyly (*ibid.,* p. 493).

reasons Watson could not expand the act by putting into it Absalom's triumphant invasion of Jerusalem: as we have seen, this invasion was intended to show Absalom's deterioration, which was more appropriate to Act III. Besides, Watson apparently planned to devote each act to either David or Absalom, not both, and Act II was David's.

Watson apparently felt, too, that he needed to show us David in actual flight, since Absalom's invasion after David's mere *decision* to flee might have left his audience in doubt as to David's position.[26] Showing us David already out of Jerusalem is, I think, the principal purpose of II.3. But what was the author to have David do during the flight? In the Biblical account, David at this time sent Chusai to spy on Absalom, and Sadoc and Abiathar to be Chusai's couriers; as we have seen, this counteraction could not be placed earlier than Act III. Thus, if the flight scene was to be more than a lamenting soliloquy (of which we had had a sufficiency in II.2), Watson had to use some of the Bible's extraneous narrative. He chose the Semei episode as needing less explanation than either the Ethai or the Siba episodes and as accomplishing more for his play.

As Robinson stated, Semei adds to the "aura of doom" in the play and emphasizes David's past wrongs, the cause of the present difficulties: "Such would be sufficient justification for his inclusion in a drama of Greek or Senecan design. Further, Semei is a contrast to the resistant but loyal Joab of the preceding scene and to the hot-tempered and loyal [Abisai], who in Scene 3 threatens to abuse Semei" (p. 191). Probably more important, the scene demonstrates David's vast tolerance and thus allows the subsequent chorus to wonder at his "memorable patience," which is likened to that of Isaac, Joseph, Gedeon, and Moses and contrasted with the savagery of David's son; and to draw a moral in a direct address to the youths in the audience. In this contrast we are prepared for the newly savage Absalom of Act III. Thus, Watson, perhaps forced by dramatic exigency to use unrelated matter, has given the offending scene apparent organic connection with his central theme, and has made it serve the function of showing David in flight.

Despite this infraction of the "rule" of unity of action, *Absalom* is almost unique in its period: contemporary plays (except, significantly, Buchanan's) were very diffuse, and even in the second half of the

[26] Robinson stated (p. 192) that the chorus in II.3 informs the audience of David's flight. But Watson's choruses do not narrate important action: they merely comment on action already made clear, and their comments in II.3 could be construed by the audience as referring to David's decision rather than his instituted action.

century, when what Boas (p. 352) called the "ordinary neo-Senecan type" — e.g., *Gorboduc* — consciously narrowed its scope of treatment, plays showing little or no unity of action were quite common. The contrast of *Absalom* with Peele's play (or with Murer's) is striking. And no doubt this unity is another reason for Ascham's praise of *Absalom;* for surely Watson, Ascham, and Cheke discussed this fundamental critical precept.

The minor unities are wanting in *Absalom.* According to the scene settings which I have supplied from the Bible, the play occurs in five rather widely separated locations. Except when the setting is Jerusalem, however, the play is obtrusively vague about location, and we should perhaps reduce this number by placing in Jerusalem the scenes (IV.2-3) which I have set in Galaad and Giloh. Robinson, indeed, thought that the first four acts were all set in Jerusalem, and Act V "in David's camp near the forest of Ephraim" (p. 188). I do not agree that II.3, whose purpose I have described as showing David's flight from the city, is set in Jerusalem, though it may not have been far from the city (see Appendix F); but even without considering this scene we have two distinct locations for the play — one too many even in a small country like Israel. Unity of time is more seriously violated. Act I is clearly a single action of a few minutes' or a few hours' duration. Before Act II, however, enough time has elapsed for Absalom and Achitophel to gather an army and march on Jerusalem — a few months at least, though there are no references to time. The action from II.1 through IV.1 is relatively consecutive, but a lapse of probably a year occurs between IV.1 and IV.2, for Absalom complains at length about the lag while his generals plan. Act V is continuous within itself (except perhaps for a short delay after V.3), and the lapse between Acts IV and V is probably small. Boas used this violation of the minor unities as an argument against Watson's authorship of the play in Stowe MS. 957 (p. 64). Robinson, on the other hand, found in *Absalom* "some concern by the author to keep the disposition of time and place clear" (p. 195). That Watson reduced the elapsed time from the forty-odd years of the Bible to something like a year may support Robinson's view; so might the very vagueness of the play when it moved from Jerusalem. Robinson pointed out (pp. 96, 102) that there was precedent in Terence and in the Senecan chorus for gaps between the acts and that Seneca's *Octavia* and *Phoenissae* gave precedent for "transitions of time or place (though not so much as a year) without benefit of chorus" (p. 193). But even these precedents cannot gainsay that *Absalom* violates the minor unities.

Far from arguing against Watson's authorship, however, this violation testifies that the St. John's humanists did not consider the minor unities laws. Both Robinson (p. 185) and Baldwin (p. 362) have clearly demonstrated that the "law" requiring identity of stage time and place with real time and place did not become effective until several decades after *Absalom* was written. Unity of time was not even proposed as law until Robortellus in 1548 argued for a twelve-hour time limit (from sunrise to sunset) and Bernardo Segni in 1549 argued for a twenty-four-hour day; and neither of these Aristotelians discussed unity of place as a rule (Herrick, pp. 78-81). At their date, the St. John's scholars would certainly have been looking in Aristotle himself rather than in latter-day commentators, and Aristotle mentioned the minor unities only incidentally: unity of place probably came out of his statement that "In tragedy it is not possible to imitate several parts of a story as happening at the same time" (Ch. XXIV; Potts, pp. 52-53). Unity of time was grafted onto Aristotle's quite incidental statement that epic and tragedy "differ in length, because tragedy tends as far as possible to keep within a single day and night or thereabouts" (Ch. V; Potts, p. 23). Among the English humanists these statements apparently caused only a feeling for the minor unities, and *Absalom* shows no more than a mere feeling for them; that it did no more did not deter Ascham from praising it highly.[27]

DICTION

Both Aristotle (Chs. XIX-XXII; Potts, pp. 44-51) and Horace (ll. 89-118) stated explicitly the necessity of using language appropriate to the matter of the poem, and the sixteenth century apparently found Seneca's language the most appropriate for tragedy: for example, Ascham excepted Seneca's "elocution" from his opinion that the Greeks "far ouer match our *Seneca*." Accordingly, Watson expanded the matter of his source mostly after the model of Seneca's rhetoric. We have already noticed Watson's long "prologue" and the long, purple narratives of his messengers; in fact, most of the scenes are marked by long speeches. Besides those long Senecan speeches, Mendell (p. 107) described three other kinds of long speeches in Seneca, borrowed from Euripides: "the extended dialogue speech,

[27] *Iephthes* observes the minor unities. So do most of Seneca's tragedies, but *Octavia* (probably not Seneca's, but used by Watson as though it were), *Hercules Oetaeus,* and the fragmentary *Phoenissae* violate one or both of the minor unities.

the argument scene, and the monologue." All of these occur in Watson. I.2 and IV.3 are devoted entirely to monologues by Achitophel, the former somewhat expository but principally a philosophical discussion of crime; the latter a mournful complaint prior to his suicide. Absalom has monologues in I.1 and I.3 in which he dispels his doubts concerning parricide; in III.1, where he declaims, Atreus-like, about his power; and in IV.2, where he complains of delays by his generals and consoles himself with vicious thoughts about David's fate. David's paraphrases of Psalms in II.2 and V.1 are monologic, though other characters are onstage. And III.2 is a monologue by Chusai, principally narrating his meeting with David. Thus, these monologues in both form and content are Senecan: Canter pointed out (p. 10, n. 5) that the three rhetorical ingredients of Seneca's plays were "description, declamation, and philosophic *sententiae.*"

Extended dialogue occurs in several places in *Absalom:* in II.3 as Semei curses David; in III.1 as Absalom and Achitophel discuss how best to make permanent the divorce of son and father; and in IV.1 as Chusai delivers instructions to Abiathar and Sadoc. Extended argument occurs in I.1, I.3, and II.2, but most strikingly in III.3, where Achitophel and Chusai argue before Absalom as to the best course of action. Boas commented that this debate "prolongs the scene unduly, but it reveals a genuine gift for vigorous rhetorical argumentation, which would have been still more effective had it been more tersely phrased" (p. 359). The cause for Boas' complaint is that Watson expanded by some fifteen times the arguments which Chusai and Achitophel used in the Bible, then without authority had each man repeat his position a second time, and finally added a third debate (which in the Bible was concerned, as we have seen, with David rather than Absalom) on whether Absalom should take the field.

Three of the argumentative scenes (I.1, I.3, and II.2) do not use long speeches so much as they do Senecan stichomythia. Characteristic of these stichomythic dialogues is a rapid-fire series of one-line (or occasionally half-line) moral epigrammatic commonplaces, each echoing some word from the preceding line. This type of dialogue was the closest approach which Seneca made to natural speech (Mendell, pp. 116-123), and the device held great appeal for the sixteenth century and also for Watson, who used stichomythia in virtually every act. In the stichomythic passages and in longer speeches as well as in the choruses, Watson used scores of *sententiae,* not usually taken from Seneca but repeating the same moralistic truisms which Seneca belabored.[28] No doubt Sidney had such moral statements in mind when he praised Seneca's "well-sounding phrases" and "notable morality."

Another common rhetorical device in *Absalom* is the extended simile, in nearly every case drawn from nature. As a few of many instances we may note Absalom's vow (III.1.87 ff.) that wolves will be at peace with sheep and grain will grow from the sea before he is reconciled with his father; his comparison (I.3.152-153) of the way his mind resists proper counsel with the way a reef withstands the sea; and Chusai's suggestion (III.3.173-175) that an army be raised as numerous as the sands of the sea. The last simile was taken from the Bible (*2 Kings* xvii.11); the first two, along with others, from Seneca (*Thyestes* 476 ff. and perhaps some other passages).

In not all of his Senecan rhetoric did Watson actually use Senecan phraseology. For instance, few of the stichomythic passages were borrowed from Seneca; the device itself was sufficiently Senecan. But we have already seen that a very significant number of passages were based on Senecan wording: Absalom's speeches based on those of Atreus and Medea; Achitophel's on speeches in *Phaedra,* etc. Several scenes open with a Senecan quotation. In the first act hardly three consecutive lines lack Senecan echoes. Later the proportion diminishes, but no very extended passage is without its borrowings. These borrowings range from the mere epithet to the whole line or more, as we have seen; sometimes a rather long Senecan passage was used, especially, it would seem, when there had been no significant borrowing for a time. Typically, Watson did not use these Senecan passages verbatim; he rearranged phrases or even ideas, he interwove Scriptural and other wording, and in general he fitted the borrowed material to his own pattern. His use of the borrowed phrases is a reflection of the literary temper of his age. I suppose the proportion of borrowing from different plays is also somewhat reflective of the taste of the age. Of at least 270 lines in *Absalom* which are significantly based on Senecan lines, borrowings are especially heavy from *Phaedra;* heavy from *Medea;* moderate from *Octavia, Hercules Oetaeus,* and *Thyestes;*

[28] Watson conveniently labeled a number of his commonplaces with a marginal *c,* all but one in the first act. I have not found a common storehouse of the commonplaces which Watson used, and I have found few of them individually in early commonplace books. I suspect that he compiled them himself from his primary reading. Incidentally, since Seneca was not generally taught in the grammar schools in Watson's age, Watson must have got his Seneca at the university; see T. W. Baldwin, *William Shakspere's Small Latine and Lesse Greeke* (Urbana, Ill., 1944), II, 553.

light from *Phoenissae, Oedipus,* and *Troades;* and very light from *Hercules Furens* and *Agamemnon* (see Appendix E).

Watson's Latin is not Golden; it is scarcely Silver. He tried to make his vocabulary largely Senecan, but he did not hesitate to use late Latin words when he needed them; I have noted a few of these in the Notes to the Translation. He also allowed a number of syntactical and grammatical errors to creep into his Latin. We may mention only a few of them as examples: *ne . . . irrita* instead of the standard *noli irritare* or *ne irrites* (I.3.148); a nominative absolute (II.3.98-99); an occasional wrong case (*ex itinere factum* [for *facto*]: III.2.13) or gender (e.g., I.1.21); many subjunctives with *si* clauses, even those expressing simple condition, and on the other hand many indicatives in subsequent parallel *si* clauses when the first has used the subjunctive; and a number of indicatives in indirect discourse (II.3.133-134) or in result clauses (III.1.19). Watson frequently used simple future verbs where we would expect either an imperative or a subjunctive and was quite inconsistent in his use of past and historical present tenses in passages describing action. And sometimes, especially in the anapestic choruses and the stichomythic passages, the thought is so compressed that its meaning is obscured (e.g., I.1.65).

Some of these errors are no doubt the result of poetic exigencies: the compression and the *ne . . . irrita,* for example. Others are probably the result of carelessness: the unparallel verb forms, for example. But neither of these explanations will suffice for all the instances, or for the many not mentioned. The errors, then, would seem to belie Ascham's repeated references to Watson as one of the most learned men of his time; and one might wonder whether the errors contributed to Watson's failure to have the play published. I rather suspect, however, that their significance lies in reflecting what the learning of Watson's time was: in general, that learning extended to a thorough knowledge of the thoughts and structures of classical authors, but not to a careful precision in grammatical points. Even the Latin of Erasmus is not completely free of tarnish. The fact is that sixteenth-century standards, especially early sixteenth-century standards, in both English and Latin grammar were not what our standards are; and Ascham's praise of a play which contains "errors" is proof of this difference in standards. Illustrative of the difference in standards is that the change in pronunciation of Greek which the St. John's group fought so hard to introduce is today regarded as being a change to an incorrect pronunciation. In any case, Watson was much more interested in linguistic decorum than in syntactical nicety — and he achieved that decorum by imitating Seneca well.

METRICS

Aristotle, describing Greek practice, decreed that the iambic trimeter of all meters was fittest for drama (Ch. IV; Potts, p. 22). Horace agreed for the Romans (ll. 79-82). The iambic trimeter was the principal meter of Seneca's tragedies, and Ascham praised Seneca's metrics over those of the Greeks. It is not surprising, then, that *Absalom* was written chiefly in iambic trimeters. Boas complained of the "monotonous versification" of the play (p. 64). And, to be sure, the superficial figures lend support to his opinion: of the 2,253 lines of the play, some 1,845 are iambic trimeters; the proportion (82 per cent) is somewhat higher than that in Seneca.[29] So does the rather high proportion of end-stopped lines in the play (except in the anapestic portions) seem to support Boas. However, anyone who had taken the trouble to analyze the meter could hardly have called Watson's versification monotonous. In many ways he strove for variety, and he achieved it. In the choric odes his most obvious means was to vary the meters from one chorus to another. Although his principal choric meter (163 lines) is that which is most frequent in Seneca, the anapestic dimeter, it does not have a majority: there are 94 sapphic hendecasyllabics (IV.2.75-123, 125-169), 78 lesser asclepiads (II.3.68-145), 45 choriambic glyconics (III.3.346-390), two iambic trimeters (closing the play), and one anapestic monometer (IV.2.124) — nearly all of these being Senecan variations as well. The internal structure of a number of these meters also shows variety: in the anapestic dimeters of *Absalom,* for example, occur all the permitted variants — dactyls in the first or third foot, spondees anywhere — and some forbidden patterns, such as a dactyl in the second or fourth foot or an iamb or pyrrhic somewhere in the line.

[29] See the detailed analyses, with distribution tables, of Ladislaus Strzelecki, *De Senecae Trimetro Iambico Quaestiones Selectae,* Polska Akademja Umiejętności Rozprawy Wydziału Filologicznego, LXV (Krakow, 1938), and of Max Hoche, *Die Metra des Tragikers Seneca. Ein Beitrag zur lateinischen Metrik* (Halle, 1862). It is important to realize, however, that their statistics were drawn from better texts than were available to the sixteenth century: the better textual tradition (E) was not discovered until 1640. Sixteenth-century editions were printed from manuscripts of the A tradition; see Rudolf Peiper and Gustav Richter, eds., *L. Annaei Senecae Tragoediae,* Bibliotheca Teubneriana (Leipzig, 1867), p. iii. One of the biggest weaknesses of the A manuscripts was metrical.

Watson's greatest efforts for variety, however, occurred in his iambic trimeter. Here again he occasionally substituted different metrical patterns in the iambic trimeter passages: besides a few irregular or defective lines, there are twenty-one trochaic tetrameter catalectics, all in the epitasis (III.1.34-44, 47-52, 61-63, 72); two dactylic hexameters (III.1.88, 90); and two mournful spondaic lines (V.3.136, 147). Apparently he even constructed a few speeches stanzaically (e.g., IV.1.1-16). The mixing of meters is in distinct violation of the Aristotelian epic principle that "it would be an even worse blunder [than writing a heroic poem in a nonheroic meter] to mix meters, in the manner of Chaeremon" (Ch. XXIV; Potts, p. 53). But the mixing has the full authority of Seneca behind it: Seneca's iambic trimeters are interrupted by trochaic tetrameter catalectic passages (*Medea* 743 ff.; *Oedipus* 227 ff.; *Phaedra* 1210 ff.) and occasionally by dactylic hexameter lines. And Aristotle did not oppose the mixtures in tragedy.

In internal structure Watson took advantage of all the licenses he was permitted — and again a few others besides. The pure iambic line, consisting of six iambs, is very rare in Latin literature except in *iambographi* like Catullus, and it was not generally considered proper for tragedy; there are no such pure iambics in *Absalom,* though there are some lines with five iambs. In classical practice the most common iambic trimeter pattern is that showing iambs in the second, fourth, and sixth feet and spondees in the rest: Horace, for example, explicitly permitted this variation so that the iambic line "tardior . . . paulo, graviorque veniret ad auris" (l. 255). This pattern is frequent in *Absalom.* In addition, these spondees are permitted by the theorists to be resolved into any feet having an equivalent number of *morae;* thus, the odd feet of the line admit an anapest or dactyl as well as the spondee.[30] The iambs of the second and fourth feet are universally permitted to be resolved into tribrachs, but the sixth foot has to remain an iamb (or a pyrrhic, which by *syllaba anceps* is the equivalent of an iamb). The combinations of these permitted variations, singly and in groups, allow an almost infinite variety of acceptable iambic trimeter patterns, and Watson used many of them.[31] We may note here, too,

[30] Some theorists did not permit the anapest in the third foot, and Hoche and Strzelecki found few such anapests in the E versions of Seneca. A *mora* is the amount of time used in uttering a short syllable (breve); a long syllable contains two *morae.* The limitations imposed on the even feet of the iambic trimeter line came about because there was only one long, in the iamb properly found there, to be resolved — that into a tribrach.

[31] Hoche (p. 11) found and listed fifty-eight different combinations of individual feet in Seneca's iambic trimeter (E version).

the variety of caesuras in *Absalom:* most occur in the normal places — the third or fourth foot — but they sometimes fall in the second or fifth foot, or often in both. Finally should be mentioned Watson's frequent metrical tricks, many of them intended to add variety as well as a higher poetic effect: e.g., alliteration, synizesis, syncopation, and diplasiasmus.

Most of these practices were permitted by all or nearly all metrical theorists. But to a rather surprising extent Watson ran into conflict with the standard theorists in a number of his attempts to achieve variety. For example, more than a dozen verses contain spondees in the second or fourth foot, and Horace, among others, had specifically stated that the iamb "non . . . de sede secunda/ cederet" (ll. 257-258). Sometimes Watson used a dactyl, a tribrach, and an anapest consecutively, causing seven straight breves, and there are a number of instances of five consecutive breves—generally considered poor metrics. There are even a few examples of the worst violation against iambic trimeter verse: the scazon, a verse containing a spondee in the sixth foot. Second in gravity only to the scazon is a trochee in this line, and Watson has some of those. There are a few hypercatalectic lines (which Watson himself labeled), resulting in an anapest in the sixth foot. Less serious are the hundreds of anapests in the second and fourth feet of the iambic trimeter lines (though some can be avoided by syncope if we do not assume a concomitant lengthening of the syllable before the syncopated one). I have reserved discussion of these until last because they have special significance.[32]

It will be recalled that Ascham ascribed Watson's reluctance to publish his play to the fact that "twise or thrise" it had an anapest *in locis paribus:* "A smal faulte, and such one, as perchaunce would neuer be marked, no neither in Italie nor France" (*Scholemaster* [1570], fol. 57*v*). The phrase *in locis paribus* seems not to have been well understood by modern critics of Ascham. John E. B. Mayor, for example, gave what purported to be a concrete illustration of Ascham's poor judgment: he pointed out that in Buchanan's *Iephthes* "an anapaest is found in the fifth place three times in the first twenty lines."[33] While his observation is true, and while his strictures on Ascham's judgment may be well taken, his illustration is unfortunate: the fifth foot is not a *locus par* and was almost universally held acceptable if it contained an anapest; Seneca has many such anapests. The *loci pares* are the second, fourth, and sixth feet, and *Absalom* has not two or three

[32] See Appendix D.

[33] In his edition of *The Scholemaster* (London, 1863), p. 571.

anapests there but hundreds. Perhaps Ascham's memory of the exact degree of the "smal faulte" had faded by the 1560's; perhaps he was deliberately minimizing the infraction (and not even mentioning the more serious faults described above) in order not to cancel his praise of the play; or perhaps he was ironically pointing to a minor flaw in his friend's "Imitation" while really intending the more serious ones which he did not mention.[34] Whatever Ascham's motives, the anapests are still there in *Absalom,* and we may well consider the sixteenth-century critical attitude toward this metrical problem.

In the absence of a much-needed thorough analysis of the whole problem of metrics in the Renaissance, our conclusions must remain tentative; for the status of criticism concerning metrical questions was at this time very unsettled. Restricting ourselves to the specific question of where anapests were to be allowed in the iambic trimeter line, we can show disagreement not only in the critics of the sixteenth century but also in the grammarians of more authoritative times. Part of the confusion was due to vagueness in some critics as to whether they were discussing comic or tragic meter, for the comic dramatists were invariably granted more license than were tragedians; part of it, too, was caused by a failure to distinguish between the practice of the more ancient Latin writers and that of the later Latins; no doubt the defective texts of Seneca and other authors contributed to the confusion because the texts did not always agree with theoretical dicta; and perhaps the biggest cause of confusion was the general failure to distinguish between the practices of the Greeks and of the Romans, between the iambic trimeter and the senarius. This last confusion has special application to Thomas Watson. The Greek iambic line, because it was scanned in dipodies, was called trimeter and had more severe requirements for its even feet than did the Latin line, which was scanned in single feet and accordingly was allowed more license.[35] And some sixteenth-century writers knew of this distinction: hence, we find Iodocus Badius Ascenius advising writers to follow the practice of the Greeks rather than that of the Romans, who permit too many licenses.[36] But perhaps more critics thought the names trimeter and

[34] Not too likely because of the lapse of time after the play's composition and Watson's changed status (he was now in confinement). By the same token I doubt Boas' suggested explanation (p. 63) that Ascham was trying to induce Watson to publish his play: Watson was in little position to publish it if he had intended to.

[35] See William Ross Hardie, *Res Metrica: An Introduction to the Study of Greek and Roman Versification* (Oxford, 1920), pp. 68 ff.

[36] *Quinti Horatii Flacci De Arte Poetica Opusculum Aureum ab Ascensio Familiariter Expositum* . . . (Paris, 1505), fol. XXXII*r*.

senarius were simply variant names for the same verse form: thus, William Lily, who allowed (*rarius*) even a spondee in the *loci pares,* headed his discussion "Trimetrvm sive senarivm";[37] Avantius, who permitted few licenses, discussed "Versus Senarii uel trimetri iambici";[38] and even Erasmus spoke of "Iambico trimetro, qui & senarii dicuntur a numero pedum."[39] Significantly, Thomas Watson, who identified the meter of nearly every scene of *Absalom,* interchangeably used the terms "Trimetri Iambici," "Trimetri," "Senarii," and (an almost oxymoronic term) "Trimetri Senarii" to describe verses having identical structure. In view of all this confusion, it should not surprise us to find almost as much confusion as to whether the anapest was acceptable in the even feet of the iambic trimeter line.

A Renaissance writer turning to ancient authority could find one for almost any position which he wanted to hold. Apart from the factors of confusion noted above, there were two basic schools among the ancient critics: the prototype school (of which some prominent members were Heliodorus, Hephaestion, and Juba) and the derivative school (including Terentius Varro and his followers, Caesius Bassus, Terentianus, and Diomedes). The prototype school held that eight basic types of verse were developed independently of each other; the derivative school held to the much more reasonable opinion that nearly all meters were derived, ultimately, from either the dactylic hexameter or the iambic trimeter by the processes of *adiectio* (addition), *detractio* (subtraction), *concinnatio* (joining), and *permutatio* (permutation).[40] By and large, the prototypists seem to have presented more lenient views of what was permissible; but eventually the derivativists took over majority critical opinion. It seems rather doubtful, however, that Renaissance writers would have known of all these factors; hence, there was probably a tendency simply to look at individual authorities without regard for any school to which they belonged. Among those ancient authorities advocating the more lenient practice in the handling of the anapest we may mention Hephaestion,[41]

[37] [William Lily], *A Shorte Introdvction of Grammar Generally To Be Vsed* ([London], 1567); Scholars' Facsimiles & Reprints (New York, 1945), sig. [G7]*v*.

[38] "Dimensiones," *Scenecae* [*sic*] *Tragoediae* [Venice, 1517], sig. Aii*v*.

[39] "De Metris," *P. Terentii Afri Comoediae* (Cologne, 1535), p. 4.

[40] Richard Volkmann, *Rhetorik und Metrik der Griechen und Römer,* 3rd ed., by H. Gleditsch and Caspar Hammer, Handbuch der klassischen Altertumswissenschaft, II (Munich, 1901), 70.

[41] 'ΕΓΧΕΙΡΙΔΙΟΝ ΠΕΡΙ ΜΕΤΡΩΝ ΚΑΙ ΠΟΙΗΜΑΤΩΝ. *The Enkheiridion of Hehfaistiown Concerning Metres and Poems,* tr. Thomas Foster Barham (Cambridge, 1843). The first edition of Hephaestion (fl. A.D. 150) was with Gaza's

Marius Plotius (otherwise known as Marius Claudius Sacerdos),[42] and Atilius Fortunatianus.[43] Some writers contradicted themselves: C. Marius Victorinus, who is especially interesting because he claimed that his work was copied from Aphthonius (of whose metrical views we otherwise know nothing), in one place said that the anapest was acceptable *in locis paribus* but in another was willing to allow only the iamb and the tribrach.[44]

By and large those ancient writers whom the sixteenth century most highly esteemed held to the more rigid view. Of course this view was implicit in Horace's demand (made specifically in connection with spondees) that the iamb not "de sede secunda/ cederet, aut quarta" (ll. 257-258), but all the commentators seem to have interpreted this statement only in its significance to the spondee, not in relation to the tribrach or anapest. Diomedes admitted no license except the tribrach and the pyrrhic in the even feet, and he even went so far as to make the iamb alone acceptable in the fourth foot (though he granted comedians wider license).[45] Diomedes was one of the most widely

---

Greek grammar in 1526, but Philologus knew him in 1505. Hephaestion qualified his license (p. 144): ". . . in the *even* [feet are admitted] . . . an iambos, tribrakhy, and anapaist: this last, with the comedians, frequently; but with the *iambopoioi* and tragedians, more rarely." Elsewhere he was less accommodating (p. 147): ". . . the metre does not in the even places admit the spondee, neither ought it [by resolution] to admit the anapaist. . . . The *iambopoioi* . . . and tragedians . . . employ it but seldom."

[42] "De Metris Liber," in Helia Putschius, ed., *Grammaticae Latinae Avctores Antiqvi* (Hanover, 1605), col. 2641; Heinrich Keil, ed., *Grammatici Latini* (Leipzig, 1857, 1855-80), VI, 415-546; Thomas Gaisford, ed., *Scriptores Latini Rei Metricae. Manuscriptorum Codicum Ope Subinde Refinxit* (Oxford, 1837), pp. 242-301: "In secunda vero & quarta parte . . . illos ponere debemus qui ex breui incipiunt, iambum, tribrachum, anapaestum."

[43] "Ars de Carmine," Gaisford, pp. 342-343; Keil, VI, 278-304; Putschius, cols. 2692 ff. (But Putschius leaves out an essential *non.*) The lenient view was still being presented three centuries after Atilius, as seen in an anonymous eighth-century manuscript fragment "De Iambico Metro" (Codex Parisinus 7530; Keil, VI, 629).

[44] "Ars Grammatica . . . de Orthographia & Ratione Metrorum," Putschius, cols. 2525, 2570-71. The selection is also found in Keil, VI, 79 ff., and Gaisford, pp. 106 ff. The work was first printed in 1537. See Volkmann, pp. 74-75. Victorinus (not to be confused with two other grammarians of the same name) late in life became a Christian and wrote several works on religion which might have made him (and his metrical work) better known to the Christian world. He lived in the fourth century (William Smith, ed., *Dictionary of Greek and Roman Biography and Mythology* [London, 1850-51], III, 1258-59.

[45] "De Oratione et Partibvs Orationis et Vario Genere Metrorum Libri III," Putschius, col. 503. The selection is in Gaisford, pp. 479 ff., and Keil, I, 503 ff. Diomedes lived in the fourth century or later (Volkmann, p. 75). Like several other authors, Diomedes used *sinister* and *dexter* to refer to even and odd feet, respectively.

published critics in the sixteenth century and certainly was influential: I know of at least thirteen printings of his work between 1476 and 1530. Also influential in the sixteenth century (because of his commentaries on Vergil) was Servius, whose *Centimetrum* was first printed in 1473 and many, many times reprinted. Servius was equally firm in permitting only comedians much license.[46] Highly interesting because John Cheke mentioned him as becoming available at Cambridge in the 1530's is Terentianus, who was printed as early as 1497 and went through six other editions by 1533; and his view is quite unbending in allowing only the iamb and tribrach in the even feet.[47]

We find, however, sixteenth-century writers who adopt both the more and the less rigid principles. Benedictus Philologus, an editor of Seneca, Terence, and Horace, used the Greek Hephaestion for authority that the Latin iambic trimeter line admits in the even feet the iamb, tribrach, and anapest. While he was concerned with comic meters in this essay, he made it clear that the licenses allowed comedians are not these, but the additional ones of having in all places indifferently these feet plus dactyls and spondees. For tragedies, he explicitly stated, "Erit . . . probabilis Iambicus uersus aptusque . . . si secundum, et quartum pedem, non alios feceris quam Iambos, aut eum, qui Tribrachus, aut Anapaestus nominatur, quoniam sunt pares."[48] Another early Senecan editor, Aegidius Maserius, said that in the iambic trimeter line the second and fourth feet take an iamb, an anapest, or a tribrach.[49] On the other hand, another Senecan editor, Hieronymus Avantius, called on Seneca's example to support his view that the

[46] "Ars de Centvm Metris," Putschius, cols. 1817-18. It is also in Gaisford, pp. 376-377, and Keil, IV, 457 ff.

[47] "De Literis, Syllabis, Pedibus, et Metris," Putschius, col. 2432. It is also in Keil, VI, 390 ff. Terentianus flourished around A.D. 300. We may also mention the stern view shared by Flavius Mallius Theodorus and the Venerable Bede. Theodorus, who flourished in A.D. 400, called the verse *metrum iambicum hexametrum* ("Liber de Metris," Gaisford, p. 543; also in Keil, VI, 593-594); he seems not to have been printed in the sixteenth century. Bede was printed in 1504 and 1519 ("De Metrica Ratione Liber Unicus," Putschius, col. 2378). Another writer, Franciscus Niger, apparently described the practice of *iambographi* rather than of tragedians, for he thought the best line to be composed entirely of iambs (*Grammatica* [Basel, (1500)], fol. LXXIX*r-v*).

[48] "De Pedibus Iambici Metri," *Terentius in Sua Metra Restitvtvs* (Florence, 1505), sig. [a7]*v*-[a8]*r*. The phraseology suggests some confusion in terminology, as does Philologus' reference in another passage to the anapest and tribrach as *pares*. But elsewhere he spoke of the iamb, tribrach, anapest, dactyl, and spondee as *quinque pedes*.

[49] "De Tragici Carminis Metro," *L. Annei Senecae Tragoediae Pristinae Integritati Restitutae* [Paris, 1514], fol. CCLXVII. In a Latin poem appended to his essay he used some anapests in the even feet of his trimeter lines.

anapest was not permissible in the even feet.[50] And apparently Ascham agreed with this view.

I believe that some degree of sanity can be derived from this bedlam of varying opinions. It seems very likely that the attitude toward the anapest *in locis paribus* changed in direct proportion to the advance of the new learning. My analysis seems to indicate that the generally "conservative" critics of the sixteenth century allowed more license than did the generally "liberal" critics, who were the advocates of the harsher principles[51] of the new learning. The respectability of the more rigid rules apparently increased as the respectability of the new learning increased, and as the classical critics like Horace and Terentianus came to be more and more influential. The development is clouded by overlapping of thought: thus, the authors named in the preceding paragraph are not very far apart in time, yet their views are quite different. The development is also clouded by long lapses of time between the writing and the printing of some important essays. For example, Hieronymus Avantius, in Fabricius' Seneca (1566), felt compelled to rebut the view of a "vir eruditissimus & amicissimus" who had recently ("nuper") expressed the view that anapests were acceptable in the even feet; but Avantius had certainly been dead for some time when Fabricius used his essay, and so far as I have been able to determine, no earlier form of the essay survives. Thus, we are likely to think that Avantius was referring to some mid-century opponent, whereas he had probably been disputing with someone forty years or more earlier.[52] As an additional problem, the grammarians used by the sixteenth century seem to contradict this apparent development. Robert Whittinton, one of the older grammarians whom Lily generally supplanted by the 1530's[53] and therefore just possibly a grammarian

[50] "De Carmine Iambico Trimetro," in Georgius Fabricius Chemnicensis, ed., *L. Annaei Senecae Tragoediae* (Leipzig, 1566), p. 423.

[51] The phrase is Peiper and Richter's, p. iiin. They were referring to Avantius' Aldine edition of Seneca (1517).

[52] "De Carmine," pp. 429-430. Little is known of Avantius' life, but he studied belles-lettres under Antonio Partenio Lacise from 1485 to 1488; edited Lucretius in 1500 and Seneca in 1517; and was named professor at Padua in 1493 (Conti Giammaria Mazzuchelli Bresciano, *Gli Scrittori d'Italia cioe Notizie Storiche, e Critiche Intorno alle Vite, e agli Scritti dei Letterati Italiani* [Brescia, 1753-63], I, Part 2, 1226-27). Joseph Thomas (*Universal Pronouncing Dictionary of Biography and Mythology,* 5th ed. [Philadelphia, (1930)], p. 232) said that Avantius was born about 1460 and was still alive in 1534. I do not know to whom Avantius was referring, but his failure to mention the dispute in "Dimensiones" (1517) suggests that it arose after that date.

[53] Baldwin, *Small Latine,* II, 690.

whom Watson used in Durham early in the 1520's,[54] laid down the rule for the "Novum [iambicum tragicum]" as requiring iambs and spondees in the odd feet and iambs alone in the even (with the added license of *syllaba anceps* in the sixth).[55] And Lily's *Shorte Introdvction* considerably later was so lenient as to allow even a spondee in the even places.[56] However, these grammarians do not seem to have been influential at all on metrical practice or opinion. For Whittinton, following the rules of the Latin *iambographi,* thought that the best iambic line consisted entirely of iambs, and no other author whom I have seen in the sixteenth century followed him. And Lily's apparently not well-informed permission to use spondees *in paribus* was assuredly not accepted by Renaissance theorists.

On the other hand, there are some rather solid indications of a trend such as I have theorized: after 1517, Avantius' essay "Dimensiones" (or, in 1566, his "De Carmine") was the only one printed with Senecan editions, whereas earlier editions had had essays by Philologus and Maserius. Significant, I think, of a trend toward less lenient rules is Avantius' statement in "De Carmine" (pp. 429-430) that he had himself been deceived, with everybody else, on this question of the propriety of anapests in his younger days ("adolescentior") — obviously before 1517. Furthermore, in 1549 the handbook which was to become the metrical bible, Rudolphus Gualtherus', was published; and it presented the more rigid rules.[57] And we must not overlook Ascham's mid-century statement about Watson's anapest. It will perhaps be pertinent to mention here George Buchanan's rules for the iambic trimeter line, though they were not published until late in the century:

[54] Where Watson attended grammar school is not known. For the system at Durham Cathedral see Baldwin, *Small Latine,* I, 166-170.

[55] *De Syllabarum Quantitatibus Opusculum* ([London], 1519), sig. [2Cviii]*r*. In the passage referred to there is some confusion in the use of *choreum:* once it is made synonymous with the trochee (as in Quintilian) and made permissible (in older poets) in the odd feet; in the next phrase it is listed along with the anapest and iamb as permissible in the even feet and would seem, then, to mean the tribrach. But there is no question about the newer poets: they use "in secundo, quarto pede iambum; in sexto, iambum vel pyrrhichium."

[56] The prosody section which proceeds under Lily's name was apparently written by Thomas Robertson and probably dates before 1532, when Robertson's supplemented version of Lily first appeared (Baldwin, *Small Latine,* II, 697). Its lenience, then, may reflect an older view of iambic trimeter rules, but Robertson does not show much knowledge of the subject about which he is writing.

[57] *De Syllabarvm et Carminvm Ratione, Libri Dvo* (Zurich, 1549), fol. 92*r*. He allowed the anapest only in the first and fifth feet, not even in the third. For the position of Gualtherus in the century see Baldwin, *Small Latine,* II, 392.

for the "Versus Iambicus Acatelecticus trimeter" he allowed the anapest only in the odd feet and admitted nothing but the iamb and the tribrach into the even feet.[58] I think it is especially significant that Terentianus brought his stern view into the hands of Thomas Smith and John Cheke shortly after 1535 — apparently just before *Absalom* was written (Mullinger [1884], p. 55). Terentianus had great influence on these scholars' opinions concerning Greek pronunciation, and he probably influenced their metrical judgments too; and from their apical position at Cambridge they and their follower Ascham may have looked with some disdain on the failure of Watson to follow Terentianus' principles in the matter of the anapest.[59]

Perhaps Watson's anapests were the result of careless writing; but Watson's many revisions belie any charge of undue negligence. Perhaps they were the result of ignorance or disinterest; but Watson was far from ignorant, and his interest in metrics has been amply demonstrated. Perhaps Watson took quite literally Aristotle's opinion (Ch. I) that imitation, not meter, makes a poet. But the truth, probably, is that Watson did not share the newer metrical opinion. As we have seen, he was a humanist but in at least some areas a conservative one; and it is quite possible that he sympathized with the older opinion of the propriety of anapests, despite the contrary opinion of the recently more-reputable Latin authorities. That he may have tried to make his play acceptable to Smith and Cheke (and Terentianus) may be indicated by the fact that in the early scenes a few of his revisions apparently were motivated by a desire to eliminate an offensive anapest; such, for example, must have been his reason for reversing the first two words of the first line. But, except occasionally when he could eliminate an anapest by merely transposing two words, he soon gave up these attempts, and in fact he seems to have had something of a fondness for the anapest in the fourth foot, where above all some critics (e.g., Diomedes) had frowned on it. In any case, I feel rather certain that these anapests, being (even from the "liberal" point of view) among his least serious though certainly his most frequent metrical infractions, were not the reason (or at least not the main reason), as Ascham said they were, for Watson's reluctance to publish

[58] George Buchanan, *De Prosodia Libellvs* (Edinburgh, [?1595]), sig. C2.

[59] Of course the sixteenth century did not settle the question once and for all. In 1797 the great Richard Porson (in the "Praefatio" to his edition of Euripides' *Hecuba*) took strong issue with Richard F. P. Brunck, editor of Aeschylus, Aristophanes, Euripides, and Sophocles, for saying that the anapest could appear in the even feet. Porson, in fact, would have allowed it only in the first foot.

his play. The real reason I do not pretend to know — nor do I care much.[60]

SUMMARY

We have seen that Watson with obvious deliberation attempted to follow the important dictates of Aristotle and Horace and the more important example of Seneca. As such his play is an important tool in the exegesis of the critical standards of Ascham and his fellow humanists at St. John's College, Cambridge. We might sum up Watson's motives by saying that in language, plot, and diction Watson was fundamentally concerned with *decorum,* that most important critical doctrine.[61] *Decorum* meant, among other things, appropriateness of style and language to subject matter and avoidance of mixtures of tone and characters. That it was important to Ascham is indicated by his several uses of the term, as in the passages quoted in this chapter. That it was important to Watson is indicated by the technique of *Absalom.*

One may argue about the results. F. S. Boas made a number of favorable comments about the play, but tempered nearly all with unfavorable ones. He spoke of Watson's "genuine gift for vigorous rhetorical argumentation" in the debate in III.3, but complained of the length of the argument. He spoke of Watson's "power of selecting and arranging material," but weighed against it the "frequently diffuse verbiage" and what he called the author's "monotonous versification." He called Chusi's description of the battle in Act V "a vivid piece of narrative," but was disturbed by the messenger's "tedious circumlocution." And, comparing *Absalom* with Peele's *David and Bethsabe,* he found that, generally, "the Latin play profits by comparison with the English" because of its "dexterous arrangement of material . . . concentration of interest, and, above all . . . psychological insight"; but he allowed Peele "far more sense of beauty and a finer ear for rhythm" and superiority in "sensuous imagery," and he praised Peele for avoiding Watson's "cardinal sin of diffuseness." He also thought Peele's play to be superior in moral import (Boas, pp. 333, 352, 359, 362-365). No one would claim that *Absalom* is a masterpiece, and some of Boas' complaints are undoubtedly justified by an absolute standard. But

[60] The play was possibly no more than an exercise in "Imitation," never intended for publication. James Upton (1711, p. 175n.) suggested as a reason "either an Unwillingness to appear in Print, or a Dissatisfaction with the Times, he being one of the ejected Bishops."

[61] Cf. the details of the foregoing analysis with the points discussed by Herrick, pp. 48-57.

some of them I consider to be absolutely groundless: Watson's verse is not monotonous, as I have shown, and his poetry, while not "sensuous," lyrical, or rhapsodical, achieves true beauty in some of its natural images and particularly in David's speeches in Act V. As for moral import, I hope that my analysis has shown that morality was in fact Watson's primary interest in writing the play. Finally, if Peele's play is less marred by diffuseness of thought than is Watson's, it makes up for it by diffuseness of plot. Fundamentally, Boas' most serious objection to *Absalom* was to its rhetoric, which he variously described as "diffuse," "tasteless," and "lurid." Thus, he was concerned over the "vituperative epithets" which Semei hurls at David in II.2; and he was most deeply disturbed by Chusi's circumlocution in V.3 (pp. 64, 353, 356, 363). But much of Watson's writing, especially, must not be judged by our standards, for Watson did not know them — and even Boas conceded, though with too little emphasis, that "the Renaissance standard in such matters was different from our own" (p. 64). The historical importance of the play is that it clarifies for us what that standard was. Watson was consciously trying in every way to make his play Senecan,[62] and to make it accord with certain Horatian-Aristotelian doctrines. In doing so he was answering the demands of his scholastic peers.[63] He used the matter and the manner of "Gods holie Bible" and the matter and the manner of Seneca. John Cheke said that any student who did that "must nedes proue an excellent man"; and Ascham called Watson's play an excellent imitation. The only fair judgment of *Absalom,* considering its plot, thought, characterization, and — yes, its rhetoric, is that for its age and for its place as our first true tragedy from England it is a truly remarkable work; and the phrase "for its age" should not be taken as an apology.

[62] Not the least Senecan quality, incidentally, is the relative stasis of the scenes. Of course, the excessive interest in rhetoric contributed to this lack of movement.

[63] I hope that my analysis has also rebutted Boas' argument that *Absalom* is not "scholarly" enough to have been written by Thomas Watson. Boas also said that the present play is not "monumental" enough to have been Watson's play (p. 64), but I confess that I don't know what that means.

CHAPTER FIVE

THE METHOD OF THIS EDITION

TEXT

In the Latin text I have attempted to reproduce faithfully the intentions of the author; hence, I have copied his Latin with a minimum of emendations. I have not, however, attempted to make a perfect transcription of the manuscript. The punctuation of the manuscript consists largely of a period at the end of nearly every line; of occasional commas; of colons between protases and apodoses of similes and conditional sentences; and of virtually identical points marking queries and exclamations. For greater clarity I have freely changed the punctuation, usually silently. Where the change involved a query or exclamation and some other mark;[1] where I substituted a major stop for an absence of any mark; or where some locally significant condition was present (as where Boas had a mark significantly different from mine), I have noted the change in the Textual Notes. I have silently raised lower-case letters or lowered capitals of the manuscript where I have deemed such action necessary. I have expanded all contractions: where the missing letters were represented by some symbol in the manuscript (¯ for nasals, ꝰ for *-us*, ę for *-ae-* and *-oe-*,[2] ꝗʒ for *-que*, etc.), I have supplied the letters silently. Where the missing letters are not represented in the manuscript I have added them in square brackets [ ] and have noted the emendation in the Textual Notes. As the one exception to this principle, I have not normally mentioned in the Textual Notes expansions of abbreviated speech prefixes, though in the text I have put the supplied letters into square brackets. Except for the proper names of the dramatis personae, I

[1] Because Watson (and his time) used the query and exclamation almost interchangeably, I have ignored the substitution of one for the other.

[2] The sixteenth century often used *-ae-* and *-oe-* interchangeably. In expanding the abbreviation for these digraphs, I have used whichever form is more common for the given words.

have not attempted to normalize Watson's inconsistent spellings or to improve his "incorrect" spellings. Thus, unless some special circumstance is present (such as a confusion of two words, e.g., *letum* and *laetum*), I have preserved the manuscript's spellings: *-e-* for *-ae-* or *-oe-* and vice versa (*faelix* for *felix, hec* for *haec*); *-c-* for *-t-* (*ocium* for *otium*); double consonant for single consonant or vice versa (*suppremo* for *supremo, oportunius* for *opportunius*); *-y-* for *-i-* (*desydero* for *desidero*), etc. In the Textual Notes I have given the more common equivalent for unusual spellings which I think might be confusing. In a very few instances I have corrected Watson's grammar (gender, case, number, tense, or mood), but only where I felt that the error would impede clarity. These changes and (except as indicated) all others are noted in the Textual Notes. Except for the changes mentioned, I have scrupulously avoided emendations; for instance, I have not emended merely for the sake of the meter, even where the meter is clearly defective. And my only transpositions are those which the author himself clearly authorized. Watson's method of indicating transposition was to put an *a* over the word or beside the line which should go first, a *b* over or beside the word or line which should go second, etc. I have abided by these notations and by other authorial notations affecting the text; and I have entered all significant authorial notations in the Textual Notes. Of course the author's scene headings (act and scene numbers and identification of characters and meter) are entered at the head of each scene; I have supplied (in square brackets with a notation in the Textual Notes) such information as is wanting in the headings of some scenes. In the right margin I have marked the line with which each manuscript page begins; these numbers do not take into account Watson's occasional rearrangement of lines.

TEXTUAL NOTES

The scope of the Textual Notes, found at the foot of the Latin text, has been made partially clear by the above discussion. A very considerable portion of the Textual Notes records significant authorial revisions. Generally, all revisions which were substantive and were not obvious corrections of scribal blunders are considered significant and are entered in the Textual Notes. Whenever a revision seems substantive, I have entered the fact of revision even if the original reading is illegible. The reader should be aware that my readings of canceled word(s) are sometimes open to question, though I have usually shown, by means of shaped brackets ⟨ ⟩ or a query, any doubt which I have had. Especially in cases where more than one word was revised or where a revision occurred in more than one stage, it has often been impossible to reconstruct with certainty what the stages of revision were, even when the individual words are all legible; in such cases I have always given what I regard as the probable sequence.

I have noted variant readings from the extensive excerpts in Boas (pp. 352 ff.), and from the few lines quoted by Churchill and Keller (230 ff.). I have, however, recorded only some of their punctuation variants: I have ignored all differences except those involving a major stop (semicolon or period) and either a comma or no punctuation; those involving a query or an exclamation and any other mark; and those involving a colon and any other mark. When I have recorded a punctuation variant from one of these sources, I have also shown what the manuscript punctuation is. The sigla are *Boas, Ch,* and *MS.* Since Boas is inconsistent in his expansion of the manuscript's abbreviations, I have noted all instances where his treatment of an abbreviation differs from mine; Ch expands all abbreviations silently, and I have not noted these expansions.

The method of noting these items is as follows. All entries are by line numbers. Transpositions of lines and notations of authorial markings are entered by line numbers alone. Equivalent forms are entered with the manuscript reading immediately after the line number, thus: hec = haec. All other entries use a lemma (word or words copied exactly from the printed text, including square brackets if any) followed by a single bracket]. The lemma sometimes includes only the first and last words of a lengthy passage, separated by an ellipsis (. . .); in such cases the note may record variants to the words given or it may record a variant of the whole passage. If the note records an authorial revision, I have separated the original manuscript reading from the lemma by a derivation sign ⟨ immediately after the bracket]. If the revision was made in several stages, I have recorded the stages in reverse order, the eldest reading appearing last; I have shown the direction of the sequence by placing a derivation sign ⟨ before each of the stages, thus: furor armet] ⟨ furor armat ⟨ furor. Occasionally in a note recording a revision of a longer passage, I have indicated a second-stage revision of a single word within the passage by placing the alternate word within square brackets immediately after the revised word; within the square brackets and before the alternate word I have placed a derivation sign ⟨ or ⟩, depending upon whether the alternate word represents an earlier or a later stage, thus: tante gravatam] ⟨ et quot [⟩ quantae] molestiae *etc.* If the note records an emendation or a variant reading in Boas or Ch, the manuscript reading or the variant (or both in order) follows immediately after the lemma and is identified with the appropriate siglum; if the manuscript reading and my reading are the same, the siglum *MS* follows the bracket after the lemma and precedes the other variants. Such notes are distinguished from notes showing authorial revisions by the *absence* of a derivation sign, thus: integras;] integras *MS* integras, *Boas*. Normally a note records only one type of variant; if both a punctuation and a spelling variant, for instance, are to be recorded for the same word, I have usually put the variants into separate notes. However, if both an emendation or variant and an authorial revision are to be recorded at the same place, I have sometimes included both types in one note. In these cases I have noted the emendation or variant first according to the method outlined above and have shown the previous stages of the manuscript reading in parentheses following the siglum *MS;* the derivation sign ⟨ or ⟩ within the parentheses indicates the direction of the revision, thus: Bibul[a]e] Bibule *MS* (⟨ Bibulis). Where there is more than one note to a line, I have separated them by a single bar |. After the last note to a line (even if there is only one note to the line) I have placed a double bar ||. When a note records an authorial revision in which an earlier stage of the reading was left incomplete, I have often attempted to conjecture what the full original reading would have been if completed; I have shown my conjecture in square brackets immediately following the incomplete reading and have marked it with an asterisk, thus: violare] ⟨ turba [*turbare]. A *pair* of shaped brackets ⟨ ⟩ indicates an illegible letter or words; where I have been able to guess what the illegible parts were, I have placed my conjectured reading within the shaped brackets. A query preceding the derivation sign or in parentheses following the original reading indicates doubt either as to the accuracy of the transcription or as to whether a true revision occurred at all. I have put into italics all editorial comments and sigla and into roman all textual matters.

Besides the sigla given above, the following abbreviations appear in the Textual Notes:

/	end of verse	*p.h.*	heading showing persons in scene
abbrev.	abbreviation		
ad loc.	at the place cited	*pn.*	punctuation
incl.	including	*prob.*	probably
m.h.	metrical heading	*s.d.*	stage direction
om.	omitted	*s.h.*	(act and) scene heading
orig.	original(ly)	*s.p.*	speech prefix
		var(r).	variant(s)

TRANSLATION

> . . . euen the best translation, is, for mere necessitie, but an euil imped wing to flie withall, or a heuie stompe leg of wood to go withall: soch, the hier they flie, the sooner they falter and faill: the faster they runne, the ofter they stumble, and sorer they fall [Ascham, *Scholemaster* (1570), fol. 51*v*].

My intention has been to try to present Watson's *Absalom* — or as much of it as I could capture — in a language understood by much of the world rather than in one understood by almost none of it. I have put the translation into prose because I am not a poet and because I felt that I could more easily capture the flavor of the original in prose. That original is, as we have seen, highly rhetorical and unconversational. Accordingly, I have put the translation into English which is rhetorical and unconversational and so far as possible have made the translation quite literal. Naturally, I have had to make some changes because of the differences between Latin and English syntax and also because of the author's lack of clarity at times. Hence, I have occasionally substituted proper names where the Latin has only pronouns; I have tried to improve the coherence of the play with occasional supplied transitions; I have eliminated some of the unclear figures which are natural to Latin but quite unnatural in English (e.g., "sad iron" as a figure for a weapon); I have usually tried to make consistent Watson's inconsistent tenses; and I have obviously not been able to reproduce the Latin participle for participle, phrase for phrase, etc. But I have attempted to make no changes beyond those necessary for clarity or English literateness; in particular, I have usually avoided the kind of general paraphrase which would be necessary to make *Absalom* "good" according to modern standards of prose style. I hope, therefore, that my translation presents, not a new work either better or worse than the original, but an old work which has been virtually unknown heretofore and which is historically important enough to be better known.

Much of what I have said in the Introduction and of what I shall say in the Appendices is an attempt to explain exactly how Thomas Watson set about putting his play together — what gods he was serving. If I have been successful, the world should know more, not only about this play, but about the temper of the age which produced it — and that is perhaps even more important.

ABSALOM:
LATIN TEXT AND TRANSLATION

[ABSALOM

Dramatis Personae

ABSALOM, *third son of David (by Maacha, daughter of Tholmai, King of Gessur): rebel against David and later King of Israel*

DAVID, *son of Jesse (Isai): King of Israel*

ACHITOPHEL *of Giloh: formerly advisor of David and now of Absalom against David*

IOAB (JOAB), *son of Sarvia (sister of David): David's military leader; benefactor of Absalom until the latter's rebellion*

CHUSAI: *friend of David and subversive advisor of Absalom*

ABISAI, *son of Sarvia (sister of David): follower of David*

SEMEI, *son of Geva and relative of Saul: factional enemy of David*

SADOC, *son of Achitob: a priest* } *spies for David*

ABIATHAR, *son of Achimelech and grandson of Achitob: a priest* } *spies for David*

ACHIMAAS, *son of Sadoc* } *couriers faithful to David*

CHUSI } *couriers faithful to David*

NUNTIUS (MESSENGER)

SPECULATOR (WATCHMAN)

POPULUS (PEOPLE)

CHORUS

Scene. *Jerusalem and Environs; Desert near Bahurim; Galaad; Giloh; Mahanaim*

Time. *Ca. 1036 B.C. to ca. 967 B.C.*][1]

Title] David and Absalom. by Johan Bale *MS* (*in modern hand on fol. 1r*) || Dramatis Personae, Scene, and Time] *Om. MS*

[1] For the dates see Fallows *et al.*, I, 29-30. But Watson probably intended the action to cover a year. For a discussion of the settings and time see Appendix F. Some of the historical information given in the Dramatis Personae is not available from the play and has been supplied from the Bible. Apart from the alterations in characters discussed in the Introduction, the only other significant changes which Watson made in Biblical characters were of omission: for example, in the Bible Abisai was leader of one third of David's army.

[ACTUS PRIMUS.] SCENA PRIMA. [*fol. 1v*]

ABSALO[M]. IOAB.

Trimetri Iambici.

[ABSALOM.] Animus adhuc vexatur excusso metu,
tante gravatam miseriae mentem premunt
fessoque segnes excutit somnos dolor.
Hinc laesa nostro crimine voluntas patris,
illinc atrox fratris perempti mors mihi
somnum excutit, ita vtrinque maerore opprimor.
Huius tamen sororis iniuria necem
compensat, et magna ex parte aerumnas levat.
Illum tuus reduxit mecum in gratiam
favor benignus, meque iterum patriae dedit
(si quae tuis adsit dictis solida fides).
Quid profuit nocentem retulisse huc pedem
et tuta statim liquisse presidijs loca?
Si omnis residat eius pectoris tumor
et iam furentis animi aestus deferbuit,
cur prohibet aspectum veterum irarum memor? [*fol. 2r*]
Gradus est futuri finis vnius mali.
Sin pertinax in pectore iam condat odium
nec caecus iras animus tumidas posuit,
rigido recludat nostra ferro pectora
strict[o]que corpus ense mactatum cadat:
optatior mors est, mali finem adferens,
quam vita languidis sepulta miserijs.
Quis ferre contemptum patris recte potest?

I.1.s.h.] Scena 1ª. *MS* || P.h. Absalo[m]] Absalon *MS* || **1-10.** *Printed in Ch, incl. varr.* || **1.** S.p.] *Om. MS* | Animus adhuc] ⟨ Adhuc animus || **1-3.** Animus . . . dolor] ⟨ Heu quot malis quantisque obrutus asto miser/ et quot [⟩ quantae] molestiae mentem exagitant meam/ nec vllam adesse quietem cupienti sinunt *Ch queries* asto || **2.** tante = tantae || **3.** excutit . . . dolor] ⟨ excutiunt . . . mihi || **4.** nostro] ⟨ nostra (?) || **4-5.** *After each line a trefoil, both canceled* (*see I.1.10, 13, 16, 17*) || **5.** fratris perempti] ⟨ perempti fratris || **6.** *First two words obscured by stain* (*or erasure*?) || **9.** Illum] -u- *obscured by modern ink stain* || After **10.** *A trefoil* || **12.** pedem] pedem? *MS* || **13, 43, 57,** etc. presidijs, penas, Ceca, que = praesidijs, poenas, Caeca, quae (*a very common spelling of* -ae- *words; hereafter I shall note the spelling only under unusual circumstances*) || **13.** statim liquisse presidijs] ⟨ presidijs liquisse statim || After **13.** *A trefoil* || Before **16** and **17.** *Trefoils* || **18.** pertinax . . . iam] ⟨ triste adhuc in pectore | condat] ⟨ condet (?) | *A heavy score extends from beneath the last word into the right margin* || **19.** *A light score begins in the left margin and ends beneath the first word* || **21.** *To the left of the line an* X | strict[o]que] strictaque *MS* ||

[ACT I.] SCENE 1.

[Jerusalem. Before the Royal Palace.]

[Enter] ABSALOM [and] JOAB.[1]

[ABSALOM.] Though my fear[2] has been dispelled, my heart is still troubled: such great torments weigh upon my overburdened mind, and even in my weariness my sorrow drives away the tardy sleep. On the one hand my father's affection, offended by my crime, on the other the cruel death of my murdered brother — these things disturb my sleep: thus from both sides am I smothered with sadness. But my sister's injury counterbalances this murder and in large measure lightens my distress. Him your gracious support has reconciled to me,[3] and me it has restored to my homeland — if any solid trust may be put in your words. But to what avail have I returned my erring footstep hither and left places continually made safe with garrisons? If all the swelling passion of my father's heart subsides, and if indeed the heat of his raging soul has now cooled down, why does he forbid my seeing him as if mindful of old angers? The end of one evil is but the onset of another to come. But if he still conceals within his breast an obstinate hatred and if his secret heart has not put aside its swelling angers, let him lay open my breast with his sharp blade and let my body fall, cut down by his drawn sword. Better death bringing an end to evil than life overwhelmed with heavy adversities. Who can bear patiently the contempt of his father?

[1] The scene is based on *2 Kings* xiv.32-33, with verse 32 in particular being expanded into a long stichomythic dialogue (Boas, p. 352).

[2] The fear of retribution during his three-year exile in Gessur. J. S[tudley] rendered this Senecan line (*Hercules Oetaeus* 712) "So yet my wit be tocksicate, although my feare be gone" (*Tenne Tragedies,* ed. Thomas Newton [London, 1581]; Tudor Translations [London, 1927], II, 219).

[3] Actually, according to the Biblical account, Joab had not interceded until the king was already "comforted concerning the death of Amnon" (*2 Kings* xiii.38) and "the king's heart was turned to Absalom" (*2 Kings* xiv.1). In ignoring these Biblical statements and later making Joab speak of David's grief as continuing, Watson gave Absalom better motivation for his later actions: if the play had mentioned David's softening of heart, Absalom's later complaints of David's hypocrisy (I.3) would be patently fallacious.

IO[AB]. Frena dolorem, atque illicitos questus doma.
Quin verba pectoris parum sani premis?
Pium patris luctum violare non decet.
Nescis dolores quot violenta mors facit
Amnonis, vnici patris solatij,
nam tempore ipso iam vetus crescit malum.
Nunc ne tua sepultos dolores concitet [*fol. 2v*]
facies timet, ac iras lacessat pristinas:
malum receptum semper est nocentius,
dolor recrudescens gravius incenditur.
AB[SALOM]. At vivere in patria ignobilem miserrimum est.
IOAB. In servitute exul cruciatur miserius.
AB[SALOM]. Tutus domi est, charis qui amicis vtitur.
IO[AB]. Tutus quis est, qui sibi patrem infensum timet?
AB[SALOM]. Iam mihi quïetum verba retulerunt tua.
IO[AB]. At quem movere rursus aspectus potest.
AB[SALOM]. Si placeo, cur patris frui aspectu vetor?
Sin displiceo, quid amplius vitam traho?
Caedis ego factae debitas penas luam,
nam servitutem morte mutarem libens.
Mori iuvabit: servitus pena est mihi.
IO[AB]. Servum vocas qui quod placet agit libere? [*fol. 3r*]
AB[SALOM]. Quemcumque contemptum videas, servum scias.
IO[AB]. Vocemus abiectum, scelus qui pessimum
conflavit, in terras profectus exteras,
liber remisso iam scelere reducitur?

25. doma.] doma, *MS* || **27.** violare] ⟨ turba [*turbare] || **29.** Amnonis] ⟨ Ammonis (?*scribal*) || **35.** misserimum est] ?⟨ miser || **36.** cruciatur] ⟨ latere est || **38.** qui sibi] ⟨ qui | timet?] timet. *MS* || **41-45.** *Printed in Boas* || **41.** patris frui aspectu] ⟨ conspectu patris frui || **43.** factae] *MS* (*abbrev.*) facte *Boas* || **44.** mutarem libens] ⟨ mutare placet || **45.** servitus . . . mihi] ⟨ poena servitus mihi est || **46.** qui] ⟨ qu⟨e *or* o⟩ [*quem *or* quod] || **48.** abiectum] ⟨ adiectum | scelus . . . pessimum] ⟨ scelere . . . pessimo ||

JOAB. Bridle your sorrow, and your unseemly complaints subdue. Why not suppress these mouthings of your maddened heart? It is not proper to profane the pious mourning of your father. You do not know how many sorrows the violent death of Amnon, your father's only comfort,[4] causes him, because even now his old grief grows stronger. Now he fears that sight of you will stir up his hidden sorrows and provoke his former angers:[5] the hurt which he has received is ever more injurious, and sorrow which breaks out afresh is kindled more seriously.

ABSALOM. But in my own country to live a lowly life is very wretched.

JOAB. An exile is tormented more wretchedly, in servitude.

ABSALOM. One is safe at home who enjoys the companionship of his loved ones.

JOAB. Is anyone safe who fears a father hostile to him?

ABSALOM. Already your words have restored me to his favor.

JOAB. But sight of you can arouse him again.

ABSALOM. If I am welcome, why am I forbidden to enjoy the sight of my father? But if I am not welcome, why do I prolong my life further? Let me pay the penalty required for a committed murder, because this servitude I would willingly exchange for death. Dying will be pleasant: this bondage is torture to me.

JOAB. A bondman do you call one who does freely whatever he pleases?

ABSALOM. Whomever you see scorned, know he is a slave.

JOAB. Should we call scorned one who has committed the worst crime and who, having gone forth into foreign lands, is brought back free, his crime already forgiven?[6]

[4] Apart from describing David's prolonged grief over Amnon's death (*2 Kings* xiii.31, 37), the Bible gives no authority for this description of Amnon except perhaps in its reference to David's love for him "because he was his first-born" (*2 Kings* xiii.21). Incidentally, this part of the sentence is wanting in sixteenth-century English Bibles.

[5] For the first of several notable times, Watson supplies psychological motivation for an action which in the Bible (*2 Kings* xiv.24) is narrated without motive: "But the king said: Let him return into his house, and let him not see my face."

[6] To avoid ambiguity, whenever the last line on a page does not correspond to the end of a speech or paragraph, the last line is aligned at the right regardless of its length.

Abiectus est qui vel nocens patriam tenet?
Nunc ergo languescat dolor implacabilis;
prorsus recedat impetus animi ferox,
nam quod patri placet ferendum est filio.
AB[SALOM]. Ipsi voluptati obsequi iuvenem decet:
dulcis voluptas frena numquam sustinet.
IO[AB]. Ceca est voluptas que rationem labefacit:
rationis est regere, voluptatis regi.
AB[SALOM]. Pectus gravatum scelere rationem exuit.
Scelus refricatum alterum irritat novum:
semper oculis fraternus occurrit cruor, [*fol. 3v*]
foedum nequeo crimen removere pectore.
Scelus occupandum est dum mihi fervet manus.
IO[AB]. Num quid grave in patrem statues sanctissimum?
AB[SALOM]. Malum esse oportet qui reiecit filium.
IO[AB]. At impium minime tulisse debuit.
AB[SALOM]. Raptum sororis cede pius vlciscitur.
IO[AB]. Est regis improbos gravi pena affici.
AB[SALOM]. Verum sororem fratris est vlciscier.
IO[AB]. Nullus quidem affectus, furor potius fuit.
AB[SALOM]. Animo obsequi iuvabat.
IO[AB]. At rabido tamen.
AB[SALOM]. Quodcumque libuit, id licebat principi.
IO[AB]. Quodcumque rectum erat licuit, non impium.
AB[SALOM]. Tulissem invltus tam pudendam iniuriam?
IO[AB]. Tibi grandiorem gratus omisit pater.

51. vel] ⟨ cum || 52. languescat] ⟨ languescit | dolor implacabilis] ⟨ dolor intolerabilis ⟨ in [*intolerabilis dolor] || 57. labefacit] ⟨ labet (?) || 63. Scelus] ⟨ Se (?*scribal*) || 64-78. *Printed in Boas* || 67. Raptum . . . pius] ⟨ Pius . . . raptum | cede = caede || 72. licebat] ⟨ li⟨⟩ [?*libuit] ||

Is he scorned who, though a criminal, lives in his native land? Now, therefore, let your implacable passion die down; let the fierce turmoil of your mind be completely assuaged, for what pleases the father must be borne by the son.

ABSALOM. It is right that youth indulge its own pleasure: sweet pleasure never submits to bridles.

JOAB. Blind is that pleasure which impairs the reason: it is the role of reason to rule, of pleasure to be ruled.

ABSALOM. A heart burdened with wickedness casts off reason. One crime scratched open again inflames another, a new one. The blood of my brother is always before my eyes; I cannot cleanse the foul crime from my breast. My father's wickedness must be prevented while my hand is still hot.[7]

JOAB. You won't decide something harmful against your most holy father?[8]

ABSALOM. Evil is necessary because he has rejected his son.

JOAB. But an undutiful son he ought never to suffer.

ABSALOM. It is a dutiful one who avenges with death the rape of his sister.

JOAB. It is the king's place to inflict heavy penalty upon the wicked.

ABSALOM. A sister, however, it is the brother's place to avenge.[9]

JOAB. That was not love; no, it was madness.

ABSALOM. I was happy to indulge my passion.

JOAB. But it was madness nonetheless.

ABSALOM. Whatever he pleased, that was permitted a prince.

JOAB. Whatever was right was permitted, not what was wicked.

ABSALOM. Should I have endured unavenged so shameful a wrong?

JOAB. Your dear father overlooked an even greater wrong for you.

[7] Such seems to be the meaning of Watson's paraphrase of Seneca's *Hercules Oetaeus* 435, which ends *perge* [E versions: *perage*], *dum feruet manus.* Studley seems to have missed the point of the line: "Now must thou set thy hands on worke, too 't while thy hands bee hot" (*Tenne Tragedies,* II, 209). Frank Justus Miller rendered the line "His [i.e., Hercules'] crime must be forestalled; act while thy hand is hot!" (*Seneca's Tragedies,* Loeb Classical Library [Cambridge, Mass., 1953], II, 219).

[8] It was, of course, a capital offense to take undutiful action against a father (*Exodus* xxi.15, 17). And Absalom's father was also the anointed ("most holy") minister (king) of God. In Jewish and English life, divine right of kings was important.

[9] "In all cases where polygamy is allowed, we find that the honor of a sister is in the guardianship of her full brother, more even than in that of her father, whose interest in her is considered less peculiar and intimate. We trace this notion even in the time of Jacob (Gen. xxxiv:6, 13, 25, *sq.*)" (Fallows *et al.,* I, 29).

AB[SALOM]. Minime remittit supplici vultum negans.
IO[AB]. Dolor mora lenitus aspectum feret.
AB[SALOM]. Lentas nimium supplex moras numquam feret. [*fol. 4r*]
IO[AB]. Quod vis mora impetrare sobrietatis est,
id perdere praecipiti impetu dementie est:
caeca temeritas semper comes est insaniae.
At cum parentis non videre tui faciem
tam sit molestum, pectoreque curas tibi
tantas recondat, vt reditus e Syria,
ira dolo patris expedita, author fui,
ita cohibito luctu videndum iam dabo,
vt post nimium diutinas absentias
iam fiat aspectus redeunti gratior.
Ergo profectam temere comprimas vocem
dira rabie quam fundit armatus calor.
In te cogita quam amore fertur anxio
quem tantus adhuc fratris miseri tenet dolor.
Insueta pietas pectus ingratum occupet.
Pars sanitatis velle sanari fuit.
Gradu citato regis augustam domum
peto, relaturus quis illi sit animus. [Exit]
AB[SALOM]. Vitam libentius miser profunderem
quam ferre longae languidas poenas morae.
Quid fluctuo prostratus? Quid segnis moror?
Est aliquid audendum. Preces captos decent,
virtus superbos: cuncta cunctantem impediunt.

79. Quod vis] ⟨ Quodvis || **80.** id . . . est] ⟨ id impetu perdere celeri dementiae est | dementie = dementiae | *Beginning with this line the pages become more crowded: the first five sides (of text) average 15.4 lines, the remaining fifty-three sides (incl. short pages) 41.1 lines* || **81.** comes est insaniae] ⟨ sequitur insaniem || **82.** faciem] ⟨ vultus || **83.** curas tibi] ⟨ molestias || **85.** ira] ⟨ ⟨o⟩ (*scribal*) || **92.** tenet dolor] ⟨ dolor tenet || **93.** Insueta] ⟨ Nunc sancta || **95.** augustam] Augustam *MS* || **96.** S.d.] *Om. MS* || **98.** languidas poenas] ⟨ poenas [?⟨ poen⟨ ⟩] languidas || **101.** impediunt] ⟨ obruunt ||

ABSALOM. No, he has not forgiven me, denying his face when I beg for it.

JOAB. With time the assuagement of his sorrow will bring you his face.

ABSALOM. Too long delays a suppliant will never endure.

JOAB. To accomplish what you wish by waiting is the part of prudence; to lose it by precipitate haste is the part of madness. Blind rashness is always the companion of madness. But because not seeing your father's face is so irksome and because it instills in your breast so many cares, now, just as I was the instigator of your return from Syria once your father's anger had been softened by my guile,[10] so will I grant your seeing him once his mourning has been curbed; thus may the sight of him now be the more pleasing to you returning after a too long absence. Therefore suppress these rashly uttered words which your passion, armed with dreadful madness, pours out. Within yourself consider with how troubled a love he suffers, whom such a deep sorrow for your unfortunate brother still grips. Let an unwonted piety take possession of your ungrateful heart. The will to be healed is the first part of health.[11] I will quickly go in to the royal home of the king and report back what his feelings are.

[Joab goes into the palace]

ABSALOM. In my wretchedness, I would pour out my life more willingly than suffer the heavy penalty of long delay. Why do I abjectly vacillate? Why do I lazily delay? Something must be dared. Pleas befit captives; force, the proud — but all things impede the irresolute.

[10] See I.1, n. 3. The guile was Joab's use of a woman of Thecua to persuade David by means of an analogy that he should permit Absalom's return from Gessur (*2 Kings* xiv.1-21).

[11] Watson's verb is perfect rather than present. The line is quoted from Seneca's *Phaedra* 249, which Studley rendered "much health it is, if will to health encline" (*Tenne Tragedies,* I, 145); Miller (Loeb, I, 339) translated it "The wish for healing has ever been the half of health." Joab obviously means that Absalom's desire for reconciliation is a symptom of proper love for his father.

Quid tam diu gnatum aspicere differt suum?
Non tempore ipso iam moriens dolor vetat,
sed intus odium plus novercale imbibitum.
Id arguit pre caeteris contemptio
plusquam feralis: pluris inimicos facit,
vel filium vultu placido indignum putat.
Hos forma contemptus recusat, et decor
vultu refulgens: non amat virtus potens
sperni, impatientes sunt lacertis mollibus
fortes tori. Istas sceptra decorarent manus
veneranda, servitute diadema aptius
molli et per humeros dividuae latos comae.
Aetas iuvenilis semper vsa prosperis
et abstinens malis gravi insolita est iugo.
Quin verba premae: regius cardo strep[i]t.
[Introit IOAB.]
Iam a rege quid narretur anxius expeto.
IOAB. Cecidit acerbus luctus, et semet dolor [*fol. 4v*]
remisit ipse, visque preterita occidit.
Maestos sacrato pectore questus abdidit:
animos minuit, et filij amplexus petit.
AB[SALOM]. Credenda si narres, dolet et facti pudet.
Sin ficta vultu prodere imbellis timor
edocuerit, impetus retineri non potest.
Animum patris tentare sedatum libet. [Exeunt]

103. Non] ⟨ Non vel || **107.** vultu placido] ⟨ placido vultu || **111.** manus] ⟨ manus. || **115.** et . . . iugo] ⟨ iugo insolita est (*prob. to be followed by new thought*) || **116.** *Apparently added interlineally some time after completion of l. 117* | premae = preme | strep[i]t] strepet *MS* || After **116.** S.d.] *Om. MS* || **119.** remisit] ⟨ remittit (?) || **120.** Maestos] ⟨ Maestas (?) || **122.** narres] ⟨ narras (?) || **125.** S.d.] *Om. MS*

Why so long does he put off seeing his son? Not his grief, already dying in due course, forbids it, but a hatred conceived within himself which is worse than a stepmother's. His worse than deadly scorn of me in relation to others proves it: he makes more of his enemies, while his son he deems unworthy of a gentle look. My fine physique and the comeliness glowing in my face protest against these scorns. My powerful strength does not like to be contemned; the strong muscles in my soft arms are impatient. A venerable scepter should grace these hands; more fitting than servitude would be a diadem and hair divided over my broad shoulders.[12] Youth ever accustomed to prosperity and abstaining from evils is unaccustomed to the heavy yoke.

[The palace door opens]

But soft! the royal hinge creaks.[13]

[Enter JOAB from the Palace.]

[To Joab] Now I am anxious to know what is reported from the king.

JOAB. His harsh grief has died down, and his very pain has abated; its former force has withered. Sad complaints he has put away from his consecrated heart. He has diminished his passions and seeks the embraces of his son.

ABSALOM. If what you say may be believed, I am sorry and ashamed of my deed. But if fond awe has taught you to deceive with a feigned countenance, my violent passion cannot be restrained. I would test this calmed spirit of my father.

[They go into the palace]

[12] We are told (*2 Kings* xiv.25) that "in all Israel there was not a man so comely and so exceedingly beautiful as Absalom: from the sole of the foot to the crown of his head there was no blemish in him." For the hair, see Appendix G.

[13] Watson seems to have thought of David's home as palatial: note *augustam domum* at I.1.95 as well as the Senecan *regius cardo* here. Actually, the Bible invariably speaks of the royal residence merely as a house.

[ACTUS PRIMUS.] SCENA SECUND[A].

ACHITOPHEL.

Trimetri [Iambici].

ACHITOPHEL. Quem tot malis finem daturus est deus?
Aut quis nefandorum scelerum esse potest modus?
Nihil diu durare violentum potest.
Quisquis nimium se credulum laetis dedit
is sorte mutata gravius premitur ruens.
Hos dura questus exprimunt mihi tempora,
quibus miseri gravamur aeque singuli.
Fortuna res vt voluerit humanas rotat.
Hic scelera regnant, venere dominatur potens
turpi libido. Sancta pietas exulat.
Hinc orta longa est facinorum series, doli,
fraudes, nefanda stupra, caedes horridae.
Vitium sorori — o facinus! — oblatum est piae.
Ex insidijs frater peremptus concidit.
Hostis suo cruentus est gnatus patri.
Nocens in exilium redigitur filius.
Victo rediens parente contemptus iacet,
afflictus vndique vt videat vix impetrat.
Quod omnibus patet negatur filio.
En supplici aspectus parentis non datur.
Quis tot scelerum formas referre vnus valet?
Aut quis potest de tot malis dari exitus?
Difficile nimis est animum ab ira fervidum
deflectere; quin in omne nefas preceps ruit.

I.2.s.h.] Scena 2 *MS* || **P.h.** Achitophel] ⟨ Achitophell || **M.h.]** Trimetri *MS* || **2.** nefandorum] ⟨ necum (?) || **3.** *Apparently written over a former line which was erased beyond legibility* || **4.** credulum] ⟨ craedulum | dedit] ⟨ debit || **10-12** (Sancta . . . horridae). *Printed in Boas* || **11.** longa est] ⟨ est longa || **13.** *Written after l. 14 and marked for insertion here. Watson's standard method of marking such transpositions was to put an* a *before the line (or above the word) intended to be first, a* b *by that intended to be second, etc.* | piae] ⟨ suae || **16.** Nocens in exilium] ⟨ In exilium nocens *(the* a *is over* Nocens, *the* b *over* exilium; *metrics and syntax demand that* in *follow* Nocens, *and Watson surely meant the* b *to include the entire prepositional phrase as a unit)* || **19.** patet] ⟨ datur || **20.** En] ⟨ Vel || **21.** valet] ⟨ potest || **22.** dari] ⟨ dare ⟨ esse ||

[ACT I.] SCENE 2.

[Jerusalem. Before the Royal Palace.]

[Enter] ACHITOPHEL.

ACHITOPHEL. What end will God grant to so many evils?[1] What can be the limit of wickedness? No violent enterprise can long survive. Whoever has allowed himself to be too credulous in his circumstances when favorable, when he falls is oppressed the more grievously by his changed lot. Hard times force these complaints from me, times in which we are all oppressed, equally wretched. Fortune twirls human affairs as she wishes. Here crimes reign; powerful lust governs with base venery.[2] Holy piety is exiled. Hence is sprung the long series of crimes: the treacheries, frauds, heinous debaucheries, horrid murders. Rape was committed — O horrible deed! — on a pious sister. From ambush a brother fell murdered. A bloodstained son is an enemy to his father. The guilty son into exile is banished. After his father is appeased, he returns and lies scorned; distressed at every turn, he is scarcely permitted to see his father. What is open to all is denied the son: lo, the sight of his parent is refused the suppliant. Who has the strength to bear alone so many kinds of crime? Or from so many evils what outcome can be given?

It is very difficult to divert a heated mind from its anger; nay, it rushes headlong into every wickedness.

[1] There is no Biblical authority for this scene. According to *2 Kings* xv.9-10, Absalom instituted his conspiracy in Hebron rather than in Jerusalem, and he sent for Achitophel only after taking the initial steps himself (*2 Kings* xv.12).

[2] Presumably Achitophel is referring to David's lust for Bethsabe and his treacherous slaying of Urias and to the lust of Amnon and the fratricide by Absalom. But the Roman Catholic Watson may have intended a covert allusion to the divorce of Henry VIII and other courtly impiety and to the "hard times" imposed on "oppressed" Catholics by the Royal Injunctions of 1535, the deposition of Metcalfe as Master of St. John's, the martyrdoms of Fisher and More, etc.

Contemptus auget non facinus aufert malum.
De[s]ertus improbus gravius ardere solet:
vt arduis fera montibus intractabilis
non nisi sagaci ac pervigili mitescere
cura potest, fit asperatate atrocior,
sic scelera dum spernuntur augentur magis,
eadem pietate et obsequio facile cadunt.
Varij casus multorum animum firmant meum: [*fol. 5r*]
quartus hominum fratris fera occidit manu,
dirum tamen redundat in caput scelus
autoris: incerti laris dum errat vagus
Lamech cruentato ense transfixus iacet.
Dolore coniunctum scelus vt ignis vorax
extingui in adolescentia numquam potest
sed ampliores continuo vires capit.
Tanta facinorum segete que tandem quies
speranda? Suspectos habent magna exitus.
Sed ecce gressum rapidus admovet Absalo[m]:
vultu dubio, quid pectore abditum gerit.

[ACTUS PRIMUS.] SCENA TERTIA.

ABSALO[M]. ACHITOPHEL.

Trimetri [Iambici].

ABS[ALOM]. Credat ne quisquam tanta posse tam pium
lingua facieque patrem simulata fingere
virtutis almum qui refert nomen bonae?
Tandem quis apud illum tenere locum precor
fraudes, dolos et insidias turpes putet?

26. De[s]ertus] Defertus *MS* || **29.** asperatate = asperitate || **31.** facile] ⟨ cito || **34-35.** caput scelus/ autoris] ⟨ caput scelus/ authoris ⟨ caput autoris/ *(revised before l. 35 was begun)* || **36.** Lamech] ⟨ Lamechi | transfixus iacet] ⟨ cruentatus iac [*iacet] || **40.** tandem] ⟨ nobis || **41.** speranda] ⟨ optanda || **42.** gressum] ⟨ gr⟨a ⟩ (?) | rapidus] ⟨ regia | Absalo[m]] Absalon *MS* || **43.** gerit] ⟨ tegit ⟨ gerit

I.3.s.h.] Scena 3[a] *MS* || P.h. Absalo[m]] Absalon *MS* || M.h.] Trimetri *MS* || **1-2, 6-11.** *Printed in Boas* || **1.** Credat ne = Credatne | tam pium] ⟨ fingere || **2.** lingua] ⟨ ore | fingere] *MS* figere *Boas* | fingere] fingere? *MS* || **3.** bonae?] bonae *MS* || **4.** Tandem quis] ⟨ Quis | precor] ⟨ putet? ||

Scorn increases rather than removes evil villainy. A wicked man forsaken is wont to be more sorely inflamed. As a savage beast from the rugged mountains cannot be made tame except through wise and ever watchful care and becomes more fierce with harsh treatment, so crimes, while they are scorned, are increased the more. But those same crimes readily give way before affection and indulgence. The several misfortunes of many men strengthen my conviction. The fourth man falls before the barbarous hand of his brother, but the dreadful crime redounds upon the head of its author: while he wanders a vagrant of uncertain home, he is slain, transfixed by the bloodied sword of Lamech.[3] Like a voracious fire, crime, when compounded with sorrow, can never be extinguished in a youth, but continually takes on greater force. What respite is at length to be hoped for from so great a harvest of crimes? Great affairs have uncertain outcomes.

But look, Absalom is hurriedly approaching. His expression is uncertain, but he has something concealed in his heart.

[3] The fourth man (literally, the "fourth of men") was Abel, second child of Adam and Eve and therefore the fourth human (*Genesis* iv.1-2). For Lamech see Appendix H.

[ACT I.] SCENE 3.

[Jerusalem. Before the Royal Palace.]

[Enter] ABSALOM [from the Palace.] ACHITOPHEL [Stands Apart.][1]

ABSALOM [Aside; pausing occasionally and fluctuating between anger and calm]. Would anyone believe that a father so pious, a father who rehearses the beautiful name of true virtue, could with his tongue and his face conceive such gross pretenses? Pray, who, I ask, would think that deceits, treacheries, and infamous craftiness would hold a place with him?

[1] Achitophel has remained onstage, but Absalom obviously does not see him until l. 79. Again for this scene there is no Biblical authority.

Vt ficto odium vultu tegebat pertinax!
Mens aliud a lingua loquebatur subdola,
nec vt aliâs index animi sermo fuit:
vultus quietus at venenum mens tegit.
Suspecta mihi sunt blanda nimium colloquia.
Oscula meras blanditias mihi reputo.
Non hoc solitum est. Graviora pertimuit scio:
semper potentis est comes regni timor,
secura numquam est aula sublimis metu.
Quin si timeat, timoris ego caussas dabo.
Metui potentes non alios metuere decet.
Obscurus, ignavus latui nimis diu:
pennas diu nido reconditas semel
exerere iuvat, iucundum enim quod liberum.
Sequere anime impetum: facinus aude aliquod
quod nulla taceat posteritas mortalium.
Iam te para et animos inertes excita.
Penitus valeat contentus exiguis modis:
novum molestae quere vindicte genus,
antiqua non placent mihi. Iam faxo sciat
quam triste sit animis generosis exilium,
viresque quam resum[a]t abiectus dolor.
Iuvat inquinatum scelere fraternum caput
ferro amputasse. Istec stupri poena levis.
Delictum adhuc quodcumque factum est dicitur.

6. pertinax!] *Boas* pertinax. *MS* || 11. *Added in the margin* || 13. semper potentis est] ⟨ potentis est semper || 14. sublimis] ⟨ magnifica || 16. Metui] ⟨ Me (*blotted*) Metui || 19. exerere] ⟨ excutere || 20. anime = animae || 24. vindicte = vindictae || 27. resum[a]t] resumit *MS* ||

Behind his feigned visage how he concealed his stubborn hatred! His mind spoke something other than his treacherous tongue, and his speech was not, as at other times, a token of his thoughts: his face was calm, but his mind was hiding poison. His too smooth speeches are to me suspicious. I consider his kisses mere flatteries of me. This is not his accustomed way. He dreaded, I know, more serious actions:[2] fear is ever a companion of powerful sovereignty, and an exalted palace is never free from terror. Well, if he be afraid, I will give him reasons for fear. It is right that the strong be feared, not fear others. Obscure and unrecognized, I have lain hidden too long. It is pleasing for once to stretch out my wings long concealed in the nest, for what is free is happy. Follow the violent impulse of your mind, Absalom: dare some evil deed about which no son of men may be silent. Now prepare yourself, and arouse your inert passions. Away that inward contentedness with mere trifling means: seek a new kind of grievous revenge — the old kinds do not appeal to me. Now I shall make my father know how sad is exile to noble minds and how grief scorned takes on renewed strength. I am glad that with my sword I lopped off my brother's head befouled with wickedness. It was a light punishment for rape. That which has been done up to now is called a crime.

[2] I.e., more serious than those that I have already done. This account of the reconciliation is Watson's own (Boas, p. 353); the Biblical description in its entirety reads: "Absalom was called for, and he went in to the king, and prostrated himself on the ground before him: and the king kissed Absalom" (*2 Kings* xiv.33).

Graviora factis non rudis mens concipit:
ferro paterna sunt fodienda pectora, [*fol. 5v*]
populosa tum perdenda dolis gens Israel.
Frangi facile vltrix ira, flecti non potest:
sceleri scelus addend[u]m est. Dolor nescit modum.
Quo rapior — hei mihi! — contremuit pectus gelidum
vbi pietas, vltro in patrem gnatus ferar?
Frangit animos nomen paternum turbidos.
Hic cur pereat? Ad coepta deficiunt manus.
Ingratus hos impune contemptus feret?
Ingratus ergo iam pereat: non est pater
qui omnem penitus in filium affectum exuit.
Discat patris quid sit. Merito cadat suo.
Vitae mihi author qui fuit ero illi necis?
Illi ne fundam sanguinem mihi qui dedit?
Haud vsitatum a mi absit hoc dirum nefas.
At mortuo rex patre celebrabor potens,
nam rapta tenentur sceptra multo gratius.
Iudaeaque mihi victa serviet ferax.
Non est honor: tantum titulus est nominis,
vanus superbos decipiens splendor viros.
Gratus tamen, et qui facere felices potest.
Quid, anime, dubitas? Sequere quo rapit impetus:
vt cimba quam ventus rapit huc, illuc aestus
aquae tumidus dubiaque cui pareat potius
incerta distrahitur locis contrarijs,

32. ferro . . . pectora] ⟨ paterna fodienda ense sunt mihi pectora || **35.** sceleri . . . est] ⟨ sceleri num dandum est scelus, ira (*incomplete*) | addend[u]m] addendem *MS* || **36.** mihi!] mihi, *MS* || **38.** turbidos.] turbidos *MS* || **40.** hos] ⟨ ergo || **42.** affectum] ⟨ affectus || **44.** *A small horizontal mark precedes the line* || **46-226.** *Small mark beneath 46, marking the fifteenth line from the top of the page; later marks count off blocks of lines at 76, 86, 116 (?), 126, 136, 156, 166, 176, 196, 206, and 216; ll. 146, 186, and 226, each the last line on its page, want marks. See note at I.3.234* || **48.** nam rapta] ⟨ raptaque | multo] ⟨ longe || **53.** dubitas?] dubitas, *MS* || **55.** aquae tumidus] ⟨ contrarius | dubiaque] ⟨ dubiusque ?*Read* dubiusque | potius] potius, *MS* (⟨ potius: [*orig. marking end of first half of simile*]) ||

But my not inexpert mind conceives graver ones than those already performed. My father's breast must be gouged with this sword, then the teeming race of Israel must be destroyed by treachery. Vengeful rage cannot easily be broken or bent: crime must be added to crime. My sorrow knows no bound.

Alas, whither am I transported that, while conscience shudders at the coldness in my breast, I a son should willingly move against my father? That name "father" overcomes my wrought-up passions. Why should he die? My hands are inadequate for these undertakings.

Will he ungraciously carry on these mockeries of me without punishment? Well, then, let the ungracious fellow die. He is not a father who has so thoroughly cast away all love for his son. Let him learn what the part of a father is. Let him die for his punishment.

But am I to bring death to him who brought life to me? Shall I pour out the life's blood of him who gave life's blood to me?[3] Nay, let this unaccustomed and terrible evil depart from me.

But once my father is dead I shall be proclaimed a mighty king, for scepters violently snatched are held much more gratifyingly. And fertile Judea, once conquered, will serve me.

This is not honor: it is only the glory of renown, empty splendor deceiving proud men.

But it is pleasing splendor, nonetheless, and it can make men happy. Why, O my soul, do you waver? Where the impulse leads, follow. As a ship which is rushed this way by the wind and that way by the swelling tide of water and is doubtful which it ought to obey, is in its uncertainty eventually torn apart in dangerous places,

[3] Cf. David's similar question at V.2.35-36. David's answer, of course, is the opposite of Absalom's.

ita animus hinc pietate at illinc impetu
rapitur in incertum. Meliora comprobo,
peiora tamen sequor. Latet intus nescio
quid intimis absconditum precordijs.
Quocumque volentem hec me nova vis rapit, sequar:
incertus, amens, mente vecordi feror.
ACHITOP[H]EL. O numen eternum, hos habebunt exitus
exempla dura? Nullus est scelerum modus?
Semper ne crescit aliud ex alio nefas?
En quo veniet frenis solutus impetus!
Continuus in rabiem dolor exibit feram.
Qualis patrum fugiente nostrorum duce
pharao spolijs superbus ablatis furens [*fol. 6r*]
in mare periturus precipiti cursu ruit,
talis minaci fronte recursat vndique:
vultus furoris signa vesani tenet,
minas anhelo ex pectore profert turgidas,
vix spiritus verbis faciendis sufficit.
In ore formas omnis affectus gerit:
cogitat, minatur, sistit, aestuat, dolet.
Quodcumque sit, magnum aliquid attentat gemens:
quam primum animus constituit iratum aggredi.
O clara David progenies, animos doma.
Gressus citatos siste. Parce iam minis,
ne tam rabido incautus furori prebeas
temet regendum. Nam facile vincet malum
primum exorienti qui resistet fortiter.

63. Achitop[h]el] Achitoplel *MS* (*scribal*) || **65.** Semper ne = Semperne || **66.** impetus!] impetus. *MS* (⟨ impetus?) || **75-76.** *Printed in Boas* || **79.** *Orig. followed l. 80 (or was added there for insertion here)* || **80.** Gressus] ⟨ Gradum *or* Gressum ||

so my heart, on one side by duty, on the other by passion, is dragged into uncertainty. I approve the better course, but follow the worse. Within me, in my innermost heart, lies hidden I know not what. Wherever this new force carries me, with all my will I shall follow: uncertain, witless, I am borne along by a mind destitute of reason.

ACHITOPHEL [Aside]. O Lord eternal, will harsh punishments have these results? Is there no limit to perfidies? Must one evil always grow out of another? Look whither violence, loosed from restraints, will go. Continuous sorrow will mount up into savage madness. As when the leader of our fathers[4] was fleeing, proud Pharaoh, raging because his spoils had escaped, with precipitate haste rushed into the sea to die, so Absalom with a threatening countenance runs about. His face holds signs of furious anger. He pours out turgid threats from his panting breast, he has scarcely enough breath to speak. In his visage every emotion takes form: he ponders, he threatens, he grows determined, excited, sorrowful. While he laments, he is conceiving something or other, something gross. I must approach this raging man forthwith.[5]

[Advances and addresses Absalom] O famous progeny of David, restrain your passions. Halt your hurried steps. Now leave off threats lest you recklessly surrender yourself to be ruled by such savage rage. For whoever shall vigorously resist evil as it first arises will easily overcome it;

[4] Moses (*Exodus* xiv.21-31).

[5] Literally, "My mind is made up to approach" etc.

Nulla est malo medicina firmato moris:
declivis onere praecipitatur rota suo,
at colle suppremo cito tardari potest.
Hos qui casus efficit tumores expedi.
Qui tegitur ignis moritur extinctus brevi.
ABSA[LOM]. Non capiet vllum consilium magnus dolor.
Preceps paterni rapior in penas doli.
Ego ne fidem dextra mihi obstrictam manu
iterum solutam segnis, invltus perferam?
Bibule prius numerus arenae non erit
priusque rapaces esse desinent lupi
quam noster hic cessabit incassum furor:
sed crescet vt ignis flatibus adiutus vagis.
ACHITO[PHEL]. Quo pergis, amens? Monstra parturis nova?
Quid seculum rude insolitum doces nefas?
ABS[ALOM]. Nullus taceat vnquam quod hic faciet dies.
ACHIT[OPHEL]. Nihil in parentem temere decerni decet.
ABS[ALOM]. Sic nec parentem blanditiae probum decent.
ACHITO[PHEL]. Apertum amoris indicium fuisse puta.
ABS[ALOM]. Non est amor verus trepido iunctus metu:
qui metuit odisse solet, amor metu caret.
A[C]HI[TOPHEL]. Tu caussa metus es: culpa ad autorem redit.
ABS[ALOM]. A me malam rem si timeat, malam dabo.
ACHITO[PHEL]. Regenda potius est iuventus fervida.
ABS[ALOM]. Imo magis obsequenda dum vires habet. [*fol. 6v*]
ACHIT[OPHEL]. Vires penitus ratione seiuncta nocent.
ABS[ALOM]. Fortuna iuvat fortes, recusat desides.

86. suppremo [= supremo] cito tardari] ⟨ cito summo retardari || **91.** Ego ne = Egone | mihi obstrictam] ⟨ pellectam || **93-96.** ***Printed in Boas*** || **93.** Bibule [= Bibulae]] ⟨ Bibulis *Boas reads* Bibulis || **97.** nova?] nova, *MS* || **101.** blanditiae probum] ⟨ blanditiae doli ⟨ doli blanditiae || **104.** odisse . . . caret] ⟨ odit, amor timoris est expers || **105.** A[c]hi[tophel]] Acchi. *MS* || **108.** Imo magis] ⟨ Illi est magis ⟨ Illi magis es [*est] || **109.** Vires . . . nocent] ⟨ Prudentia plerumque semota nocent || **110.** recusat] ⟨ repellit ||

but there is no remedy for an illness well established through negligent delays. On the roll a wheel is hastened downward by its own weight, but at the top of a hill it can be quickly stopped. Discharge these calamitous tumors. A fire which is covered dies, soon extinguished.

ABSALOM. My anguish will not accept any counsel. Headlong am I being swept into vengeance for my father's treachery. What, should I unruffled, unavenged suffer that the faith which was pledged to me with his right hand[6] is now broken again? Before this rage of mine shall abate unavailingly, the multitude of bibulous sands shall cease to be, and wolves shall cease to be ferocious: nay, rather my rage will grow like a fire fanned by shifting winds.

ACHITOPHEL. Whither do you purpose, you madman? Are you pregnant with new monstrosities? What unwonted wickedness do you teach an innocent age?

ABSALOM. Let no one ever keep silent about what this day will bring.

ACHITOPHEL. Nothing should be rashly resolved against a parent.

ABSALOM. By the same token, blandishments do not befit a proper parent.

ACHITOPHEL. Suppose these "blandishments" were an open display of love.

ABSALOM. True love is not yoked with quaking fear. Who fears is wont to hate; love is free from fear.

ACHITOPHEL. You are the cause of his fear: the blame returns to its instigator.

ABSALOM. If he fears evil from me, I will give him evil.

ACHITOPHEL. Your hot youth ought rather to be governed.

ABSALOM. On the contrary, it ought to be humored more while it has strength.

ACHITOPHEL. When reason is severed, strength is baneful.

ABSALOM. Fortune aids the bold, rejects the indolent.

[6] The allusion is not clear.

ACHIT[OPHEL]. Fortuna caeca est, aequa cum virtus abest.
ABS[ALOM]. Numquam caret virtute magna qui potest.
ACHIT[OPHEL]. Nullus datur in furore virtuti locus.
ABS[ALOM]. Virtus valido mihi omnis in ferro iacet.
ACHIT[OPHEL]. At rectius in animo bonis condi solet.
ABS[ALOM]. Ferrum mihi dulce est.
ACH[ITOPHEL]. Sed vtenti grave.
ABS[ALOM]. Spretus iacebo?
ACHIT[OPHEL]. Lege vetita est vltio.
ABS[ALOM]. Lex sordet.
ACHIT[OPHEL]. At violantis est vindex deus.
ABS[ALOM]. Diu moratur.
ACHIT[OPHEL]. Poena dilata gravior.
ABS[ALOM]. Impune non feret.
ACHIT[OPHEL]. Pietas aliter docet.
ABS[ALOM]. Toleranda non sunt.
ACHIT[OPHEL]. Genitor est, ferendus est.
ABS[ALOM]. An patiar invisum miserijs opprimi?
Pedibus iacentem proteret scio. Non feram.
ACHIT[OPHEL]. Morbum tenere prima salutis est via.
Magnum ex levi caussa paras scelus, exitus
incertus, aggressu arduum, autori grave,
dedecore et ancipiti periculo obsitum.
Si quod patris sit vultus et vox blandior
tutum facinus credas et alienum metu,
erras: parentum in liberos cura est sagax,
nam plurimae sunt regis aures et oculi.

113. Nullus] ⟨ Num [*Numquam] || **114.** valido mihi] ⟨ mihi | iacet] ⟨ latet || **116.** Sed] ⟨ At || **122.** opprimi?] ⟨ opprimi: || **123.** proteret] ⟨ proter⟨-ret⟩ || **125.** paras scelus] ⟨ scelus paras || **127.** ancipiti] ⟨ diro ||

ACHITOPHEL. Fortune is blind, being favorable even when virtue is wanting.[7]

ABSALOM. One who has strength is never lacking in great virtue.

ACHITOPHEL. No room is given for virtue in madness.

ABSALOM. My entire virtue lies in my strong sword.

ACHITOPHEL. But more properly, among the good, is it wont to be stored in the mind.

ABSALOM. The sword is sweet for me.

ACHITOPHEL. But dangerous to the user.

ABSALOM. Shall I lie spurned?

ACHITOPHEL. Vengeance is forbidden by law.

ABSALOM. The law is worthless.

ACHITOPHEL. But of its violator the avenger is God.

ABSALOM. He delays too long.

ACHITOPHEL. Punishment delayed is the more severe.

ABSALOM. My father shall not escape unpunished.

ACHITOPHEL. Duty teaches otherwise.

ABSALOM. Conditions cannot be tolerated.

ACHITOPHEL. He is your father, he must be tolerated.

ABSALOM. And should I suffer myself to be hated and oppressed with miseries? If I cower at his feet, I know he will crush me. I will not bear it.

ACHITOPHEL. The first rule of health is to check disease. A great crime you are planning for little cause — its outcome doubtful, difficult to begin, serious to its instigator, beset with shame and perilous danger. If, because your father has a somewhat gentle voice and countenance, you believe that your wicked act will be safe and free from his apprehension, you are wrong: the attention of parents to their children is keen, and many are the ears and eyes of a king.

[7] In ll. 111-114, the stichomythy plays on the two meanings of *virtus:* strength, as Absalom means it, and virtue, as Achitophel uses it.

Sed vt sceleris successus accidat. Bonus
quid ille vasti conditor mundi, arbiter
rerum omnium, author Iudaice gentis deus,
tantum nefas latere invltum vnquam sinet?
Est acer in peccata vindex tetria:
sic impia fetens libidine Sodoma
consumpta flammis sulphure commixtis iacet.
Quot milia patrum murmure obstantes deo
varijs eremo mortibus cesi cadunt?
A Moÿse protervus duce deficiens Chore
alta voragine vivus absorptus perit.
Gravia sceleratis verbera incutit deus.
Restat molestus consciae mentis pavor
animusque numquam tutus, et semet timens.
Compesce scelus ipsis odiosum belluis.
Nefanda sacro pectore exturba precor, [*fol. 7r*]
neque dominum criminibus irrita novis.
ABS[ALOM]. Desine loqui. Vera esse quae memoras scio,
sed ratio victa est: mente dominatur furor,
et sana pellit consilia sui impotens.
Vt aequori cautes resistit aspera
vndasque salientes remittit longius,
sic pestifera mens bella cum rectis gerit:
sanos fugio monitus, fugiendos appeto.
Quid conor impedire vincentem impetum?
Patiar mihi quemcumque exitum casus dabit.

132. successus accidat] ⟨ accid [*accidat] successus | accidat. Bonus] ?*Read* accidat bonus. || **134.** omnium] ⟨ p [*primus] | Iudaice [= Iudaicae]] ⟨ Iudaici || **135.** nefas latere] ⟨ nefas labi ⟨ labi nefas || **137.** fetens] ⟨ infamis || **147.** sacro] ⟨ sacra (?) | precor] ⟨ precor (*canceled, then written again*) ⟨ ocyus || **148.** irrita] ⟨ irritat (?) || **150.** sed] ⟨ iam ||

But grant that the crime come off successfully: why will the good Lord, great Founder of the vast world, Judge of all things, Creator of the Jewish race — why will He ever allow so gross a wickedness to go unavenged? He is a fierce avenger of foul sins. Thus Sodom, stinking in its impious lust, lies low, consumed by fire mixed with brimstone.[8] How many thousands of our elders who offended the Lord by murmuring lie in the wilderness, smitten in their several deaths? Cruel Core, deserting his leader Moses, perished, swallowed up alive in a deep pit.[9] The Lord inflicts heavy punishments on sinners. The grievous quaking of a guilty conscience awaits you, and a soul never safe, even fearing itself. Check this crime hateful to the very beasts. Drive out the wickedness from your sacred breast, I pray, and do not provoke the Lord with new crimes.

ABSALOM. Enough! What you remind me of I know to be true, but my reason has been overcome. Madness reigns in my mind, which, having no control of itself, turns away sane counsel. As a rough reef withstands the sea and hurls the leaping waves far back, so my baleful mind fights against proper things. I avoid sound warnings, seek those things which ought to be shunned. Why try to control this overpowering passion? I shall endure whatever result the future shall give.

[8] *Genesis* xix.24.
[9] *Numbers* xvi.1-35.

Sed ocyus iam tolle consilium irritum.
Obsecro monstri quicquid horrendi paro
id pectore secreto premas reconditum,
huiusque te quod aggrediar ducem dato.
ACHI[TOPHEL]. Si stercore careat, ingenuam presto fidem,
sin te furor armet in patrem, scelus est fides.
Istud penitus horreo facinus et execror.
ABSA[LOM]. Quo me furibundae miserum adigis insaniae?
Intus alitur vis ignium et vires capit.
Ô nullo adhuc satiate supplicio dolor,
iam quaere formas incogitatas hactenus,
expromeque odia: nescio irasci satis.
Iste an pater poenas mihi luet prius,
vterque nocens, vterque mihi contrarius?
Hanc nulla poena aut sanguis explebit sitim.
Omnia videntur tarda properanti ad nefas.
Quatiam, traham, turbabo, cunctaque eruam.
ACHITO[PHEL]. Quid ago? Vis animum gemina dubium trahit:
cedam ne furioso? an resistam fortiter?
Scelus vocat hinc, illinc patria, princeps, deus.
Cedam meliori: facinus aspernor malum.
At huius adhuc ardescit in peius furor.
Vt vritur stipula igne supposito levis,
ita hic negando nova alimenta concipit.
Recta malesanus consilia reijcit, fugit.
Edet ruinas, praecipitabit omnia.
Regnum occupabit, et neci quos vult dabit.
Quid fluctuor? Vite profecto consulam.

159. paro] ⟨ apparo || **161.** te quod] ⟨ quod || **162.** stercore] ⟨ scelere ?*Read* scelere (*see Appendix E*) || **163.** armet in] ⟨ armat in ⟨ in || **170.** prius, [prius *MS*]] ⟨ horridas? || **171.** contrarius?] contrarius. *MS* || **176.** cedam ne = cedamne | furioso? . . . fortiter?] ⟨ furioso et sceleris princeps ero? || **177.** illinc] ⟨ ill⟨uc⟩ || **178.** meliori:] meliori *MS* || **179.** ardescit] ⟨ ardescet || **182.** malesanus = male sanus || **183.** *Orig. followed l. 184 (or was added there for insertion here)* || **185.** Vite = Vitae ||

But quickly now, away with your vain advice. Whatever dreadful and monstrous deed I plan, I beseech you to keep it hidden in your secret heart; and give yourself as leader of this enterprise which I shall undertake.

ACHITOPHEL. If it is free from filth, I offer frank loyalty. But if your rage brings you to arms against your father, loyalty on my part is a crime. Within myself I shudder at that wickedness, and I despise it.

ABSALOM. In my wretchedness why do you drive me into raging madness? The force of the fires is nourished from within and takes on more force. O grief, not content with any punishment yet devised, now seek methods heretofore unthought of. And bring forth your hatreds: I know not how to be sufficiently enraged. Shall Achitophel or my father first pay the penalty to me — both inimical, both opposed to me? No punishment, no blood will quench my thirst. All things seem slow to one hurrying toward crime. I will harass, plunder, confound, destroy everything.

ACHITOPHEL [Aside; pausing often in irresolution][10] What am I to do? Divided passion pulls my doubtful mind: shall I yield to the madman or strongly resist him? Crime beckons me on this side; country, ruler, and God on that. I shall yield to the better course: I reject evil perfidy.

But Absalom's rage still burns toward the worse course. As a light reed is consumed when fire is applied, so this madness from rejection receives new nourishment. The madman rejects correct counsels, flees from them. He will produce ruin, destroy everything. He will seize authority and put to death whomever he wishes. Why do I waver? Truly I shall look to my life.

[10] This confused speech, obviously an aside through l. 203, reflects Achitophel's confused state of mind. In essence the main factors arguing against his support of Absalom are his honor and his fear of retribution; those arguing for that support are that he has little choice under the pressure of Absalom's madness; that he could do nothing to prevent the crime anyway, whereas he might be able to help Absalom restore stability; and that David's rule promises to continue in its present corrupt course.

Scelus expiandum est: vivere posthac non datur.
Cur in alienum facinus incurram sciens? [*fol. 7v*]
Cur parricidae similis ac demens ero?
Quod cogitur crimen perhiberi non solet:
nemo coactus peccat, at sponte est nocens;
turpi furiosus error a culpa vacat.
Iustum, prophetam, regem, amicum deseram?
Ingratus, impius, scelestus non ero.
Quid si maneam? Prohiberem advltum iam nefas?
Servare regem nemo periturum potest,
nec vllus vsquam esset miseriarum modus.
Istoc aliqua regnante speranda est quies,
et vetera patriae iura stabiliet potens.
Eandem ego quam cum patre tenebo gloriam,
et rara quam prestabo in adversis fides
mihi ampliores secum amicitias paret,
scelusque placari potest. Quidnam facis?
Ô anime! gloriae coactus serviam.
Hic si furialis impetus possit regi,
in me nihil erit quod fidem damnes meam,
sin omne prorsus consilium iratus fugis,
nolo sciens in fata ruere propria.
Infrenis ira prospicere rectum nequit.
Vt caecus extensa viam quaerens manu
in recta raro flectit errantem gradum,
iratus ita claro rationis lumine
orbus viam quam quaeritat non invenit:
Error vagus semper furoris est comes.

186. vivere . . . datur] ⟨ vita revocatur numquam || **187.** sciens?] sciens? ? *MS* || **189.** solet:] solet *MS* || **192.** Iustum . . . regem] ⟨ Regem . . . sacrum || **193.** scelestus non ero] ⟨ ero, non faciam volens || **194.** maneam?] maneam, *MS* || **195-201.** *Printed in Boas* || **198.** potens.] potens *MS* || **202.** facis] ⟨ facit || **204.** possit regi] ⟨ regi potest || **210.** flectit] ⟨ flectet ||

Crime must be atoned for: to live at ease thenceforth is not permitted. Why shall I rush deliberately into another's crime? Why shall I be as foolish as the parricide?

What is forced is not wont to be accounted a crime: no one sins under duress; by one's will is he wicked. An error of madness is free from culpable blame.

Shall I abandon right, prophet, king, friend? I will not be ungrateful, unfaithful, villainous.

What if I should remain faithful? Could I prevent a crime which is already well advanced? No one can save the doomed king, nor would there ever be any end of the present miseries. With Absalom ruling some peace is to be hoped for and as ruler he will establish the ancient laws of the country. I shall hold the same position of honor as I held under his father; and the rare loyalty which I shall render in troubled times should prepare for me even greater friendship with him, and the crime can be mitigated. What, then, do you do? O my soul! Under compulsion I shall serve my glory.

[To Absalom] If this dreadful violence can be controlled, there will be nothing in me which you may charge against my loyalty. But if in your rage you straightway avoid every counsel, then I do not wish to rush knowingly into certain death.[11] Unbridled anger cannot perceive what is right. As a blind man seeking the way with his hand extended seldom diverts his wandering course into the right places, so an enraged man, bereft of the clear light of reason, does not find the course which he seeks. Inconstant Error is always a companion of madness.

[11] Absalom's eventual refusal to follow Achitophel's counsel (III.3) precipitates his catastrophe and Achitophel's suicide.

ABSALOM. Ira modo paterni avida saturetur sanguinis
voti nec impos, quodlibet possim pati —
bonum, malum, quodcumque consilium exequar.
ACHITO[PHEL]. Quod praevidetur facile declines malum,
gravius enim premit subito quod accidit.
Vultus oportet grati amoris praeferas.
Sermo tacitos ne prodat incautus dolos.
Vulgi temeritas pollicitis capitur cito:
nullum populo malum rudi presentius
quam iuncta blanditijs celebris potentia.
Nec est sceleri locus hic faci[e]ndo commodus:
procul moventur rapida bella tutius,
hosti velox ne fama cito praenunciet.
ABSALOM. Quin iam paratis ensibus nosmet damus? [*fol. 8r*]
Lentas patitur numquam vltio, vindex moras. [Exeunt]

CHORUS.

Anapestici Dimetri.

Scelera dum non reseras tetra,
sed grassari sinis impune,
vires capiunt semper validas
et quotidie magis augescunt.
Quis facinus quis nimis horrendum
differt, iterum peccare docet.
Cecus dolor est percitus ira:
animi nullos patitur frenos
mortemque trucem non timet, enses
cupit in ipsos obvius ire.

214. avida] ⟨ avidas || **216.** exequar] ⟨ feram || **224.** est] ⟨ est ⟨s⟩ | faci[e]ndo] faciundo *MS* || **225.** procul] ⟨ proculo (?) || **226.** velox ne] ⟨ ne velox || **227.** paratis . . . damus] ⟨ geratur res paratis ensibus || **228.** S.d.] *Om. MS* || **229 ff.** *The "parts" of the chorus are marked as follows:* a *229-238,* b *240-249,* c *250-261,* d *262-271,* aπ *272-280,* b *281-284,* c *285-287. The* π, *here as elsewhere, may have indicated a turning of the chorus, or it may have marked the second round of speeches; but it does seem to suggest acting* || **233.** Quis facinus quis] ⟨ Quisquis facinus ?*Read* Facinus quisquis || **234-274.** *Small mark beneath 234, marking the eighth line from the top of the page; but, since the heading of the chorus occupies the equivalent of two lines, the mark must indicate the space used by ten lines. Later marks count off blocks of lines at 244, 254, and 274; l. 264, the last line on the page, required no mark. See note at I.3.280* || **237-238.** enses/ . . . ire] ⟨ ire/ . . . enses ||

ABSALOM. Only let my anger, greedy for my father's blood, be glutted and not cheated of its desire, and I could endure any fortune, I would follow any counsel, good or bad.

ACHITOPHEL. One may easily divert an evil which is foreseen, but that evil which comes up suddenly smites more gravely. You must wear the visage of dear love. And let no incautious speech betray your secret guiles. The rashness of the mob is quickly captivated by promises: no evil is more powerful among the ignorant people than renowned authority combined with flatteries. Also, this place is unfavorable for committing a crime: violent battles are more safely waged far away so that no swift report can quickly inform the enemy.

ABSALOM. Why not devote ourselves now to our ready swords? The avenger and his revenge never endure long delays.

[They go]

CHORUS

So long as you do not disclose heinous crimes, but allow them to go unpunished, they assume ever greater strength and every day increase. Whoever spreads too horrible wickedness teaches transgression in return. Blind is sorrow when excited by anger: it allows no reins on passion and does not fear grim death, but is eager to advance even against swords.

Furit Absalom non aliter quam
tigris parvis orba catellis,
nemus vmbrosum saeva pererrans.
Ruit in sancti fata parentis.
Pereat misere pia naturae
quisquis violat iura parentis.
Dum non fratris plectitur atrox
caedes miseri, iamque remissa est,
fit supposito fomite maius
facinus crudele et genitoris
in caput audax stringitur ensis.
Vt si intrasses specus opacum
qua via ducat caeca tenebris
quoque relicto magis in vmbras
lumine pergas, magis infernae
te vallabunt tenebre euntem,
ita profundo fedi baratro
vitij quisquis semel occlusus
seque nec extricare laboret
in nova peior scelera rumpit,
et preteritum facinus longe
sequitur peius, seque sceleribus
pravis semper vincere tentat.
Vt qui madido saepe volutus
coeno sordes retinet plures
et continuo mage polluitur,
sic qui sceleris rapitur visco [*fol. 8v*]

240. tigris parvis] ⟨ vrsa pusillis || **241.** pererrans] ⟨ pererrat || **243.** misere] ⟨ quisquis || **247.** maius] ⟨ maior || **254.** vallabunt] ⟨ circumstant | tenebre = tenebrae || **255-256.** fedi . . ./ vitij] ⟨ vitij . . ./ miseri || **255.** baratro = barathro || **258.** peior] ⟨ peios (*scribal*) ⟨ semper ||

Absalom rages not otherwise than a tigress robbed of her small cubs and savagely roaming the shadowy woods. He rushes toward the death of his holy parent. Let perish wretchedly whoever violates the pious laws of our mother nature. While the frightful murder of his unfortunate brother is not punished and has already been forgiven, a spark has been touched off and a more cruel crime is formulated: against the head of his father is his presumptuous sword drawn.

If you enter a dark cave where runs a path hidden in shadows and if, leaving the light behind, you go even farther into the shadows, the underground darkness will surround you more as you proceed; just so anyone who has once been locked in the deep abyss of foul vice and does not endeavor to free himself, becoming more evil bursts into new crimes. A much worse wickedness follows the earlier one, and he ever seeks to destroy himself with his vicious crimes.

As one who, having often rolled in wet mud, retains some of the filth and becomes more and more befouled, so one who has been ensnared in the birdlime of crime

foedius vt sus olet et crimen
magis in ipsis sordibus auget,
nam cui pectus scelere onustum est,
quid aliud quam scelera cogitet!
Qui flagitijs semel oblinitur
ipsis pice tenacius haeret.
  Ô perfide consultor regis,
ita ne dominum deseris, atque
saevo homicidae iunctus adhaeres?
Veteres magni fecit amicos
prisca vetustas, nec credebat
esse nova potiora veteribus.
Quorsum instigas sponte furentem?
Satis insanit. Sine: retentis
illi magis est opus habenis.
  Quid consilium possit vtranque in
partem, iuvenes discite prompti.
Caetera multis mala contingunt:
est virtutis nullus abvsus.
  Deus immensi conditor orbis
scelera quevis cito rescinde
atque optatam redde quietem.

ACTUS SECUNDUS. [SCENA PRIMA].

NUNCIUS. CHORUS.

Trimetri Iambici.

NUNTIUS. Ô lenta nimium consilia instanti malo. [*fol. 9r*]
Quicumque regi et patriae optatis bene,

266. et crimen] ⟨ obscena || **272.** regis] ⟨ David || **273.** ita ne = itane || **276.** credebat] ⟨ credebant || **280.** illi] ⟨ illis | *Beneath this line is a small mark like those counting lines, but apparently not having the same purpose*

II.1.s.h.] Actus Secundus *MS* || P.h. Nuncius = Nuntius ||

smells worse than a hog and fosters more crime in that very foulness, for when one's heart is burdened with wickedness what other than crimes could he think of! He who is once besmirched with scandalous acts sticks in them more tenaciously than in pitch.

O perfidious adviser of the king,[12] do you so forsake your lord and clutch onto a fierce murderer? On old friends his venerable old age put great value and did not believe that new things are preferable to old. Whither do you urge the madman, and by choice? He is mad enough. Leave off. He has more need of tightened reins.

O all ye youths, be quick to learn what counsel is worth both pro and con. Otherwise evils befall many people. There is no using up of virtue.

O God, Creator of the vast world, quickly remove these crimes, if Thou wilt, and restore desired peace.

[12] Achitophel. "Lord" and in the next sentence "his" refer to David.

ACT II. [SCENE 1.]

[Jerusalem. Before the Royal Palace.]

CHORUS [Remains Onstage. Enter] MESSENGER.[1]

MESSENGER. O too tardy are the counsels for the present evil. Any of you who wish well to the king and the nation,

[1] Presumably the chorus remained onstage throughout the play. The frame of this scene and the material in the messenger's first speech are based on *2 Kings* xv.13. After this speech, however, Watson turned to the earlier verses (1-6) of the Biblical chapter to describe the blandishments used to recruit the rebel armies, thus intensifying Achitophel's role in the rebellion; see Introduction, p. 55. The remainder of the messenger's report is, as Boas noted (p. 354), Watson's invention.

defendite vrbem: magna pernicies adest.
Arcete regia hostis ignitas faces.
Rabidi cohortes en glomerantur vndique,
populi furor cruentus ecce vrbi imminet,
cuncti sequuntur signa violenti ducis:
decem copulant sese tribus; non sunt minae —
virus rabies expromit, extingui nequit.
Vt flumina parvis orta sparsim fontibus
tandem spatiosum confluunt in alveum
et in rapidum sese pelagus fundunt simul,
ita aere fulgentes, catervatim casis
passim relictis, exeunt: exercitus
iam cogitur apum densa velut examina.
CHORUS. Quis bella crudus hostis horrenda inchoat?
NUNTIUS. Nulli regionem hanc allophyli invadunt truces:
natus domi istas excitat tragoedias.
Furibundus Absalom coegit agmina:
scribit gladiatorum legiones integras,
in prelia cunctos vndique populos agit.
At ille qualis fulvus insanit leo,
torva rigentem fronte conquassans iubam,
ardens oculos vultusque torquet igneos.
In bella strennuos retrudit milites,
ipsosque castra iam propius muros premunt,
cohortibus cunctas praeoccupant vias.
Vix vnus evasi vt referrem hec nuntius.

5. Rabidi] ⟨ Rapidi || 7. ducis] ⟨ ducit | ducis:] ducis *MS* || 10-35. *Lines of page are counted by small marks beneath 10, 15, 26 (see note at II.1.20), and 35; another mark appears beneath 45 on the verso* || 13. casis] ⟨ pagis || 14. passim] ⟨ pag [*pagis] || 16. *The MS s.p. is* chorus ad, *presumably meaning that the* a *and* d *sections of the chorus spoke the speech together* | bella crudus] ⟨ crudus bella || 17-21. *Printed in Boas* || 17. allophyli] Allophyli *MS, Boas* || 19. Absalom] *MS* Absalon *Boas* || 20. *Added interlineally, apparently after completion of l. 26 and before completion of l. 35 (since the score beneath 26 now marks off eleven lines and that beneath 35 compensates by marking off only nine)* || 22. fulvus] ⟨ torvus || 25. retrudit] ⟨ animatur || 26. ipsosque] ⟨ ips⟨a⟩que || 27. cunctas] ⟨ cunnctas (*scribal*) ||

defend the city: great destruction is near. Ward off from the palace the enemy's firebrands. Behold, rabid throngs are assembling everywhere. See, the cruel madness of the people threatens the city. All are following the banners of a violent leader. Ten tribes are united; these are not mere threats — their madness exudes poison and cannot be extinguished. Just as streams sprung from scattered small springs at length flow together into a wide channel and united pour forth into a raging ocean, so, gleaming with bronze, the people go forth, everywhere leaving their homes in droves. Now an army is assembled as dense as swarms of bees.

CHORUS. What rude enemy begins these horrible wars?

MESSENGER. No wild foreigners invade this region: one born in our home stirs up these tragic doings. Raging Absalom has brought armies together: he enlists whole legions of swordsmen; he leads all peoples everywhere into battle. But he himself rages like a tawny lion shaking its bristling mane about its savage face; inflamed, he twists his face and rolls his flashing eyes. He hurls his bold soldiers into the wars, and now they push their camp nearer to our very walls. They completely occupy all the roads with their throngs. I alone barely escaped, a messenger to bring back these tidings.

CHORUS. Quod queso nefas inceptat indomitus, doce?
In quem cruentus arma capit rebellia?
NUNTIUS. Caeca interitum rabies patris turpem petit,
valida in parentem est facta coniuratio.
Bonos neci designat, improbos favet.
Animo potentia regna tumido concipit:
morte patris imperium superbus somniat.
Vrbem occupabit, qui resistent occident.
Furor impatiens vt lepra serpit latius.
CHORUS. Num quae gravis a patre imposita est iniuria? [*fol. 9v*]
NUNTIUS. Nulla, nisi quia non laesit, offendit pater:
horum scelerum caussa est priorum impunitas.
CHORUS. Libenter aerumnas miseri audiunt suas:
effare quomodo quove consilio, precor;
tanta facinora numquam potuit fatuus furor
fecisse recte: alios sibi authores habet.
NUNTIUS. Armatus est consilio Achitophel potens,
olim columen nunc proditor regni vagus:
cuncta arbitrio et nutu gubernantur suo.
Omnes ab eo pendent vt aliquo numine:
vt corniger totum antëit aries gregem,
turbae obsequenti cuncta quae vult imperat:
eo loquente et ponitur et crescit furor.
Primum aequitate, iustitia, tum muneribus
simplicia plebis corda sollicitat cito,
improvidos dolis et astu fascinat:

29. *Before the s.p. is an* a, *identifying the "part"* | inceptat] ⟨ incepta⟨s⟩ || **30.** quem] ⟨ quem f [?*filius] | rebellia] ⟨ rebellis || **37.** impatiens vt] ⟨ v [*vt] impatiens || **38, 41.** *Before the s.p.'s are an* a *and* a c, *respectively, identifying the "parts"* || **43.** *Orig. s.p.* Nuntius (*ll. 43-44 added to chorus' speech as afterthought*) || **46.** proditor] ⟨ predator [= praedator] | vagus] ?⟨ va⟨r⟩ [*varius] || **47-67.** *Groups of ten lines from top of page marked off with small scores beneath 47 and 67 and with a dot before 56; see note at l. 56* || **47.** arbitrio] ⟨ arbetrio (*scribal*) || **53.** sollicitat] ⟨ sollicitas (?) | cito] ⟨ rudis ||

CHORUS. Pray tell me, what wickedness does this wild man undertake? Against whom does the villain take up rebellious arms?

MESSENGER. His blind madness seeks the sinful destruction of his father: a mighty conspiracy has been formed against his parent. He marks the good for death, befriends the bad. In his overweening mind he conceives powerful rule, presumptuously dreams of empire gained by the death of his father. He will seize the city; those who resist will die. His impatient fury, like leprosy, creeps far and wide.

CHORUS. Has no grave injury been imposed on him by his father?

MESSENGER. With none did his father harm him — unless it was by not injuring him at all. The impunity of Absalom's earlier crimes is the cause of these new ones.

CHORUS. Willingly do the wretched listen to their own miseries. Pray tell us, how? By what counsel? Such gross villainies his foolish frenzy could never have carried out successfully; he has others to advise him.

MESSENGER. The prince is armed with the counsel of Achitophel, once the support, but now an errant betrayer, of the kingdom: all things are managed by his decision and at his nod. All things depend on him as on some god. As a horned ram goes before the whole flock, so he commands of the subservient throng whatever he wishes. When he speaks, their fury is both implanted and nurtured. First with urbanity and gentleness, then with bribes he quickly wins the simple hearts of the people; by tricks and cunning he bewitches the un-

"Quis iudicem me constituet," ait, "omnibus
iusta vt graves lites dirimam sententia?
A rege quis est qui constitutus iudicet?"
His blanditijs miros amores omnium
allexit, hijs noxia venena miscuit.
Hoc virus animos dulce penetravit rudes:
mox singulas mittuntur in patriae plagas
qui tristia belli signa deferrent trucis.
Iam flexilis mestum tuba profudit sonum,
raucus resonantem clangor implet aëra.
Regnavit Absalom: vna vox est militum.
Fremitus populi currentis anhelus perstrepit.
Quae caussa sit inflatae rogatur buccinae.
Confluit atrocis plebs avara prelij.
Factum approbant, multi in scelus vetitum ruunt.
Vt immeritae bonos dare neci gestiunt!
Alij timore perciti ornabant fugam:
plebis ferinam concitae rabiem stude[n]t
vitare. Alij se antris recludunt concavis
melius taciti furore, sperant, mortuo.
Sed nil iuvat: in bellum rapiuntur impium,
cunctosque nolentes, volentes pertrahunt.
Altis coruscae montibus ardebant faces, [*fol. 10r*]
ignesque passim signa flammivomi pagis
belli dabant: protinus in armis cuncti erant.
Hic pollicitis turbam tenebat concitam:
predas spospondit egregias victoribus.

55-57. *Quotes om. MS* || **55.** ait] ⟨ inquit | omnibus] ⟨ gravem || **56.** *Written after l. 57 and marked for insertion here* || **65.** vna] ⟨ ois [*omnis] || **70.** gestiunt!] gestiunt. *MS* || **72.** stude[n]t] studennt *or* studeunt *MS* (*scribal*) || **73.** recludunt concavis] ⟨ recondunt concavis (recludunt, *over which is an* a, *is in margin following* concavis, *over which is a* b) || **78.** *A heavy score beneath last word* || **81.** victoribus] ⟨ victor⟨um⟩ ||

suspecting. "Who," he says, "will set me up as judge to stop these oppressive strifes with a judgment just to all? Who is there appointed by the king who could settle them?" With these blandishments he entices astonishing devotion from everyone. Their devotion he infuses with baleful venoms. This sweet poison penetrates their simple minds: soon they are sent into the various regions of the nation to carry the sad banners of savage war.

Already the curled trumpet has poured forth its mournful sound;[2] its hoarse vibration fills the echoing air. Absalom has taken command; his only word is of soldiers. The panting noise of people running resounds. They ask what the cause is of the blowing of the trumpet. The people come together in throngs, eager for terrible battle. They approve of what is done. Many rush into this forbidden crime. How they long to deliver good people to an undeserved death! Others, fear-stricken, prepare to flee: they are eager to avoid the animal madness of the aroused crowd. Still others shut themselves up in hollow caves, better hidden, as they hope, from the deadly fury. But nothing helps: they are caught up into impious war; all are dragged into it willy-nilly. Blazing firebrands burn on the high mountains, and everywhere flame-vomiting fires give notice of the war to the country folk. Directly they are all in arms.

Absalom keeps the mob aroused with promises: he pledges excellent booty to them if they are victors.

[2] Apparently not the trumpet of battle, but that by which Absalom announced to all the tribes of Israel that he had taken command (*2 Kings* xv.10). The epithet "curled" is classical and does not necessarily describe Jewish trumpets accurately. In the following passage, as in several other descriptions in the play, the tenses in the Latin are quite inconsistent.

Si qui imperij exitiale vitabant iugum,
regi studentes, continuo exigua novis
[est] preda militibus: reluctantes domant
tormenta, servitus, rapina, incendia.
Pugnant vel impij, vel orbantur pij.
Se postea in turmas numerosas dividunt,
ducibus statim traduntur omnes bellicis.
Prata procedit acies, dux it[i]neris;
sequuntur animosae phalanges ordine.
Pulvis nebulam glomeratus effecit nigram;
teretes galeae toto micabant aethere;
hastae speciem sylve gerebant horridae;
peditum resonus vastum fragor caelum ferit;
claras referunt incurva voces littora:
audire diceres sonora tonitrua.
Ipsam tenere se putant victoriam,
laetosque securi triumphos somniant
vt dividunt predas, honores deferunt,
opes parant, novam gerunt rem publicam.
Omnes avaris divitias animis hiant.
Iam diceres rerum potitos omnium.
Quo propius accedunt, eos securitas
maior tenet, propinquitas animos facit.
Iam iam irruent. Sed quid moror sanctissimum
regem gemendi facere certum nuntij? [Exit]

82-83. vitabant . . . novis] ⟨ vitabat [⟨ vitabant ?⟨ vitat] . . ./ regis bonae et contrariae studens parti || **84.** [est]] sunt *MS* || **84-85.** reluctantes . . . incendia] ⟨ domant incendia/ tristia reclamantes tormenta [⟨ tormentus], servitus || **86-97.** *Marks beneath 86 and 97 and a dot beside 107 set off ten-line groups from top of page; see note at ll. 96-98* || **88.** ducibus . . . bellicis] ⟨ statim suis traduntur omnes ducibus || **89.** procedit] ?⟨ precedit | it[i]neris] iteneris *MS* || **92.** aethere;] aethere *MS* || **93.** sylve = sylvae || **94.** peditum resonus] ⟨ strepentium || **95.** claras] ⟨ liquidas | incurva] ⟨ fumosa || **96-102.** *Printed in Boas* || **96-98.** *Line 96 was added after l. 98 and marked for insertion here; at the same time Watson (perhaps carelessly) marked ll. 97-98 for transposition, but then canceled the markings* || **96.** diceres sonora tonitrua] ⟨ tonitrua s [*sonora diceres] ⟨ terrifica putes tonitrua || **98.** somniant] somniant. *MS, Boas* || **100.** opes . . . publicam] ⟨ novas gerunt respublicas, ob o [*opes] || **101.** *Orig. followed l. 102 (or was added there for insertion here)* | Omnes] ⟨ C [*Cuncti] | hiant] ⟨ trahunt || **106.** S.d.] *Om. MS* ||

If any, out of loyalty to the king, shun the deadly yoke of Absalom's authority, immediately their reward from the new soldiers is skimpy:[3] torments, slavery, rapine, and fire subdue the reluctant. Either they fight as rebels, or as loyalists they are bereft. Next they are divided into many companies, and all are forthwith handed over to military leaders. The vanguard moves forward into the fields, the leader of the march, then the bold phalanxes follow in order. The stirred-up dust forms a black cloud. The polished helmets light up the whole sky. Their spears look like a grim forest. The resounding din of the infantry strikes the broad firmament; the curved seashores echo the loud shouts: you would say you were hearing noisy thunderbolts. They think they already have the victory, and, free from care, they dream of happy triumphs as they divide the spoils, parcel out the honors, prepare for power, and form a new government. They are all eager, their minds greedy for wealth. Now you would say that they have taken over everything. The nearer they approach, the greater unconcern holds them; nearness makes them bold. At any moment they will make their attack.

But why do I delay apprising the most holy king of this mournful message?

[Messenger goes into the palace]

[3] Litotes for the punishments listed in the next clause.

CHORUS.

Anapestici [Dimetri].

Quod presidium patres fidum
satis invenient, si paricidae
gnati pergant esse cruenti?
Desine crudos trepidus hostes
amplius vllo vitare metu:
ipsa domestica scrutare magis —
anguis in ipso limite tegitur.
Familiare malum magis vrit.
Rationem natura negavit
brutis, verum non pietatem:
homines dira nunc feritate
longe a tergo bruta relinquunt.
Quid nova mundo scelera obtrudis? *[fol. 10v]*
Criminis atri desine turpis
author haberi. Crimina saepe
talia sequitur exitus atrox.
Deus amabilis, arbiter aequi,
rabidum iustis pelle furorem
qui tua solum numina colunt.
Turbam penitus perde rebellem,
reprobos iusta diffunde manu:
sine te spes est nulla salutis.
Surge, nefandi sceleris vltor:
culpa dignam concipe bilem,
deprime tumidis colla superbis.

M.h.] Anapestici *MS* || **107** ff. *The "parts" of the chorus are marked as follows:* d *107-122,* aπ *123-128,* bπ *129-143,* c *144-150* || **114.** *Beneath the line a score into left margin* || **116.** *So heavily revised that stages of revision are impossible to reconstruct with certainty; sequence prob. as follows:* brutis, verum non pietatem (*final form written twice*)] ⟨ brutis, att⟨am⟩en non pietatem ⟨ brutis, att⟨am⟩en haud pietatem ⟨ brutis, attribuit pietatem (*clearly earliest form*) || **125.** ?*Score beneath last word* || **128-148.** *Marks beneath ll. 128, 138, and 148 set off groups of ten lines from top of page* ||

CHORUS.[4]

What certain protection will fathers find sufficient if sons turn out to be bloody parricides? No longer shun uncivilized enemies, trembling with fear. Rather, examine our own domestic affairs: a serpent is concealed within our very boundaries, and an endemic illness is graver. Nature denied reason to brutes, but not loyalty; men now far surpass brutes in abominable savagery. Why do you thrust new crimes on the world? Cease being accounted the base author of malicious crime. A terrible outcome often follows crimes of this nature.

Lovable God, Judge of Right, drive away this rabid fury from the just who honor only Thy will. Destroy completely the rebellious throng; disperse the false with Thy just hand. Without Thee there is no hope of salvation.

Arise, Avenger of heinous crime. Conceive an anger worthy of the fault; weigh down the necks of the ambitious proud.

[4] The occurrence of a lyrical ode elsewhere than at the end of an act (of which there is another instance in IV.2) is rather unusual; but it has the authority of Seneca's *Agamemnon* 589-658 and *Octavia* 761-777, and of lyrical speeches by Thyestes at *Thyestes* 920-969 and Alcmena at *Hercules Oetaeus* 1862 ff.

Vindex ausus sterne malignos.
Scelera irritas nova misericors.
Vltio quid tam sero moratur?
Isto gravius scelus expectas?
Pia naturae iura recusat:
facit atrocia bella parenti,
agit in rabiem miseram plebem,
vivida spernit decreta patrum,
nova docet flagitia mundum.
In te pessima, dominum, admisit,
in te saevus tela paravit:
cur in penas dextera cessat?
  Gravius punit crimina tardus.
In se rursus tela redibunt,
in se subdola retia tendit,
cadet in ipsas quas facit artes:
mala in autorem cuncta redundant.
Que mala regi parturit ipsi
proprio solum pariet damno.
  Ferrea nobis deus est turris,
dux est validus, saxea rupes,
inde auxilium petimus omnes.
Praebe afflictis quam ambimus opem
fortisque tuam protege plebem.
Regem serva quem vnxeris ipse. [*fol. 11r*]
Nostra exaudi vota, precamur,
vita, salus, spes, via, protector.

132. sterne] ⟨ st⟨ ⟩r (*scribal*) || **139.** spernit] ⟨ tollit || **140.** docet] ⟨ doce⟨s⟩ (?) || **141.** pessima] ⟨ cr⟨ ⟩s⟨t⟩as || **144.** crimina] ⟨ scelera || **146.** tendit] ?⟨ tendet || After **147.** *Canceled line (doubtfully a predecessor of l. 148):* vertetur dolor in caput eius || **154.** afflictis] ⟨ precamur || **155.** plebem.] plebem *MS* || **156.** ipse.] ipse *MS* || **157.** Nostra] ⟨ Vestra

As an avenger, scatter these evil undertakings.[5] By pitying, Thou excitest new crimes. Why does vengeance delay so long? Dost Thou await a crime more serious than this? Absalom flouts the pious laws of nature; he makes atrocious war against his parent; he drives the people into wretched madness; he scoffs at the living precepts of his elders; he teaches the world new disgraces. Against Thee, O Lord, has he committed the most serious crimes; against Thee has the miscreant readied his spears. Why does Thy right hand delay punishments?

When slow, He punishes crimes more heavily. On himself will Absalom's spears turn back; against himself does he stretch out his treacherous nets; he will fall into those very artifices which he devises. All evils redound onto their author. Whatever evils he conceives against the king he will bring forth only to his own damnation.

God is an iron tower for us; He is a strong leader, a hard rock whence we all seek aid. Show Thy afflicted the aid which we entreat, and with Thy strength protect Thy people. Save the king whom Thou Thyself anointed. Hear our prayers, we pray, our Life, our Health, our Hope, our Right Way, our Protector.

[5] *Ausus* as a fourth-declension noun occurs in Petronius (*Harper's Latin Dictionary*); it is not given in Cooper's *Thesavrvs.*

[ACTUS SECUNDUS.] SCENA SECUNDA.

DAVID. IOAB. cum POPULO.

Iambici Trimetri.

DAVID. Quid, summe deus, stipata crescunt agmina
quae rebus afflictum vndique insultant malis?
En pestifero in caput ore coniurant meum,
nostrae nefarias insidias vitae parant.
Cur me indocili populo dare pastorem velis?
In me immeritum maledicta fundunt impia
et convitijs lacerare pergunt asperis:
"Illi in deo spes nulla superest," inquiunt,
"nulla ex deo salutis adest fiducia:
desperat opem," aiunt, "en facile iam vincitur."
Verum tua vanos arguet potentia:
te terribilem iaculis clypeum opponam omnibus.
Tu sola servi imbellis extas gloria:
virtus tenuitatem tua illustrat meam.
Ergo dominum verbis precabor vindicem
hoc dum rapido vexor malorum turbine,
et audiet de monte respectans sacro
nec servulum sinet ope frustrari sua.
Securus antea plurimo discrimine
versabar: integris iacebam noctibus,
me alto salute posthabita somno dedi;
tutus tamen oriente surgebam die
nec obruerunt quae mihi instabant mala.
Dominus potenti servat illesum manu,
cunctis sibi fidentem periculis liberat.

II.2.s.h.] Scena 2ª. *MS* || **1-38.** *Source identified in MS as* psalmus 3us; *verses numbered as follows:* 1 *before l. 1,* 2 *before 6,* 3 *before 11,* 4 *before 15,* 5 *before 19,* 6 *before 26,* 7 *before 31,* 8 *before 34. Apparently Watson used an unnumbered Psalter and did not count the heading of Psalm iii as Verse 1, for his numbering is always one behind that of numbered Psalters* || **1.** deus] ⟨ deûm | agmina] agmina. *MS* (⟨ agmina?) || **5.** *Added after l. 6 and marked for insertion here* || **6.** In . . . impia] ⟨ In me impio sermone fundunt opprobria || **8-10.** *Quotes om. MS* || **13.** sola] ⟨ v [*vnus *or* vna] || **17.** sacro] ⟨ suo || Beneath **18.** *A small score into the left margin (the only one on the page): it is twenty-one verses from the top of the page (not counting the canceled version of l. 6), but Watson may have thought of it as marking the equivalent of twenty-five lines, since the headings to Scene 2 occupy the equivalent of almost four lines* || **22.** tutus . . . die] ⟨ omni tamen discriminae [= *and perhaps* ⟩ discrimine] surgebam liber | surgebam] ⟨ surgebus (*scribal*) || **23.** mihi] ⟨ me ||

[ACT II.] SCENE 2.

[Jerusalem. Before the Royal Palace.]

[Enter] DAVID [and] JOAB with PEOPLE [of Jerusalem.][1]

DAVID. Why, O God on high, do the crowded throngs increase that leap up against me and afflict me with evils everywhere? Behold, in their pernicious mouths they plot against my head and devise wicked treacheries against my life. Why shouldst Thou wish to give me as a shepherd to a rebellious people? Against me undeserving they pour out impious curses, and they begin to lash me with harsh taunts: "For him," they say, "no hope in God is left; no assurance of salvation from God remains. He despairs of power," they say; "behold, now he is easily conquered." But Thy power will prove them wrong. I shall set Thee before me as an awesome shield against all darts. Thou remainest as the only glory of Thy peace-loving servant: Thy strength shows up my weakness. Therefore I shall beseech the avenging Lord with words while I am harassed by this violent vortex of evils. And He shall hear, looking down from His holy hill, and shall not allow His humble servant to be deprived of His strength. Before this I lived free of great danger. I lay through entire nights and gave myself to deep sleep, my safety a matter of small worry; yet safe I arose at the dawn of day, and these evils which now beset me did not strike me down. The Lord with His powerful hand keeps unhurt and frees from all dangers whoever trusts in Him.

[1] The scene opens (through l. 35) with an iambic trimeter expansion of Psalm iii; see Introduction, p. 50. Watson then returned to the Biblical narrative (*2 Kings* xv.14), but, as Boas noted (p. 355), "the dramatist makes a notable departure from his source." According to *2 Kings* xv.15, "the king's servants said to him: Whatsoever our Lord the king shall command, we thy servants will willingly execute," and this verse is indeed spoken by Populus at II.2.149-150 of *Absalom*. But Watson made Joab first argue vigorously against the flight. The dispute allowed Watson to emphasize the contrast between the good David and his rebellious son.

Non ergo quantumvis numerosas hostium
timebo turmas: obvium opponam caput
vel millium armis. Surge nunc, deus Iacob:
gratum petenti confer auxilium mihi,
et redde quam salutis expugnant opem.
Antehac mihi infestos tua percussit manus,
et facile dentes conterebas impios,
purae vnicus defensor innocentiae.
Non militum munere posita est securitas
nec in hominum armis sita: sed domini est salus.
Est ille vitae restitutor perditae.
A te sacra in cunctos fluit benedictio,
et in tuum venit alma populum gratia.
Certum est furorem plebis hostilem fuga [*fol. 11v*]
vitare: mihi salus aliunde non venit.
Pastor populum non caede dispergam fera.
Quam omnes perirent melius est vnum mori:
hunc solum avidis armis requirunt sanguinem,
me caeteris tranquilla erit pax mortuo.
Cedam. Exitum quemcumque tolerabo libens.
IOAB. Factum hoc veneranda stirpe Iesseia, edite!
Et summa quam tuo favore authoritas
sum consecutus et hec mea experientia
amorque et in quod nunc vocaris periculum
verba haec vel invito exprimunt mihi aspera:
turpem ducis summi fugam non approbo.
Regem fugabit parricida pessimus?

28. nunc] ⟨ mihi || **29.** gratum] ⟨ c [*confer] || **33.** purae] ⟨ almae || **38.** venit alma] ⟨ alma venit || **41.** Pastor . . . fera] ⟨ Dira . . . pastor || **43.** *Small score beneath* sanguinem || **46.** edite] ⟨ educe | edite!] edite, *MS* || **47-49.** *Added in the margin, apparently sometime during the writing of ll. 81-88; see note at II.2.51-88* || **48.** hec mea] ⟨ mea hec || **50.** exprimunt] ⟨ excutit || **51-54.** *Printed in Boas* || **51-88.** *Small scores beneath ll. 51, 61, 71, 81, and 88 (the last compensating for the added ll. 47-49) set off groups of ten lines from top of page; Watson originally miscounted and put a mark beneath l. 52. See note at II.2.100-178* ||

Therefore I shall not fear the squads of enemies, however numerous. I shall expose my head to their weapons, yea even of thousands. Arise now, God of Jacob: confer Thy gracious aid upon me Thy petitioner, and restore the treasure of safety which they wrest from me. Before this, Thy hand beat dangers away from me, and easily didst Thou grind down their wicked teeth, Thou only Defender of chaste innocence. My safety is not placed in the province of soldiers nor located in the arms of men: nay, salvation is of the Lord. He is the Restorer of lost life. From Thee flows holy blessing onto all, and into Thy people comes nourishing grace.

I have resolved to escape the enemy's fury in flight with my people.[2] For me personally, safety comes from no other course; as a shepherd, I will not scatter my people in terrible slaughter. Than all should perish it is better that one die. Only this blood of mine do they seek with their eager weapons; when I am dead, tranquil peace will belong to the rest. I shall withdraw. I shall endure the outcome gladly, whatever it may be.

JOAB. This act, your Majesty, from the reverend son of Jesse? Both the very great authority which I have enjoyed by your favor[3] and my experience and love, even in what you now call danger, force these harsh words from me, though I am reluctant: I do not approve of base flight by the supreme leader. Will the meanest parricide put a king to flight?

[2] Literally, "by the flight of my people." This must be the sense, though the position of the words makes it appear that David wanted to avoid the hostile fury of the people.

[3] "And David reigned over all Israel. . . . And Joab the son of Sarvia was over the army" (*2 Kings* viii.15-16).

Ego si recuses bella iam contra inferam:
belli integrum cervici onus incumbet meae.
Ferro nefarios tollere infesto pium est,
et patriam truci tyranno liberas.
In summum habebit regna blasphemus deum?
Legis violator, legis vltor habebitur?
Quid iam sceleratus debita poena vacat?
Dedisse prestat. Sera furenti est vltio.
Qui temeritate fertur in preceps furor
nec consilium factis adhibet vllum suis,
quam facile sedula potest cura opprimi!
Non te probrosam victoria frequens fugam docet.
Quam strennui parva cecidere hostes manu!
A te quot acri proelio fusa agmina!
Vt horridum vasto Goliam corpore:
durum clypeo armatum caput septemplici
crebro rotatim stridulum amentum vibrans,
tua hec lapillo invalida percussit manus.
Qui debili vires tibi nervosas dedit
quando leonem vrsumque scernebas puer
mitem arietem medio rapientes de grege,
idem pusillis roborabit copijs
in impium patris sitientem sanguinem
et in manus bello tibi prostratum dabit.
Hosti resistamus: tua est victoria.
DAVID. Quamvis salutem saevus expugnet meam,
nostro est tamen dilectus animo filius.

54. cervici . . . meae] ⟨ cervici . . . meo (?) ⟨ humeris . . . meis [?⟨ meum] || **58.** vltor] ⟨ author || **64.** probrosam] ⟨ trepidam || **65.** strennui] ⟨ strennua || **67.** corpore:] corpore *MS* || **69.** *Orig. followed l. 70 (or was added there for insertion here)* || **73.** rapientes] ⟨ rapientem || **76.** tibi] ⟨ cito || **77-88.** *Printed in Boas* || **78.** saevus] *MS* servus *Boas* ||

If you decline, I will now carry the war against them; the whole burden of the war shall lie upon my neck. It is proper to wipe out the wicked who bear hostile arms,[4] and you free the nation from a cruel tyrant. Is a blasphemer against God on high to rule the kingdom? Is a violator of the law to be regarded as an avenger of it?[5] Why is one already polluted free of deserved punishment? It were better for him to have paid it. Too late is the revenge on this ranter. Headstrong madness which is borne along in recklessness and applies no deliberation to its deeds — how easily it can be overcome with careful thought!

Your frequent victories do not teach you shameful flight. How the bold enemies fell before your humble hand! How many battle lines were routed by you in fierce fighting! What of the fearsome Goliath with his huge frame![6] His hard head was protected by a sevenfold shield; and your weak hand, brandishing a whizzing slingshot round and round, smote it with a tiny stone. In your weakness One gave you sinewy strength when you, a mere boy, saw the lion and bear seizing the gentle ram from the midst of your flock;[7] He will likewise strengthen you with your meager troops against that impious one who thirsts after his father's blood. Into your hands He will deliver him, prostrated before you by war. Let us resist the enemy; the victory is ours.

DAVID. However savagely he endangers my safety, he is still my son, esteemed in my heart.

[4] I interpret *Ferro . . . infesto* as an ablative of specification rather than of instrument.

[5] *Scil.*, as a king is regarded.

[6] *1 Kings* xvii.4-51.

[7] Recalled by David at *1 Kings* xvii.34-36.

IOAB. Num nomen habebit parricida filij?
DAVID. Nefas abhorreo; charus est gnatus tamen.
IOAB. Es dignus (o rex, pace quod dico tua)
in cuius omnes vsque coniurent caput:
hac lenitate scelera plura provocas.
DAVID. Potest tamen ad frugem recipere se bonam,
nam saepe mota nube candida fit dies.
IOAB. Nulla eius est spes qui ad nefas obduruit:
est semper advltus morbus incurabilis.
DAVID. Mentem pietas humana victam retrahet.
IOAB. Rabies pie[ta]tem dira transcendit probam.
DAVID. Eo magis sanos fugisse oportuit.
IOAB. Eo magis insanos domare oportuit.
DAVID. In filij pater exitium numquam ferar. *[fol. 12r]*
IOAB. Quid, si patri malus exitium gnatus ferat?
DAV[ID]. Vincit pater vt aetate sic patientia.
IOAB. Hanc ergo patiendo retunde iniuriam.
DAVID. Iniuriam qui in filium pulsat, facit.
IOAB. Iniuriam qui filij fert, provocat.
DAVID. Prestat tulisse quam intulisse iniuriam.
IOAB. Sed dum pateris vitae rationem non habes.
DAVID. Satius mori est quam prole laesa vivere.
IOAB. Gnato studens, patriam occupandam deseris.
DAVID. Pugnae studens, plebem domini ledam magis.
IOAB. Plebem magis tumida tyrannis opprimet.
DAVID. Custos fidelis plebis est dominus suae.
IOAB. At interim tu ne fuga tentes deum.

80. parricida] ⟨ ⟨ ⟩ (*apparently first letter of different word, illegible*) || **84.** lenitate] *MS* levitate *Boas* || **90.** pie[ta]tem] pietatatem *MS* (*scribal*) | transcendit probam] ⟨ ⟨p⟩ [*probam transcendit] || **94-95.** *Added in the margin, apparently after l. 130 was written and before l. 138 was written (since the ten-line markings do not compensate for the added lines until l. 138; see note at II.2.100-178)* || **94.** Quid] ⟨ Non | ferat?] ferat. *MS* || **95.** Vincit] ⟨ Vincet || **96.** Hanc . . . patiendo] ⟨ Hanc ergo tolerando ⟨ A te pater tantum [?tantam] || **100-178.** *Beneath l. 100 a small score marks off ten lines from the last such mark, at l. 88 (not incl. the added ll. 94-95); Watson no longer counted merely from the top of each page. Further ten-line marks appear beneath ll. 110, 120, 130, 138 (compensating for the added ll. 94-95), 148, 158, 168, and 178 (the last four on verso). For continuation of the numbering see note at II.3.6-58* ||

JOAB. Is a parricide to have the name "son"?

DAVID. I abhor the crime, but I love the son.

JOAB. O King, saving your displeasure with what I say, you deserve that everyone should go on banding together against your head: by this policy of leniency you provoke more crimes.

DAVID. But he might bring himself to moral virtue, for often does a day become clear after its cloudiness has cleared.

JOAB. There is no hope for one who has hardened in his wickedness: an incurable disease is ever aggravated.

DAVID. Human duty will bring back his senses and win him over.

JOAB. His dreadful madness overbalances proper duty.

DAVID. The more it behooves the sane to flee.

JOAB. Rather, the more it behooves them to subdue the insane.

DAVID. As a father I will never be moved to the destruction of my son.

JOAB. Why, if an evil son intends destruction for his father?

DAVID. A father prevails as much by forbearance as by his age.

JOAB. Then prevent this injury by forbearing.

DAVID. He who strikes out against a son creates an injury.

JOAB. He who tolerates an injury from a son provokes injury.

DAVID. It is better to suffer an injury than to give one.

JOAB. But so long as you forbear you show no consideration for your life.

DAVID. It is better to die than to live by smiting a child.

JOAB. In your eagerness for your son, you forsake the nation, which ought to be looked after.

DAVID. If I were eager for battle, I should do more injustice to the people of the Lord.

JOAB. A domineering despotism will oppress the people more.

DAVID. The Lord is a faithful guardian of His people.

JOAB. But meanwhile do not test God by fleeing.

DAVID. Imo resistendo cito offendam deum.
IOAB. Non si saluti perniciem amoveas tuae.
DAVID. Salus cita melius retinebitur fuga.
IOAB. Speranda iusto est omnibus bello salus.
DAVID. Extincta magno est omnibus bello salus.
IOAB. Omnis subigitur facile motus turbidus.
DAVID. Motus violentus est timendus omnibus.
IOAB. Illis duces, ordo, arma desunt. Quid times?
DAVID. Cuncta haec satis ministrat impotens furor.
IOAB. Preceps ruit omnia consilia spernens furor.
DAVID. Graviore laedit clade quod preceps ruit.
IOAB. Confusa parvis dissipantur copijs.
DAVID. Nobis coactus non adest exercitus.
IOAB. Domini recessit ex animo potentia?
DAVID. Ille omnipotens cunctis tuetur miserijs.
IOAB. Hoc ergo servum proelio tuebitur.
DAVID. Hec plaga praeterita ob scelera inflicta est mihi.
IOAB. Num quis tibi vates ore predixit sacro?
DAVID. Eius iterum sermone renovas memoriam
quod numinis Nathan minister rettulit,
iussu cadente nobili Vria meo:
"Numquam e tuis gladius recedet aedibus
domino quod Vriae neglecto coniugem
acceperis. Sed suscitabit de domo
tua malum, idque fiet omnibus palam."
Haec ergo nunc authore clades est data
deo; hec nefandi sceleris est poena adhibita:

107. Imo = Immo | cito] ⟨ optimum || **108.** saluti perniciem] ⟨ perni [*perniciem] saluti | perniciem] ⟨ pernicies || **115.** impotens] ⟨ vnicus || **125.** sermone . . . memoriam] ⟨ verbis memoriam renovas || **128-131.** *Quotes om. MS* || **132.** nunc] ⟨ mihi || **133-134.** *Smearing of the ink while wet makes lines difficult to read* ||

DAVID. On the contrary, by resisting I should immediately offend God.
JOAB. Not if you are removing a peril to your safety.
DAVID. My safety will be maintained better in swift flight.
JOAB. Safety for all is to be hoped for in a righteous war.
DAVID. The safety of all is extinguished in a large war.
JOAB. Every seditious movement is easily put down.
DAVID. A violent action must be feared by everyone.
JOAB. They lack leaders, organization, and arms. What do you fear?
DAVID. All these his unbridled fury adequately ministers.
JOAB. His fury rushes rashly, scorning all counsels.
DAVID. It strikes with more severe calamity just because it rushes rashly.
JOAB. Disorganized affairs are routed with few troops.
DAVID. We have no army assembled.
JOAB. Has the power of the Lord slipped your memory?
DAVID. Almighty God protects in all misfortunes.
JOAB. Then He will protect His servant in this battle.
DAVID. This blow has been visited upon me because of my past crimes.[8]
JOAB. What, has some prophet advised you with a holy speech?
DAVID. With your words you recall again my memory of that which Nathan, the minister of God, reported after the noble Urias fell by my order: "Never from thy house shall the sword depart because, neglecting the Lord, you have taken the wife of Urias. But He shall raise up evil out of thy house, and that will happen in the presence of all."[9] Thus, this misfortune has been given by God the Father; this penalty has been invoked because of my wicked crime:

[8] As stated in the Introduction, p. 50, this is thematically important. But David has been made to seem reluctant to state this truth, finally doing so only after Joab's arguments have overpowered his earlier evasive positions. Note, incidentally, from the scornful tone of Joab's answer here that he thinks David to be rationalizing.

[9] The prophecy here quoted, which is alluded to by Semei in II.3, is at *2 Kings* xii.1-14. Robinson (p. 191) observed that a Terentian commentator would have called David's recollection of Nathan's prophecy "excellent *oeconomia,*" for Absalom fulfills another part of the prophecy (concerning David's concubines); see III.1.

iam e propria in nostrum caput exurgit domo
haeres patris. Domini nihil irritum redit.
Eius suävia verbera aeque perferam:
ab eo profecta mihi videntur dulcia.
Nolo misericordi deo resistere.
Non est repellendum quod imponit iugum:
numquam negabit fortiter ferenti opem.
Fugiamus ergo: est nulla mansuris salus.
Gravis ruina vrbi imminet: cuncta obruet,
nemo truces furentis effugiet manus.
Fugam parate, surgite, exite ocyus
ne nos gladio cunctos minaci devoret. [*fol. 12v*]
In vrbe trucidandum relinquite neminem:
immitis est ensis cruentus sanguine
crudisque nescit parcere pinguis cedibus.
POPULUS. En adsumus prompti libenter exequi
quaecumque servis rex suis praeceperit.
DAVID. Summe Abrahae deus, populo qui me vnxeras
regem futurum, perpetua qui foedera
pacis mihi promiseras tecum fore,
quique inclyta Israelis ornasti domo,
cur servulum penitus ope destituis tua?
Ecce haec tuum querela pertingit thronum:
presentia prostrato mihi auxilia petit.
Cuncti patres in numina sperabant tua,
nec in tua periere fidentes ope.
Hanc ne protervus devoret animam leo,

141. est] ?⟨ et || **144.** surgite, exite] ⟨ exite, surgite || **145.** minaci] ⟨ cruento || **160-167.** *Printed in Boas* || **160.** leo] *Boas* Leo *MS* ||

now from my own home the heir of the father rises up against my head. Nothing of God's proceeds without plan. His kind punishments I shall endure with equanimity: since they come from Him, they seem sweet to me. I do not wish to resist merciful God. The yoke which He imposes must not be shunted off: He will never refuse strength to one who bears His yoke bravely. We shall flee, then; there is no hope for us if we remain. Heavy ruin hangs over the city: Absalom will destroy everything; no one will escape the savage hands of the madman.

[To the People] Prepare for flight; arise; leave quickly, lest he devour us all with his threatening sword. Leave no one in the city to be slaughtered: his terrible sword is gory with blood and, already besmeared, does not know how to refrain from merciless murders.

PEOPLE. Behold, we are here, ready to follow willingly whatever the king orders his servants.

DAVID. Great God of Abraham, Who didst anoint me as the people's future king,[10] Who didst promise me that everlasting treaties of peace would exist with Thee, and Who didst honor me with the celebrated race of Israel, why dost Thou utterly deprive Thy humble servant of Thy help? Behold, this complaint reaches Thy throne and seeks immediate aid for me in my prostration. Our fathers all placed their trust in Thy divine will, and confident in Thy strength they did not perish. Let not the savage lion devour this soul,

[10] *1 Kings* xvi.13, *2 Kings* ii.4.

sed cornua potens frange monstrosae ferae
quae fraudibus rapit malignis filium
in scelera, et in omne precipitem trudit nefas.
Ô omnibus portentum Achitophel bonis,
quo turpibus infrenem dolis animum trahis?
Volens ab incepto facinore sisteret
ni verba sontem provocassent impia.
Eius cogitata dulcis infatua deus,
et reprobum iam consulenti animum dato.
Vrbi et mihi consilium nociturum dissipa.
En in meum vt vitulus tener insultat caput.
Rictum vt canis in me rabidus aperit suum,
casses tetendit, virus effudit latens:
iusto nefandus insidiatur sanguini.
Sed qui intima hominum corda scrutaris deus
et facile cunctas hominis agnoscis vias,
ex vnguibus me agnum leonis eripe
et perpetui mecum memento foederis.
Si non placeo, quodcumque tibi visum est bonum,
vel vita vel interitus, mihi gratus accidet. [Exeunt]

[ACTUS SECUNDUS.] SCENA TERTIA.

SEMEI. DAVID. ABISAI.

[Trimetri Iambici.]

SEMEI. Egredere, monstrum, vir Belial, vir sanguinum,
cruore numquam sordido bufo satur,
vorax homicida caede laetans horrida.
En sanguis in caput redundat proprium —

161. sed] ⟨ et || **163.** precipitem] *MS* praecipitem *Boas* || **164.** Achitophel] ⟨ Achotophel || **170.** *Added after l. 171 and marked for insertion here* | Vrbi et] ⟨ Vncto || **172.** rabidus . . . suum] *The stages of revision can only be conjectured:* ⟨ rabidus extendit suum ⟨ avidum aperit vorax || **174.** insidiatur] ⟨ inse (?) || **176.** agnoscis] ⟨ agnoscit || **177.** agnum] ⟨ ⟨er⟩ [*eripe] || **180.** accidet] ⟨ accedet (?*scribal*) | S.d.] *Om. MS*

II.3.s.h.] Scena 3ª *MS* || M.h.] *Om. MS* || **1-3.** *Printed in Boas* || **2.** numquam] nūquam *MS* nunquam *Boas* | bufo] *MS* (⟨ h [?]) fuso *Boas* || **3.** caede] ⟨ strage ||

but break the horns, O mighty God, of the monstrous beast which, by evil treacheries, rushes my son into crimes and pushes him headlong into every perfidy. O Achitophel, monster to all good people, why do you divert his unbridled mind with wicked deceits? Willingly he would leave off his villainy thus begun had not your impious words provoked the criminal. O sweet Lord, make Achitophel's ideas appear foolish, and make his reasoning faulty as he now deliberates.[11] Dissipate the plan which will do harm to the city and to me. Look, he leaps at my head like a young bull. He opens his jaws against me like a rabid dog. He has set out traps. Lurking for me, he has poured out poisons. The villain lies in ambush awaiting my just blood. But Thou, O God, Who hast scrutinized the innermost hearts of men and easily knowest all the ways of men, deliver me, a lamb, from the claws of the lion, and be mindful of Thy everlasting pact with me.[12] If I displease Thee, whatever seems proper to Thee, be it life or death, will please me.

[David and Joab lead the people off]

[11] *Reprobus,* a late Latin word (*Harper's Latin Dictionary* = "false, spurious"), is not given in Cooper's *Thesavrvs.*

[12] As Boas recognized (p. 356), David's final prayer is based on phrases in Psalm xxi (xxiii in Boas' Bible), "and by an ingenious application of its imagery David is made to ask for Absalom's deliverance from the monster Achitophel."

[ACT II.] SCENE 3.

[The Desert near Bahurim.]

[Enter] DAVID [Flanked by] ABISAI [and Other Followers.] SEMEI [Enters from Bahurim and Throws Stones at David.]

SEMEI. Come out,[1] monster, man of Belial, man of blood; toad sated with blood that was never base; greedy homicide, rejoicing in horrid murder. Behold, the blood redounds onto your own head —

[1] That is, come out from the throng of people so my stones can get to you. But for the possibility that he means "Come out from Jerusalem" (in which case the action of II.2-3 is continuous), see Appendix F. The source of the scene is *2 Kings* xvi.5-13, where the former meaning seems to be intended. Watson's only freedom with the source is that he "elaborates with zest the vituperative epithets of the original . . . and adds a gruesome prophecy of God's vengeance upon David" (Boas, p. 356). Semei being of the family of Saul, his cursing of David had its genesis in the long strife between David and Saul, whose death did not end the quarrel; see *2 Kings* ii-v. Watson probably had this factionalism in mind when he had Joab warn David against continued grieving in V.4.42-45. Naturally, Watson ignored the grudge which inspired David's dying hint to Solomon to "bring down [Semei's] grey hairs with blood to hell" (*3 Kings* ii.9).

Saül et eius quam vorasti familia[e],
cuius tyrannus regna durus occupas.
In nobilem, atrox, irruisti regiam.
Sed rapta dominus regna vindex abstulit:
per filium iustus tuum te vlciscitur.
Hic membra frustatim tua divellens dabit
rodenda partim canibus, alia edacibus
dirupta corvis, alia vastabunt maris
portenta, in auras alia sparget foetidas —
monstris cadaver turpe proijciet feris.
ABISAI. Cur impijs regem canis hic opprobrijs [*fol. 13r*]
lacerat et in vnctum convicia domini vomit?
Linguam viri non extrahemus improbam?
Hic ensis animam strictus abripiet ream.
Foedum scelesto sanguine aspergam solum.
Tantam protervitatem invltus auferet?
DAVID. Patiens minas iactare mitte turgidas:
hoc iam ferendum dominus imponit iugum.
Ne tristia linguae frena adhibeas garrulae,
nec morte quamvis debita hominem punias,
et hec quietis tela reconde nescia.
ABISAI. Quis prurientem retrahere potest manum
quin hanc loquendi vindicet petulantiam?
DAVID. Temet refrena. Nam huius impudentia
in nos flagellandos pius vtitur deus.

5. familia[e]] familiam *MS* || **6-58.** *A score beneath l. 6 marks ten lines from the last score (counting two lines for the scene headings) at II.2.178; further scores appear beneath ll. 16, 27, 38 (the latter two marking off eleven lines each, prob. by error), 48, and 58. See note at II.3.73-134* || **6.** durus] ⟨ dura || **10-14.** *Printed in Boas* || **10.** Hic] *MS* Sic *Boas* || **12.** vastabunt] ⟨ depascent || **13.** foetidas] ⟨ foetidat || **15.** Abisai] *MS* Abishai *Boas* || **19.** scelesto] ⟨ scelestum || **20.** auferet] ?⟨ auferit || **21.** Patiens minas] ⟨ Minas patiens || **24.** *In the left margin are four dots in a diamond shape. Some early printed editions of Seneca used varying patterns of two to five dots beside choric lines; I do not know their meaning* || 25. hec] ⟨ iam ||

the blood of Saul and of his family which you devoured, whose rule you, a harsh tyrant, hold. Onto his noble throne you forced your way, you vicious man. But the avenging Lord has taken away your stolen realm: through your own son does just God wreak vengeance upon you. Absalom will rend your limbs asunder piecemeal. Part he will give to the dogs to be eaten, other severed parts to the gluttonous crows; the monsters of the sea will ravage other parts; others he will cast out into the stinking winds; the ugly torso he will toss out for savage beasts.

ABISAI. Why does this dog tear at the king with his insolent insults and vomit abuse upon the anointed of the Lord? Shall we not cut out the wicked tongue of the man? This drawn sword will rip out his criminal soul. I will spatter the ground filthy with his criminal blood. Shall he commit such great boldness unavenged?

DAVID. Forbear; let him throw out his turgid threats: now this yoke the Lord imposes for me to bear. Do not put stern checkreins on his talkative tongue, and do not punish the man with death, however much deserved. And put away these senseless weapons of death.[2]

ABISAI. Who can restrain my itching hand from avenging this petulance of speaking?

DAVID. Restrain yourself: his impudence pious God uses to scourge me.

[2] Although David in the Biblical account forces Abisai to "Let him alone that he may curse as the Lord hath bidden him" (*2 Kings* xvi.11), he does not mention specific weapons. Watson may have had in mind the insistence of Jesus in the Garden of Gethsemane that his follower "Put back thy sword into its place; for all those who take the sword will perish by the sword" (*Matthew* xxvi.52); cf. *Absalom* I.3.116. In Christian doctrine, of course, David prefigured Christ. For one notice of the parallel between David and Christ in general and, in particular, between David's tolerance of Semei and Christ's of his arresters, see Erasmus' *In Tertium Psalmum Paraphrasis* (*Opera Omnia,* V [Utrecht, 1703], cols. 235-236).

Gnatus avidas furore dentes exerens,
circumfremit vorare conatus patrem:
odit, lacessit, lacerat, exagitat, premit,
iugulum parentis ense fodiendum petit.
Hunc ergo non mirum est maledictis prosequi,
nec si salutem pace defoetam bona
hostis venenato ore devoveat meam.
Rabie i[n]nocentes sinite sectari fera.
Quae libeat immerito mihi obijciat probra.
Nos forte visitabit afflictos deus
et, omnia iustis convicia vertens bene,
pacem malorum turbine discusso dabit.
Nos singuli rectam taciti instemus viam.
SEMEI. Vtinam hic lapis cerebrum penitus ruptum exprimat
vel vulnere cervicem resolvat putrido!
Iugulum gladiolo praebe foedandum meo,
strages bonorum facere qui magnas soles.
Ne dulcis aura donet afflatus tibi;
te tenebrae euntem semper obducant nigrae,
nec ignis, aqua, aër, tibi det nec tellus iter,
nec flebili dolore mens vnquam vacet.
Tremente oberres ore mendicans cibum.
Quis non nitentem monstro huïc lucem invidet?
Vtinam hoc rapiant cadaver vltores equi,
vel fulmen artus dilaniet saevum tuos,

33. fodiendum] ⟨ mactandum (*over* mactandum *a canceled letter, doubtfully a* b *indicating an original intention to reverse* mactandum petit; fodiendum *is in the margin after* petit, *but metrics require reading it before* petit, *and Watson probably had to write it in the margin because of lack of interlineal space*) || **37.** Rabie . . . sinite] ⟨ Sinite . . . rabie (rabie *underscored*) | i[n]nocentes] inocentes (*with a semicircular, or double-nasal, mark over the first syllable*) *MS* (?⟨ nnocentes) || **40.** vertens] ⟨ vertet || **41.** malorum . . . dabit] ⟨ hodie discusso daturus turbine || **44.** putrido!] putrido. *MS* || **48-56.** *Printed in Boas* || **52.** huïc] *MS* huic *Boas* || **53.** Vtinam hoc] ⟨ Vtinam ||

My son, baring his eager teeth in madness, roars out his attempts to devour his father: he hates me, attacks me, tears at me, torments me, oppresses me; he seeks to slash the throat of his father with his sword. It is no marvel, then, that this man pursues me with curses nor that this enemy with poison tongue curses my safety, which is devoid of pleasant peace.[3] Be guiltless, and let him pursue me with his savage madness: since I am innocent, let him hurl at me whatever insults he wishes. Perhaps God will visit us in our affliction, and, righting all these revilings against the just, will give peace, once the uproar of evils has been ended. Let us all press on in silence along the proper road.

[David and his followers start to leave]

SEMEI [Pursuing them and throwing rocks]. Would that this rock might spatter your brain, utterly splitting it, or lay open your neck with a rotten wound! Hold out your neck so that I may hack it with my sword, for you are accustomed to committing great slaughters of the good. May no sweet air give its breath to you. May black shadows always cover you in your travels. May neither fire, water, air, nor earth give you passage.[4] And may your mind never be free of weeping sorrow. May you wander begging for food with trembling mouth. Who does not begrudge the bright light of day to this monster? Would that avenging horses might drag your body, or that fierce lightning might rip your joints apart,

[3] *Defoetus,* which is not given in Cooper's *Thesavrvs,* is listed by *Harper's Latin Dictionary* as a past participle of *defoedare,* "to defile." I have rendered it "devoid" on the authority of Francis Holyoke's *Dictionarivm Etymologicvm Latinvm* [London, 1633]. Holyoke ascribed the word to "Quidam" texts of Ovid and translated it "past bringing forth young, void, empty."

[4] The four elements of the universe; the conception is classical. Cf. II.3.60 and V.4.28.

vel membra rapidae vrenda tradantur pyrae,
vel spiritus tenax laqueus claudat viam.
Ô sanguinis crudelis absorptor pij,
ô patriae exitium, lues, pestis bonae,
fuge, mortifera numquam reditura bestia.
In te irruunt elementa, filius, deus.
Coenum fuge immundum, omnibus os impudens.
Deforme corpus scopulus confringet cavus,
ipsumque saniem pondus exprimet nigram.
Vultum ab odioso sol reflectit denegans.
Protrita nusquam perdito patet via:
praerupta saxa sanguineo obsistunt viro.
A cede non te foeda servabit fuga. [Exeunt]

CHORUS.

Asclepiadici.

Non hostes faciunt tanta pericula,
nec te fata premunt, rex, adamantina.
Expromit veteres maximus, optimus
iras et scelus hoc corripiet tuum.

55. vrenda tradantur] ⟨ vret [?vrent] traden [*tradenda] || **61-67.** *Added, with s.p.* Semei, *after l. 145; perhaps it was intended to remain there, but the facts that it was written after Watson had drawn a heavy line ending the scene with l. 145 and that such post-choric speeches are very rare indicate that it was meant to follow l. 60* || **61.** Coenum . . . immundum] ⟨ Coenum fuge impu [*remainder of line to read* *impudens os omnibus immundum (?)] ⟨ Olens fuge cenum || **62.** scopulus] ⟨ sco scopulus (*Watson apparently changing his mind about the word to write and then changing it back again*) | confringet] ⟨ effringet || **64.** Vultum . . . denegans] ⟨ Vel vultum odioso . . . denegans ⟨ Vel sol odioso se reflectit [⟨ reflectet] vultum negans || **65.** perdito] ⟨ pert (*scribal*) || After **67.** *Canceled line:* Opima vultu regna purga iam tuo || **67.** S.d.] *Om. MS* || M.h. Asclepiadici] ⟨ Asclepeadici (*scribal*) || **68-130.** *The "parts" of the chorus are divided as follows:* a *68-78,* b *79-108,* c *109-130,* πd *131-145. Orig., ll. 109-130 stood between the present ll. 78 and 79 (and the "parts" were orig.* b *109-130 and* c *79-108). Apparently Watson then started to move ll. 109-130 before the present l. 68, for he changed the* b *before 109 to an* a; *but that move was not completed, for the* a *before 68 was left unchanged. Finally, canceling the* b ⟩ a *before 109 and the* c *before 79, he wrote in their place* c *and* b, *respectively* || **69.** fata premunt] ⟨ fata premunt fa [*fata (*intending to reverse the words by canceling the first* fata)] ⟨ fata premunt ||

or that your limbs might be committed to a raging pyre for burning, or that a tight noose might shut off the passageway of your breath! O cruel leech of pious blood; O ruin, plague, bane of our good nation — flee, you death-bringing beast, and never return. The elements, your son, and God are falling upon you. Flee, you foul and filthy fellow; your face is shameless to everyone. A hollow-faced cliff will shatter your hideous body, and your very weight will squeeze out your black and filthy blood.[5] The sun turns away its face from your hateful person, refusing to shine. There is no smooth path anywhere for you in your desperation; steep rocks obstruct your way, you blood-stained man. Your shameless flight will not save you from slaughter.

[David and his followers make their way out, Semei following]

CHORUS.

Not enemies cause such great dangers, and not the inflexible fates oppress you, O King. The Greatest and Best reveals His ancient angers and will reproach your wickedness in this manner.

[5] David actually died a natural death (*3 Kings* ii).

Est poenas dominus mitis in horridas:
peccantem quatiet, comminuet minus; [*fol. 13v*]
confringet penitus corda rebellia,
prostratos, humiles recreat, excitat;
inflatis animis parcere nescius,
aufertur tumidis gratia blandiens;
lentus novit opem ferre iacentibus.

72. Est] ⟨ E⟨t⟩ ?*Read* Et (*but see III.2.31, where the reading is clearly* est) | horridas:] horridas *MS* (*appropriate to orig. reading* Et) || **73-134.** *Beneath l. 73 a score marking ten lines from the last score, at l. 58 (counting the chorus heading as occupying the equivalent of two lines and ignoring added ll. 61-67, which had not been written when the score was made). Further ten-line groups are marked with alternating scores and dots at ll. 114 (which does not account for added l. 77; see note ad loc.), 124, 82, 92, 102, and 134; these markings set off the lines according to their physical order in the MS, not according to their revised order. For a different kind of mark, see note at l. 108. Added ll. 61-67 and 77 never were compensated for in Watson's numbering. He began renumbering with the next act; see note at III.1.20-130* || **76-77.** inflatis . . . blandiens] ⟨ inflatis animis [⟨ ani⟨ ⟩ (*scribal*)] parcere nescius,/ aufertur [⟨ aufertus (*scribal*)] . . . blandiens (*second line added marginally*) ⟨ nescit zelotypus parcere tumidis (*only one line*). *The revisions were made (and l. 77 added) after completion of the remainder of the scene, for the line numberings do not account for the added line; see note at ll. 73-134* || **78.** novit] ⟨ novis (*?scribal*) ||

The Lord is gentle when it comes to horrid penalties: He will beat the sinner, but not crush him; He will completely shiver rebellious hearts, but He restores and arouses the prostrate and the humble; not knowing how to spare puffed-up souls, He withdraws His gentle grace from the pompous, but being flexible He knows how to bring aid to the abject.

Lignorum patiens pertulit Isaac
fascem, quo fieret victima flebilis.
Solvendum iugulum supposuit volens
mactantis gladio mortifero patris,
sed numquam dominus negligit optimus
fidentes sibi: ovem quam pater immolet
servato puero vepribus obtulit.
Vt fratrum facinus fatidicus tulit
Ioseph nec veniam supplicibus negat,
ira nec miseros percitus vltus est,
sed pravos onerat muneribus bonis,
sic sedat Gedeon providus asperos
quaestus quod habuit filius Ephraim
et mentes patiens mitigat incitas.
Sic fratrem Mariam murmurat, in ducem
Mosen verba loquens impia sedulo,
quam feda dominus percutiens lepra
e castris, populo separat integro:
septem continuos proijcitur dies,
sed mitis precibus dux dominum rogans,
a morbo penitus sana reducitur.
Sic David genitor iam fugit e domo
dum trux bella parat fervida filius —
cui ne vim faciat bella reliquerit.
Hic patrem gladio persequitur fero, [*fol. 14r*]

84. quam pater immolet] ⟨ vepribus obtulit || **85.** puero] ⟨ pe (*scribal*) || **89.** sed pravos] ⟨ ingratos || **93.** Mariam] ⟨ Mariah || **95.** feda . . . lepra] ⟨ lepra [*lepra . . . feda] || **97.** septem continuos] ⟨ ad septem penitus || **98.** mitis] ⟨ Moses | precibus dux dominum] ⟨ d⟨o⟩m⟨inum⟩ dux ||

Patiently Isaac carried the bundle of wood by which he would be made a lamentable victim. Willingly he laid out his neck to be cut off by the death-bringing sword of his sacrificing father. But never does the very good Lord forsake those who are faithful to Him: He produced among the briers a sheep for the father to sacrifice, saving his son.[6] The prophet Joseph endured the perfidy of his brothers: he did not deny forgiveness to them when they asked, and did not, aroused by anger, take vengeance upon them in their wretchedness, but loaded those misguided men with fine gifts.[7] Just so did the provident Gedeon calm the harsh complaints which the sons of Ephraim had and patiently appeased their wrought-up passions.[8] Thus Miriam murmured against her brother, speaking deliberately impious words against the leader, Moses. The Lord, afflicting her with horrible leprosy, exiled her from the camp and from all the people. Seven whole days she was in exile; but, the gentle leader beseeching the Lord with prayers, she was returned completely healed of the disease.[9] Thus David the father now flees from home while his wild son prepares hot wars — the father has forsaken war so as not to use force against the son. The son pursues his father with savage sword;

[6] *Genesis* xxii.1-14.
[7] *Genesis* xxxvii, xlii-xlv.
[8] *Judges* viii.1-3. The Latin reads, literally, "the son of Ephraim."
[9] *Numbers* xii.

alter deposuit tela minacia.
Hic ferrum quatiens strinxerit in patrem,
affectus bonus hunc edocuit fugam.
Hic iam morte patris vult reus effici,
ille vt sit fugitat filius innocens.
Ô regis memorandam patientiam,
hac caelum petitur stelligerum via:
istaec sola bonum conciliat deum,
est hec mente quies vnica languidis,
afflictis validum corpore pharmacum.
Sola est sollicitis meta doloribus.
Debetur domini summa benignitas.
Adversis recreat solum animus bonus,
mens placat patiens rebus in asperis.
Fit laetis homini dulcis amenitas.
Mens lenis placide sustinet omnia,
mens lenis gracilem pauperiem levat.
Lumen magnificis divitijs parat.
Illi iuncta modo munditіes placet:
haec numquam regerit crimina noxia,
haec non obstrepera est convitiantibus,
nullum persequitur scommatibus malis,
hec semper fugitat iurgia tetrica,
nullum flagitijs nobilibus notat,
fortis verba boni consulit aspera.
Quid multis, miseris innocua est quies,
curarum domina est, leticiae comes.

Beneath **108.** *A score apparently indicating the end of the out-of-order section of the chorus and of the* b *section* || **115.** Debetur] ?*Read* Deletur || **129.** quies] ⟨ que (*scribal*) || **130.** leticiae = laetitiae ||

the father has laid aside his threatening weapons. The son has unsheathed his sword, brandishing it at his father; a fine goodwill has taught the father flight. The son now wishes to become a criminal by the death of his father; the father quickly flees so that his son may remain guiltless.

O the memorable patience of the king! By this course is starry heaven sought. Only this patience gains the favor of the good Lord. It is the only peace for the weak in spirit, and for the afflicted in body a strong medicine. It is the only end to anxious cares. To it is due the very great bounty of the Lord. Only a spirit which is good under adversities revives; only a mind which is patient under difficult circumstances makes for peace. In prosperous times the result for man is — sweet delight. A temperate mind endures all things calmly; a temperate mind lightens lean poverty. It prepares a life of magnificent wealth. Purity united with this moderation is pleasing: it never directs harmful crimes; it is not noisy with people railing, and none does it pursue with evil mockings; it ever avoids crabbed quarrels, and none does it accuse of notorious vices; it constantly puts a good interpretation on harsh words. In short, it is the guiltless respite from misfortunes, the ruler of cares, the companion of joy.

Hic fortem, Iuvenes, discite spiritum,
hic exempla viri sumite strennui.
Quid debet fieri rebus in omnibus
hic miles stupidos non rudis instruit.
Haec vobis operum forma imitabilis.
Solus perpetuo doctor habebitur,
solus perpetuo qui celebrabitur:
hec servate avidis mentibus abdita,
hec rursus memores promite cum est opus.
Ex hac invenies magna levamina.
Faelices facit haec: attonitis quies,
aerumnasque levat; presidium bonis,
abiectis decus est insuperabile.
Frangit dura potens hec patientia,
virtuti assiduus perpetuo comes.

ACTUS TERTIUS. [SCENA PRIMA].

ABSALOM. cum POPULO. ACHITOPHEL.

Trimetri Iambici.

ABSALOM. Iam strennui gradum prohibete milites:
nolo relictam funditus vrbem evertere.
Hic imperium regale fundabo meum:
haec alta regis scaeptra tenebit civitas,
hic nobile aeternum propagabo genus.

137. solus] ⟨ ⟨h⟩ solus [?*hec *miscopied from l. 138*] || **145.** *Added as an afterthought after Watson had drawn a heavy score across the page beneath l. 144 to mark the end of the scene; a somewhat smaller underscore beneath l. 145 separates it from the lines (61-67) added beneath it. The first of these two markings cuts through part of l. 145* | virtuti . . . comes] ⟨ virtutique comes non fatigabilis | perpetuo] ?⟨ perpetue | *Watson's troubles with this page are reflected in a large doodle in the right-hand margin*

III.1.s.h] Actus 3us *MS* || **1.** Iam . . . milites] ⟨ Iam g [*gradum strennui . . . milites] ⟨ State, strennui pedem revocate [⟨ rec] milites | milites:] milites *MS* (*earlier version* milites.) || **2.** evertere.] evertere *MS* || **3.** meum:] meum *MS* || **4.** scaeptra = sceptra ||

Here, O youths, learn to know a strong spirit; here take to heart the example of a strong man. This not inexperienced soldier[10] teaches the ignorant what ought to be done in all circumstances. This sort of works is worthy of your emulation. Only that teacher will be forever retained who alone is forever honored: lock up these secrets in your eager minds; remembering them again, call them forth when there is need of them. From patience you will find great solace. It makes people happy: a respite for the confounded, it lightens cares; a defense for the good, it is the paramount dignity for the abject. This powerful patience, always a diligent companion to virtue, shatters misfortunes.

[10] David.

ACT III. [SCENE 1.]

[The Outskirts of Jerusalem.]

[Enter] ABSALOM with [His] PEOPLE [and] ACHITOPHEL.[1]

ABSALOM [To his people]. Now halt, valiant soldiers. I do not wish to overturn the deserted city from its very foundations. Here I shall found my royal empire; this noble city will hold the great scepter of King Absalom; here I shall propagate for all time my glorious line.

[1] The scene has only the sketchiest source in the Bible, which contains none of the exultant boasting that Watson gave Absalom as a sign of his deterioration. *2 Kings* xvi.15 states: "Absalom and all his people came into Jerusalem, and Achitophel was with him." The following verses relate the initial audience of Chusai with Absalom, which Watson postponed until III.3; for the present scene Watson next skipped to *2 Kings* xvi.21-22. Besides adding Absalom's boasts and fierce threats, Watson solidified the motivation for Achitophel's advice that the son defile the father's concubines: when Absalom orders his soldiers to search Jerusalem, he notices a hesitation to follow his orders (l. 53), which Achitophel explains is due to their fear of reconciliation. The Biblical motivation, though the same, is much less concrete. As Boas said (p. 357), "The dramatist has shown skill and psychological insight" in leading up to the climactic advice concerning the concubines.

Non gladius vrbem frigidus, alium petit,
quem querit ad penas cruentus, vindices.
Armis superba Hierusalem maestis fremet,
vtrumque curvis mare onerabo classibus,
Iudaica meo tellus sonabit milite
ferrumque districtum micabit vndique
et cuncta ruina flebili implebo loca
ni detur invisum mihi mactandum caput.
Nulla vrbs validis praecincta passim moenibus, [*fol. 14v*]
nec sylva secretis cavernis obsita,
nec astra turres vel penetrantes splendida,
nec maria, nec clivosa montium iuga
patrem integrum a mucrone servabunt meo
quin ensis hic invisa rump[a]t viscera,
quin sanguinem crassum peremptus expu[a]t.
Tum quisquis infestum mihi clam proteget
nec prodet hacipsa trucidandum manu,
huic poena crudelis geminabitur nimis,
in quo sceleris exempla statuam pessimi.
Deformis hanc iam vastitas vrbem tenet:
a moenibus qui hostes feroces arceant
desunt — fuga vitae probrosa consulunt.
Sic avida vindictae ira saturari nequit.
Eius cruore, non fuga ignis pectore
conclusus extinqui potest: crescit malum
monstro gravius, illi nihil poenae est satis.
Quid author es? Regnum ne fortis occupem,
an bellicis armis fugientem persequar?

10. meo] ⟨ mea || **14-20.** *Printed in Boas* || **16.** astra] ⟨ coela || **19-20.** rump[a]t . . . expu[a]t] rumpet . . . expuet *MS, Boas (with "sic")* || **20-130.** *The twentieth line of the act (not counting headings) is marked with a small score; following ten-line groups are marked with alternating scores and dots at ll. 30, 40, 50, 60, 70, 80, 90, 100, 111 (physically the 110th line of the scene; see note ad loc.), 120, and 130. See notes at III.1.138 and III.2.10-50* || **21.** proteget (?)] ⟨ protegit || **31.** nihil poenae] ⟨ poenae nihil || **32.** es?] es, *MS* | occupem,] ⟨ occupem? ||

My sword is not so spiritless as to attack a city; it seeks another, whom it demands, bloodthirsty for avenging punishments. Proud Jerusalem will rumble with my dreadful weapons, I shall cover every sea with my curved ships, the land of Israel will resound with my soldiery, my busy sword will flash everywhere, and I shall saturate all places with grievous ruin — unless his hated head is surrendered to me for destruction. No city protected on all sides by strong walls, no woods filled with hidden grottoes, no towers even if they reach the glittering stars, no seas, and no craggy yokes of mountains will keep my father safe from my sword, will keep this blade from ripping into his hated vitals or keep him from spewing out his thick blood in death. Then whosoever secretly protects this enemy from me and does not give him over for execution by my very own hand, for that one will be compounded the cruelest punishment; I shall hold him guilty of the gravest crime.

[To Achitophel] An unnatural emptiness now possesses this city: those who should ward off fierce enemies from the walls are missing; they look to their lives in ignominious flight. My anger, so hot for revenge, cannot be satisfied. By his blood, not by his flight, can the fire confined within my breast be extinguished. The illness grows more oppressively than a monster; no punishment is sufficient to satisfy it. What do you advise? Should I occupy the kingdom in force, or with warlike arms pursue the fugitive?

ACHITOPHEL. Iam fatigat[a]m gravi plebem labore recrea:
refice defessum molesta ac aspera populum via.
In parentem incerta plebis corda confirma cito.
Varia vulgi saepe mutatur rudis sententia:
vt nigrantes ventus in diversa nymbos discutit,
efficiunt sic vulgus incertis sedere sedibus
hinc metus, hinc favor. Levi momento aguntur mobiles:
ergo primum regna fortis vacua victor posside,
militumque iam vacillantes tibi animos attrahe,
nec sinas torpore mentes fluctuare turbidas.
Consilium postea quieti, de parente inibimus.
ABSALOM. Omnes capacem validi in vrbem invadite:
arcem tenete destinatam principi.
Cuncta sollertes loca inquirite: domos scrutemini
singulas, vsquam doli ne collocentur callidi,
ne fuga eliciant citata in insidias improvidos.
Tum cavas furtim cavernas excutite omnes st[r]ennui.
Mox profundas opere vestigate fossas sedulo,
vt ademptis prorsus malis tuti ingrediamur fraudibus.
Quid ocyus iussa haec dubitatis exequi?
Dic, qua vagantes plebis animi mobilis
mecum in patrem ratione firmari queant?
ACHITOP[HEL]. Largis avidae mentes capiuntur premijs:
levis labor erit quem sequuntur munera,
promptos opum spes efficit vel desides,
optata curas pellit affluentia.
Ad quod nefas non dulce lucrum perpulit?

34. fatigat[a]m] fatigatum *MS* || **39.** sedibus] ⟨ ⟨de⟩ sedibus || **47.** sollertes] ⟨ seduli | scrutemini] ?⟨ scrutamini || **50.** st[r]ennui] strnennui *MS* (*scribal*) || **51.** vestigate fossas] ⟨ fo [*fossas] vestigate || **54.** mobilis] ⟨ concitae ||

ACHITOPHEL. For the present, rest your rank and file, wearied from heavy toil; revive your people, exhausted from the dangerous and hard journey. Quickly confirm against your father the unstable hearts of the commoners. The wavering sentiments of the rude mob are often changed: as the wind disperses black clouds in different directions, so on the one hand fear and on the other favor cause the common herd to be irresolute. They are fickle and are swayed for small cause. Therefore first take possession of the empty kingdom as a mighty conqueror, and win over to your cause the now vacillating minds of the soldiers; and do not allow their minds, once aroused, to waver with listlessness. Later, when we are at leisure, we will take up a plan concerning your father.

ABSALOM [To his people]. All ye valiant men, invade this great city; take this citadel destined for your leader. Warily investigate all places. Search all the homes, lest some ingenious tricks be devised and lest their hasty flight lure us unawares into an ambush. Then all of you diligently hunt out privily dug hideouts. Immediately and with diligent labor discover any deep trenches. Thus, when all evil treacheries are removed, we may go forward safely.

[The soldiers stand in uncertainty]

Why don't you follow these orders immediately?

[The soldiers go out]

[To Achitophel] Tell me how the wavering minds of the fickle mob can be strengthened toward me and against my father.

ACHITOPHEL. Greedy minds are won with great liberality: labor is light if followed by rewards. Anticipation of wealth makes even the lazy eager; hoped-for affluence disperses doubts. To what deed has sweet lucre failed to incite?

Ergo se quae civium fortuna restat aedibus,
ea sit fructuosa avaris praeda iam centurrijs.
Praebe iam gustum rapinarum, novae victoriae [*fol. 15r*]
fructum: sciant futura belli praemia,
quibus cito stomacha incitabis fervida.
Quam in bella divitijs rapiuntur ebrij!
Hijs in scelus quodvis retrudes artibus.
ABSALOM. Assentior. Cupidos beabunt munera
grata et malum quodcumque persuadent nefas:
optata cunctis iam patebunt premia,
et singuli fructus laborum perferent.
Attamen periculis veremur vt fidi sient:
de mente certi, de fide incerti sumus.
Hec iam sapientia tua mihi expedi.
ACHITOP[HEL]. Magnus parenti affectus est cum liberis,
nec ira temere concita est durabilis,
sed saepe parva occasione extinguitur;
natura saepe plus potens iniurias
conterit acerbas et recipit in gratiam:
pietas premit iras vsque recurrens noxias.
Hoc turba solum facta segnior timet:
hic suspiciosus corda refrenat metus.
Verentur (ira deposita iam mutuo,
iterum reducta pristina concordia)
illi impiae vt defectionis sint rei
et det nefandi turba penas criminis.

61. se quae] ⟨ quae iam || **62.** centurrijs] ⟨ centurijs || **63.** gustum rapinarum] ⟨ rapina [*rapinarum gustum] || **64.** fructum: sciant futura [*pn. emended*]] ⟨ fructum futurum, sciant || **65.** cito] ⟨ cito (*canceled, then rewritten*) || **68.** Assentior] ?⟨ Assentio⟨ ⟩ || **72.** Attamen . . . sient] ⟨ Sed periculis [⟨ pr] veremur valde fidi [?⟨ t⟨ ⟩] ne sient || **82.** metus] ⟨ timor || **85.** illi impiae vt . . . sint rei] ⟨ ne turba tum . . . sit rea ||

Thus, whatever of the citizens' fortune remains in the temples, let it now be profitable loot for my greedy companies.[2] Now gratify their taste for plunder, the fruit of a recent victory. Let them know the rewards of war which will be theirs, and with these rewards you will quickly arouse their hot desires. When men are drunk with riches, how they are rushed into wars! By these arts you will induce them into any crime at all.

ABSALOM. Done. Pleasing rewards will make the covetous happy and will inspire them to any evil deed. The desired booty now will stand open to them all, and everyone will carry off the fruits of his labors. However, I fear that they won't be faithful in times of danger: though certain of their disposition, I am uncertain of their reliability. Now, in your wisdom, advise me about this.

ACHITOPHEL. Great is the affection of children for a parent; and their anger, though casually aroused, is not lasting, but is often quenched at the slightest opportunity. Nature, often more powerful, wipes away their harsh injuries and restores natural feelings. Loyalty, ever recurring, suppresses their harmful angers. The mob is made somewhat hesitant only by this; it is afraid, and this suspicious fear restrains their hearts. They fear that, if sometime your anger is mutually put aside and the old concord once again restored, they will be held guilty of impious treason and the mob will pay the penalties for this heinous crime.

[2] Here as elsewhere Watson's terms for the soldiers are Roman. But in the advice to loot the temples, which is not in the Bible, the Romanist Watson was possibly incorporating a bitter topical allusion to the rape of the monasteries which accompanied the Reformation.

ABSALOM. Ver sordido iungetur autumno prius,
torrida nymbosae brumae miscebitur aestas,
foecunda spumoso mari surget seges,
conveniet pelago furibundus ventus amaro,
ab axe frigido tepens flabit notus,
cum pecore muto placida pax erit lupis
quam sit odioso cum parente gratia.
Nec vlla feruorem hora lenibit meum
nec hoc odium vllum comprimet tempus: patris
in perniciem segnis magis accendit mora.
ACHITOPHEL. Haec cuncta norunt, sed vacillant interim,
et de exitu incerti dubia pendent fide.
Sin corda tecum firmiora iam velis,
est caede maius aliquod audendum scelus.
Semper sceleribus scelera firmantur novis.
Quin aliud audes facinus atrocissimum?
Vetera satis non sunt: novum attenta nefas,
pacem vt penitus cum patre desperent bonam.
ABSALOM. Quid caede pessima gravius dici potest?
Et iam patrem regno, bonis, honoribus,
vita quoque spoliamus. Hijs gravius potest
patrare quisquam? Haec non videntur maxima?
Si maius agnoscis, doce: faciam lubens.
ACHITOPHEL. Si vera nobis fama venit credulis,
servant relictam concubinae regiam,
et praeda sola sunt fugatis caeteris.
Ergo torum stupro paternum pollue:
tecum palam commisceantur ordine.

88. brumae] ‹ bre || **89.** mari] ‹ e mari || **93.** gratia.] gratia *MS* || **95.** vllum . . . tempus: patris [*pn. emended*]] ‹ vnquam . . . tempus meum || **97** (Haec . . . norunt). *Printed in Boas* || **98.** pendent] ?‹ pendunt ?*Read* pendunt || **102.** Quin . . . audes] ‹ Aliquod aude | atrocissimum?] atrocissimum, *MS* ?*Read* atrocissimum. || **103.** novum . . . nefas] ‹ gravius novum aggredi || **105.** dici] ‹ dice [?*diceri *by error*] || **106-107.** bonis, honoribus,/ vita] ‹ domo, vita, bonis/ (*revised before next line was started*) || **108.** quisquam?] ?‹ quisquam, || **110.** *Added after l. 115 for insertion here* || **113.** torum] ?‹ ⟨p⟩ || **114.** commisceantur] ‹ commiss ||

ABSALOM. Sooner shall spring be united with barren autumn, hot summer be mated with cloudy winter, a fertile cornfield spring up from the frothy main, a raging wind come in from a calm sea, the warm south wind blow from the frigid north, and a placid peace exist between wolves and a tranquil flock than I shall have a reconciliation with my hateful father. No season will temper my heat, no lapse of time will curb this hatred; the slow delay inflames me even more toward the death of my father.

ACHITOPHEL. All this they know, but they are uneasy for all that, and, uncertain of the outcome, they remain of doubtful loyalty. But if you wish their hearts to be firmer toward you now, you must dare a crime greater than murder. Crimes are always confirmed by new crimes. Why not dare another atrocity, the worst? The old ones aren't sufficient; try a new wickedness, so that your people will completely despair of a reconciliation with your father.

ABSALOM. What can be called worse than the most heinous kind of murder? Even now we strip my father of his kingdom, his goods, his honors, even his life. Can anyone commit something graver than these? Do these not seem the greatest? If you know a worse one, teach me; I will gladly do it.

ACHITOPHEL. If a true report has come to me — and I believe it — the concubines are living in the deserted palace,[3] and they are the only prizes left, since everyone else has been put to flight. Then defile your father's bed with debauchery; make them lie with you publicly, one after another.

[3] "And the king went forth, and all his household on foot. And the king left ten women his concubines to keep the house" (*2 Kings* xv.16).

Quid iam nefandos concubitus pius times?
Quid membra quatiunt, artus et stringit rigor? *[fol. 15v]*
Num denuo priora abhorres conscius?
Non animus ad flagitia adhuc obduruit?
ABSALOM. Quamvis torum impia patris libidine
fedare dicatur scelus gravissimum,
si quid tamen manaret inceptis boni
pulso vel hoc pudore conflarem scelus.
ACHITOP[HEL]. Tam enorme, foedum, immane, crudele, improbum
perhibetur vt de pace desperent nova:
extincta credent prorsus omnes foedera.
Penitus erit praerepta spes concordiae,
tecum in patrem omnium manus firmabitur:
auspicia prompti tua sequentur singuli,
tuti imperio quodcumque patrabunt tuo.
ABSALOM. Haec inscio recte populo possunt agi.
ACHITOP[HEL]. At quae videntur propalam movent magis:
testes oculi sunt firmiores auribus.
Iubebis aedito domus solario
regi statim regale tentorium erigi,
quo cuncta factum plebs videat nefarium.
Tum perpetuas credet inimicitias fore.
ABSALOM. Quin iam violamus patrios thalamos stupro?
Non est morandum, iam esse factum oportuit. [Exeunt]

120. dicatur] ⟨ dicitur || **121.** quid] ⟨ quod || **126.** Penitus] ⟨ Omnis || **127.** manus firmabitur] ⟨ roborabitur manus || **129.** tuti . . . tuo] ⟨ quodcumque tuti vno patrabunt verbulo || **130.** agi.] agi *MS* || **133.** aedito = edito || **134.** tentorium erigi] ⟨ tentori⟨um ——fog⟩ (*the final reading is written in a dark erasure stain and is underscored*) || **135.** nefarium *is underscored* || **136.** credet] ⟨ crede⟨nt⟩ || **137.** stupro?] ?*Read* stupro! || **138.** esse factum] ⟨ violatum | S.d.] *Om. MS* | *Beneath the line a score apparently marking the end of the scene, but perhaps indicating ten lines (eight of verse and two in the next heading) beneath the last such mark*

Now why do you piously fear these wicked intimacies? Why do your limbs quake and rigor stiffen up your joints? What, do you newly shudder scrupulously at your earlier deeds? Hasn't your spirit by now become hardened to shameful acts?

ABSALOM. Although defilement of my father's bed with impious lust be called the gravest of crimes, yet, if any good would proceed from such undertakings, I would perform even this crime, ignoring the shame.

ACHITOPHEL. So gross, wicked, dreadful, cruel, and monstrous is this deed regarded that the people will despair of a new reconciliation; all will thenceforth believe that the bonds are broken. Their deep-rooted apprehension of a reconciliation will have been plucked away; the hands of everyone will be made resolute for your cause and against your father. They will all eagerly follow your commands; being safe, they will do anything by your command.

ABSALOM. These things can be done effectively without the knowledge of the people.[4]

ACHITOPHEL. But those things which are seen openly are the more moving: the eyes are more reliable witnesses than the ears. Give order that on the sunny top of the house a royal tent be set up at once for the king, so that all the rout might see the nefarious deed performed.[5] Then they will believe that your enmity will be perpetual.

ABSALOM. Well, why not violate my father's couches with defilement? There must be no delay; it must be done at once.[6]

[They go into Jerusalem]

[4] Apparently Absalom intends *inscio* to mean "without the *firsthand* knowledge of." Or perhaps he means *populo* to suggest, not his soldiers as usually, but the nonmilitary (and uncommitted?) general populace.

[5] In fulfillment of Nathan's prophecy (*2 Kings* xii.11), this part of which David did not tell Joab about in II.2.

[6] Absalom still religiously follows the advice of Achitophel, as he had promised he would. Thus, Achitophel still shares the brunt of the villainy with the prince.

[ACTUS TERTIUS.] SCENA SECUNDA.

CHUSAI.

Trimetri Iambici.

CHUSAI. Ô rebus hominum fata semper tristia
cum saeviunt et cum favent aeque mala.
Nulla est penitus mortalium securitas?
Quam cuncta sint caduca iam doctus scio,
quam quodque fragile, quam sit aeternum nihil.
O conditor, iam numen appello tuum.
Tuane nobis hec veniunt potentia?
Istec invltus scelera fers ac misericors?
Quam lentus vltione crudeli abstines?
Te regis invictus animus moveat boni!
Sortem sibi benignus vt fert asperam!
Vt sustinet et adversa patitur omnia!
Nam nuper ex itinere fact[o] obviam
excelsum olivae qua teretes montem tegunt,
perculsus amici calamitate flebili,
eius gravi permotus infortunio
cuius salutem praefero vitae propriae,
tantas miserias impatienter perferens,
non potui aperto temperare affectui.
Non impetum poteram tenere fervidum
quin se genas fund[a]nt rigantes lachrimae,
et vda tingunt ora manantes mihi. *[fol. 16r]*
Maeror tepentem possidet vultum gravis:
vestem violenta sordidam trivi manu,

III.2.s.h.] Scena. 2ª. *MS* || *P.h. and m.h. reversed in MS* || **6.** appello] ⟨ attestor || **9.** crudeli] ⟨ vindice || **10.** boni!] boni. *MS* || **10-50.** *Lines marked in groups of ten (starting from l. 1) with scores beneath ll. 10, 20, and 40 and dots beside 30 and 50. For continuation of the numbering see note at III.3.6-336* || **12.** et] ⟨ vt | omnia] ?⟨ i || **13.** ex] ⟨ et | fact[o]] factus *MS* || **21.** se] ⟨ mihi | fund[a]nt] fundunt *MS* (⟨ rumpunt) ||

[ACT III.] SCENE 2.

[The Outskirts of Jerusalem.][1]

[Enter] CHUSAI.

CHUSAI. O, in human affairs, destiny is always disagreeable, equally bad when it rages and when it favors. Is there utterly no freedom from care for mortals? I know from experience how fleeting all things are and how fragile, how nothing is eternal. O Founder, now I call upon Thy will. Is it by Thy power that these things come to us? Dost Thou unavenged and even pitying suffer these crimes? How dost Thou unconcerned refrain from cruel revenge? Let the unconquered soul of the good king move Thee! How he bears benignly a fortune harsh to himself! How he tolerates and endures all these adversities! For recently, after a trip made to meet him where the smooth olives cover the high mountain,[2] I was dejected by the lamentable catastrophe of my friend and deeply moved by the grave misfortune of him whose safety I prefer to my own life. Abiding such great miseries impatiently, I could not restrain myself from open emotion. I could not contain my hot passion, that the tears would not pour down my cheeks; flowing down they wetted my damp lips. Heavy sadness took possession of my flushed face. I tore my soiled clothes with a violent hand,

[1] The conversation between David and Chusai reported in this scene occurs in a very similar form at *2 Kings* xv.32-36. But the soliloquy by Chusai is of Watson's invention: according to *2 Kings* xv.37, after his meeting with David, "Chusai the friend of David went into the city."

[2] Mount Olivet, which lies a few miles directly east of Jerusalem.

et horridum atro cinere foedavi caput.
At ipse maesto me ore lugentem videns,
"Quid te," inquit, "ô fidelis amice, conficis?
Cur te malis caussa mea afflictas modis?
Punit deus, non perdit; abiectos premit,
non opprimit; miseros cruciat, non dissipat:
est mitis in poenas deus culpabiles,
eius leve quidem corripientis est onus:
dulce nimium noli iugum deponere.
Haec fortiter prompti feramus omnia.
Hic me relicto, saevum adibis filium
(me nil iuvare poteris): eius abdita
animi erues secreta, pro sapientia
tua potes consilio Achitophel malo
resistere, tum quodcumque rex decreverit
vterque statim factus sacerdos certior
per filios nobis renunciet suos."
Hec fatus, huc efferre nolentem pedem
coëgit. Vtinam tanta mentis, consili,
[s]apientiae esset vena, vt astu vel dolo
possem rebellionis authorem trucis
fraudum laqueis circumvenire debitis.
Sed haec potens omnia deus daturus est:
recto eius vnius regimur arbitrio.
Sed luctus, aegritudo, squalor, lachrimae,
et maesta ponenda est facies: vultus mihi
simulandus est hilaris quibusvis artibus
vt me novo possem insinuare principi. [Exit]

27-41. *Quotes om. MS* || **29.** perdit] ⟨ perdet | abiectos] ⟨ cul [*culpatos *or* culpabiles] || **29-30.** perdit; abiectos premit, non opprimit; miseros cruciat,] perdit, [?] abiectos premit non opprimit, miseros cruciat *MS* (⟨ perdit abiectos, premit non opprimit miseros, cruciat) || **33.** dulce nimium noli] ⟨ noli dulce nimium || **36.** eius] ⟨ ist⟨i⟩c || **39.** tum] ⟨ et *or* et tum || **44.** [s]apientiae] fapientiae *MS* (*scribal*) (?⟨ c) || **51.** est hilaris] ⟨ hilaris est || **52.** S.d.] *Om. MS*

and I dirtied my shaggy head with black ash.[3] But, seeing me lamenting with a sad expression, he said, "Why destroy yourself, faithful friend? Why do you vex yourself on my behalf in this terrible way? God punishes but does not destroy. He presses hard on the abject, but does not crush them. He torments the wretched, but does not shatter them. God is gentle when it comes to blameworthy punishments; when He reproaches, the burden is light indeed. Do not put off His very sweet yoke. Let us eagerly and bravely bear all these things. Leave me here, for you can avail me nothing; go to my fierce son; elicit the hidden secrets of his mind. Out of your wisdom you can combat the evil counsel of Achitophel. Then, whatever the king decides, immediately inform one of my two priests; through their sons they will relay it to me."[4] So saying, he ordered me to make my reluctant way here.

Would that there were in me such a vein of intelligence, counsel, and wisdom that by cunning or trickery I might entrap the author of this savage rebellion in deserved snares of deception. But all these qualities God almighty will grant; we are ruled by the just will of Him alone. But sorrow, grief, mourning appearance,[5] tears, and sad countenance must be put aside; I must pretend a happy face, by whatever arts I can, so that I may ingratiate myself with the new ruler.

[He goes into Jerusalem]

[3] Signs of mourning. See *2 Kings* xv.32; cf. *2 Kings* iii.31.

[4] The priests are Sadoc and Abiathar; their sons Achimaas and Jonathan.

[5] Literally, "filthiness"; cf. n. 3. Cooper's *Thesavrvs* (s.v. "Squalor") cited Cicero, Quintilian, Apuleius, and "Metellus ad Ciceronem" for this meaning and suggested the translations "The mourning estate" or "Mourning countenance."

[ACTUS TERTIUS.] SCENA TERTIA.

ABSALOM. CHUSAI. ACHITOPHEL.

Senarij.

ABSALOM. Quis orbe vasto regnat aequalis mihi?
Nunc vota prosperis satur implevi mea:
sublime patris teneo nunc solium senis,
et turba nostro obedit famularis nutui.
Quid restat? Animum abunde placavi meum —
Non est satis: adhuc vivit infestus pater.
Quam sanguineo letarer eius funere.
Non tuta pulso regna rex teneo metu.
CHUSAI. Regem suus invictum veneratur servulus
et ad genua prosternitur clementia.
O festa servo optata mihi semper dies,
gnatus patri qua regna succedit tenens!
Eterna felici opto regi tempora,
regni quietum semper expeto statum.
Rex multa magnus secla vivat integer, [*fol. 16v*]
cui opto meliora quam patri charissimo.
Sedem deus confirmet aeternum tuam.
ABSALOM. Hanc candido refers amico gratiam?
Et patriae et patris dolose proditor,
num deficere te rebus adversis amor
verus docuit? Fortuna amicitiam gravis
diremit? Assentator es vilis. Patrem
cur deseris fidum tibi semper, transfuga?
Cur nunc parenti ingratus ad me deficis?

III.3.s.h.] Scena. 3ª. *MS* || *P.h. and m.h. reversed in MS* || **5.** restat?] restat, *MS* | Animum] ⟨ Anim⟨o⟩ | meum—] meum *MS* || **6-336.** *Beneath l. 6 a score marking ten lines from the last mark, at III.2.50 (counting eight verse lines and two lines of headings [equivalent, not incl. blank space]). Through l. 336 every tenth line is marked with a score or a dot, alternately. (Line 55 is marked with a dot because it is ten lines below l. 46 in the physical order of the MS; see note ad loc.) Beside l. 206 Watson wrote the number* 20. *A small mark at l. 211 was canceled, as was another at l. 254. The count is interrupted after l. 336 (see notes at III.3.345 and 385). A new count begins in Act IV (see note at IV.1.10-60)* || **10.** prosternitur] ⟨ provolvitur || **12.** regna] ⟨ re [*regna] regna (*perhaps scribal; possibly Watson started to change the word, then restored it; or if, as it appears, there is another letter beneath the canceled* r [?*an* o], *perhaps Watson began a different word, then started to write* regna *over it, but rewrote it for clarity*) | tenens!] tenens. *MS* || **13.** felici opto] ⟨ magno exopto || **14.** regni] ⟨ regna || **20-21.** rebus . . . verus] ⟨ verus . . . rebus || **22.** Assentator es vilis] ⟨ Adulator es levis (?) ⟨ Adulator levis ||

[ACT III.] SCENE 3.

[Jerusalem. The Royal Palace.][1]

[Enter] ABSALOM [and] ACHITOPHEL [from One Direction and] CHUSAI [from Another. ABSALOM Seats Himself on the Throne. ACHITOPHEL and CHUSAI Stand Apart.]

ABSALOM [Aside]. Who in the wide world rules as the equal of me? Now sated with prosperity I have fulfilled my vows: I now hold the high throne of my old father, and the crowd of servants obeys my nod. What is left? I have abundantly pleased my spirit— No, it is not enough: my hated father still lives. How I would be pleased by his bloody pyre! Though king, I do not hold safe dominion with fear expelled.

[CHUSAI Comes Forward and Falls Prostrate before ABSALOM.]

CHUSAI. His Majesty's humble servant venerates the unconquerable king and prostrates himself at his knees for mercy. O happy day, a day which this servant has always eagerly desired, the day on which the son succeeds his father in the seat of empire! May the king have everlasting prosperity; may the condition of his kingdom be ever peaceful.[2] May the great king live hale for many ages. May his lot be better than was his very dear father's. May God strengthen thy throne forever.

ABSALOM. Is this the thanks you return to an honest friend? You treacherous betrayer of both my fatherland and father, has true love taught you to defect in hard times? Has his grave fortune destroyed your friendship? You are a vile toady. Deserter, why do you forsake my father, who was always faithful to you? Why do you now, thankless to my father, desert to me?

[1] The opening speech, from Seneca, shows Absalom developed into an arrogant usurper. The dramatist then introduces Chusai's meeting with Absalom, including Absalom's rebuke, from *2 Kings* xvi.16-19. But, as stated in the Introduction, the material is consolidated as to its incidents and greatly expanded in dialectic.

[2] That is, long live the king. Literally, "I desire that time be eternal for the happy king; I long for an ever peaceful status of his kingdom."

CHUSAI. Ne spernat abiectum precor rex optimus.
Dum mihi tenuis vsura lucis suppetat,
dum corpus hoc vitae tueatur spiritus,
subiectus illi vni libenter serviam
quem dominus et plebs tota regno praeficit.
Est charus ille, patria tamen est charior:
non regi ego quantumvis amicum preferam,
privatus vsque est post habendus principi.
Iam tota praefectura delata est tibi,
hoc auspicijs latum imperium exurgit tuis.
Regni deus tibi has habenas contulit.
Tibi ergo eandem quam patri obstringo fidem,
totum obsequio me promptus addicam tuo.
Quem elegit vniversus Israel ego
solus relinquam contumax, vanus, miser?
Nec in aliam regnum domum traducitur,
sed filius idem haeres paternus obtinet.
Quid est igitur quod quis merito succenseat?
Quodcumque divino obtigit beneficio,
id recte alacres laetis feramus mentibus.
Mecum vt patri necessitudo arctissima
fuit, ita servus filio fidissimus
ero. Nulla fraus est: simplicitas est candida.
Ne, oro, repellas pedibus abiectum tuis.
ABSALOM. Crudelitas regno minime obtento decet:
tum nemo suspicione damnari potest.
Prodesse miseris: magnificum hoc reges habent.

25. precor rex optimus] ⟨ rex o [*optimus] precor || **27.** dum . . . spiritus] ⟨ communis hic dum me regat vitae spiritus || **33.** delata] ⟨ collata || **35.** contulit.] contulit *MS* || **38-41, 45-47.** *Printed in Boas* || **44.** feramus] ⟨ feran⟨du⟩m || **47.** simplicitas est candida] ⟨ sed rudis simplicitas ||

CHUSAI. I pray that the very good king will not spurn me in my abjection. So long as any little use of the light of day remains to me, so long as this body maintains a breath of life, I shall freely serve as a subject to him alone whom the Lord and all the people set over the kingdom. Your father is dear, but my country is dearer: I would not place a friend, however dear, above the king; a private citizen must always be held secondary to the ruler. Now the whole government has been delivered to you; this vast realm rises to your commands. God has conferred these reins of government upon you. To you, therefore, I owe the same allegiance as before I owed to your father. Entirely to your service I do readily dedicate myself. Whom all Israel has chosen shall I alone — obstinate, vain, and wretched — reject? Not to a different house has the reign been transferred; no, the father's heir, indeed his son, succeeds to it. What is there, then, that anyone could justifiably find fault with? Whatever has happened under divine blessing we should, to be proper, bear eagerly and with happy spirits. As my relationship with the father was very close, so to the son will I be a most faithful servant. This is no trick: it is simple truth. Do not, I pray you, repel me abject at your feet.

ABSALOM. When a kingdom is scarcely secured, cruelty is fitting, for then no one can be done an injustice in suspicion. But kings have this sublime purpose: to aid the wretched.

Hec vera laus est nulla quam rapiet dies.
Quamvis mihi timendus appares, tamen
nolo superbo miserias premere pede.
Nolo genuis calcare prostratos meis,
sed misericors dictis fidem adiungo tuis,
et supplicem te protegam fido lare.
Tua modo non suspecta sit deinceps fides. [*fol. 17r*]
CHUS[AI]. Hanc tibi animam, o rex, iure mancipatam habes.
Ne mors quidem caussa vnquam acerba erit tua.
ABSALOM. Procede, prudens splendidi regni comes:
de proelio quod consilium tardus dabis?
Paternum avara iam sitit mens sanguinem,
nec amplius penas cruentas deferet.
ACHITOPHEL. Languet mora brevi solutus impetus,
nec pristinas laxus semel vires tenet.
Illud bene fit quicquid suo fit tempore.
Tum longiores quo fugienti das moras,
eo indies hic redditur securior,
nam tempus interim putatur remedium.
Id ergo mature facias si quid facis
fessae via dum dissipantur copiae.
Nec tota plebs hoc proelio vexabitur,
nec regia nunc erit opus presentia:
paucis ego sumptis virorum millibus
parvaque stipatus corona militum,
hac nocte passibus fugientem persequar
longis, et opprimam parato exercitu.

53. mihi timendus] ⟨ t⟨i⟩m [*timendus] mihi || **55.** *Added after l. 56 for insertion here* || **59.** Chus[ai]] ⟨ Achitophel (*changed before ll. 59-60 were written, which were never intended for Achitophel, for whom they are inappropriate*) || **62.** dabis] ⟨ capis || **63.** Paternum] ⟨ Cruentum || **65-71.** *Printed in Boas* || **66.** laxus] ?⟨ laxa [*laxas] || **69.** indies = in dies (*Boas' reading*) || **73-74.** *Written after l. 75 and marked for insertion here* ||

This is truly praiseworthy policy which no coming day will wipe out. Although you seem worthy of my fear, yet I do not wish to trample on your miseries with a haughty foot. I do not wish to tread upon those who prostrate themselves before my knees. Rather, pitying, I place trust in your words, and I shall protect you, as you plead, in my trusted retinue. But let your loyalty, in turn, be above suspicion.

CHUSAI. My life you have, O King, delivered up to you by my oath. Not even death for your sake will ever be harsh.

[He withdraws to a side of the throne room]

ABSALOM [To Achitophel]. Come forward, wise companion of my splendid rule.

[ACHITOPHEL Comes Forward.]

What counsel do you belatedly give concerning the battle? My greedy mind still thirsts for my father's blood and will no longer put off the bloody punishments.

ACHITOPHEL. Passion, once loosed, languishes after a short delay and, once relaxed, does not retain its former strength. Whatever is done in its season is done well. Thus, the longer the delays you give the fugitive, the safer he is rendered day by day, for meanwhile time is regarded as a healer. Therefore, if you do anything, you should do it quickly while his troops are scattered, weary from their journey. And not all the people will be bothered with this battle, nor will your royal presence now be required: I shall gather a few thousand men and, accompanied by this small band of soldiers, shall this very night pursue the fleeing enemy with forced marches, and I shall put him down with my ready army.

Iam lassa servi membra singuli trahunt,
iam plurima omnes languidi sunt de via.
Dulcem quietem potius exoptant fera
quam bella: somnus marte fessis gratior.
Cladem fuga iam non opinantur gravem,
cunctique turbato gradiuntur ordine.
Tum facta nostrorum repente excursio,
continuo in hostes imparatos irruens,
populum cruenta strage terrebit levem,
et plaga dissipabit a tergo data.
Hic praecipiti fuga saluti consulet,
ille arduis fugiens latebit montibus,
pars dura foveis fata depellent cavis,
alij reversis in fugientes vultibus
sese esse nostrarum simulabunt partium:
plebs vniversa se in trepidam dabit fugam.
Rex, auxilio iam prorsus orbatus bono,
facile avidas in hostium veniet manus.
Hoc ense cogam animam nocentem ponere:
ferro gravi transfossus efflabit cadens.
Dispersa plebs, tanquam veniente grex lupo
pastore mortuo, locis passim vagis
seclusa, placato hoste cito reducitur.
Improvidi est plebem ferire innoxiam: [*fol. 17v*]
non arma sponte sed coacta sustulit,
nec tu populum omnem sed rebellem queritas.
Tuis pater ceptis resistit vnicus:

85. Tum] ?⟨ Tam || **90.** arduis . . . montibus] ⟨ arduis semet ⟨pre⟩ fugiens latebit | latebit] ⟨ latebet (*scribal*) || **91.** dura foveis fata] ⟨ fata speluncis ||

Now his every servant drags his tired limbs along; now they are all weak from too much travel.[3] Sweet rest they desperately desire rather than fierce battles; to the exhausted, sleep is more pleasing than war. Now, in flight, they do not expect severe disaster, and they are all moving in disorder. Thus, the sally of our men, suddenly made and abruptly falling upon the unprepared enemy, will terrify the lightly armed people in a cruel slaughter, and the blow delivered from their rear will scatter them. One man will look for safety in headlong flight; another, fleeing, will hide in the rugged mountains; some in hollow caves will ward off harsh death; others, with their faces turned backward among the fleeing, will pretend that they are of our faction. The whole rout will give themselves to fearful flight. The king, now utterly deprived of effective help, will easily fall into the eager hands of his enemies. With this sword I will force him to lay down his noxious life; he will fall and breathe his last, transfixed by my heavy sword. A dispersed mob, scattered without order in uncertain positions, like a flock whose shepherd is dead when a wolf is coming, is readily led forth when its enemy is placated. It is unwise to strike out at the blameless rank and file: not by choice, but under force do they bear arms. And you seek, not the entire populace, but the one rebel. Your father alone resists your efforts;

[3] "And the king and all the people with him came weary, and refreshed themselves" at Bahurim after the incident with Semei (*2 Kings* xvi.14); see n. 5.

hunc queris vnum, pace redeant caeteri
a te data, nam lenitate vel impios
vinces. Minime proterva victorem decet
saevitia: alios virtute vinces mascula,
teipsum domabis nobili clementia.
De te quid iniqui posteri dicant vide:
vivax ob hoc bene iudicabit memoria,
haec mitia statim exempla sument posteri,
haec clara laus nullo peribit seculo.

ABSALOM. Divina me responsa iam audire arbitror.
Mihi visus est hic sermo prudentissimus.
Iam video sparsam caede plebem pallida,
turmas fugatas et cavernis abditas.
Parentis obversatur ante oculos rubens
sanguis, nocenti et a iugulo abscissum caput,
populique reduces pace servati mea.
Accinctus hoc salubre consilium exequar.
At re gravi alios consulere sapientis est.
Tentare multos forsitan erit vtile.
Prodeat amicus patris olim candidus,
nunc hostis insolens futurus, Chusaï.
Parvam repente hic suadet armandam manum
cuius erit illeipse imperator strennuus:
qua continuo illum persequendum duxerit,
solum et relictum plebe dispersa opprimet,
quo mortuo salvos reducet caeteros.
Rectene nobis an secus dictum putas?

108. Minime proterva] ⟨ Proterva minime || **111.** iniqui] ⟨ i⟨n?⟩ ⟨ aeque | vide:] vide *MS* || **115.** me] ⟨ mihi | arbitror] ⟨ a⟨ e?⟩ || **119.** rubens] ⟨ trucis || **121.** mea] ⟨ aurea || **125.** Prodeat . . . candidus] *Stages of revision prob. somewhat as follows:* ⟨ Amice patris olim candide (*defective*) ⟨ Huc olim [⟨ Olim] amicus patris at nunc proditor ⟨ Prodi [*Proditor] (*line unfinished*) || **126.** Chusaï] ⟨ vndique ||

him alone you seek. Let the others return under a truce granted by you, for by lenity you shall win over even the disloyal. Violent cruelty befits a conqueror not at all. Others you shall conquer with manly strength; yourself you shall overcome with noble clemency. Consider what an unfavorable posterity will say about you: enduring memory will judge you well because of this. These unharsh examples posterity will continually bring forward; this noble statesmanship will never die.

ABSALOM. I think I am now hearing divine answers. This speech has seemed to me to be very wise. Now I see a mob scattered in slaughter which makes them pale with fright. I see troops put to flight and concealed in caves. The red blood of my father, his head cut off from his wicked neck, and the people saved and brought back under my peace — these things hover before my eyes. Thus armed, I shall follow this sound advice.

But in an important matter it is the part of wisdom to consult others. It will perhaps be useful to examine several people. Let Chusai come forth, that once honest friend of my father who is now, unwontedly, about to be his enemy.

[CHUSAI Comes Forward Again.]

[To Chusai] Achitophel persuades me that a small band should be armed at once, of which he himself will be the valiant commander. With it he will forthwith conduct the pursuit of David; will overwhelm him, who is alone and bereft, his people now scattered; and, when David is dead, will lead back the others safe. Do you think he has spoken to me well or not?

CHUSAI. Primum hoc tua rex clementia sentiat velim:
fido profectum id corde quicquid dixero.
Aliâs dedit consilia semper optima,
hoc etsi amici sit tamen est improvidi.
Non martis ancipitem exitum considerat,
nec subdolas patris vigilis astutias
nec multiformem militum experientiam.
Tum nec latentes noctis insidias videt.
Non callidum "parva manu" patrem "opprimet."
Secum viros armis habet fortissimos
priusque semper proelio vsos prospero.
Vt vrsa partu clam dolo ablato furens
totis oberrat saltibus reconditis [*fol. 18r*]
quaerens dolosum dente furem vindice,
sic acri animosus saeviens bello parens,
manu superbam comparans victoriam,
pulsos in hostes ense grassatur truci.
Numquam hactenus domum redibat copijs
bello fugatis: quin subactis hostibus
spolijs triumphos huc relatis nobiles
victor habuit, tanta est in arte subdolus.
Et mente cu[n]cta perspicaci providet.
Novit videre in longitudinem sagax,
nec nunc media incedit caterva, vt hic putat.
Scit inde quod periculum consurgeret.
Suos relinquit ingruente vespera,
tutus cavis totam locis noctem latet.

134. profectum] ⟨ f [?*factum] || **136.** improvidi] ⟨ improvid⟨o⟩ || **137.** considerat] ⟨ consyderat || **141.** *Quotes om. MS* || **143.** prospero.] prospero *MS* || **144-145.** clam . . . oberrat] ⟨ clam dolo ablato ferox [⟨ suffurato squallida]/ furens oberrat [⟨ furit pererrans] || **146.** quaerens] ⟨ quaerit | vindice] ⟨ vindici || **148.** manu] ⟨ manum || **149.** truci.] ⟨ truci, || **151.** *To the left of the line a canceled mark* (*?an* s) | quin] ⟨ ⟨vni⟩ || **152.** triumphos] ⟨ trium⟨ ⟩ || **153.** subdolus] ?⟨ sub⟨ti⟩ [?*subtilis] || **154.** cu[n]cta] cunncta *MS* (*scribal*) | providet.] providet *MS* || **157.** quod] ⟨ quantum ||

CHUSAI. First, O King, I would wish your Grace to know this: that whatever I say is offered out of a faithful heart. At other times Achitophel has always given the best of advice.[4] But, though this present counsel is that of a friend, it is of an improvident one. He does not take into account the doubtful outcome of war, nor the shrewd tricks of your watchful father nor the wide experience of his soldiers. Again, he does not see the lurking traps of the night. He will not "overwhelm" your clever father with a "small band." With him David has men who are very brave in arms, men formerly accustomed always to victorious battle. As a she-bear whose cubs have been secretly carried off by trickery rambles through all the out-of-the-way forests seeking the treacherous thief, her tooth her avenger, so your parent, fierce and bold in hot battle and with his band of men preparing for a proud victory, moves among your repulsed enemies, his sword inspiring dread. Never up to now has he returned home with troops who have been routed in war. Rather, having put down his enemies and brought the spoils back here, he, the victor, has had noble triumphs, so crafty is he. And with his sharp mind he prepares for all eventualities. He is shrewd and knows how to see into the distant future. He does not, as Achitophel thinks, march in the midst of his troops. He knows whence some danger might arise. He has left his men at the approach of evening, and safe in hollow caves he lies in hiding the whole night.

[4] "Now the counsel of Achitophel, which he gave in those days, was as if a man should consult God. So was all the counsel of Achitophel, both when he was with David, and when he was with Absalom" (*2 Kings* xvi.23).

Vel insidias iam machinatur pervigil.
Tum separabit milites acerrimos
in subsidium secum futuros caeteris.
Alij parati aciem tenebunt fulgidam:
telis venientes eminus iactis petent;
ictum vel ensibus gravem salvi inferent,
vel tela scuto torta propellent cavo.
Si acerba clades instet, excurrent statim
auxilia opem latura, fundent obvios
quoscumque. Franget clamor animos territos,
et strage nostros dissipabunt horrida.
Non ergo parvam est vtile armari manum.
At si meo parere consilio velis,
a Dan populus iam totus vsque Berseba
Iudaicus in turmas glomeretur maximas,
vt numero arena naufragi carens maris.
Nemo tenebris deliteat innoxijs,
nec militiam subterfugiat quisquam asperam.
Optime ita mentes omnium explores vagas:
quis ducitur metu, quis affectu bono?
Tu, magne rex, denso imperabis agmini
nullique committes alij bellum hoc viro —
grave est, et ex hoc omnium pendet salus,
hinc laeta speranda est quies nepotibus.
Haec perpetuum ocium pariet victoria.
Quodsi ille non multo comitatus milite,
vt sperat, incautum subito patrem opprimet,

162. futuros] ⟨ futur⟨i⟩ || **163.** parati aciem] ⟨ aci [*aciem] parati || **164.** eminus iactis] ⟨ vsque con⟨i⟩ectis *or* con⟨v⟩ectis | petent;] petent *MS* || **170.** horrida] ⟨ impia || **173.** Berseba] ⟨ Bers⟨a⟩ba || **179.** bono?] bono. *MS* || **180.** Tu] ⟨ Tu s⟨a⟩ || **182.** grave] ⟨ gravis || **183.** nepotibus.] nepotibus *MS* || **184.** ocium = otium ||

Indeed, ever watchful, he is even now devising traps. Thus, he will separate his fiercest soldiers to be with him as a reserve to the others. Other skilled men will hold the flashing battle line: after they have thrown their spears from a distance, they will seek out the approaching soldiers; either they will deliver a mortal blow with their swords if that is safe, or else they will hurl their javelins from behind their curved shields. If harsh disaster is impending, the auxiliaries will at once rush out to bring assistance and will destroy all who come to meet them. The noise will shatter frightened minds, and they will scatter our men with horrible slaughter. It is therefore not fitting that a small band be armed.

But if you wish to follow my advice, let all the Jewish people from Dan to Bersabee now be assembled into a very large force, as countless as the sand of the ship-wrecking sea. Let no one lie hidden in safe shadows, let no one shun the hard campaign. Your Majesty, you could examine the doubtful minds of all after this fashion: who is led by fear, who by favorable sentiments? You, great King, will command right in the thick of the line and entrust this battle to no other man. It is heavy business, and upon it depends the safety of all. From it is happy peace for our grandchildren to be hoped for. This victory will engender eternal peace.

Assume that, as he hopes, Achitophel, accompanied by only a small detachment, will subdue your father, suddenly caught unawares;

quid rex sua potens faciet presentia, et
iugera frequens mille operiens exercitus?
Vt pluvius vernis cadens ros noctibus
distillat herbis incubans florentibus, [*fol. 18v*]
fallens rudes oculos micante stellula,
pondusque gramen quodque sustentat suum,
numerosa sic coacta nostrorum manus,
quocumque diris hostibus insultans loco,
vt sepe qu[a]dam dens[a] eos circumdabit
et irruens gladijs vorabit singulos:
nec fata quidem vel vnus evadet fera.
Omnes rebelles, intereant omnes simul,
nam lenitas saepe in periculis nocet:
mala est sibi ipsi quae nocet clementia.
Non vtile est salute venari levem
famam neglecta: aura levi melior salus.
Hostes cruenti non capient clementiam:
aut strennui vitam ensibus rapient tuam,
victi aut frementi marte prostrati cadent —
omnis sibi ferro aspero posita est salus.
Qui perfidus tanto hoc fuit periculo
vsque inferendae sit tibi suspectus necis.
Omnes dolori spiritum reddant tuo:
mori iubebis voce perfidos tibi,
et singuli iram hanc sanguine extinguant suo.
Hostes truces servare quae dementia est!

187. presentia, et] ⟨ presentia? || **189-197.** *Printed in Boas* || **191.** fallens] ⟨ falletque | stellula,] ⟨ stellula? || **195.** qu[a]dam dens[a]] quodam denso *MS, Boas* || **200.** sibi ipsi] ⟨ sibipsi || **203.** clementiam:] clementiam *MS* || **204.** strennui vitam ensibus] ⟨ ensibus v [*vitam strennui] || **206.** salus.] salus *MS* || **210.** perfidos] ⟨ suspectos ⟨ sp (*scribal*) || **211.** iram] ⟨ ani [*animum] | suo.] suo *MS* ||

then what will the mighty king accomplish by his presence, and what will a vast army covering a thousand jugers accomplish? Just as the rainy dew falling on spring nights drips down and rests on flowering herbs (deceiving untutored eyes as with a gleaming starlet) and every blade of grass feels the water's weight, so an assembled throng of our men, rushing with force against the dreadful enemies everywhere, will surround them as with a thick fence and falling upon them will destroy them one by one with its swords. Not even one will escape this terrible fate. Since they are all insurgents, let them all die together, for lenience is often harmful in dangerous times; that clemency which harms oneself is evil. It is of no use to seek a shining reputation if one's safety is neglected; safety is better than bright gold. Your bloody enemies will not accept your mercy: either they will rip out your life with their swords if alive, or conquered they will fall prostrated by raging war. The safety of everyone is entrusted to his own fierce sword. Any who have been faithless to you in this time of great peril you should suspect even of plotting your murder. Let all of them surrender their lives to satisfy your distress. You with a word will order those who are dangerous to you to die, and let all of them extinguish your anger with their blood. Save cruel enemies? What madness!

Si consulens vrbem sibi munitam occupet,
vel funibus trahemus obsessam brevi
vel machina excindemus eversam aenea.
Ne parvus vsquam ex vrbe restabit lapis.
Nostris nihil adversum resistet copijs,
sic nemo turmis tutus e nostris cadet:
ille vltimum quovis loco claudet diem.
ABSALOM. Ô quanta levis assentio fert incommoda!
Iam sentio horis neminem sapere omnibus.
Modo gravis persuasit huius dictio.
At nunc levis videtur, hic sapientior,
hic sermo melior est mihique tutior.
Iam intelligo nil parte statuendum altera,
sed consilium frequenter excussum valet.
Libet rogare rursum aliqua succinctius:
hic vniversum suadet Israel, manum
tu consulis parvam, horrida arma sumere.
Quod potius est nos aggredi, nunc expedi.
ACHITOPHEL. Stultum est id aggredi tumultu turbido
quod cito pusilla confici manu potest.
Iam vincitur maerore consumptus pater:
fit impotens, et plurima tabet via. *[fol. 19r]*
Hostilis est dolore fractus spiritus.
Nec plurimo vallatus est exercitu
nec optimo, sed tantum habet quos frigidus
dirae necis protrusit in fugam metus.

213. consulens vrbem] ⟨ vrbem [*vrbem consulens] ⟨ vrs (*scribal*)] || **219.** quovis] ⟨ quocumque || **222.** gravis persuasit] ⟨ persuasit gravis | dictio.] dictio *MS* || **225.** intelligo] ⟨ video || **226** (consilium . . . valet). *Printed in Boas* || **233.** pater:] pater *MS* || **236.** vallatus] ⟨ munitus ||

If David, looking to his safety, takes to a fortified city, we will besiege it and in a short time either pull it down with ropes or smash it, destroying it with a bronze machine. Not a single pebble of the city will remain standing. Nothing will stand against our troops. Likewise, no one will fall down and escape our troops: each will end his final day wherever he is.

ABSALOM. O how many troubles does easy assent suffer! Now I realize that no man is wise all the time. Just now the weighty speech of Achitophel persuaded me. But now it seems worthless, this one wiser. This speech is better and safer for me. Now I know that nothing should be decided from only one point of view; no, that counsel is valuable which is fully examined.

[To Achitophel] I would ask you a few things in turn, quite briefly. Chusai argues that all Israel, you advise that only a small band, should take up terrible arms. Now tell me what is better for us to do.

ACHITOPHEL. It is stupid to attempt with a violent tumult what can quickly be accomplished with a small band. Your father is already overcome, consumed by sorrow; he becomes weak and is wasting away from his long march. His hostile spirit has been broken by his grief. He is defended by neither a very large nor a very good army; no, he has only those whom cold fear of terrible death has put to rout.

Nec tam cito cladem futuram praevidet:
pedes — molestis impeditus sarcinis,
dolens ab animo, pallida enectus fame —
fluenta Iordanis vaga adhuc non transijt.
Quivis equitatu facile diffundet levi.
ABSALOM. Tu fare. Caussae iam tuae dabitur locus.
CHUSAÏ. Dictu facile, sed summus est factu labor.
Stultum est tenui periclitari somnio
quod firma recte conficiet securitas.
Nam saepe coniectura fallit credulos.
Dementis est praeferre certis lubrica.
Non aliter ac si quam manu teneas avem,
eam remittas spe volantis percitus.
Bellum est timendum, varius est martis casus:
pugna esse nimium nemo securus potest.
Sit iam pater dolore confectus, via
tabescat, et fortes remittat spiritus,
vt civium iam habeat solutum exercitum,
vt sint fames, maeror, molestae sarcine:
minime tamen prorsus animum abiecit suum,
nec ensibus palam obvium opponit caput.
Non oscitans vitam hostibus prodit suam.
Fortuna tristis cautiores efficit,
ne rebus, o rex, prosperis sis laxior.
Et quo magis fortuna blanditur procax,
eo tibi sit provido suspectior.

240. impeditus] ⟨ impeditis (*by attraction*) || **243.** Quivis equitatu . . . levi] ⟨ Prope est, equitatus . . . levis || **247.** recte] ⟨ bene || **249-251.** *Printed in Boas* || **250.** quam] ?⟨ qua || **255.** fortes] ⟨ fortis || **257.** sarcine = sarcinae || **260.** oscitans] ⟨ oscitat || **263.** procax] ⟨ tibi ||

Not so readily does he provide for future disaster: his infantry is burdened with heavy packs, pained by anxiety, worn down with the pallor of famine. It has not yet crossed the uncertain waters of the Jordan.[5] Anyone at all will easily scatter it with light cavalry.

ABSALOM [To Chusai]. Now you speak; room will be given for your side.

CHUSAI. This is easy to say, but is the greatest difficulty to perform. It is stupid to endanger by idle dreaming that which suitable precaution will accomplish quite well. For conjecture often deceives the credulous. It is madness to prefer slippery places to sure ones. It is as if you held a bird in your hand and, moved by a hope for one on the wing, you let it go. War is fearful, its outcome uncertain; in a battle no one can be too safe. Grant that your father is weakened by sorrow, that his march is wearing him down, that he is relaxing his strong spirit, that he now has a weak army of civilians, that there are famine, anxiety, heavy packs; yet by no means has he utterly given up his courage, nor does he openly offer his head to our swords. Not listlessly does he yield his life to his enemies. Misfortune makes people more vigilant: thus, O King, you should not be less vigilant in these prosperous times. The more favorable is wanton Fortune, the more you should suspect her, if you are wise.

[5] David has stayed at Bahurim; he "passed over the Jordan" only after receiving intelligence from Sadoc and Abiathar concerning Absalom's plans (*2 Kings* xvii.22); see IV.1. Robinson (p. 192) calls Achitophel's statement another evidence of Watson's awareness of time and place: "We are being reminded . . . of off-stage action and place as well as that of the on-stage representation."

Ne tenuibus credas supinus copijs
quod trans[f]igi turmis oportet maximis:
non est sapientis. Non putaram dicere,
nam desipit qui re iocatur seria:
sic sentio — facienda sunt tuto omnia.
ABSALOM. Potius in hanc peccare partem mavelim,
vt tutus omnia consequar, quam nunc novas
vincentibus creare turbas hostibus.
Consurget armis totus Israel feris,
et integrum iam convocabo exercitum.
Non vereor insidias, dolos, fraudes, locum,
tempus, nec hostem proelio nec turribus
praecinctum ahenaeis. Domabit funditus
iam militum pharetrata multorum manus.
Iacente funestum vrbe mactabo caput.
Hoc constitutum est de faciendo exercitu. *[fol. 19v]*
At de duce varias adhuc sententias
hausi. Quid optimum videtur dic prius.
ACHITOPHEL. Per fata dulcia, perque lucem hanc auream,
per sacra numina, magne princeps, te obsecro
vt et omnium et tuae saluti consulas:
nescis pericula tibi quanta iam imminent,
quantam tibi illud consilium cladem afferet.
Nobis eadem est tecum salus, vita, omnibus:
tuo periclitamur infortunio.
Si certum habeas in bella cunctos trudere
et omnium casum experiri vis simul,

266. trans[f]igi] transsigi *MS* (*scribal*) || **268.** nam . . . seria] ⟨ qui marte desipit iocatur serio || **275.** *Watson twice changed his mind about the order of the series of nouns:* dolos] ⟨ fr [*fraudes] dolos | fraudes] ⟨ l [*locum] fraudes || **276.** hostem] ⟨ hostes || **277.** praecinctum ahenaeis [= aheneis *or* aeneis]] ⟨ cinctus ahenaeis, re (*?unfinished word*) || **279.** Iacente] ⟨ Iacentem || **280.** exercitu.] exercitu *MS* || **285.** et omnium et] ⟨ omnibus et || **288.** eadem] ⟨ eaddem || **291.** et] ⟨ sed | casum . . . simul] ⟨ simul [?⟨ sic] . . . casum (casum *underscored*) ||

Do not carelessly trust to a few men what ought to be carried out by very large forces: it is not wise. I had not intended to say this, for he who jokes about a serious affair[6] is foolish; I feel this way: all things ought to be done safely.

ABSALOM. I would rather err on this side, that I might carry out everything safely, than create new troubles now in enemies to defeat me. All Israel will arise in savage arms, and I shall now call together a whole army. I do not fear traps, tricks, nor treacheries, his position, the time, nor the enemy himself, either in battle or when he is girded about with bronze towers. Now a force of many soldiers armed with quivers will completely crush the enemy. And when his city is laid low, I will immolate his deadly head.[7]

Such is my decision about the make-up of the army. But about the leadership I have so far heard varying opinions.[8] [To Achitophel] You first, tell me what seems best.

ACHITOPHEL. I beseech you, great prince, in the name of this golden light of life and of holy God, to consider the safety of yourself and of us all. You do not know how many perils now threaten you, how great the disaster which his counsel will bring on you. The safety and the lives of all of us are tied up with yours: by your misfortune we are imperiled. If you are resolved to thrust everyone into war, if you wish to try the fate of everyone at the same time,

[6] That is, by speaking a truism such as that which follows.

[7] Either David, the head of the enemy forces, or the collective heads of the enemy troops (pursuant to Chusai's advice at III.3.207 ff.). The sacrificial image (*mactabo*) intensifies Absalom's villainous deterioration.

[8] The Biblical dispute between Achitophel and Chusai provided the germ of the ensuing debate (*2 Kings* xvii.1, 11), but the Biblical passage which most influenced Watson here was a discussion of David, not Absalom (*2 Kings* xviii.2-4); see Introduction, p. 54.

teipsum validis servato claustris moenium
obseptum, ab omni clade prorsus liberum.
Si prosperum sit bellum, eris beatior,
sin funebre, auxilia remittes tutior.
Discrimen ingens tua feret profectio:
ne militi credas adhuc te incognito,
nam vana vento turba fertur quolibet.
Absente pugnam fortius te conserent.
Ex vrbe cuncti praesidium expectant bonum:
animos magis inflammat futurae spes opis
quam nuda regis maximi praesentia.
Iuvabit aspectus, sed auxilium magis:
quem non vident omnes, iuvantem sentient.
Si propria vel si militum securitas
tranquilla mentem, vt dixeris, moveat tuam,
si tibi tuorum grata curae sit salus,
ab hoc cruento te refrena proelio.
Non quod dubitem de prospera victoria —
in manibus est —, sed si qua clades accidat,
e menibus securus auxilia feras.
Vrgens meis impone onus cervicibus.
Ego aut redibo victor aut victus cadam.
ABSALOM. Quid agam? Vagus et incertus animi pendeo:
in varia rapiunt dicta me contraria.
Sed audiam: miror quid hijs respondeat.
CHUSAI. Hostem cruentum aliena transfodiet manus?
Non ille gladius pectore abdetur truci?

294-295, 301-304. *Printed in Boas* || **294.** prosperum] ?⟨ prosperis || **297.** te incognito] ⟨ incognito || **305.** vel si] ⟨ te vel ⟨ vel || **309-310.** victoria — . . . est —,] victoria . . . est. *MS* ||

then keep yourself shut up within the strong gates of a fortification completely safe from all the slaughter. If the battle should go favorably, well and good; but if it should go badly, you, being safe, will send help. Your going forth will carry great danger. Do not entrust yourself to a soldiery still untried by you, for the fickle crowd is swayed by any wind. If you are not present, the men will enter the battle more strenuously. All will eagerly anticipate strong support from your walled position. The hope of coming assistance will inflame their minds more than the mere personal presence of even the greatest king. Your appearance will help, but your aid will help more: whom they do not all see they will all feel is helping them. If, as you say, your own safety or the untroubled safety of your soldiers influences your thoughts, if the welfare of your people is of concern to you, keep yourself out of this bloody fray. Not that I doubt victory according to our wishes — that is in our hands — but if misfortune should occur anywhere, you, being safe, could send assistance from the fortifications. Place the heavy burden on my shoulders. I will either return victorious, or conquered fall.

ABSALOM. What should I do? I am perplexed, my mind wavering and uncertain. These opposing points of view sweep me into varying decisions. But let me hear: I wonder what Chusai's answer is to these things.

CHUSAI. Is someone else's hand to run your cruel enemy through? Will not this sword of yours be plunged into his villainous breast?

Hec spolia cedis? Alius hanc laudem feret?
Devincere est quam audire victum pulchrius.
Quod ipse feceris manu est preclarius,
namque hoc iuvat recitasse facta propria.
Magis alijs haec bella credes quam tibi?
Numquid alij est quam tibi parens infestior? [*fol. 20r*]
Quis non potenti tutus erit exercitu?
Hostes facile te crede victurum fore.
Hic etsi habeat feros, tamen paucissimos,
te multa pergentem sequentur millia.
Vt in recurvos se mare diffundens sinus,
fluvios rapaces alveo absorbet cavo,
ita singulos hostes gladijs vorabimus,
campusque totus sanguine manabit nigro.
Quid iam vacillas? Se tibi dedent protinus:
numquam ferent, domabit aspectus. Novo
non est opus auxilio: statim cedent tibi.
ABSALOM. Abrumpe verba. Dulcis hic sermo placet.
Collum iuvat ferro secare frigido
et lurida sanie repletas solvere
venas caputque pulvere palpitans
atro videre. Iam tumet mens fervida
et in doloris supplicium languet grave.
Praecordia mihi odio malo ardent intima.
Tua iam sequar consilia, at eius postea.
Laudem hec manus vel sola propriam feret.
Me maximum belli ducem omnes sequimini. [Exeunt]

319. cedis] ⟨ cedit | cedis?] cedis, *MS* || **320-322.** *Printed in Boas* || **324.** Numquid . . . parens] ⟨ Numquid [⟨ Aut] alij quam tibi pater est || **325.** potenti] ⟨ potente | erit] ⟨ est || **326.** te] ⟨ te (*canceled, then rewritten; presumably Watson started to move it* [?*after* crede]) | crede victurum] ⟨ v [*victurum] crede | fore.] fore *MS* || **331-332.** hostes . . . vorabimus,/ campusque] ⟨ strictos . . . vorabimus/ hostes (*revised before any more of l. 332 was written*) || **333.** vacillas?] vacillas, *MS* || **335.** est] ?⟨ et || **340.** fervida] ⟨ languida || **341.** doloris supplicium] ⟨ supplicium doloris || **342.** intima.] intima *MS* || **345.** S.d.] *Om. MS* | *Beneath l. 345 a score, presumably marking the division between the scene and the chorus, but perhaps marking ten lines from the last mark, at l. 336 (nine lines of verse and the one-line chorus heading). See note at III.3.385* ||

Will you give up this prize? Will another have this praise? It is more pleasant to conquer the enemy than to hear that he has been conquered. What you yourself do with your own hand is more illustrious, for indeed it is gratifying to recite one's own deeds. Will you entrust these battles more to others than to yourself? Is your parent more hateful to another than to yourself? Who will not be safe in your powerful army? Believe it, you will easily conquer the enemy. Although he has fierce men, yet they are few in number, while many thousands will follow you in your advance. Just as the sea, pouring itself into curved bays, swallows up racing rivers in its hollow bed, so we will gobble up the enemy one by one with our swords, and the whole field will run with black blood. Why do you vacillate now? They will surrender to you immediately. They will never hold up. The sight of you will defeat them. There is no need of reserve assistance; the enemy will yield to you at once.

ABSALOM. Enough words! This sweet speech pleases me. I want to sever his neck with cold steel and open his veins, filled with the ghastly corruption of his blood, and see his head convulsing in the black dust. Now my eager mind teems with excitement; it weakens under the heavy torture of anger. My very heartstrings glow with evil hatred. I will follow your advice now and Achitophel's hereafter. This hand of mine will perform its own praiseworthy deeds, yes, all alone. Me — all of you follow me, the greatest leader of war.

[They all go out]

CHORUS.

Gliconici Choriambici.

Qui spem humana ope collocant,
confisi auxilio virûm,
iactati subito gravi
tempestate cadunt cito.
Quaecumque in domino sita
spes est perpetuo manet,
nullo turbine frangitur,
nec vi concutitur mala.
Fidunt magnanimis equis
pravi menteque reprobi,
fidunt curribus arduis,
armis et rapidis rotis.
in ferro posita est salus
pugnantûm et numero virûm.
Prestanti omnia robore et
nervis praevalidis domant.
Exultant tumidis minis,
fundunt verba ferocia.
Contemnunt humiles viros:
insontes feriunt truces
inflatique bonos premunt. *[fol. 20v]*
Designare neci iuvat
quisquis criminibus vacat.
Quam rebus sapiunt malis,

M.h. Gliconici] ⟨ Glyconici || **346 ff.** *The "parts" of the chorus are divided as follows:* a *346-353,* bπ *354-376,* cπ *377-382,* d *383-390* || **348.** *Orig. followed l. 349 (or was added there for insertion here)* | gravi] ⟨ mala || **350-351.** Quaecumque . . . spes est] ⟨ At quorum . . . spes est ⟨ Quorum est . . . spes (*revised before any more of l. 351 was written*) || **359.** et numero] ⟨ numero || **360.** Prestanti] ⟨ Nervoso || **363.** verba ferocia] ⟨ ferocia verba || **366.** inflatique] ?⟨ inflati || **369.** malis,] ⟨ malis! ||

CHORUS.[9]

Those who place faith in human resources, trusting in the assistance of men, when battered by some sudden grave tempest fall swiftly. But whatever hope is placed in the Lord remains perpetually, is shattered by no whirlwind, is shaken by no evil force.

The perverse and false-minded trust in high-spirited horses, in tall war chariots, in arms, and in rapid wheels. On the sword does their safety rest and on the number of their fighting men. They subdue all things with mighty strength and powerful sinews. They boast with bombastic threats; they pour forth fierce words. They despise humble men; these savages smite the innocent and, in their pride, oppress the good. It pleases them to mark for murder anyone who is free of crimes. How wise they are in evil things,

[9] Some specific phrases from Psalms are more evident in this chorus than in most. Lines 354-357 were probably based on Psalm xix.8 (and the passage then blends into the Senecan l. 358); l. 372 is from Psalm x.7; l. 373 sounds like Psalm vii.13; l. 377 is similar to Psalm xxxii.17; l. 378 is like Psalm lxxxviii.33.

rebus desipiunt bonis!
Vt iusto insidias struunt!
Sub lingua est labor et dolor.
In quem non gladios vibrant?
Caedem trux animus sitit,
in pravis bonus artifex,
in rectis penitus rudis.
  Tandem fallet equus velox,
tandem verbere ferreo
summus percutiet deus.
Illos poena gravis manet.
Est verax deus optimus,
certum est: esse aliter nequit.
  At quisquis dominum colit
divinaque ope nititur:
non turbo quatiet rapax,
non sternet boreas tumens,
nec vis vlla furens premet.
Perstat non pede lubrico.
Poenis afficit improbos,
iustos sublevat in malis.

ACTUS QUARTUS. [SCENA PRIMA].

SADOC. ABIATHAR. CHUSAI.

Trimetri Iambici.

SADOC. Qui mitis alto numine Israel regis [*fol. 21r*]
quique populum nos eligis solos tibi,
ad filium converte sacratos tuum
vultus, salutis certa David pignora.

370. bonis!] bonis. *MS* || **376.** in rectis penitus] ⟨ virtuteque proba || Beneath **385.** *A score presumably marking the twentieth line on the page (or perhaps marking the fortieth line of the chorus and the fortieth verse line from the last mark)* || **388.** lubrico] ?⟨ lubrice || Beneath **390.** *A long underscore marking the end of the act*

IV.1.s.h.] Actus [⟨ Atus] 4us. *MS* || *P.h. and m.h. reversed in MS* || **1.** mitis] ?⟨ r [*regis] || **2.** tibi] ⟨ tuum ||

and how incapable of understanding decent things! How they devise plots against the just! Lurking beneath their speech is labor and sorrow. Against whom do they not shake their spears? The savage mind thirsts after slaughter, is an expert skilled in depravities, is thoroughly unschooled in proper things.

At length the swift horse will deceive; at length Almighty God will smite them with an iron scourge. A heavy penalty awaits them. The good God speaks truly, that is certain;[10] He does not know how to do otherwise.

By contrast, whoever worships God and leans on His divine power, no raging whirlwind will plague, no teeming north wind will lay low, no ravaging force will weigh down. He stands on a steady foot. God visits punishments on the wicked, the just among the evil He sustains.

[10] *Scil.,* in promising vengeance to evildoers.

ACT IV. [SCENE 1.]

[Jerusalem. A Secret Place.][1]

SADOC [and] ABIATHAR [Enter from One Direction and Stand Waiting for] CHUSAI [Who Approaches Them from Another Direction.][2]

SADOC. Thou Who gently rulest Israel by Thy divine will and Who choosest us alone as Thy people, turn Thy holy visage toward Thy son as a sure sign of the safety of David.

[1] In this scene Watson "returns to his Biblical source, but he again welds together detached episodes" (Boas, p. 359). For the meeting of Sadoc and Abiathar with Chusai, the Biblical narrative has only two verses (*2 Kings* xvii. 15-16) immediately after those describing the debate between Achitophel and Chusai. Watson could have spared us, as the Biblical narrator did, the additional repetition of the details of the argument which occurred in III.3.

[2] The stanzaic lyricism of the first four speeches is Watson's invention. The tone of these speeches indicates that the speakers have not yet met Chusai, and Chusai's opening words at l. 36 indicate the same thing. But if Chusai were not present throughout, Watson would probably have indicated a new scene with his entrance. (Perhaps Sadoc's speech at ll. 17-35 was addressed to Chusai.)

ABIATHAR. Plurima quietem iam exhibe passo mala.
Communis exprimit querelam hanc calamitas.
Fugere ad tuum docemur adversis thronum:
David potenti dextera afflictum leva.
SADOC. In te vnico fidit: tuum iam sentiat
levamen. Hostium timet violentiam
plusquam feralem. Cladibus succumberet
ni tua gubernans cuncta fulsisset manus.
ABIATHAR. Erepta vt animo regna tranquillo tulit?
Non regna, perditum gemebat filium:
vox querula numquam subticebat filium.
Mortem ille patris, hic filij vitam petit.
SADOC. Ab vrbe rege ineunte deserta fugam
nos, obsiti grato Levitarum grege,
arcam sacratam foederis portavimus.
Ex quo putantes caelitus auxilium fore,
vsque comites esse itineris decrevimus.
Sed noluit nos se amplius deducere:
cum archa dei praecepit vrbem repetere.
Privata mecum haec colloquia maestus habuit:
"Iam continuo in vrbem reverso, videns,
tuus tibi filius aderit Achimaas
et huius vna gnatus Ionathan comes.
Simul latebunt abditi subvrbijs.
Regis per illos facta narretis mihi.

5. mala] ?⟨ malo || **10-60.** *The tenth line of the act is marked by a dot. Following ten-line groups are marked with alternating scores and dots at ll. 20, 30, 40, 50, and 60. For continuation of the numbering see note at IV.2.3-163* || **15.** querula] ⟨ querus (*?scribal*) || **18.** obsiti] ⟨ obsito || **19.** foederis] ⟨ foeder⟨e⟩ || **25-33.** *Quotes om. MS* || **25.** reverso] ⟨ reversus | videns] ⟨ o videns (*interjection*) || **26.** filius aderit] ⟨ ade [*aderit] filius || **27.** huius] ⟨ huius h (*?scribal*) ||

ABIATHAR. Show Thy peace now to one who has suffered many evils. The common calamity forces this complaint. We are taught to flee to Thy throne in times of adversity: with Thy strong right hand lighten the affliction of David.

SADOC. In Thee alone he puts his trust: let him now feel Thy solace. He fears the more than deadly violence of his enemies. He would be overcome by calamities if Thy all-ruling hand did not support him.

ABIATHAR. How has he borne the loss of his kingdom with a calm mind? Not his kingdom, but the loss of his son he mourned; his voice, never complaining, was silent concerning his son.[3] The one seeks death for a father; the other, life for a son.

SADOC. As the king was beginning his flight from the deserted city, we, accompanied by our beloved flock of Levites, carried along the Sacred Ark of the Covenant. Thinking that help would come from Heaven through David, we decided to be his constant companions on the journey. But he did not wish us to conduct him farther; he ordered us to return to the city with the Ark of God. He sadly said to me in private, "Now, my priest, return immediately into the city. Your son Achimaas will be near you and with him his companion Jonathan, the son of Abiathar; together they will lie hidden in the outskirts. By them you should relay to me the doings of the king.

[3] *Subticere,* a late Latin word not given in Cooper's *Thesavrvs,* I have found listed only in DuCange's *Glossarium Mediae et Infimae Latinitatis,* with the synonyms *silere* and *tacere.*

At ego in eremi me occulam campestribus,
quid inde veniat tutus expectans boni.
Si placeo, me dominus reducet optimus,
sin aliter ei visum est, libens quidvis feram."
Huc ergo quaesitum venimus quid ratum
regi sit: vtinam commode succederet.
CHUSAI. Nimis benignus mihi deus vos obtulit:
contingere potuit nihil oportunius.
Rex de his nisi vestra fiat opera certior,
ab hostibus iam vivus absorbebitur.
Haec consilia subdolus Achitophel dedit:
ille ipse decem sumptis virorum milibus
hac nocte longis passibus eum persequens,
mestum, solutum, improvidum, lassum opprimet. [*fol. 21v*]
Me rursus, vt fit, postea rex consulens
in alteram perducitur sententiam:
ego, quid mali ferret subita hec excursio
et lecta militum manus considerans,
illi vt aliquid daretur interim morae,
in dubia totum prelia Israel agat,
et vt ipse persuasi imperaret vnicus.
Hec sat scio vastabit eum confusio.
Statim ergo David filios emittite,
vt ne moretur amplius campestribus,
ne forte non praevisa clades opprimat.
Vel muniat sese vel vrbem aliquam occupet:
illinc potest optata sperari salus.
Omnes ego abiens suspiciones auferam. [Exit]

32. me dominus] ⟨ dominus || **34.** quaesitum] ⟨ quaesitu || **36.** Nimis] ⟨ Semper || **37.** oportunius [= opportunius]] ⟨ commodius || **38.** de his] ⟨ iam || **46.** hec] ?⟨ ⟨p⟩ || **49.** dubia] ⟨ ⟨f⟩ || **50.** ipse] ⟨ i⟨ll⟩e || **52.** David] ⟨ regi || **57.** S.d.] *Om. MS* ||

But I will hide myself in the plains of the wilderness, safely awaiting any good news which will come from there. If I please Him, the very good Lord will restore me; but if it seems otherwise to Him, I will willingly bear whatever He pleases." Therefore we have come here to find out what plan the king has decided on. Would that we may prosper well.

CHUSAI [Coming up to Sadoc and Abiathar]. A God too kind to me has brought you; nothing more opportune could have happened. Unless the king be made aware of these things through your efforts, he will soon be eaten alive by his enemies. The wicked Achitophel gave this advice: that Achitophel himself, taking ten thousand men in a forced march, would tonight pursue David and that he would overcome a David grief-stricken, negligent, surprised, and weary. The king, as it happens, then consulted me in turn and was led into another sentiment: thinking what evil consequences this sudden sortie and this select band of men might bring about, I persuaded him that he should delay for a time; that he should lead all Israel into battles of doubtful outcome; and that he alone should have command. This tumult, I know very well, will destroy him. Therefore send your sons to David at once so that he will not delay in the plains any longer lest perchance an unforeseen disaster overwhelm him. Let him either fortify his position or take over some city; thence the desired welfare can be hoped for.

As I leave, I will draw off all suspicions.

[He goes out by the way he came in]

SADOC. Quid agimus? Hic diu morari non licet,
obseptaque via iam omnis est ad filios.
Non possumus consilia tuto prodere,
hic vndique vicatim fremente milite.
ABIATHAR. Ancilla ad hanc rem mihi domi est aptissima:
novit sapiens et nuncia recte dicere,
et milites dolosa cautos fallere.
Hec sola factum hoc si videtur perferet.
SADOC. Fit optime. Iam nunc viam instemus simul.
Servet dominus a clade fidentes sibi. [Exeunt]

[ACTUS QUARTUS.] SCENA SECUNDA.

ABSALOM cum POPULO.

Trimetri Senarij.

ABSALOM. Fervens tumentes ira distendit fibras,
ardore liquescit medulla perdita,
totumque sorbet sanguinem infelix mora,
et tabe corpus hoc fluente solvitur.
Saevire iam libet. Enecat dilatio,
exedit artus tarditas haec languidos.
Exite, lenti huius doloris vindices:
numquam placet protracta vincenti vltio.
Solum id iuvat nobis quod ex voto cadit.
Nam caetera etsi prospere eveniant, tamen
multum molestae acerbitatis continent.
Satiare et animum hunc et libidinem volo.
Vindicta lentis iuncta consumit moris.

59. obseptaque] obsepta que *MS* || **62.** rem mihi] ⟨ rem | aptissima:] aptissima *MS* || **63.** sapiens et] ⟨ facunda || **67.** S.d.] *Om. MS*

IV.2.s.h.] Scena 2ª. *MS* (⟨ 2ᵘˢ.) || *P.h. and m.h. reversed in MS* || **1.** Fervens] ⟨ Fervet | distendit] ⟨ distentit || **3-163.** *At l. 3 a dot marks the tenth line from the last mark, at IV.1.60 (not counting s.h., p.h., and m.h.). Every tenth line following this is marked with a score or a dot, alternately. For continuation of the numbering see note at IV.3.4-164* || **5.** dilatio] ⟨ cunctatio || **8.** vltio.] vltio *MS* || **10.** prospere] ⟨ prospera ||

SADOC. What are we to do? We cannot stay here too long, and every road to our sons is already sealed off. We cannot transmit these plans safely, since the military is raging everywhere here, from street to street.

ABIATHAR. There is at my house a handmaid who is very well suited for this business. She is wise and knows how to deliver messages correctly; she is cunning and knows how to deceive watchful soldiers. If you approve, she alone will take care of this action.[4]

SADOC. Very well. Now let us take to the road together. May the Lord preserve from disaster those who are faithful to Him.

[They go out by the way they came in]

[4] Thus Watson only hints at the Bible's detailed account of the difficulties which Jonathan and Achimaas had in getting the message to David (*2 Kings* xvii.17-21). Inclusion of that account would have marred the play's unity.

[ACT IV.] SCENE 2.

[Galaad. The Camp of Absalom.][1]

[Enter] ABSALOM with [His] PEOPLE.

ABSALOM [Aside]. Searing anger is stretching my swelling entrails. My marrow, undone by the heat, turns to liquid; this unhappy waiting sucks all my blood, and my body is dissolved by this flowing corruption. Now I want to rave. This procrastination exhausts me; this lagging eats away at my listless limbs. Ye laggard avengers of my anger, go forth: protracted revenge never pleases a conqueror. Only that which happens according to my will pleases me. For, although other things are turning out well, yet they hold much of my annoying vexation: I want to satisfy my passion as well as my will.[2] My desire for vengeance coupled with slow delays is consuming me.

[1] The Bible says nothing of Absalom's either chafing while the army was being raised or issuing dreadful threats against David. In the play these threats have been previously made (III.1), and Boas was partly right in saying that the "repetition of this unnatural theme, in even more repulsive detail than before, could well have been spared" (p. 360). But I do not agree that the scene adds "no new touch" to Absalom's character. This is the last time we see Absalom, and we must be perfectly prepared for the dreadful end which will be his in the description of Act V. The steady deterioration in his character must reach a climax, and this scene utterly strips the hero of sympathy. Even in III.3 there may at least have been some sympathy for Absalom, for his residual sense of honor (in rebuking Chusai for deserting David) if for nothing else.

[2] That is, my successes (presumably his winning all of Israel) satisfy my intellectual desire for power, but they emphasize my failure to satisfy my emotional desire to destroy my father.

Quantum doloris detrahit mihi vltio,
tantum dabit poenarum iners prolatio. [*fol. 22r*]
Obstare quam mihi videntur omnia!
Non vndique adsunt iam coacti milites
vtrumque crebri qui mihi obstipent latus,
nec quique partiuntur in turmas vagas,
desuntque turmarum paludati duces.
Conferta non adhuc acies producitur,
nec expediti illam sequuntur velites.
Peltis frequenti dimicantes agmine
absunt, et alas ambientes strennui
equites: nec ordo proeliandi imponitur.
Longus parandis rebus annus labitur.
Immenso vt aestuat spatio mens fervida!
Quam multa scriptores terunt iam secula,
dum debitum [m]ihi contrahant exercitum!
Labore cessant facti, opinor, desides
vel iussibus somno neglectis languido
sese dederunt: segnibus occidunt moris.
Iam iam hic probe effectis, scio, mandatis erunt:
hic impetus paulum est remittendus mihi.
Dulcem meditabor antea victoriam.
Est suave pugnas gloriosas persequi et
animo futura iam prius revolvere.
Quali nimium res prosperas vultu feram?
Tum tristis aerumnae aliquid admittam libens
quae laeticias nimis insolentes temperet,

14. doloris] ⟨ ex dolore || **21.** Conferta] ?*Read* Conserta || **23.** dimicantes] ⟨ demicantes | agmine] ⟨ agmine. || **28-32.** *Printed in Boas* || **28.** scriptores terunt] ⟨ missi conterent || **29.** [m]ihi] *Boas* nihi *MS* || **36.** Est suave pugnas] ⟨ pugnas iucundum est | persequi] ⟨ pr [*prosequi] || **39.** Tum] ⟨ Vel ||

As much of my anger as revenge will take away from me, just that much torment will this inert postponement give me. How all things seem to thwart me! No assembled soldiers are here all around to gird me on either side with their numbers or to be assigned to scouting patrols; absent are the troops' armor-clad leaders.[3] As yet no crowded battle line is drawn up, with ready skirmishers to follow it. Wanting are the men who fight with shields in the thick of battle and the quick, wing-circling cavalry. No battle plan is laid out. The long year slips away in preparations. How my feverish mind burns during the great interval! How many centuries the draftsmen wear away now while they assemble an army bound to me! Made lazy, I suppose, they are remiss in their labor or, ignoring orders, have given themselves over to languid sleep; they are killing me with their slothful procrastination —

No, they will be here forthwith, I know, with their orders properly carried out. I must a little subdue this fury. I will look ahead to my sweet victory.[4] It is pleasant to carry out glorious battles and to ponder now, ahead of time, the things that will come. With what sort of expression will I bear my very auspicious circumstances? At that time I will freely show something of sorrowful distress in order to moderate my happiness that it may not seem excessively arrogant,

[3] Literally, "leaders clad in general's garb."

[4] The following passage is one of several instances of dramatic irony in the play.

nam saepe quod nimium est molestum redditur.
Tractare miserias patris animo iuvat:
viles humi cum bestijs carpit dapes,
unda capit aquas pro aureo vola scypho,
tum dormiens patet ferarum rictibus,
pro purpura pannis supinus incubat,
brevi fugatus pallida arescet fame.
Haec poena nulla est: hactenus non sum satur.
Ensem ne funesto recondam pectore?
An horridum a trunco reliquo abscindam caput?
An precipiti pressum cerebrum excutiam casu?
An corpus equis crassum rapientibus dabo?
Frangentur artus rupe deiecti cava?
Melius nocentem laqueus astringet gulam?
Quidsi premam lapidum oneroso pondere?
Vastave disrumpam cadaver lamina?
Et lacera saevis membra proijciam lupis?
Sanie potius stillante consumam ignibus?
An tumida suffocem veneno pectora? [*fol. 22v*]
An fusa iactem viscera edenda piscibus?
An funereis torrenda supponam regis?
Prestat strepente flumine vitam extinguere?
Quid si cavo claudam huc reductum carcere,
solum esca villosis futurum vermibus?
Mortem negabo illi petitam sepius,
et debita fraudabo moribundum nece.
Vindicta vix vlla satis, et quaevis placet.
Numquam, nisi quando vota transcendit sua,
placari animus dolore vesanus potest.

43. viles] ⟨ lautos || **44.** aquas] ⟨ aguas || **53.** cava?] cava. *MS* || **54.** gulam?] gulam. *MS* || **55.** oneroso] ⟨ onerosus || **57.** lupis?] lupis *MS* || **58.** ignibus?] ignibus. *MS* || **59.** pectora?] ⟨ pectora, || **61.** An funereis] ⟨ An tabificis ⟨ Frusta [⟨ An frusta] rapidis [⟨ rapidos] || **62.** extinguere?] extinguere. *MS* || **63-64.** carcere, . . . vermibus?] carcere? . . . vermibus *MS* || **64.** solum] ⟨ vel | futurum] ⟨ futum (*scribal*) || **65.** petitam sepius] ⟨ s [*sepius] petitam ||

for often what is extreme returns as trouble. It is pleasant to reflect on the miseries of my father: he is eating wretched meals on the ground among the beasts; from a stream he gets his water — with a cupped palm instead of a golden goblet; then when he sleeps he lies exposed to the jaws of wild animals; instead of purple he lies on his back in rags.[5] Soon he will wither, confounded with the pallor of famine.

But this punishment is nothing: I am still not satisfied. Shall I bury my sword in his deadly breast? Or cut off his hateful head from the rest of his body? Or shake his brains out and crush them in a quick death? Or deliver his gross body to running horses? Or shatter his members by hurling him from a vaulted cliff? Or, better, will a noose strangle his wicked throat? How if I should crush him with the heavy weight of stones? Or shatter his carcass utterly with a huge iron plate and throw his mangled members to the savage wolves? Or shall I rather burn them with fire while the gore is still dripping? Should I choke off his arrogant life with poison? Should I toss out his scattered entrails as food for the fish? Or should I put kindling under a royal funeral pyre? Is it better to smother his life in a noisy river? How if I bring him back here and lock him in an empty prison merely to be food for hairy worms? I shall refuse death to him though he repeatedly ask for it, and when he is dying I will cheat him of his deserved death. Scarcely any revenge is enough, and any revenge whatever is pleasing. Never, except when it surpasses its vows, can my furious mind be assuaged from its anger.

[5] Ironically, Absalom is not aware that David has been supplied by friendly citizens with beds, tapestry, earthen vessels, wheat, barley, meal, corn, beans, lentils, pulse, honey, butter, sheep, and fat calves (*2 Kings* xvii.27-29).

Sed cur mihi fando moras vanus sero?
Hec omnia campis melius acta oportuit.
Iam plurimo illuc confluente milite,
acies moratur tota in armis iam arbitror.
Ergo comites lecti ducem praecedite. [Exit cum Populo]

CHORUS.

Sapphici.

Quis venit tandem miseris rogandus,
quis dabit laesis medicus levamen,
quis bonus pellet subitas ruinas
ni deus clemens ope sublevaret —
improbis vltor, miseris benignus?
Quis deum digne celebrare novit?
Qui manu mundum fabricavit omnem
conditum nutu moderatur ipso.
Non potest vlla ratione claudi
quicquid a summo domino creatur.
Sustulit mundum fluvio malignum.
Gens dedit quaevis scelerata poenas:
forma submersae fuit vna terrae,
sed Noë, vastis prohibens ab vndis
liberos tuta teneros in arca
servat illaesos. Tulit ore ramum
foederis signum stabilis columba.
Et capit pontus fluvios vagantes,
et suae terrae est homo restitutus.

70. Sed] ⟨ ⟨ ⟩ || **74.** comites lecti ducem] ⟨ d [*ducem] comites lecti | S.d.] *Om. MS* || After m.h.] *A quincunx MS* || 75 ff. *The choral "parts" are divided as follows:* a *75-84,* b *85-93,* π *94-138* (b *continuing to speak, in a different direction?*), c *139-162,* d *163-169* || **75.** rogandus,] rogandus? *MS* || **76.** levamen,] levamen? *MS* || **78.** ni deus] ⟨ ni qua || **79.** benignus?] benignus. *MS* || **87.** submersae] ⟨ stagnanti || **88.** sed . . . vndis] ⟨ sed manu Noe rapuit fidelem || **89.** arca] ⟨ archa ||

But why do I vainly create delays by talking to myself? All these things could be better performed on the field. Already a very large troop is assembling there, and the whole array, I judge, is now waiting in arms. [To his people] Therefore, my chosen companions, go on before your leader.

[Absalom and his people go out]

CHORUS.

What solicitor[6] comes at length to the wretched, what physician will give comfort to the sick, what good man will drive away sudden catastrophes if clement God, vengeful to the wicked but kind to the wretched, does not sustain us with His power? Who knows how to celebrate God worthily? He Who with His hand founded the whole world, with His mere nod rules what He founded. Whatever is created by the Lord on high cannot be ended in any way.

He supported the wicked world during the flood. Every race that was wicked has paid the penalty. One form was that of the flooding of the land, but Noah, protecting his tender charges from the broad waters in a safe ark, kept them unharmed. The intrepid dove bore in his mouth a branch, the sign of the Covenant; and the sea took the errant rivers under control, and man was restored to his land.[7]

[6] Literally, "one worthy of being sought."
[7] *Genesis* vi-viii.

Victa naturae ratio recessit 94
Isaac quando, patriarcha noster,
nascitur prorsus sterili parente. 96
Vicit humanos rubus ille sensus, [*fol. 23r*]
igne flagrans haud periens corusco, 98
quo deus Mosen famulum allocutus
misit vt victo pharaone pressum 100
liberet crudo populum tyranno.
Quanta per vilem facit ille servum: 102
induit formam colubri tumentis
virga consistens; iterum recepta 104
in manus formam veterem resumit.
Edomat regem dominus stupendis: 106
vertit in tetrum fluvios cruorem,
putrido pisces moriuntur amne. 108
Intulit raucas velut imbre ranas,
regiam foedant populumque totum, 110
foetidam Aegyptum populantur omnem.
Pulverem fecit ciniphes solutam 112
qui genus vastant animantis omne.
Misit et muscas numero carentes 114
cuncta quae tristi inficiunt veneno,
morsibus stringunt rigidis protervae. 116
Et boves atra periere peste,
tabidum cunctos violavit vlcus. 118

95. patriarcha noster] ⟨ peperit genitrix || **97.** Vicit] ⟨ Vincit | sensus] ⟨ captus || **102.** servum] ⟨ f (?*scribal*) || **105.** resumit.] resumit *MS* || **106.** Edomat regem] ⟨ Principem frangit | stupendis:] stupendis *MS* || **107** ff. *The plagues are numbered with a* 1 *before l. 107,* 2 *before 109,* 3 *before 112,* 4 *before 114 (the* 3 *and* 4 *are braced),* 5 *before 117,* 6 *before 118,* 7 *before 119,* 8 *before 125,* 9 *before 130,* 10 *before 134* || **111.** foetidam] ⟨ garrulae || **115.** tristi inficiunt] ⟨ caeco violant | veneno] ⟨ veneno ⟨et⟩ || **116.** morsibus] ⟨ morsis | protervae.] protervae *MS* ||

The normal system of nature, confounded, disappeared when Isaac our patriarch was born to an utterly sterile parent.[8] That famous bush, burning but not being consumed by the flaming fire, surpassed human comprehension — the bush from which God spoke to his servant Moses and sent him to free his oppressed people from a cruel tyrant by overcoming the Pharaoh.[9] How many things He did through His lowly servant! A rigid rod took on the form of a convulsive serpent; when it was taken into his hands, it resumed its former shape.[10] The Lord subdued the ruler with marvelous happenings:[11] He turned rivers into hideous blood; the fish died in the putrid stream. He brought in hoarse frogs like rain; they polluted the kingdom and all the people, and they ravaged all of stinking Egypt. He made the dust of the air turn into lice which devastated every kind of living creature. He also sent flies without number which infected all things with their foul poison; they viciously wounded with their sharp bites. And cattle died of an ugly disease. A corrupt sore befouled all creatures.

[8] *Genesis* xviii.10-15, xxi.1-3.
[9] *Exodus* iii.2.
[10] *Exodus* vii.9-12.
[11] In order are listed the ten plagues (*Exodus* vii-xii).

Grandinem misit nimis ille diram
ignibus mistam rutilumque fulgur; 120
occidunt herbae, cava ligna frangit,
dissipat vites pecudesque sternit, 122
et manet nudus penitus resecta
pampinus vva. 124
Ventus vrebat furibundus agros,
sustulit pennis validas locustas, 126
pervolant totam regionem inanes,
poma diffindunt lapidosa morsu, 128
nec sinunt quicquam superesse fructus.
Post tribus fecit tenebras diebus 130
ne manum quisquam poterat videre,
sed loco segnis iacuit recepto, et 132
se dedit somno pavido sepultus.
Abstulit primogenitos, trucidat 134
omnium primos catulos ferarum:
regis haud parcit solio sedenti 136
filio. Clamant viduae gementes,
singulis funus domibus iacebat. [*fol. 23v*] 138
Dividunt Mosi freta vasta sese,
per rubrum tutos mare ducit ipsos, 140
perque iter fluctus medios patebat.
Mergitur fluctu pharao tumente: 142
reprobis talis solet esse finis.
Dux viae nubes levis est diebus, 144
flamma precaessit radians in vmbra.

121. *Orig. followed l. 124 (or was added there for insertion here)* || **124.** vva] ?⟨ vna || **125.** furibundus] ⟨ violentus || **126.** pennis] ⟨ mersu || **129.** fructus.] ⟨ fructus, || **130.** Post tribus fecit] ⟨ Fecit et ternis ⟨ Fecit et tribus || **131.** videre] ⟨ vidisse ⟨ vide⟨sse⟩ || **135.** ferarum] ⟨ l⟨eonu⟩m | ferarum:] ferarum *MS* || **139.** vasta] ⟨ rubra || **142.** fluctu] ?⟨ flucta || **145.** flamma] ⟨ ignis | precaessit = praecessit ||

He sent a plethora of hard hail mixed with flashes of lightning, and the red thunderbolt. It knocked down plants and shattered hollow trees; it strewed out the vines and scattered the flocks; the tendril remained completely barren, the grapes stunted. A raging wind chafed the fields; it carried the strong-winged locusts, which flew aimlessly over the whole region and broke off the stone-centered fruit with their teeth and allowed no fruit to survive. Afterwards for three days He made darkness so that one could not see his own hand: everyone lay idle in the position which he had taken and, overcome, gave himself up to a tremulous sleep. He carried away the first-born, slaughtered the first pups of all beasts; He did not even spare the ruler's son sitting on the throne. Weeping widows wailed, and a corpse lay in every home.

The broad straits divided themselves for Moses, and he led his people safely through the Red Sea, and his course passed through the middle of the waves. But Pharaoh was swallowed by the swelling waters; such an end is customary for the wicked.[12] The leader of the journey by day was a white cloud; in the darkness a glowing flame went before the people.[13]

[12] *Exodus* xiv.21-29. Watson alluded to this event previously (I.3.68-70).
[13] *Exodus* xiii.21.

Plebe deserto sitiente sicco,
fit lacus dulcis sapor ex amaro,
caelitus tanquam pluvia madenti.
Vespera semper cecidit coturnix,
mane prebeter cibus angelorum,
decidens vt ros liquidus cadebat.
Dicitur turba dubitante, "Man hu?"
Rupe percussa fluit vnda cunctis,
quisque de petra sitiens bibebat.
Improbum serpens populum momordit,
inficit morsos tumido veneno.
Vnico aspectu cruce fixus anguis
morbidis gratam tribuit salutem.
Plura quid summi referam stupenda?
Nam deo quidvis facile est potenti.
Ergo quid factis tero verba rebus?
Solus afflictis deus est vocandus.
  Sis memor David miseri, precamur.
Se tibi totum tribuit fidelis.
Si velis, scimus, potes adiuvare.
Vir bonus numquam est ope destitutus.
Fortior cunctis manus est supremi.
Illa si pugnet, superabit hostes.
Ô deus solam petimus salutem.

146. sitiente] ⟨ sitiente, || **147.** sapor] ⟨ f⟨ ⟩ sapor (*?scribal*) || **148.** madenti] ⟨ cothurnix || **150.** prebetur] ⟨ descendit || **152.** *Quotes om. MS* | hu?] hu. *MS* || **153.** percussa] ⟨ de percussa || **158.** morbidis] ⟨ morbid⟨o⟩

When the crowd was thirsty in the dry desert, the taste of a lake was changed from bitter to sweet, as sweet as rain fallen from heaven.[14] Always at evening quail fell, and in the morning was provided the food of the angels, falling like liquid dew. The wondering crowd said, "Man hu?"[15] When a rock was struck open, water flowed out for all, and everyone thirsting drank from the rock.[16] A serpent attacked the wicked people and inflicted wounds with swelling venom, but at a single glance the serpent, fixed on a cross, restored pleasant health to the sick.[17] Why should I relate more marvels of the Supreme One? For Almighty God anything is easy. Then why do I use up words about the deeds which He has done? God alone must be called upon by the afflicted.

Be mindful of wretched David, we beseech Thee. He has faithfully given himself wholly to Thee. If Thou wishest, Thou canst help him, we know. A good man is never bereft of help. The hand of God is stronger than all. If it fights, it will overcome the enemies. O God, we ask only his safety.

[14] *Exodus* xv.23-25. The lake was Mara in the wilderness of Sur.

[15] *Exodus* xvi.13-15. *Man hu* (which supplied our word manna, the food of the angels) means "What is this?"

[16] *Exodus* xvii.6.

[17] *Numbers* xxi.9.

[ACTUS QUARTUS.] SCENA TERTIA.

ACHITOPHEL.

Trimetri [Iambici].

ACHITOPHEL. Hoccine refers ingrate nobis praemium?
Hanccine ferent consilia nostra gratiam?
Heu tetrum animus nimium paratus in scelus!
Istuc laboresne rediere seduli?
Ab optimo rege hoc meruit defectio?
O vana spes, o mens mihi nimis credula!
Hic vota mea frustrata turpiter iacent. [*fol. 24r*]
Siccine sacratam vane confirmas fidem?
Itane recepta, o impudens, praestas tua?
Famam male sanus prorsus attrivi meam.
Quorsum haec adibam mentis inops pericula?
Quorsum arma contra patriam, regem, deum
apprendi? Vtinam elinguem peperisset me parens
aut tigribus iactasset editum feris.
O impio prudentiam authori malam!
Semper sapientia est male vtenti gravis.
Quod consilij miser reporto praemium?
Quae proditionis impiae merces datur?
Vilis lateo, contemptus, abiectus, miser;
improvidus, vanus, fatuus, demens putor —
merito quidem, qui non ea praevi[d]i fore.
Omnia dolor promittit, at praestat nihil.
Quid non boni res pollicentur asperae?
Sed negligunt rursus eadem res prosperae.

IV.3.s.h.] Scena. 3[a]. *MS* || *P.h. and m.h. reversed in MS* || M.h.] Trimetri *MS* || **3.** nimium] ⟨ nimis | scelus!] scelus. *MS* || **4-164.** *A score beneath l. 4 marks ten lines (not counting s.h., p.h., and m.h.) from last mark, at IV.2.163. Every tenth line following this is marked with a score or a dot, alternately. See note at V.1.10-80* || **6.** credula!] credula. *MS* || **7.** Hic] ⟨ En || **9.** praestas] ⟨ praestat || **13.** apprendi?] ⟨ apprendi, | parens] ⟨ mater || **15.** malam!] malam. *MS* || **16.** male] ⟨ ⟨b⟩ male || **18-21.** *Printed in Boas* || **21.** praevi[d]i] praevisi *MS, Boas* || **24.** Sed] ⟨ At ||

[ACT IV.] SCENE 3.

[Giloh. The House of Achitophel.][1]

[Enter] ACHITOPHEL.

ACHITOPHEL. Is this the reward which you repay, ingrate?[2] Is this the thanks which my counsels will bring? Alas, that my mind was too ready for hideous crime! Have my diligent labors come to this? Has my desertion of the very good king merited this? O vain hope, O my too credulous mind! Here lie my desires, basely deceived. Thus emptily do you pledge your sacred honor? Do you thus fulfill your promises, O shameless one? Utterly insane, I have worn away my reputation. To what purpose did I witlessly approach these dangers? To what purpose did I take up arms against my country, my king, and my God? Would that my mother had borne me speechless or that she had thrown me to be eaten by fierce tigers! O wisdom, evil to an impious adviser! Wisdom is always oppressive for one who abuses it. What reward do I, wretched, bring back for my advice? What wages are given for undutiful treachery? I lie debased, despised, abject, wretched; I am held to be improvident, false, foolish, insane — deservedly so, to be sure, for I did not foresee that these things would happen. Suffering promises everything, but delivers nothing. What good things do hard times fail to promise? But good times in turn ignore those promises.

[1] After describing Absalom's preference of Chusai's over Achitophel's advice and narrating the report of Jonathan and Achimaas to David, the Bible in one verse (*2 Kings* xvii.23) tells Achitophel's outcome. Watson's expansion is repetitious and verbose, but it has poetic merit.

[2] The second-person pronouns in this speech usually refer to Absalom. Ultimately, of course, Achitophel blames himself, but here he blames Absalom for failing to keep his promise (I.3.216) to heed Achitophel's advice.

Quid in furore postulo constantiam?
Ego potius furore memet perdidi.
Sanus potui vixisse, non inglorius
columen dum eram regni potentis vnicum.
Coeptis potui tum restitisse noxijs
et cladibus rem liberasse publicam.
Potui paternae prodidisse necis reum
servasseque pio debitam regi fidem —
ni animum furor mihi fascinasset pertinax.
Quae tum rabies mentem fera caecavit mihi!
Quis aestuans sensus abegit impetus!
In nulla consilium merita impendi male.
O turpe factum, o flagitium nimis malum!
Hec lingua filium furentem propulit
in fata patris, hijs nefanda faucibus
fluxere verba, hoc scelera concepit caput,
istae nocentia arma sumpserunt manus.
Etsi patria alterius truci iaceat manu,
at mente nostra: cur necis vivo reus?
Dehisce, tellus, recipe funestum caput.
Corpus nefandum glutiat dirum chaos.
Vtinam voragine sorbeantur horrida
artus scelesti. Sceleribus feci viam.
Ego sum malorum solus author omnium.
Quae tristis animos infatuauit caecitas? [*fol. 24v*]
Edoctus ante tot malorum cladibus,

32. pio] ⟨ ⟨m⟩iti || **35.** sensus] ⟨ f (?*scribal*) || **37.** malum!] malum. *MS* || **38-43.** *Printed in Boas* || **42.** manu] ⟨ mente ||

Why do I demand constancy in madness? No, I destroyed myself by my own madness. If sane, I could have lived in glory while I was the chief support[3] of the powerful kingdom. I could then have resisted Absalom's noxious undertakings and saved the country from these disasters. I could have surrendered the perpetrator of paternal murder and preserved the loyalty which I owed to the pious king — if unyielding madness had not bewitched my mind. Then what a fierce madness blinded my mind! What a surging passion dispelled my senses! To no benefit did I malevolently expend my counsel. O base deed, O too evil and disgraceful act! This tongue propelled a raging son into the murder of his father; from this throat flowed those impious words; this head conceived these crimes; these hands took up those hateful weapons. What though it be by another's cruel hand that the nation lies low? It was by my plan. Why do I live, a party to the murder? Open, earth; receive my calamitous head. Let dreadful Chaos swallow this perfidious body. Would that my criminal limbs might be engorged in a horrible whirlpool. To crimes I have paved the way. I am the only author of all these evils. What sad blindness infatuated my powers of reason? After having been taught earlier by the deaths of so many evildoers,

[3] Literally, "only support." Cf. II.1.46.

hoc improbum cavisse non poteram scelus?
Non audeo vultus nocentes prodere.
Numquam nefas malo carebat exitu.
O caeca corda avido furore percita!
Vt iam ferox in fata tendit propria!
Non ipsa salus servare moriturum potest:
in perniciem recta furens ruit via.
Nihil potuit dici saluti infestius
quam quod furor iam cogit aggredi impotens.
Non auxilium, sed perniciem tantus feret
exercitus. Tumultus est presens ducis
strages: sui sibi nocebunt milites.
Mercede plebs pavida cito corrumpitur.
Aut turbulento marte sternetur cadens
aut vivus in poenas trahetur maximas.
Pro misera tum l[e]ti facies, ordo ad necem
nece gravior. Valeat nece dignus qualibet:
tam perdito vix mille mortes sunt satis.
Sed poena quae nos tum manebit horrida?
Vt animus horret conscius mortis genus!
Numquam furens satiabitur crudelitas:
vt saeviens, immanitate barbarus
victor cruento supplicio vitam trahet!
Quam saeva victoris rapiet atrocitas
ad fata miseros! Ipsa mactat memoria.
O flebilem horum principi mihi diem!
O dura mihi tormenta! Perpessu aspera

53. Numquam . . . exitu.] ⟨ Quando . . . exitu? | nefas] ⟨ nefax | exitu] ⟨ exitum || **54.** percita!] percita. *MS* || **61-62.** presens ducis/ strages] ⟨ pestis ducis./ (*one line only*) || **66.** misera tum] ⟨ misera | l[e]ti] laeti *MS* || **73.** cruento supplicio] ⟨ cruciat⟨u⟩ nos reos [⟩ reis] | trahet] ⟨ trahent || **75.** miseros!] miseros, *MS* || **76.** diem!] diem. *MS* || **77.** tormenta!] tormenta, *MS* ||

could I not have guarded against this wicked crime? I dare not reveal my guilty face. Never does evil want for an evil end.

O blind heart aroused by heated fury! How the headstrong Absalom strives for his own death now! Not Safety herself can save him from death. By an unbending road the madman is rushing into disaster. Nothing could be called more harmful to his safety than the impotent madness which drives him on. Not help, but catastrophe will such a large army bring. The impending battle will be the death of its leader. His own soldiers will be harmful to him. A timid mob is quickly seduced by a bribe. Either he will be slain, falling in the turbulent fighting, or he will be dragged alive into the gravest of punishments.[4]

Alas, then, the wretched face of death — and a road to death which is worse than death! One worthy of any death should be strong;[5] for one so lost a thousand deaths are scarcely enough. But what dreadful penalty will await us then? How my guilty conscience shudders at that kind of death! David's raging cruelty will never be satisfied. Fierce and monstrously barbaric in victory, how he will stretch out my life with a cruel punishment! How savage the conqueror's harshness which will drag us to our death! The mere thought of it slays me. O lamentable day for me, the chief of these wretches! O the hard torments awaiting me! It is not difficult to

[4] Robinson (p. 194) commented on the *oeconomia* in "Achitophel's surety that Absalom and his army are doomed."

[5] That is, should surrender and take his punishment.

nec saxa nec ferrum nec immitis chalybs.
Quae tela nostrae rigida sufficient neci?
Mortem haud vereor, sed ipsum iter torquet magis:
in me fugienda exempla statuet omnibus.
Cunis vtinam extinctus iacuissem mollibus!
Hos mens sagax turpes habebit exitus?
Vt vulnere sic mens consilio perit suo.
Quid proderit furtiva morituro fuga?
Manebo. Callum flebili obduxi neci.
Non mortis atrae, sed sceleris reum pudet.
Qua fronte David intuebor perfidus?
Aspectus ille morte quavis durior:
numquam reditum expectabo regis proditor.
Iam ferream ipsa morte praevertam necem. [*fol. 25r*]
Vixi satis, vel mille dignus mortibus.
Numquam patiar tam indigna supplicia miser
nec vivus vnquam haec membra lacerari sinam.
Ferro incubabo potius aut vitam mihi
laqueo tenaci finiam. Certum est mori.
Decreta mors est, fataque abrumpam mea.
Tetrum hac manu punire iam placet scelus.
A rege quam statui salutem tollere:
mihi eripiam, haec ipsa anima se tollet sibi.
Servare nolo mortem in alienas manus:
proprijs peribo. Queritur fati genus:
crudele vox hec sola facinus edidit;
ergo nocentis vinculo vocis viam

78. immitis] ⟨ infra | chalybs] ⟨ charibs || **80.** sed ipsum] ⟨ ad mortem || **81.** fugienda] ⟨ cruenta | statuet] ⟨ statuent (*see var. at l. 73*) || **82.** mollibus!] mollibus. *MS* || **87-90.** *Printed in Boas* || **88.** perfidus] ⟨ proditor | perfidus?] *Boas* perfidus *MS* || **91.** necem.] necem *MS* || **94.** sinam] ⟨ f (?*scribal*) || **100.** mihi eripiam] ⟨ er [*eripiam] mihi || **101.** mortem] ⟨ v mortem || **103-106.** *Printed in Boas* || **103.** edidit;] edidit *MS* edidit. *Boas* ||

endure either stones or steel or cruel arrow. But what rough tools will suffice for our death? I don't fear death at all, but the way to it torments me more. Of me David will make an example to be shunned by all. Would that I had died in my soft crib!

Will my shrewd mind have this miserable end? My mind perishes from its own counsel as if from a wound. What would furtive flight avail me, who must die? I will stay. I have hardened myself to a grievous death. A criminal is ashamed, not of his dismal death, but of his crime. With what face shall I, a traitor, look upon David? That sight would be more difficult than any death. I, the betrayer of the king, will never await his return. I would prefer death by the sword now to that death. I have lived enough — worthy, indeed, of a thousand deaths. I shall never wretchedly endure such shameful punishments, never while I am alive allow these limbs to be cut to pieces. I shall rather fall upon my sword or put an end to my life with a gripping noose.

I am determined to die. My death is decreed, and I shall rip out my own life. I am resolved to inflict my punishment now with this hand for my shocking crime. I have indeed decided to take my welfare out of the hands of the king. I shall take my own life; my soul will destroy itself on its own account. I do not wish to save my death for someone else's hands; I shall die by my own. I only think on the kind of death: this voice alone caused the cruel and evil crime; then it is proper to bind the path of that noxious voice

obstringere est aequum. Scelus concepit haec,
periat eadem: solum placet suspendium,
iam fune cervicem ligare gestio.
O chara patria, o grata tellus, iam vale.
Vale, socia nostri tori dulcissima.
Valete, mihi videnda numquam pignora.
Intelligo quam vana iam sint stemmata,
quam fluxi honores, quam caduca gloria.
Hanc vltimam vocem sodales candidi
sumite: morior prudentia infelix mea —
insania dixisse satius est mea.
Valeque lux oculis novissima meis,
et aura numquam recipienda faucibus
nostris, vale, et lumen molestum perditis.
Et sponte rumpo fata et invitus mea:
mortis futurae trudit ad mortem timor. [Exit]

CHORUS.

[Dimetri] Anapestici.

Qui dant regi mala consilia
imminet illis exitus atrox.
Numquam possunt nece carere
necis autores: vsque vtenti est
mortifer ensis. Caveat quisquis
magna gubernat: casus ab alto
gravior accidit, qui magna petit
acrius vrit ferre repulsam.
Animo sic qui monstra aggreditur
quaecumque alijs scelera anhelat,
in se merito sola redundant.

106. placet] *MS* placeat *Boas* || **109.** socia . . . dulcissima] ⟨ tori dulcis iugalis socia || **112.** fluxi] ⟨ fluxe [*fluxere] | gloria.] gloria *MS* || **114.** sumite . . . infelix mea] ⟨ accipite . . . infelix | mea—] mea *MS* || **118.** perditis] ⟨ conscijs | perditis.] perditis *MS* || **120.** S.d.] *Om. MS* || M.h.] Anapestici *MS* || **121** ff. *The "parts" of the chorus are divided as follows:* a *121-131,* b *132-144,* c *145-159,* d *160-164. Apparently inconsequential marks appear to the left of ll. 127 and 159 (both canceled)* || **121.** dant] ?⟨ dat || **130.** anhelat] ⟨ anhelant ||

with a rope. My voice conceived the crime; let it perish. Only hanging pleases me; I am eager to choke off my neck now with a rope.

O my dear fatherland, O beloved land, now farewell. Farewell, most sweet companion of my bed. Farewell, children whom I shall never see again. I know now how empty are pedigrees, how fleeting are honors, how perishable is glory. My beloved ones, hear this last utterance: I die unhappy because of my intelligence — it were better to have said because of my insanity. And farewell, this very last day to meet my eyes; and air, never to be received by my throat; and daylight, distasteful to the damned — farewell. Both by choice and against my will do I destroy my life: a fear of the death which is coming forces me to this death.

[He goes out]

CHORUS.[6]

Over those who give a king evil counsel hangs a frightful end. The perpetrators of death can never escape death: the sword is fatal, even to its user. Let whoever manages great affairs beware: the fall from a high position occurs with more seriousness; to suffer a rejection galls more fiercely one who seeks great things. Thus, whoever undertakes monstrous things, whatever crimes he breathes onto others, they will only redound — and deservedly — onto himself.

[6] Robinson (p. 194) commented that this chorus, "with typically Senecan sentiments, is significant because its words make the setting of these four acts and especially the scene of Achitophel's announcement of suicide much more than a mere place; it is an environment, a milieu, a functional part of the theme and tone of the tragic action."

Humilis valli casa profunda [*fol. 25v*]
fulmine raro sternitur atro.
Alto valida culmine turris
boream sentit saepe minacem,
saepe insano frangitur austro;
dissipat asper fulminis ictus.
Sic qui secum grandia versant,
portenta rudi mundo obtrudunt,
saepe ingenio pereunt proprio:
et quod ratio nequit humana
deus id supplet maximus. Alios
in sua coget ruere fata,
alios in tormenta reservat.
Faelix quisquis vivere tecto
poterit humili. Non admittunt
lubricos motus pauperis aedes:
illic tutus capitur somnus,
nec locus vsquam fraudibus extat.
At numquam vacat aula timore:
cunctorum illa exponitur oculis;
illic fraudes, dira libido,
fasces vani, falsumque decus —
quid non sceleris regnat in aula?
Faelix nemo est idemque senex.

145, 155. Faelix = Felix ||

A humble home in a deep valley is seldom struck by the black thunderbolt. A strong tower on a high peak often feels the threatening north wind, is often shattered by a violent south wind; the harsh blow of the thunderbolt smashes it. Thus, those who contemplate grandiose projects and who force onto the innocent world heinous things often die by their own genius. And what human means cannot do, the almighty God will fulfill. Some He will compel to rush to their deaths, others He will save for torments.

Happy is he who can live in a humble house. The dwellings of the poor do not admit deceitful actions: there one takes his sleep safely, and never is room given for trickeries. On the other hand, a palace is never free of fear: it is exposed to the eyes of all; in it are treacheries, awful lust, hollow sinecures, and false splendor — what crime does not hold sway in court? No one is both happy and old.

Fulgor tantum vocat ad aulam,
gloria inanis, tumidi honores:
tollito premia tollisque fidem.
Abijt prorsus syncerus amor.
   In parvis est iucunda quies.
Magna quietem saepe repellunt.
Vis ergo piam vivere vitam?
Abstine magnis, vtere parvis.
Animum dominus postulat aequum.

ACTUS QUINTUS. SCENA PRIMA.

DAVID. SPECULATOR.

Trimetri Iambici.

DAVID. Graves malorum o[pp]ressus insultus tuli: *[fol. 26r]*
antehac iniquis terga presserunt iugis,
tristia humeris his imposuere pondera.
Etsi premebant saepe, tamen numquam opprimunt:
numquam fideli praevalebit improbus.
Confringere novit ille cervices malas.
Vt vile foenum alto domorum culmine
quod antequam quis disciderit exaruit
fessas secantis spe anxia fallit manus,
truces malorum sic cadebant machinae.
Quamvis eram quem petere tentabant scopus,
liber tamen gravi recessi a vulnere.
Ex vnguibus sic, spero, iam rapacibus
me liberabit deus et insidias malas
dirimet penitus. Est ille protector meus.

159. abijt] ⟨ exulat || **164.** aequum] ?⟨ aequam || Beneath **164.** *A curved mark separates Act IV from the heading of Act V*

V.1.m.h.] *Between the act number and the scene number in MS* || **1-10.** *Source identified with note* psal. 128 *at top of page* || **1.** o[pp]ressus] opppressus *MS* || **6.** Confringere novit] ⟨ Concidet dominus || **10-80.** *At l. 10 a dot marks the tenth line of the scene (and, accidentally, the tenth verse from the last mark, at IV.3.164). Following ten-line groups are marked with scores and dots, alternately. For continuation of the numbering, see note at V.2.14-44* ||

Only the splendor calls one to the palace — the empty glory, the puffed-up honors. Take away material rewards and you take away loyalty. True love is completely absent.

Pleasant tranquillity is found in small affairs; great ones often dispel peace. Do you wish, then, to live a pious life? Refrain from great affairs, enjoy the small. The Lord demands a just spirit.

ACT V. SCENE 1.

[Mahanaim. The Gate of David's Camp.][1]

[Enter] DAVID [and] WATCHMAN.

DAVID. I am set upon and have borne the heavy oppressions of evil men. Hitherto they have burdened my back with hostile yokes; heavy burdens have they imposed on my shoulders. But, though they have often oppressed me, they never press me down. A wicked man will never overcome a faithful one. God knows how to shatter their evil necks. Just as worthless grass on the high roofs of houses — grass which has dried up before anyone could harvest it — deceives the weary hands of the mower with annoying promise,[2] so the base stratagems of the evil fell short. Although I was the target which they tried to hit, yet I escaped without serious wound. So, I hope, will God free me now from their snatching claws and utterly destroy their evil plots. He is my Protector.

[1] The opening is paraphrased from Psalm cxxviii. (In the 1539 Psalter, the Zurich Latin Bible, and many other Bibles the number is cxxix, but Watson's own note proves that he used one in which it was cxxviii.) There follow thirty-five lines of Watson's invention (or imitation); the rest is closely modeled after *2 Kings* xviii.24-27.

[2] The original (Psalm cxxviii.6-7) reads: "Let them [David's enemies] be as grass upon the tops of houses, which withereth before it be plucked up: Wherewith the mower filleth not his hand, nor he that gathereth sheaves his bosom." Jewish houses had flat roofs (capable of having tents built on them; see III.1.133); they were "formed by layers of branches, twigs, matting, and earth, laid over the rafters and trodden down [and] covered with a compost" (Fallows *et al.,* II, 838). The vegetation which was accidentally sowed on these roofs by the wind could not develop deep roots and withered before maturity. Sixteenth-century commentators were vague about whether the mowers who tried to gather this grass were actually trying to gather food, but Watson obviously thought that they were. And the interpretations of some writers would have admitted Watson's view: for example, see Jerome and Cassiodorus (quoted by Franciscus de Puteo, *Cathena Avrea Svper Psalmos* [Paris, 1530], sig. Piiii*r*) and M. Antonius Flaminius (*In Librvm Psalmorvm Brevis Explanatio* [Venice, 1545], fol. 251*r*).

De proelio tam sollicitus numquam fui.
Hinc, inde mentem geminus affectus trahit:
mea me salus torquet, timeoque filio.
Nostrae deo cura est salutis optimo:
servavit aliâs, nunc quoque servabit, scio.
Sed filius iam condit alto pectore
curas mihi: illius gravabit plurimum
fortuna dira. Est ille solamen meo
solus animo. Mihi crescit in adversis amor.
Quod illi acerbe fit, idem acerbum erit mihi.
Illum domabit haec, scio, clementia.
Mens victa conceptum facile ponet nefas:
pietas refrenabit paterna vel impium.
Sed nescio quid mens vana praesagit mali:
quo plura complectitur, eo timet magis.
Quam filios timet cruentos Sarviae!
Ioab nimis irati gladium novi trucem.
Expertus antea horreo crudelem virum:
Abneris animus caede perculsus fera
(qui turpiter Ioab manu occisus iacet)
huic pectori miseros timores abdidit.
Additque multum saeviens violentia
plusquam ferina. Nescit iram fervidam
comprimere: vincenti furit immitis manus.
Vtinam exijssem! Iam reduxissem integrum
si mihi data esset quam peto victoria.
Mens fluctuat nec adhuc potest consistere.

17. trahit] ⟨ trahet || **21.** alto] ⟨ ipso || **23.** dira] ⟨ tristis || **23-25** (Est . . . mihi). *Printed in Boas* || **26.** clementia.] clementia *MS* || **28.** impium.] impium *MS* || **29.** mali:] mali *MS* || **32.** trucem.] trucem *MS* || **40.** exijssem!] exijssem, *MS* || **41.** quam peto] ⟨ nobilis ||

I have never been so anxious about a battle. Divided sympathy pulls my mind this way and that: my own safety causes me concern, and I fear for my son.[3] The care of my own safety rests with God most good; He has saved me at other times, and I know He will save me now, too. But my son now is the cause of worries deep within my breast: misfortune for him will weigh upon him heavily. He alone is solace for my mind. My love for him increases in these hard times. Whatever turns out bitterly for him will likewise be bitter for me. This indulgence, I know, will overcome him. When his mind is won over, it will readily put aside the perfidy which it has conceived; duty to one's father will restrain even the impious.

But my idle mind presages some sort of misfortune; the more it ponders, the more it is afraid. How it fears the cruel sons of Sarvia! I know the grim sword of a too enraged Joab. From earlier experience I shudder at the cruelty of that man. The spirit of Abner, struck down in a savage death, has implanted these wretched fears in my breast: he lies shamefully slain by the hand of Joab.[4] And Joab's raving violence, worse than a beast's, sharply increases my fears. He does not know how to control his heated ire: when he is victorious, his hand rages immoderately. O, would that I had gone out![5] If the victory which I seek had been given me, I would already have brought Absalom back uninjured. My mind is uneasy and still cannot settle down.

[3] "The dramatist seeks to magnify the tenderness of the father, as he has heightened the ferocity of the son" (Boas, p. 361).

[4] *2 Kings* iii.22-27. Surprisingly, neither the audience nor David is later told that Joab was responsible for Absalom's death.

[5] A recollection of the Biblical discussion of whether David should take the field, which Watson transferred to Absalom.

Gnatum, o deus, iam languido serva mihi:
ex hoc iucunda vita pende[t] vnico.
Quis sancta domino templa summo construet [*fol. 26v*]
et faciet arcae nobilem sacrae domum,
quae filio mihi erit voluptas perdito?
Auget timorem mutuum periculum.
Vt avidus animus nuncium expectat bonum
torpetque prorsus frigido pressus metu!
SPECULATOR. En longius iam cerno venientem virum
celeri ferentem maximos gressus pede.
A proelio rectam huc habet anhelus viam.
DAVID. Si solus est, boni est minister nuncij:
victoria laeti redibunt caeteri,
hic missus alios laeta praecedit ferens.
Gnatum tueatur summus orbis conditor
mihique reducat clade tetra liberum.
SPECULATOR. Alium procul conspicio currentem novum.
Certat priorem concito praevertere
cursu. Vt viam longam rapido gradu amputat!
Non currit: alis mollibus raptus volat.
Iam posterior quamvis sit, hic erit prius.
Nam plurimae facit viae compendium:
errat minus, sectatur ambages prior.
Nusquam a patulo fessus recedit tramite.
Hic agilior firmo valet plus robore.
Per invia velox rapitur ardenti pede.

43. languido serva] ⟨ ser [*serva] languido || **44.** iucunda . . . vnico] ⟨ salus et vita dependent mea | pende[t]] pendent *MS (Watson carelessly neglected to change the number of the verb)* | vnico.] vnico *MS* || **45.** construet] construet? *MS* || **46.** domum,] domum? *MS* || **49.** bonum] bonum? *MS* || **50.** frigido] ⟨ frigidus | metu!] metu. *MS* || **53.** rectam huc] ⟨ rectam | viam.] viam *MS* || **54.** solus est, boni est] ⟨ est solus, est boni ⟨ solus, est boni || **63.** Iam posterior] ⟨ Posterior || **64.** facit viae] ⟨ viae facit | compendium:] compendium *MS* || **66.** a patulo . . . tramite] ⟨ a⟨b⟩ patulo [*or perhaps* *ab via] . . . tramite ⟨ patulo . . . a via | tramite.] tramite *MS* || **67.** robore.] robore *MS* ||

O God, save my son for me, who am already weak. On this alone depends the happiness of my life. Who will build holy temples to God on high and make a noble home for the Sacred Ark, what pleasure will there be for me — if my son is lost? Our mutual danger increases my terror. How my eager mind awaits good news, and how it is benumbed, completely overcome by cold fear!

WATCHMAN. Look, far off I now see a man coming, taking very long strides at a fast pace. Panting, he makes his way here straight from the battle.

DAVID. If he is alone, he is a bearer of good tidings. After the victory, the rest will happily return; this messenger precedes the others and bears happy news. May the highest Founder of the world protect my son and bring him back to me free from terrible disaster.

WATCHMAN. Far off I see a second man running. He is striving, with his swift pace, to overtake the first man. How he shortens the wide gap with his rapid step! He is not running: he is flying, moved along on graceful wings. Although he is now the runner-up, he will soon be the pace-setter. For he is taking a short cut instead of the longer way; his bearing is quite straight while the first runner is following a roundabout course. Not spent from a long bypath, he nowhere pauses to rest. This swifter man is more durable than solid wood. Through trackless places he is sprinting at a scorching pace.

DAVID. Et hic quoque nobis nuncium feret bonum:
pergrata semper esse debet celeritas,
in re mala numquam boni contenderent.
Expecto sollicitus: bonum est quicquid ferent.
SPECULATOR. Iam plurimum a tergo reliquit alterum.
Instat nec absumpto sibi quicquam favet.
Esse auguror qui propius est Achimaas,
quantum ex citato conijcere cursu licet.
DAVID. Vir ille turbatos mihi animos recreat:
antehac mihi sinistra numquam detulit.
Clemens, scio, deus vota suscepit mea.
Solator, affectum paternum respice
et intimos scrutare viscerum sinus.
In numen ambo tuum miseri peccavimus:
vnum vel exitium, vel vna vita sit —
aeque ac meam, illius salutem postulo.
Tuae voluntati resistere nolumus,
cui quemlibet parere soli convenit.

[ACTUS QUINTUS.] SCENA SECUNDA. [*fol. 27r*]

ACHIMAAS. DAVID.

Trimetri [Iambici].

ACHIMAAS. Ô prospero rex marte faelicissime,
est laude quavis superior deus tuus,
hostes profana morte consumens tibi.
Quicumque gladium in te minacem sustulit,

69. David] ⟨ S [*Speculator] (*by error*) | feret bonum] ⟨ bonum feret || **70.** semper] ⟨ nobis || **77.** recreat:] recreat *MS* || **81.** sinus.] sinus *MS* || **82-84.** *Printed in Boas* || **82.** peccavimus:] peccavimus *MS* peccavimus, *Boas*

V.2.s.h.] Scena 2[a]. *MS* || *P.h. and m.h. reversed in MS* || M.h.] Trimetri *MS* || **1.** faelicissime = felicissime ||

DAVID. And this one too will bring us good news. Swiftness ought always to be associated with pleasantness. If the situation were bad, these good men would never vie with each other. I can hardly wait. Whatever they will bring is something good.

WATCHMAN. Now he has left the other man very far behind. He hurries onward and, though exhausted, shows himself no mercy. I think the nearer one is Achimaas, so far as I can determine from his hurried run.

DAVID. That man eases my troubled spirits: before this he has never brought me bad news. Kind God, I know, has heard my entreaties. Comforter, consider my fatherly emotion and examine the innermost feelings of my child. Against Thy will we have both transgressed wretchedly:[6] let us have either a common death or a common reprieve. I ask that my welfare be the same as his. We are unwilling to resist Thy will, which alone it befits anyone to obey.

[6] Another reminder of David's plot against Urias and of Watson's moral purpose.

[ACT V.] SCENE 2.

[Mahanaim. The Gate of David's Camp.][1]

ACHIMAAS [Enters and Greets] DAVID.

ACHIMAAS. O King, most fortunate in successful battle, your God is beyond any praise; He destroys your enemies in unholy death. All
those who raised a threatening sword against you

[1] This scene is closely modeled on *2 Kings* 28-30; but ll. 28-43 are original and are among the finest in the play.

vim principi malam cruentus inferens,
aut debita iam clade prostratus iacet
aut dissipatus se pavidae mandat fugae.
Victoriam primus reporto nobilem.
Hic maximam clemens deus potentiam
ostendit. Hoc pia fine cernitur fides.
DAVID. Quid? Filius num vivit Absalom mihi?
An mortuo perennis accrescit dolor?
Hoc fare primum, caetera queram postea.
ACHIMAAS. A Ioab huc belli allegatus principe,
tantum rediens vidi tumultum turbidum.
Clamor repente concitatur absonus.
Coguntur hostes pede salutem concito
quaerere, sequuntur ensibus a tergo tui
fulgentibus. Sternuntur vt oves morbidae.
Omni cadentum fremitus auditur loco,
cunctique devicti nemus vmbrosum petunt.
Sylva omnis, Absalom fugatur, perstrepit.
Victoriae signum sonabat buccina,
suosque Ioab vndique sparsos convocat.
Parcatur Israel fugato praecipit
et integram plebem domum reducerent.
Hoc affero certum, nihil aliud scio.
DAVID. Haec ampliores suspiciones inferunt
curasque mihi pallenti adaugent lividas.
Victoria mira est victi vbi quaeritur salus.
Vt propriam sic illius desydero:

6. iacet] ⟨ cadit || **14-44.** *Beneath l. 14 a score marks the twentieth verse from the last mark, at V.1.80. A score beneath l. 20 (marking the twentieth line of this scene and of this page) was canceled. Further ten-line groups (counting from l. 14) are marked with a dot at 22 (physically the twenty-fourth line of the scene; see note ad loc.), a score at 34, and a dot at 44. For continuation see note at V.3.8-144* || **14.** allegatus] ⟨ alligatus || **15.** tantum] ⟨ tantum huc || **21.** -victi *is lightly underscored* | petunt.] ⟨ petunt, || **22.** *Orig. followed l. 24 (or was added there for insertion here)* || **26.** reducerent] ?⟨ reduceret || **30-31, 34-36.** *Printed in Boas* || **31.** desydero] *MS* desidero *Boas* ||

and bloodily advanced their evil power against their sovereign, either lie prostrate now in deserved death or are routed in terrified flight. I am the first to report a noble victory. This kind God shows His very great power. In this result is your pious faith perceived.

DAVID. What? Does my son Absalom live? Or does my continual sorrow increase by his death? Tell me this first; I will seek the rest later.

ACHIMAAS. I was sent here by Joab, the leader of war. On the way I saw only a confused tumult. Suddenly there is a noisy clamor. The enemy are forced to seek safety on frightened feet. Your men follow behind them with swords flashing. They are strewn out like sick sheep. Everywhere is heard the noise of falling men, and all the conquered seek a shady grove. The whole woods resounds. Absalom is routed. The trumpet sounds the signal of victory, and Joab calls together his men, who are dispersed far and wide. He orders them to spare routed Israel and to conduct all the people home safely. This much I can report for sure; I know nothing more.

DAVID [Aside]. These things make my suspicions stronger and increase my leaden cares, and I grow pale.[2] A victory is remarkable in which the safety of the conquered is desired. As I desire my own safety, so I desire his:

[2] The dramatist has labored hard, not altogether successfully, to make David's slow realization of the truth dramatically effective.

est filius, quid aliud egissem parens?
Paterni animi delere non possum notas.
Quid tam paternum est quam studere liberis?
Quis proteget si ego sator expugno ferus?
Vitam semel dedi. Necem rursum inferam?
Quamvis alij possunt, ego nequeo tamen:
probis inhumanum est. Sequantur ceteri
libidinem. Istud cogit affectus patris.
Nulla, o deus, tuis vacabit laudibus
dies, perennis erit tui celebritas.
Te laude vivaci celebrabunt posteri,
nobis opem qui praebuisti perditis.
Huc a loco iam tu recede paululum.
Hic certiora vt arbitror iam deferet.
Animus benignas vsque retractat preces.

32. parens?] parens. *MS* || 35. ego sator] ⟨ sator

he is my son; what else could I do as a parent? I cannot erase the marks of a father's mind. What is so fatherly as to be zealous for one's children? Who will protect him if I, his begetter, savagely destroy him? Once I gave him life. Am I to give him death in turn? Though others can, I cannot: to the just-minded that is barbarous. Let others do what they will; this course of mine a father's love compels.

O God, no day will be devoid of praises of Thee; celebration of Thee will be perpetual. With vigorous praise will posterity extol Thee; Thou hast provided strength to us who are destitute.

[To Achimaas] Now you withdraw a little from this place — over this way.[3] This man, I think, will now report more definite news.

[Achimaas withdraws]

My soul continually renews its gentle prayers.

[3] See Introduction, pp. 60-61.

[ACTUS QUINTUS.] SCENA TERTIA. [*fol. 27v*]

CHUSI. DAVID.

Trimetri [Iambici].

CHUSI. Vocem procacem lingua rumpit gestiens.
Optata mentis adfero, rex optime:
evicimus fortes, fugantur perfidi.
DAVID. Proloquere, gnatus obijt an vivit valens?
Hoc expedi primum, ac metu me libera.
CHUSI. Vtinam inimicis sors eadem esset omnibus
nunc qualis immitem premit tibi filium.
Melius valet quam regis hostis debuit

V.3.s.h.] Scena. 3ª. *MS* || *P.h. and m.h. reversed in MS* || M.h.] Trimetri *MS* || **3.** perfidi] ⟨ caeteri || **7.** premit] ⟨ premet || **8-147.** *After l. 7 the following eighteen lines were written, then canceled (see Introduction, p. 57); most were used later, as indicated:*

7^{a}	Poenas dedit, nam debito laeto [= leto] occubat.	[*not reused*]
7^{b}	DAVID. Iam frigidus passim haeret [⟨ haerit] in venis cruor.	[7^{b}-7^{k} *later*
7^{c}	Vox haec vt ensis improbus mentem ferit:	*became, ver-*
7^{d}	omnes animae sensus mihi prorsus abripit.	*batim, V.3.*
7^{e}	O gnate, quis te casus infaelix premit [⟨ premet] ?	*130-139, and*
7^{f}	Quae dira gnati fata prorupit manus?	7^{h} *was used*
7^{g}	Quae bestia tam crudelis est author necis?	*a second*
7^{h}	Ô Absalom fili mi, fili mi Absalom.	*time as*
7^{i}	Quid saeva mors in eum furis, parcens mihi?	*V.3.147*]
7^{j}	Quis, gnate, dabit vt morte supplerem vices,	
7^{k}	vitam libenter [⟨ libens iam] morte redimerem tibi.	
7^{l}	Vt fata tulit, effare mortis ordinem.	[*not reused*]
7^{m}	Omnes miserias mens cupit amplecti simul.	[*not reused*]
7^{n}	CHUSI. Vt singuli vrbem liquimus fausto gradu,	[7^{n}-7^{r} *later*
7°	iter citatis suscipientes [⟨ suscipiendes] passibus,	*became, ver-*
7^{p}	nec longius adhuc certa progressis loca	*batim except*
7^{q}	praescripsit omnibus ille qui primas tenet	*for the last*
7^{r}	praefectus, insignemque pugnandi ordinem.	*word, V.3.*
		12-16]

A score beneath 7^{a} *and a dot by* 7^{k} *mark the tenth and twentieth lines (before cancellation) beneath the last mark, at V.2.44* || **8-144.** *A score beneath l. 8 marks the tenth line beneath the last mark, at V.2.44 (after cancellation of the eighteen lines above). Following ten-line groups are marked with scores and dots, alternately, at ll. 18, 28, 38, 48, 58, 68, 78, 88, 98, 109 (ten lines not counting added l. 108), 118 (nine lines to compensate for added l. 108; see note ad loc.), 134 (ten lines before the orig. l. 121 was expanded into seven [ll. 121-127; see note ad loc.]), and 144. A mark by l. 126 indicates the tenth line beneath l. 144 (not counting l. 148, which was added later, but counting V.4.1, which ll. V.3.121-127 follow in the physical order of the MS). For continuation of the numbering see note at V.4.10-50* ||

[ACT V.] SCENE 3.

[Mahanaim. The Gate of David's Camp.][1]

CHUSI [Enters and Greets] DAVID.

CHUSI. My exulting tongue speaks with a bold voice. I report your heart's desires, best King: in our strength we have conquered completely; the wicked are routed.

DAVID. Tell me, has my son fallen, or is he alive and well? Tell me this first, and free me from fear.

CHUSI. Would that all enemies would suffer the same fate as that which now burdens your hard son. He is in better condition than an

[1] The first nine lines are a virtual transcription of *2 Kings* xviii.31-32. The description of the battle is expanded from the sketchy account in *2 Kings* xviii.6-8. Watson's details are "purely imaginary" (Boas, p. 361), though he may have been influenced by some classical historian: as Boas noted (pp. 361-363), the order of battle was after the "discipline of the Romans." Boas complained of the goriness of the description. The account of Absalom's death, when finally given, is introduced by an invented account of Absalom's fear and by a Senecan description of the fatal tree; Seneca's *Phaedra* also colored the description of Absalom's death throes. Also found in the scene are *2 Kings* xviii.9 and 33. To conceal from David Joab's part in Absalom's death, Watson represented *2 Kings* xviii.10-15 only by the afterthought of Chusi (l. 128).

et qui saluti patris insidias tulit.
De proelio fabor prius, de hoc postea:
sic debitum servabo narrandi ordinem.
Vt singuli vrbem liquimus fausto gradu,
iter citatis suscipientes passibus,
nec longius adhuc certa progressis loca
praescripsit omnibus ille qui primas tenet
praefectus insignemque pugnandi statum:
rorarios statim, expeditos, velites
prima locat acie, hostium vim fervidam
armis refracturos levibus; tum proximum
locum obtinent densi tumultuarij,
lato ferentes pectore loricas graves,
robur clypeati sustinentes agminis.
Saltum Ephraim vix dum ferox exercitus
contigerat, et cunctis statuisset ordinem
cum subito totum cernimus Israël procul [*fol. 28r*]
longis gradum celerem ferentem passibus.
Preceps ruunt in bella visis hostibus.
Vago locis clamore neglectis fremunt.
Vt grando sulcis calamitosa concavis
recepta agros frigore rigentes operit,
sic vasta totam turba tellurem tegit.
Stulti duces minime morantur bellicos.
Discors populi tumultuantis editur
sonus, vt duobus obsitum scopulis fretum
quod saeva ventorum rabies exasperat.

11. narrandi] ⟨ narranda || **12-16.** *See note at ll. 8-147* || **12.** liquimus] ⟨ li⟨b⟩ || **14.** longius] ?⟨ long⟨e⟩ || **17.** statim] ⟨ primum || **21.** pectore] ⟨ pect⟨u⟩s || **22.** clypeati] ⟨ clypiati || **29-31.** *Line 31 orig. preceded l. 29. Just possibly Watson did not orig. intend to write l. 30, for he put a comma after* concavis; *but he wrote l. 30 before transposing the lines, for he changed the pn. after* operit *from a period to a comma, presumably at the time of transposition. Watson tried to rearrange the lines by means of preliminary letters (a* b *before 31 and apparently* a*'s before both 29 and 30, one of them prob. erroneous), but then canceled the letters and rewrote l. 31 in its present position* || **31.** sic vasta] ⟨ Immensa (*revised at time of transposition*) ||

enemy of the king, and one who has planned treacheries against his father's safety, ought to be. I shall tell about the battle first, about him later; thus I will observe the proper order of narrating.[2]

We left the city one by one at a goodly pace, beginning our march with quickened steps. We had not gone far before our commander, who was leading the way, assigned to all their predetermined positions and a remarkable fighting order. First he stations in the front line the quick *rorarii* and *velites,* ready to shatter the hot force of the enemy with light arms.[3] The heavy troops in close order hold the next position, wearing thick cuirasses on their broad chests and representing the main strength of the shield-bearing troop. When our fierce army had scarcely reached the forest of Ephraim and would have set everything in order, suddenly, far off, we see all Israel making a quick march with long strides. When our men have seen the enemy, they rush headlong into battle.[4] Abandoning their positions, they break forth in a collective shout. As a disastrous hailstorm covers the fields, filling the hollow furrows and encrusting the ground with cold, so this vast throng of men covers the whole ground. The leaders do not foolishly restrain our battle-eager men. The jarring sound of a people in tumult comes forth, as if from a strait situated between two rocks and made rough by the wild fury of the winds.

[2] This device allows Chusi to describe everything to the audience. The authority is probably some rhetorical principle learned in grammar school. For instance, under "Descriptio," Aphthonius (*Rhetorica Progymnasmata* [Paris, 1541], fol. 17*v*) advised, "Qui personas intendit describere, vt a primis ad vltima procedat, opus est, hoc est, a capite ad pedes. Res autem, ab ijs quae ante eas fuerunt, & quacunque ab illis solent euenire." Chusi goes from the general to the particular according to chronological sequence.

[3] *Rorarii* and *velites* were Roman light-armed troops, skirmishers.

[4] Watson is not very clear in distinguishing which army is doing what in this passage.

Praeter numerum nobis timendum erat nihil.
Huic galea capiti cava tuendo defuit.
Hic pectus armat strennuum et multiplici
defenditur thorace, nudus caetera.
Illum facit balista securum aerea.
Hic fidit arcui, illi fundae nititur.
Sunt quos relictis gladius armis protegit.
Hic missilem manu ferox hastam quatit.
Alter validam gerit bipennem dextera.
Nudus alius mucrone pugnabat brevi.
Nemo fuit arma qui gerebat integra:
qui scutum habuit telo carebat missili.
Armare tam subitus tumultus neminem
potuit. In ipso constitit numero salus.
Stant eminus. Telis petentes horridis
tam parvulam manum vorare gestiunt.
Ipsam ante pugnam animis habent victoriam
et proelij curas supini sedulas
omnes reponunt. Postea instant acrius,
vrgent feroces, impetunt contrarios,
et comminus pugnam cruentam conserunt.
At nos modestum contra tollentes gradum
primo petentium repellimus impetum,
mox ictibus anhelos validis aggredimur —
prosternimus forti haud bene armatos manu.
Securi vt alta fronte percussi boves,
dum pede vacillant, huc et huc dubij ruunt,

37-41. *Printed in Boas* || **38.** strennuum] ⟨ candidum || **39.** nudus caetera] ⟨ ce [*cetera] nudus || **40.** balista = ballista | balista securum] ⟨ s [*securum] balista || **46-47.** *Printed in Boas* || **52.** habent] ⟨ ⟨pe⟩ || **57.** modestum] ⟨ mon (?*scribal*) || **59.** anhelos validis] ⟨ v [*validis] anhelos || **61.** Securi vt alta] ⟨ Duri vt securi ||

Aside from the enemy's number, we had nothing to fear. On this one the hollow helmet to protect the head is missing; this one covers his bold chest and is protected by a manifold breastplate, but is bare over the rest of his body. The bronze ballista makes that one safe;[5] this one relies on a bow while that one trusts to a sling; there are some, their armor left behind, whom a sword protects; one fierce man shakes a spear in his hand; another swings a stout battle-axe with his right hand; another fights with a short sword and has no armor. Not one wears full armor: he who has a shield lacks a spear. So sudden an assault allows no one to arm; the enemy's safety consists only in his number.

The enemy stand at spear distance. Attacking with their dreadful spears, they long to devour so tiny a band. Before the battle they have victory in their thoughts, and carelessly lay aside their vigilance about warfare. Now they rush in very fiercely; they press in savagely and attack their antagonists, and hand to hand they join the bloody fray. But we, increasing our moderate pace against them, first repel the assault of the attackers and soon with our strong swords take the initiative against our gasping foes. We overcome those ill-armed men with our mighty force. Just as bulls struck with an axe on their high foreheads stagger and dazedly rush about,

[5] Though Watson's description is shifting from defensive armor to offensive weapons, the ballista hardly seems parallel to the hand weapons listed below. But in many small details Watson was careless.

sic occidere vulnera passi plurima.
Hic calcitrans humum tepentem sanguine
aspergit. Ille exhalat atro vulnere
coactus animam. Alter supinus vertice
terram moribundo pulsat. Hic tetrum vomit
cruorem. Et huius ense tra[ns]fossum est latus.
Huic viscera in humum ventre disrupto fluunt —
campo cadentum gemitus amplo perstrepit.
Passim iacebant amputata brachia. [*fol. 28v*]
Hic capita linguis palpitant trementibus.
Illic cadens iaculum momordit asperum.
Tepido solo stagnabat obscaenus cruor.
A tergo erat saltus profundus arbutis,
virgulta cuiquam ob implicita vix pervius.
Aegre patebat inter arbores via,
quo viribus totis recepta conferunt
se clade: sternuntur manentes funditus.
Saltum salutis singuli caussa petunt,
at nos furenti persequentes dextera
nullo sinebamus loco quiescere:
in invium victos adegimus lucum.
Hijs obstitere vtrimque gladius et nemus,
at gladius immitis pepercit nemini:
se saltui cunctos dederunt horrido.
E rupe praecipites cava multi occubant:
huic dum cadit, leves anima in auras abit;
scopulis caput duris resultat alteri;

63. vulnera passi] ⟨ passi vulnera || 65. aspergit] ⟨ aspersit || 66. vertice] ⟨ vertic⟨i⟩ || 68. tra[ns]fossum] trafossum *MS* | latus.] latus *MS* || 69. fluunt—] fluunt *MS* || 71-74. *Printed in Boas* || 75. arbutis] ⟨ arbu⟨c⟩is ||

so they fall from many wounds. This man, writhing, sprinkles the cool ground with his blood; that one gasps out his breath, smitten with a black wound; another, thrown backwards, beats the ground with his dying head; this one vomits his hideous gore; the side of this one is pierced with a sword; the entrails of this one flow onto the ground, his belly slashed open. The groaning of men falling on the broad field makes a great roar. Here and there lie cut-off arms; here heads convulse, their tongues trembling; there one man, as he fell, swallowed his sharp javelin. Dreadful gore stood in pools on the cool ground.

At their backs was a deep forest of arbute trees, scarcely passable by anything because of the entangled thickets. With difficulty a path was opened among the trees, where they betook themselves with all their might. They had been defeated; the survivors were totally prostrated. One by one they sought this woods for safety, but we, pursuing them with our raging right hands, allowed them nowhere to rest; into the hostile thicket we drove the conquered. On one side sword, on the other thicket beset them. But the inexorable sword spared no one; they gave themselves all to the fearful thicket. Many lie dead from headlong falls from a vaulted cliff: the life of one passes into the thin air as he falls; another's head bounces against the hard crags;

alijs adesus ora deformat lapis.
Luxata quidam membra moribundi trahunt,
et oris atro vulnere vanescit decor,
turpemque signat sanguinea viam nota.
Multos secant medios refracti stipites.
Alios subito virgulta rumpunt aspera.
Hinc alter hirsutis laceratur vepribus,
illinc comas rami frequentes auferunt.
Mors obviam fugientibus venit vndique.
DAVID. De filio iam potius audirem meo.
Haec antea mens cogitabat omnia.
Haec mitte, narra quod rogo paucissimis.
CHUSI. Casus superat omnem repentinus fidem.
Relictus hic suam in suis poenam videt:
proprium suorum morte supplicium timet.
Formidat et tristem meditatur exitum.
Mox, martio insiliens equo, preceps fugit:
densum in nemus viam capes[s]it proximam.
E capite laxa galea dum fugit cadit.
Ingens stat arbor nemoris obscuri decus,
prae caeteris altissima exerens caput.
Tabida vetustas concavum absumpsit latus.
Viburna truncum lenta putridum ambiunt.
Ramosque late annosa fundit tortiles:
imamque terram paene tangunt penduli.
Sub hac equo vectus fugaci, protinus
ramo recurvo inhaeret infaelix caput. [*fol. 29r*]

93. signat] ⟨ signum | nota] ?⟨ not⟨ ⟩ || **95.** subito] ⟨ subi⟨o *or* d⟩ (*scribal*) || **99-101.** *Printed in Boas* || **100.** omnia.] omnia *MS* omnia, *Boas* || **101.** paucissimis] ⟨ paucissimys || **103.** suam] ⟨ p [*poenam] || **105.** Formidat] ⟨ Iam pavet | tristem] ⟨ suum (tristem *recopied in margin for clarity*) | exitum.] exitum *MS* || **106.** insiliens] ⟨ insili⟨a⟩ns || **107.** capes[s]it] capescit *or* capestit *MS* || **108.** *Added marginally after l. 109 was written, but before l. 118 was written (see note at V.3.8-144)* | cadit.] cadit *MS* || **110.** caput] ⟨ capunt (*scribal*) || **114.** penduli] ⟨ pendulos ⟨ pensiles | penduli.] penduli *MS* ||

the water-polished rock mutilates the faces of others.[6] Some of the doomed drag their disjointed limbs, and the beauty of their features disappears in ugly wounds: a gory trail marks their hideous path. Broken trees cut many through the middle, and others the sharp thickets suddenly tear open. One man is slashed by the rough brambles on one side, and on the other the thick branches rip away his hair. Death comes to meet them wherever they flee.

DAVID. About my son I would rather hear now. All these things my mind has thought of before. Never mind them; in as few words as possible tell me what I ask.

CHUSI. His sudden downfall surpasses all belief. Left alone, he sees his own penalty in his men; from their deaths he fears his own punishment. He is terrified and ponders his sad outcome. Then, leaping on a war horse,[7] he takes to headlong flight; into the dense thicket he takes the shortest way. As he flees, his loosened helmet falls from his head.[8]

A huge tree stands, the glory of that dark glade, the tallest, lifting its head above all the others. Consuming age has split its arched sides. Clinging viburnums surround its decayed trunk. And this aged tree spreads wide its gnarled branches: hanging down, they almost touch the very ground. As Absalom is carried beneath this tree by his fleeing horse, suddenly his unlucky head becomes locked in a bent limb.

[6] That is, some expired in the air, some smashed themselves on the cliff as they fell, others crushed themselves on the rocks at the foot of the cliff.

[7] Not the royal mule of the Bible (*2 Kings* xviii.9), but a gallant war horse.

[8] Thus freeing Absalom's hair for the tree.

Fit pensilis ramo involutis crinibus
nodos ligat suo sequaces pondere;
pendentis animal a genibus elabitur,
dominum relinquens pendulum qua iusserit.
Metus fugit. Vox deficit. Suspiria
educit alta ex intimis precordijs.
Stant fixa capiti colligato lumina:
maestum intuetur. Spuma sordens defluit
ex ore, faucibus retentis, livido.
Nec potuit abiectas manus attollere.
Heu facinus aspectu, magis dictu grave!
Telis decorum pectus abruptum tribus.
His vidi oculis, stillante multo sanguine.
DAVID. Iam frigidus passim heret in venis cruor.
Vox haec vt ensis improbus mentem ferit:
omnes animae sensus mihi prorsus abripit.
Ô gnate, quis te casus infelix premit!
Quae dira gnati fata prorupit manus?
Quae bestia tam crudelis est author necis?
O Absalom fili mi, fili mi Absalom!
Quid saeva mors in eum furis, parcens mihi?
Quis, gnate, dabit vt morte supplerem vices?
Vitam libenter morte redimerem tibi.
O dulce pignus, o mihi charissimum,
heu saeva l[e]ti forma, mortis et genus.
Post filium l[e]to datum vixi diu:
gnatos parentes praegredi boni solent.

120. iusserit.] iusserit *MS* || **121-127.** *Expanded from an orig. one line (which followed l. 120 and was followed by present l. 128):* Metus fugit. Eheu facinus aspectu grave (*a large square inked after* fugit *canceled some short word*). *Watson canceled the line and wrote the marginal note* quere postea (*"see below"*). *He wrote the seven expanded lines after V.4.1 and marked them for insertion here. See notes at V.3.8-144 and V.4.10-50* || **127.** grave!] grave. *MS* || **128.** Telis] ⟨ Vidi | tribus.] tribus *MS* || **129.** multo] ⟨ tepido (tepido *not canceled, but presumably replaced*) || **130-139.** *See note at V.3.8-147* || **133.** premit] ⟨ prem⟨e⟩t || **136.** Absalom!] Absalom. *MS* || **138.** dabit] ⟨ dabis || **141-142.** l[e]ti . . . l[e]to] laeti . . . laeto *MS* || **143.** *Printed in Boas* ||

It happens that, as he hangs from the limb, by his very weight he ties tight knots in his tangled hair.[9] His mount slips out from his dangling knees, leaving his master hanging where the master guided him. His fear disappears; his voice fails; he drags forth deep sighs from the depths of his breast; his eyes stare, fixed in his fast-held head; he looks upon his doom. Foul froth flows from his livid mouth through his drooping jaws. He cannot raise his lowered hands. Alas, terrible thing to look at, worse to speak of! His fine breast is pierced by three spears! With these eyes I saw him while his blood still dripped freely.

DAVID. Now my congealed blood sticks fast throughout my veins. Your words strike my mind like a wicked sword; they completely rip out all the feelings of my soul. O son, what an unhappy outcome oppresses you! What hard hand dashed out the life of my son? What beast is the author of so cruel a murder? O Absalom, my son, my son Absalom! Why, savage death, do you rage against him, sparing me? Who, my son, will grant that I may take your place in death? Your life I would willingly ransom with my death. O sweet child, O my most beloved, alas the savage appearance of death — alas the kind of death! I have lived a long time since my son was given to death: good parents are wont to precede their children in death.

[9] See Appendix G.

Amara vivo est aura vitalis mihi,
ingrata lux est clara cupienti mori.
Vitae huius idem erit et doloris terminus.
O Absalom fili mi, fili mi Absalom!
O mors doloris vna perpetui comes! [Exeunt]

[ACTUS QUINTUS.] SCENA QUARTA.

IOAB. DAVID.

[Trimetri Iambici.]

IOAB. Quid, gloriose pater, gemis muliebriter?
Num filij nefanda facta comprobas?
Quid sordibus, querulusque lamentis iaces?
Victoris animosam refringis gloriam
si debitus defletur hostis exitus.
Quod gaudium in reducta erit victoria
si iusta pena parricidae plangitur?
Dolore perfundis redeuntem exercitum. [*fol. 29v*]
Ora omnium immutas salutem qui tibi
suo periculo peperere indebitam.
Hoc omnibus plane indicas hijs lachrimis:
hostiliter quam te odientes diligas,
quantumque temet protegentes oderis.
Quis non videt quam nos cupias iam mortuos
quando vltionem tam moleste hostis feras?
Quid impium iuste peremptum fles virum,
qui sydera, terram scelere complevit [s]uo?

147. *See note at V.3.8-147* | Absalom!] Absalom. *MS* || **148.** comes!] comes. *MS* | *Line apparently added after s.h. of V.4 was written, for it is crowded by the s.h., and the* S *of* Scena *overlaps it. It was prob. added after the rest of the play was written, for the line numbering apparently never compensates for this added line. See note at V.4.10-50* | S.d.] *Om. MS*

V.4.s.h.] Scena. 4^{a}. *MS* || M.h.] *Om. MS* || **2.** comprobas] ⟨ comprobat || **10-50.** *A dot by l. 10 marks the tenth line (in the physical order of the MS) beneath the mark at V.3.126 and the twentieth line beneath the mark at V.3.144 (not counting the added l. 148); it accidentally marks the tenth line of V.4. Following ten-line groups are marked with scores and dots, alternately, at ll. 19 (only nine lines, perhaps compensating for the added line V.3.148, but prob. merely a miscount [possibly caused by the canceling and rewriting of l. 18], for the mark at l. 50 compensates for the shortage here), 29, 39, and 50 (eleven lines; see above)* || **15.** feras?] feras. *MS* || **16-17.** *Added after l. 18 was written; l. 18 (and its s.p.) was canceled and then rewritten to make room for the added lines* || **16.** virum,] virum. *MS* (⟨ virum?) *Perhaps l. 17 was a second afterthought* || **17.** [s]uo] fuo *MS* ||

The breath of life is bitter to me living; the bright light of day is unpleasant to one desiring to die. The end of my sorrow will be one with the end of my life. O Absalom, my son, my son Absalom! O death, the only companion of my everlasting sorrow!

[All go out]

[ACT V.] SCENE 4.

[Mahanaim. A Room over the Gate of David's Camp.][1]

[Enter] JOAB [and] DAVID.

JOAB. Glorious father, why do you weep like a woman? Do you sanction the heinous deeds of your son? Why do you lie in mourning garments, complaining with cries of grief? You spoil a victor's proud glory if this weeping is over the deserved end of the enemy. What joy will there be in the victory which is brought back if the just punishment of a parricide is a cause for lament? You bathe the returning army with sadness; you change the expressions of all those who effected your safety at their own peril and beyond the call of duty. You plainly reveal to all by these tears how much you value those who hate you as an enemy and how much you hate those who protect you. Who does not see how you desire us all dead now when you bear so ill the vengeance taken upon your enemy? Why do you bewail the impious man justly slain, who surfeited heaven and earth with his crime?

[1] This scene is based rather closely on *2 Kings* xix.1-7. The later part of the Biblical account, which relates David's difficulty in regaining the throne and tells of the strife between Juda and Israel, is outside the scope of Watson's play.

DAVID. Victum cupivi, sed necatum nolui.
Quis triste ferrum pectori inseruit ferox
et se scelestum iussa contemnens pia
fecit? Sequar gnatum. Querelis sufficit
vix tempus vllum; gemere paulisper sine,
hoc aliqua quamvis parva defesso est quies.
IOAB. Arbor parentem est vlta, non exercitus:
haec sola vindicat paternam iniuriam.
Non milites, sed ligna rami denegant
illi salutem. Cur eum luges pater
quem nec fretum nec terra nec aura mobilis
vivum nec extinctum libenter sustinent?
Depone luctus. Statue maerori modum.
Numquam tuus erat filius qui tam pio
absimilis est patri. Meruit hunc exitum.
DAVID. Vultus oberrant vsque pendentis mihi:
oculis recurrit flebilis imago meis.
Gnatum perennis sequitur occisum dolor:
numquam intolerabiles satis aerumnas querar.
IOAB. Abrumpe questus. Solve grates debitas
victoribus. Belli redit fructus tibi.
Populi fuit periculum, tua est salus.
Procede, vultus mitte lamentabiles.
Maestos tua caussa reducito milites.
Ni feceris, iam singuli te deferent,
regalem honorem conferentes alteri.
Hic, arbitror, tibi luctus erit acerbior:
et vita et omni honore defuncto simul.

19. ferox] ferox? *MS* || 21. fecit? Sequar] ⟨ Sequar | fecit?] fecit, *MS* || 22. paulisper] ⟨ paulo || 23. defesso est quies] ⟨ est quies [*est quies defesso] || 24-29. *Printed in Boas* || 38-39. Belli . . . fuit] ⟨ Certaminis fructus tibi/ redit, populi est || 38. tibi.] tibi *MS* || 39. periculum] ?⟨ periculo ||

DAVID. I desired him conquered; I did not want him killed. What fierce man thrust that wretched steel into his breast and rendered himself villainous by despising my benevolent commands? I shall follow my son. Scarcely any amount of time is sufficient for my lamentations. Permit me to weep a little while: in my weariness, this is some respite for me, however small.

JOAB. The tree, not the army, avenged the parent; it alone avenged the injury of the father. Not the soldiers, but the wood of that bough denied him safety. Why do you, his father, mourn him whom neither the sea nor the land nor the mobile air is willing to sustain, either alive or dead?[2] Lay aside your weepings; set an end to the mourning. He never was your son who was so unlike his pious father. He deserved this end.

DAVID. The features of him hanging there hover continually before me; his pitiful image recurs before my eyes. Perpetual sorrow follows the death of a son: I could never complain enough of the unbearable calamities.

JOAB. Break off your complaints. Pay the thanks due the victors. The fruit of war returns to you. The risk was the people's, the safety is yours. Come now, away with these doleful faces. For your own sake recall your sad soldiers. Unless you do, they will now desert you one by one, conferring on another the honor of kingship. This, I think, will be an even more severe sorrow for you: having both your life and your every honor destroyed at once.

[2] ". . . the dramatist adds a fine imaginative stroke when he makes the Israelite captain urge that David should cease to mourn for one whom Nature herself has punished and cast out. . . . The conception is, of course, not Hebrew but pagan, and is the main instance in the play of the author's classical studies influencing not merely his technique and imagery but his thought" (Boas, p. 363).

DAVID. Vultum docet fingere rigida necessitas.
Nobis eundum est chara quo patria iubet. [Exeunt]

CHORUS. [*fol. 30r*]

[Dimetri] Anapestici.

Vrget rapida saepe ruina,
numquam opprimitur splendida virtus:
manet annosum semper in aevum.
Numquam caruit caeca ambitio
fine nefando: scelera irritat
atque malorum condit acervum.
Tentatio quevis bono cedit bene.
Malus malum semper requirit exitum.

FINIS.

46-55. *Printed in Ch* || **46.** David] *Ch makes the s.p. a part of the verse* || **47.** S.d.] *Om. MS* | *Beneath the line a long score separates the scene from the chorus* || M.h.] Anapestici *MS* || **48** ff. *The "parts" of the chorus are divided as follows:* A *48-50,* B *51-53,* C *54,* D *55* || **48.** *Orig. followed l. 49 (or was added there for insertion here); Ch printed ll. 48-49 in the physical order of the MS, together with the* b *and* a *indicating transposition* | Vrget] ?⟨ Vrges || **50.** aevum] ⟨ ⟨ ⟩ || **52.** nefando] ⟨ pudendo || *Beneath* Finis *a heavy underscore across the page*

DAVID. Stern necessity teaches me to feign a face; I must follow the course which my beloved country bids.

[They go out]

CHORUS.[3]

Consuming ruin is often threatening, but splendid virtue is never overcome. It always endures into ripe old age.

Blind ambition has never lacked a wicked end: it provokes crimes and creates a heap of evils.

Any temptation yields easily to good.

Evil always demands an evil end.

THE END.

[3] ". . . the universal neo-Senecan habit of ending plays as did the Greeks, and as Seneca did not, by a choric utterance, is demonstrably due to the one single instance of its employment in Seneca's dramas [*Hercules Oetaeus*]" (Kastner and Charlton, I, xliv-xlv).

APPENDICES

A. A LATIN POEM BY THOMAS WATSON

This poem was prefaced to Joannes Setonus, *Dialectica* (London, 1545), sig. Aiiii*r*-*v*. The meter is elegiac strophes: i.e., dactylic hexameter lines in which the alternate lines want two syllables (the so-called pentameter). Watson's handling of the meter is perfectly regular: he makes no substitutions except the spondee, which is permissible in the hexameter anywhere except in the fifth foot and in the pentameter anywhere except in the fourth and fifth feet.

Magnum est exacte nouisse elementa loquendi,
  Et plane sensus discutere ambiguos.
Imprimisque styli concinnum fertur acumen,
  Et rebus prudens ponere iudicium.
A veris, pulchrum est certo distinguere falsa,
  Artibus ingenuis excolere ingenium.
Pro summa rerum naturas scire putatur,
  Sermonem multis perpetuare modis.
Quid non quantumuis clarum sapientia vincit
  Vrbes quae vastas, quae fera bruta regit?
Iis aptum concinnat iter dialectica cunctis,
  Os, animum, linguam, format, et ingenium.
Huius praesidio, fines ars quaeque tuetur,
  Prae reliquis claro nomine digna ducis.
Sordibus, aut tenebris, ante hac oppleta iacebat,
  Nunc quantum, admota luce, nitoris habet!
Hanc operam rudibus praebet Setonus alumnis,
  Ornanda hac aetas arte tenella venit.
Est breuis, est clarus, palmam merito feret, vt qui
  Miscuerit lumen cum breuitate pari.
Si fructum ex studiis vllum speraueris, istum
  Quin emptum paruo conteris aere librum?

B. THE SPELLINGS OF BIBLICAL NAMES

Following are some of the proper names used by Watson in *Absalom* with some conclusions about the spellings of these names in the sixteenth-century Latin Bibles which I have seen.

Absalom (35 times in the play; the exclusive spelling from I.3.214 on) and *Absalon* (3 times in the play): the former spelling predominates in the Bibles.

Achitophel (the only spelling in the play except for two or three scribal errors): in the Bibles a heavy favorite over such alternative forms as *Achitofel, Achi-tophel,* and *Achithophel.*

David: the only spelling in Watson and the Bibles.

Ioab: the only spelling in Watson and the Bibles.

Chusai (the only spelling in the play, but sometimes a diaeresis appears over the *-i,* even in speech prefixes): a heavy favorite in the Bibles over an alternative *Husai.*

Abisai: the only spelling in Watson and the Bibles.

Semei: the almost exclusive spelling of the Bibles, though *Simei* and *Simhi* occur.

Sadoc: the spelling of most Bibles, but some have *Sadoch, Sadok,* etc.

Abiathar: the only spelling in the play and the spelling of nearly all Bibles.

Achimaas: a few Bibles have variant spellings such as *Ahimaas.*

Chusi: half a dozen Bibles confuse *Chusi* and *Chusai* under the same spelling.

Abrahae (genitive, II.2.151): no Bible which I have seen used oblique forms.

Amnonis (genitive, I.1.29): very few Bibles have oblique forms.

Berseba (accusuative, III.3.173; the name may have been altered from *Bersaba*): no contemporary Latin Bible had the *-eba* spelling, but a few English Bibles did.

Chore (nominative, I.3.142): only six of the Bibles checked have this spelling over *Core* or some other alternative, one of the Bibles being the 1531-35 Paris Bible identified in Chapter III (B.M. shelfmark 3015 aa 21).

Hierusalem (nominative, III.1.8): the spelling of most Bibles is *Ierusalem,* but eight, including the two Paris ones identified in Chapter III, have Watson's spelling.

Mariam (nominative, II.3.93, altered from *Mariah*): almost all Bibles have *Maria,* a few *Miriam;* none has *Mariam* (nominative).

Moses (nominative, II.3.98, canceled), *Mosen* (accusative, II.3.94; IV.1.99), *Mosi* (dative, IV.1.139), and *Moÿse* (ablative, I.3.141): virtually all Bibles spell the name *Moyses* and use oblique forms.

C. THE CAREERS OF JOHN CHEKE AND ROGER ASCHAM AT ST. JOHN'S COLLEGE

Sir John Cheke was admitted a fellow of St. John's College on May 26, 1529, and commenced M.A. in 1533 (*D.N.B.*). Thereafter he was at Cambridge during most of the period until July 10, 1544. Of course he was away for short periods occasionally: in 1534-35 he and others were granted a grace "abesse ab omnibus exequiis missis et congregationibus ex statuto" (Searle, p. 296), presumably because they were on some university mission; on October 3, 1536, Cheke, George Day, and Nicholas Metcalfe were appointed college proxies to appear before the king's commissioners regarding the oaths of succession and supremacy (Baker, I, 104, 359), but this may have been at Cambridge. Ascham's Letter XXI (Giles, I, Part 1, 46-49), to Cheke, indicates that Cheke was away around March 25, 1543 (or, as Giles dates the letter, 1544). But there is no evidence that these were extended absences. On the other hand, there are clear indications that Cheke was present in several of the crucial years: in 1534-35 as an *examinator questionistarum* (Searle, p. 291); in 1537-38 as an auditor (Mary Bateson, ed., *Grace Book β Part II Containing the Accounts of the Proctors of the University of Cambridge, 1511-1544,* Cambridge Antiquarian Society, Luard Memorial Series, III [Cambridge, 1905], 218); on November 6, 1538, when he and Ascham *et al.* are supposed to have signed a letter to Alban Langdaile (Baker, I, 462; I have not seen the letter); in 1539-40 as the last master of the glomery (Searle, p. 341; Baker, I, 30); in 1540-41 as one in charge of food purchases (Searle, pp. 358-359); in 1541-42, when he was paid twenty shillings as public orator (Bateson, p. 238); and in 1542-43 as *examinator questionistarum* (Venn, *Grace Book* Δ, p. 2) and public orator (Bateson, p. 245). That Cheke was at Cambridge in 1543-44 is implicit in his being called from there in July, 1544.

The records for Roger Ascham are as follows: in 1534-35 he was paid three shillings four pence for copying an instrument "de senescalli academiae officio" (Bateson, p. 193); in 1536-37 he took his M.A.; in July, 1537, he "possibly composed, and in part copied" a letter from the college to Lord Cromwell (Baker, I, 353); in 1537-38 he was paid ten shillings "for wrytyng chartoures in the blak booke" (Bateson, p. 212) and six shillings eight pence for copying certain letters to London (Bateson, p. 215); on November 6, 1538, he may have been one of the twenty-seven signers of a letter to Alban Langdaile (Baker, I, 462); in 1539-40 he was an *examinator questionistarum* (Searle, p. 342), he was paid twenty-six shillings eight pence for a mathematics lecture (Bateson, p. 226), and he served as surety for his brother Anthony (Bateson, p. 229). Also in this last year he was working for the election of Thomson to a fellowship (Letters V, VI, VII; Giles, I, Part 1, 6 ff.). The dating of Ascham's absence thereafter is so complex that I shall explore it in a separate study.

If we consider these records and those previously given (Chapter II) for Watson, we can surely reject George Saintsbury's statement (p. 333) that 1535 was the earliest date when Watson, Cheke, and Ascham were all at Cambridge.

D. SOME NOTES ON THE METRICS OF *ABSALOM*

Apart from the metrical headings to the scenes and choruses, Watson himself labeled the trochaic tetrameter catalectic passages at III.1.34-44, 47-52; the spondaic line at V.3.147; a scazon at I.3.186 (label canceled after the line was revised); and a hypercatalectic line at II.1.52 (with anapests in the fourth and sixth feet). In addition, just possibly the trefoils in I.1 (see Textual Notes) marked lines about which there was some metrical question.

As an illustration of the extent to which Watson used anapests in the second or fourth feet, I present here a list of the lines in the first scene which contain such anapests. The scene is roughly typical of the play as a whole: **I.1.**10, 13, 16, 18, 19, 25, 27, 28, 32, 34, 47, 52, 57, 62, 64, 73, 78, 80, 81, 84, 86, 87, 88, 90, 92, 103, 107, 110, 113, 114, 121, 122, 124.

Following is a list of some of the more serious faults in Watson's iambic trimeter verse. I present here only the lines which Watson made final; many of his revisions were apparently motivated by metrical errors which abound in the earlier versions of many lines. Other issues besides those involved here were of course in doubt: for example, Gualtherus (sig. 92*r*) and Avantius ("Dimensiones," sig. Aii*v*) condemned the tribrach in the fifth foot, but others did not; Watson has several such tribrachs (e.g., I.1.11). But the items which I list are those which were most universally regarded as defects. It should be added that some of the errors may have been deliberate licenses (e.g., the spondees in Absalom's opening complaint); some others seem to have been caused by ignorance, not of metrical requirements, but of the length of certain kinds of syllables (e.g., Watson apparently construed all adverbs ending in *-e* to have a short *-e*); finally, Watson may have intended syncope of certain syllables, without an attendant lengthening of the short syllable.

Anapests in the sixth foot: **I.1.**82, 101, 104; **I.3.**16, 36, 55 (in this line all feet except the first are anapests), 102; **II.3.**49.

Spondees in the even feet; if in the sixth foot, the line is a scazon: **I.1.**8, 9, 11, 14, 15, 65, 89 (scazon), 99, 123; **I.3.**29, 54 (scazon); **II.1.**27; **III.3.**5, 252 (scazon); **IV.2.**61 (scazon); **IV.3.**1, 8; **V.2.**35; **V.3.**57.

Miscellaneous defects: **I.1.**12 (dactylic fourth), 35 (dactylic second with syncope of *vivere*), 75 (pyrrhic fourth), 84 (trochaic fifth), 91 (molossic first); **I.3.**10 (tribrachic sixth), 29 (trochaic fifth), 76 (amphimaceric first); **II.1.**89 (anacrusis); **II.2.**64 (seven feet with a dactylic fourth); **III.3.**4 (amphimaceric third), 339 (five feet); **IV.1.**25 (fifth foot lacks a syllable); **IV.2.**1 (pyrrhic second); **V.3.**30 (trochaic fifth).

Watson's choric meters are somewhat more regular than his trimeters. But I have not thoroughly analyzed sixteenth-century critical attitudes toward these meters; hence, a listing of Watson's errors in these meters would be misleading. Similarly, I do not list the several faults in Watson's trochaic tetrameter (Act III).

I have made sample analyses of the iambic trimeters of a number of neo-Latin plays roughly contemporary with Watson's. Nearly all use anapests, spondees, and even trochees in the wrong places; of course, most of them are not true tragedies, though some of them tried to be. Only the following plays follow the rigid metrical rules better than does Watson's play: George Buchanan's *Iephthes sive Votum, Tragoedia* (Paris, 1554); Erasmus' translations of Euripides' *Hecuba* and *Iphigenia* (Vienna, 1511); and (surprisingly) Jacobus Zovitius' *Didascalvs. Comoedia* (Cologne, 1541). The other plays which I have sampled are John Foxe's *Christvs Trivmphans, Comoedia Apocalyptica* (Basel, 1556); Jacobus Schoepperus' *Tentatvs Abrahamvs* (Cologne, 1564) and *Ectrachelistis, sive Ioannes Decollatus, Tragoedia* (Cologne, 1546); Nicholas Grimald's *Christus Redivivus, Comoedia Tragica* (Cologne, 1543) and *Archipropheta* (Cologne, 1548); and Antonius Thylesius' *Imber Aureus, Tragoedia Nova* (Antwerp, 1546).

E. ILLUSTRATIONS OF WATSON'S "IMITATION"

In this appendix, I have used the following abbreviations of Seneca's plays: *Ag.* (*Agamemnon*), *HF* (*Hercules Furens*), *HO* (*Hercules Oetaeus*),

M. (*Medea*), *Oc.* (*Octavia*), *Oe.* (*Oedipus*), *Pha.* (*Phaedra*, or *Hippolytus*), *Pho.* (*Phoenissae,* or *Thebais*), *Th.* (*Thyestes*), *Tr.* (*Troades*). ⟨ means "taken from" or "based on"; "cf." indicates a parallel or a likely source. Only Renaissance editions should be used to check these parallels, for their readings are frequently different from those of modern editions. The line numbers for Seneca are those of Peiper and Richter. Frequently a word in a borrowed passage has colored Watson's wording in adjoining lines, but I have not normally noted these instances. By and large, I have noted only clear borrowings of at least a major portion of a line. Except for special circumstances, I have not noted parallels with authors other than Seneca, or citations of passages by Renaissance lexicons and collections of "flowers."

As I stated in the Introduction, Watson labeled a number of his lines as commonplaces, using a small *c* for that purpose. Following is a list of the lines so marked, with such indications as I have found of their sources or of parallel statements.

I.1.94 (⟨ *Pha.* 249), 100-101 (⟨ *Th.* 193-194, *HO* 1786; cf. *M.* 159), 114-115 (cf. Ovid, *Metamorphoses* II.162); **I.2.**3-5 (⟨ *Tr.* 258-259, 1-3; cf. *Th.* 939), 25-26 (contrast Morris Palmer Tilley, *A Dictionary of the Proverbs in England in the Sixteenth and Seventeenth Centuries* [Ann Arbor, Mich., 1950], E208), 37-39 (no parallel found); **I.3.**13-14 (cf. *Pha.* 982; the thought is frequent in *Tr.* and *Th.*), 34 (⟨ *Th.* 199-200; cf. *M.* 203), 84 (cf. Erasmus, *Adagia,* in *Opera Omnia,* II.8.21; Tilley, M860), 88 (contrast Tilley, F265), 104 (cf. *Tr.* 290, 870-871; Tilley, S468, S474; Hubertus Scutteputaeus, ed., *Senecae . . . Sententiae* [Antwerp, 1576], p. 369), 119 (cf. Erasmus, *Adagia* III.9.27; Tilley, V25), 124 (no parallel found), 189-191 (⟨ *HO* 885-886, 983; cf. *HF* 1237, Tilley, S475), 208 (⟨ *Oc.* 866 or *Tr.* 279-280), 213 (parallel not found), 217 (cf. Tilley, D29, H54), 218 (parallel not found), 222-223 (parallel not found); **IV.3.**16 (parallel not found).

The following list shows other Senecan borrowings by Watson not indicated by him.

I.1.1 (⟨ *HO* 712), 3 (⟨*HO* 1402-03[?]), 7-8 (⟨ *HO* 1494), 14 (probably ⟨ *Oc.* 876), 15 (⟨ *HO* 275-276), 17 (⟨ *HF* 208-209), 25-26 (⟨ *HO* 275-277), 30 (cf. *Pha.* 101), 45 (⟨ *Oc.* 108), 47-48 (⟨ *HF* 463-464), 63 (⟨ *HO* 435), 72 (cf. *Tr.* 335, *Oc.* 453-454), 80 (cf. *Tr.* 250, *HF* 975), 89 (⟨ *Oc.* 99b), 98 (⟨ *Pho.* 46), 99 (cf. *Ag.* 108-109, *Tr.* 657, *Pha.* 719), 108-109 (⟨ *Pha.* 657), 110-111 (⟨ *Pha.* 653), 113 (cf. *Pha.* 394-395), 116 (⟨ *M.* 174, 177), 120 (probably ⟨ *M.* 150-151), 121 (partly ⟨ *M.* 175).

I.2.1-2 (partly ⟨ *HF* 205-207, *Pha.* 670; cf. Vergil, *Aeneid* I.199), 6-7 (cf. *Oc.* 431), 8 (⟨ *Tr.* 259-260, *Pha.* 978-980, 1123-24), 9-10 (⟨ *Oc.* 432-433), 10 (⟨ *Oc.* 160), 11-12 (⟨ *Oc.* 143-144), 22 (cf. I.2.1), 23-24 (⟨ *M.* 203-204; cf. *Absalom* I.3.34), 32 (cf. *Oc.* 929), 35 (⟨ *M.* 20-21), 41 (⟨ *HO* 714; cf. *Pha.* 1123 ff.), 42 (cf. *Tr.* 518), 43 (cf. *Tr.* 522-523).

I.3.1-2 (cf. *Tr.* 608-609), 5 (cf. I.2.11), 6-7 (cf. *Tr.* 933), 20-21 (⟨ *M.* 895, *Th.* 192-194), 22 (⟨ *M.* 902), 24 (⟨ *M.* 898-899; cf. *Th.* 255 ff.), 25-27 (⟨ *M.* 905-906), 28-29 (⟨ *M.* 911-912, 901), 30 (⟨ *M.* 904-905), 31 (⟨ *M.* 908-909, 915), 35 (cf. *Th.* 255), 36 (⟨ *M.* 926-927, *Th.* 260-262), 37 (⟨ *M.* 929-930; cf. *M.* 943), 38 (cf. *M.* 425-426), 41 (⟨ *M.* 934-935; cf.

M. 465), 46 (⟨ *M.* 931-932, 899), 48 (cf. *HF* 341-342, 399), 50-51 (cf. *Tr.* 271-273), 53 (⟨ *M.* 895), 54-58 (⟨ *M.* 939-943), 59-60 (⟨ *M.* 917-918), 61 (probably ⟨ *M.* 953), 62 (cf. *M.* 941 ff.), 65 (cf. *Th.* 25 ff., especially 30-32), 68-70 (material Biblical, construction ⟨ *M.* 382 ff.), 71-72 (⟨ *M.* 385-386), 73-77 (⟨ *M.* 386-387, 390-391, 395), 78 (⟨ *M.* 444), 79 (⟨ *Pha.* 129 and/or *Pha.* 413, *M.* 175), 80 (⟨ *HF* 772, *M.* 174), 81-82 (⟨ *Pha.* 131-132), 82-83 (⟨ *Pha.* 132-135), 89 (⟨ *M.* 155), 91-92 (⟨ *M.* 398-399), 93-96 (⟨ *M.* 401, 403, 406-407, 412-413; for part cf. *Pha.* 569, 572-573), 97 (cf. *HF* 772, 1033, *Pha.* 142, *Oe.* 724a-725), 99 (⟨ *M.* 423-424; cf. *Th.* 192-193), 100 (⟨ *Oc.* 440), 103 (⟨ *M.* 416), 107 (⟨ *Oc.* 446), 110 (⟨ *M.* 159), 112-113 (⟨ *M.* 160-61), 114 (cf. *HF* 342, *Oc.* 456), 116 (cf. *Oc.* 456), 122-123 (probably ⟨ *Oc.* 455, 462-463), 128-130 (⟨ *Pha.* 145-147, 152), 132-135 (⟨ *Pha.* 149-159; phrases parallel to *Pho.* 655, *Oc.* 488, *HF* 205, *HO* 1173), 144-145 (⟨ *Pha.* 162-163), 146 (⟨ *Pha.* 165-166), 147 (⟨ *Pha.* 130, revised last word ⟨ *Pha.* 165), 149 (⟨ *Pha.* 177-178), 150-151 (⟨ *Pha.* 179-180, 184-185), 152-153 (⟨ *Pha.* 181-183, 580-582), 155 (cf. *Pha.* 178-179, 699), 157 (⟨ *Pha.* 138, assigned to Phaedra in sixteenth-century editions), 159-160 (⟨ *HO* 476-477), 162-163 (⟨ *HO* 480-481), 164 (probably ⟨ *Pha.* 566), 166 (probably ⟨ *Pha.* 101-102), 167-169 (⟨ *HO* 295-298; cf. *M.* 898-899, *Absalom* I.3.24), 173 (⟨ *Ag.* 426), 174 (⟨ *M.* 424-428), 175 (⟨ *Tr.* 642), 177 (⟨ *Tr.* 643), 185 (partly ⟨ *Tr.* 657), 186 (originally ⟨ *Pha.* 264), 190 (probably ⟨ *HO* 885-886), 191 (⟨ *HO* 983), 192-193 (cf. *HO* 1027-29), 195 (cf. *Pha.* 265), 202-203 (cf. *Tr.* 661-662), 204 (cf. *Oc.* 858), 205 (⟨ *Oc.* 863), 206 (cf. *Oc.* 873), 207 (cf. *Oc.* 364), 209-212 (⟨ *Pho.* 1-6, perhaps partly ⟨ *Oe.* 997), 227 (probably ⟨ *Pha.* 616), 228 (cf. *HF* 588, *Oc.* 365-366), 235-238 (⟨ *M.* 591-594), 239-241 (⟨ *M.* 862-865), 242 (⟨ *Oc.* 363).

II.1.1 (⟨ *Oc.* 820), 2-3 (⟨ *Oc.* 780-781, *M.* 670; cf. *M.* 978), 4 (⟨ *Pho.* 322 or 540-541), 5-6 (⟨ *Oc.* 781-783), 7 (cf. *Pho.* 541-542), 8 (⟨ *Pho.* 323; cf. 326), 9 (idea ⟨ *Oc.* 783-784; cf. *Tr.* 107), 10-12 (idea probably ⟨ *Pho.* 540 ff.), 13 (⟨ *Pho.* 544-545), 21 (⟨ *Pho.* 325), 22-24 (⟨ *Oe.* 919-921), 25-26 (⟨ *Pho.* 325-326), 41-42 (probably ⟨ *HO* 754-755), 87 (probably ⟨ *Pho.* 391, the context of which may have colored *Absalom* II.1.62-65), 89 (⟨ *Pho.* 419), 91 (⟨ *Pho.* 394), 92 (cf. *Pho.* 398, 414), 94 (cf. *Pho.* 395-397, 415), 115-116 (cf. phrasing but not idea of *Oc.* 868-870).

II.2.45 (cf. *Pha.* 138), 46 (⟨ *Pho.* 320), 56 (cf. *Pho.* 642), 59 (probably ⟨ *Oc.* 851, 855; 846 may have colored *Absalom* II.2.39), 60 (probably ⟨ *Oc.* 872-873), 61 (⟨ *Oc.* 838), 62 (probably ⟨ *Oc.* 873), 142 (though the idea is Biblical, cf. *M.* 427, *Tr.* 685), 147-148 (cf. *Tr.* 350-351).

II.3.10 (probably ⟨ *Pho.* 448), 14 (cf. *HF* 434, *Th.* 747-748), 43 (⟨ *Tr.* 1115-16), 44 (⟨ *Oe.* 138-139), 45 (cf. *Ag.* 972-973), 47 (probably ⟨ *Oe.* 37), 51 (cf. *Th.* 2), 53, 56 (cf. *Pha.* 1068-69, 1086), 55 (cf. *Tr.* 1108-10), 58 (probably ⟨ *Tr.* 892-893), 62 (probably colored by *Tr.* 1117 and *Pha.* 1026, 1071, 1094), 63 (cf. *M.* 732, the context of which may have colored *Absalom* II.3.59), 66 (cf. *Tr.* 1084-85), 110 (⟨ *Oc.* 476), 145 (probably ⟨ *Pha.* 1077).

III.1.2 (probably ⟨ *Ag.* 912), 8 (⟨ *Th.* 180-181), 9 (⟨ *Th.* 181-182), 10 (⟨ *Th.* 184-185), 11 (⟨ *Th.* 183-184), 12-13 (tonally ⟨ *Th.* 180-189; cf. *Th.* 21-22, 244), 14-18 (partly ⟨ *Th.* 185-187), 20 (cf. *Th.* 245), 21 (⟨ *Th.*

188-189), 25 (cf. *HF* 701), 30-31 (cf. *Pha.* 143), 31-32 (cf. *Th.* 252-254), 53 (cf. *HO* 538), 87-93 (cf. I.3.93-95; partly ⟨ *Th.* 478-482; cf. *M.* 401 ff., *Pha.* 568 ff., *Oc.* 222-226, *HO* 1582-86), 100 (⟨ *Ag.* 29 or *Th.* 193-194), 103-109 (tonally ⟨ *Th.* 244 ff.), 115 (cf. *Ag.* 30), 116 (cf. phrases in *Tr.* 168, *Pho.* 530, *Oc.* 862).

III.2.1-2, 11 (⟨ *M.* 431-432).

III.3.1 (probably ⟨ *Th.* 885), 2 (⟨ *Th.* 912-913), 3 (⟨ *Th.* 887), 4 (partly ⟨ *Th.* 901), 5 (⟨ *Th.* 889), 6 (⟨ *Th.* 890), 7 (generally ⟨ *Th.* 890-891), 8 (cf. *Th.* 887), 11 (probably ⟨ *Th.* 970-971), 17 (probably ⟨ *Th.* 971), 47 ff. (some phrases perhaps ⟨ *Th.* 473 ff.), 51-52, 57 (⟨ *M.* 222-225; *vera laus* ⟨ *Th.* 211), 54-55 (⟨ *M.* 252-253), 81-82 (cf. *HF* 925-926), 203 (⟨ *Oc.* 835, which probably colored *Absalom* III.3.200), 206 (cf. I.3.114, *HF* 342, *Oc.* 455-456), 209 (⟨ *Oc.* 829), 210 (⟨ *Oc.* 497-498), 211 (⟨ *Oc.* 830), 212 (⟨ *Oc.* 495-496; cf. *Oc.* 864), 244 (⟨ *M.* 202), 283 ff. (cf. *Pha.* 246-248), 358 (⟨ *HF* 342).

IV.1.1-4 (though probably based on Psalm lxxix, cf. *HF* 741, *HO* 1290).

IV.2.1 (⟨ *HO* 1220-22), 2 (⟨ *HO* 1219-22), 3 (cf. *HO* 1223), 4 (⟨ *HO* 1230), 5 (cf. *HO* 825), 6 (⟨ *HO* 1226-27 or *HO* 914), 43 (cf. *Th.* 450-451), 44 (cf. *Pha.* 518-520), 45 (probably ⟨ *Pha.* 520-521), 46 (⟨ *Th.* 909), 47 (perhaps ⟨ *Pha.* 515), 48 (probably ⟨ *Th.* 913 or 889), 49 (cf. *Pho.* 490), 50 (cf. the thought in *Th.* 727-729 and the wording of *HF* 1025-26), 51 (perhaps ⟨ *HF* 1007), 68 (perhaps ⟨ *Th.* 912), 70 (⟨ *M.* 281), 76 (cf. *Ag.* 491).

IV.3.1 (cf. *Oc.* 333-334), 18 (cf. *Oe.* 104-105), 19 (perhaps tonally suggested by *Th.* 176-178), 33 (cf. *Oc.* 792), 34 (cf. *Th.* 27-28), 44-45 (⟨ *Pha.* 1238), 56 (cf. *Pha.* 265, in a passage which probably influenced much of the tone and some of the words of Achitophel's speech), 66-67 (⟨ *Oe.* 180-181; cf. *Oe.* 127, *Absalom* IV.3.80), 69 (probably ⟨ *Pha.* 1228), 80 (cf. IV.3.66, but the line is aphoristic: see Quintilian, *Institutio Oratoria* VIII.v.5), 83 (cf. *HO* 714), 83 (cf. IV.3.56), 89 (probably ⟨ *Oc.* 108-110), 91 (⟨ *Pha.* 254), 92 (cf. IV.3.65-66), 95-96 (⟨ *Pha.* 258-259, *HO* 895; cf. *Absalom* IV.3.102), 101 (perhaps ⟨ *HO* 972), 102 (⟨ *Pha.* 258), 109 (cf. *HF* 309-310, *Pha.* 864), 132-133 (⟨ *Pha.* 1132-33), 134-136 (⟨ *Pha.* 1128-31; cf. *Ag.* 93, *HO* 710, *Th.* 391 ff.), 137 (⟨ *Pha.* 1132; cf. *Tr.* 394-395), 145-147 (cf. *Pha.* 1138-39, *Oc.* 895-896), 149 (cf. *Tr.* 482, *M.* 564), 152-154 (⟨ *Pha.* 981-989), 155 (⟨ *HO* 643), 156 (⟨ *HO* 617).

V.1.17 (cf. *Tr.* 642, *Oe.* 207), 23-24 (cf. I.1.29, *Tr.* 703-704), 29 (cf. *HF* 1148, *Pho.* 278-279, *HO* 745), 49-50 (⟨ *Tr.* 623-624), 53 (cf. *Pho.* 432), 62 (cf. *Pha.* 1141-42).

V.2.21 (perhaps ⟨ *Oe.* 608-609).

V.3.1 (cf. *Pha.* 995), 7^{a}, canceled (⟨ *Pha.* 997), 7^{1}, canceled (partly ⟨ *Pha.* 999), 12-14 (⟨ *Pha.* 1000-1001), 25 (transitional phrase ⟨ *Pha.* 1007), 26 (⟨ *Pha.* 1001), 61-63 (⟨ *Oe.* 337, 342-344, where it is not a simile; perhaps partly ⟨ *Pha.* 1036-38; cf. *HO* 798 ff.), 88 (cf. *M.* 304), 89 (⟨ *Pha.* 1093-94), 90 (⟨ *Pha.* 1095), 91 (⟨ *Pha.* 1097), 92 (⟨ *Pha.* 1096), 93 (⟨ *Pha.* 1107), 94-96 (⟨ *Pha.* 1099, 1102-04), 97 (⟨ *Pha.* 1094), 109-110 (⟨ *Oe.* 542-543, 532-533; partly colored by *Tr.* 1075, *Th.* 655-656), 111 (⟨ *Oe.* 535-536; cf. *Th.* 651, *Oe.* 148, 358), 112 (tonally but not phraseologically perhaps ⟨ *Oe.* 536 ff.), 113 (⟨ *Oe.* 534-535), 115-116 (cf. *Oe.* 534-535, *Pha.* 1096), 117-118 (⟨ *Pha.* 1085-87), 119-120 (Biblical, blended with

Pha. 1088-89), 130 (perhaps ⟨ *Oe.* 585-586), 141 (cf. *Tr.* 783), 142-143 (probably ⟨ *HO* 896-897).

V.4.17 (⟨ *Pha.* 1211), 19 (partly ⟨ *Pha.* 1177), 30 (perhaps ⟨ *HF* 206-207), 34 (cf. *Th.* 281-282, *Oc.* 683-684).

This list does not exhaust Watson's borrowings. There are, for example, several passages which seem to reflect Ovid (I.1.19-20, I.3.39) or Cicero (I.1.2, 55, 97). One interesting parallel exists between V.4.28-29 and Quintilian, *Institutio* VIII.v.22. Watson intended the line to heighten Absalom's tragic end, but Quintilian scorns the sentence as ridiculous: he says it was taken from a scholastic theme in which a man, ruined by the barrenness of his land, is then shipwrecked. In addition, there are scores of proverbs, which can be found in Erasmus, Tilley, and elsewhere. The Biblical source colored the wording of the play, of course, as has been amply demonstrated in the Introduction or as can be seen by looking at a Vulgate version of the Bible. The quotations from Psalms discussed in the Introduction need not be detailed here. I have not identified Watson's Psalter, and there is some evidence that he used more than one (perhaps a multiple version like *Quincuplex Psalterium* [Paris, 1509]) or an eclectic one. A number of versions were available, including three translated by Jerome: the Gallican (used in the Vulgate); the Roman; and the Hebrew (*iuxta Hebraicam Veritatem*). (For convenient versions of all three see vols. XXVIII and XXIX of Migne's *Patrologia Latina.* For Biblical manuscript variants see *Collectanea Biblica Latina,* X [1953], and XI [1954], and *Biblia Sacra iuxta Latinam Vulgatam Versionem,* X [Rome, 1953].)

A few interesting miscellaneous parallels will conclude the list: **I.1.**35 (cf. Erasmus' *Hecuba* [*Opera Omnia,* I, col. 1137D]: *Heu servitus ut semper est miserrima*); **I.2.**34-35 (cf. *Josue* ii.19, *Oc.* 431); **I.3.**58-59 (cf. *Romans* vii.15-20, Tilley B325); **II.1.**28 (⟨ *Job* i.15); **II.3.**25 (cf. *Matthew* xxxvi.52, *John* xviii.11); **II.3.**79-80, 83-84 (phrasing and some of thought ⟨ *Genesis* xxii.6-7, *Hebrews* xi.17); **III.3.**90-91 (cf. *Apocalypse* vi.15-16); **IV.2.**90 (cf. *Wisdom* xix.6); **IV.2.**160 (cf. *Genesis* xviii.14); **IV.3.**125 (cf. *Matthew* xxvi.52).

But the play's Senecanism is its most striking stylistic feature, and the parallels noted above illustrate this feature.

F. PLACE AND TIME IN *ABSALOM*

As I stated in the Introduction (Chapter IV), *Absalom* does not observe the minor unities. Below is the scene-by-scene evidence of place and time disposition in the play:

I.1. The Biblical setting (*2 Kings* xiv.31) was Absalom's house. But Watson obviously moved the scene near the king's home, as shown by Absalom's hearing the royal hinge creak (l. 116) and by Achitophel's entrance hard upon Absalom's entrance into the palace. Robinson (p. 189) mentions l. 116 as reflecting an "awareness of the setting."

I.2-3. Scene 2 occurs during the few minutes of Absalom's stay in the palace. These two scenes are continuous, for in I.2.42-43 Achitophel notes the approach of Absalom (in a speech which Robinson [p. 190] called "a *paraskeue* for the next scene"), and Absalom's entrance marks Scene 3.

That we are still before the palace is clear, because Absalom has just come from there and is still upset because of his meeting with David. And Achitophel's references to "Here" (I.2.9) and "This place" (I.3.224) clearly indicate Jerusalem. The latter line, part of Achitophel's advice that they not begin the rebellion in Jerusalem, may have been an oblique apology for the necessity of later disunity of place. In the Bible, some forty years elapsed between Absalom's reconciliation with David and his rebellion (*2 Kings* xv.7); in the play, it is a matter of minutes or, at most, hours.

II.1. Evidently enough time has elapsed for an army to be raised by the rebels, but there are no explicit references to time. The location is certainly still before the palace, where the chorus intercepts the messenger on his way in to report to David.

II.2. That the setting is Jerusalem is obvious from David's discussion of whether to flee Jerusalem; and since Populus is present (presumably the people of Jerusalem), I assume that we are still before rather than within the palace. Robinson (p. 190) observed that "the continuity between scenes is still fairly tightly preserved. [After II.1] the messenger moves into the palace to deliver the news of the rebellion. The chorus intervenes to allow time for such news to be delivered, and David appears in Scene 2 to decide his plans."

II.3. According to the Bible (*2 Kings* xvi.5), "King David came as far as Bahurim" before Semei "came out from thence" and accosted him. I have accordingly set the scene near Bahurim, "a place not far from Jerusalem beyond the Mount of Olives, on the road to the Jordan" (Fallows *et al.*, I, 229). But there are no explicit references to time and place. Is it possible that Semei's opening "Come out," which in the Bible meant out from among his followers, is intended by Watson to call David out from Jerusalem?

III.1. Robinson (p. 192) observed that "references to time and place are still present in Act III." "The chorus at the end of Act II . . . tells us that David now flees hurriedly from home. So Act III, Scene 1, has Absalom and Achitophel in command of Jerusalem." But that III.1 is not set in the heart of Jerusalem is indicated by Absalom's halting his troops (l. 1) and then ordering them to "invade the great city" (l. 45). Presumably not much time has elapsed between II.3 and III.1.

III.2. The soliloquy by Chusai does not occur in the Bible, and the scene's only indication of setting is that David orders Joab to make his way "here" —i.e., Jerusalem. He has obviously just arrived, and Robinson (p. 192) noted as an instance of Watson's awareness of time and place the fact that Chusai has just met David outside Jerusalem.

III.3. I have set the scene within the royal palace in Jerusalem because that seems the only appropriate place for such a discussion as this. If the reference to the throne (l. 3) is not figurative, it may indicate some sort of scenery (a chair?) in the St. John's production. Clearly the behavior of Achitophel (standing apart until summoned forward and thus, strangely, not commenting on Chusai's proffer of assistance) and of Chusai (withdrawing until summoned forward again) is appropriate to a royal throne room. Robinson (p. 192) called the mention of the throne another evidence of Watson's awareness of time and place.

IV.1. The Biblical setting (*2 Kings* xv.29) is Jerusalem, and Watson obviously followed the Bible; more precise location is not possible, though the sons of Sadoc and Abiathar are in the suburbs (l. 28). Sadoc has just come from David's camp and "It is apparent that in time the action is still proximate to that of Act III, since Chusai tells Sadoc that he has kept Absalom from following Achitophel's advice of moving against David 'tonight' [l. 42]" (Robinson, p. 192).

IV.2. The scene, without Biblical authority, has only vague indication of location: at l. 63 Absalom considers bringing David back "here" — i.e., Jerusalem (?) — to rot in prison. But his discussion of the battle plans sounds as though it should occur in camp; besides, at the end of III.3 he was apparently ready to leave Jerusalem. Accordingly, I have hesitantly set the scene in Galaad, where the Biblical Absalom had his camp. Robinson set both this and the next scene in Jerusalem. A considerable space of time has been necessary for all Israel from Dan to Bersabee to be armed. Thus, Absalom's general complaints about delay, including the figurative mention of elapsing centuries (ll. 28-29), and more especially his perhaps literal mention of the slipping away of the long year (l. 26) give the audience a sense of time. Perhaps these statements are another indication of Watson's feeling for what later became the unity of time. Robinson (p. 192) commented that the "great jump in time . . . comes between scenes, not between acts where, according to classical traditions, it would have been more acceptable."

IV.3. According to the Bible (*2 Kings* xvii.23), Achitophel "went home to his house and to his city [Gilo]" to die, and in the play Achitophel addresses his family and friends. But we do not have to assume the presence of family and friends; perhaps his words are apostrophic. The Bible does not state where Achitophel took the *resolution* to die — and that is the *materies* of this scene. I have doubtfully set the scene in Gilo, but Watson could have pictured Achitophel as being still in Jerusalem. So thought James Robinson (p. 194), who pointed to Achitophel's refusal to flee before David's return. But the discussion of flight is in negative terms and probably referred to flight from the country, not from the city. Perhaps by his obtrusive vagueness as to location, Watson was again paying service to the unity of place. The time of the scene can only be guessed as about the same as IV.2.

V.1-3. That the three scenes are continuous is clear from the discussions at the ends of V.1 and V.2 of the approach of messengers whose entrances mark the succeeding scenes. There is no explicit mention of location, but the arrival of the messengers hot from the battle makes a setting in David's camp very likely; and such is the setting of the Bible (*2 Kings* xviii.24-27). By the way, there is no unanimity among Bibles as to whether *mahanaim* is the name of a city or simply a common noun for camp. The time of the scenes can be inferred as not long after Act IV.

V.4. In the Bible this interview occurred in "the high chamber over the gate" (*2 Kings* xviii.33). With no great assurance I have placed Watson's scene there, necessitating the exit of all characters after V.3. Presumably a short time has elapsed since V.3, for the soldiers have become restless.

G. THE MANNER OF ABSALOM'S DEATH

In Watson's play Absalom's head is described as becoming caught in a crooked limb; thereafter his long hair became entangled in the limb, making it impossible for him to escape. Then three spears were thrust into his body (V.3.115-118, 128). Watson pointedly ignored the Bible's identification of Joab as the one responsible for slaying David's son against the father's wishes. Even more significantly, the references to Absalom's hair are an interpolation into the source, where the head but not the hair becomes locked in the branches of a tree.

Watson has prepared for this tragic end as early as the first scene (I.1.113), when he made Absalom wish for long hair. The wish was anachronistic, for it was a wish for the long hair of Tudor nobility rather than the short hair of the commoner. The Hebrews — except for the Nazarites, young persons, and later Solomon's horse guards — wore their hair short and regularly cut it with scissors (Fallows *et al.,* II, 753). The wish was not even accurate, for in the Bible we are told that Absalom "was polled once a year, because his hair was burdensome to him" (*2 Kings* xiv.26). But the wish was effective dramatic irony because of the fate which Watson was planning for his hero in the thickets of Ephraim. Perhaps the irony was intensified by the messenger's comparison (II.1.22-23) of Absalom to a lion shaking its mane.

Actually, though the Bible gave no authority for Watson's handling of the incident, there was a tradition at least as old as Josephus that Absalom's hair was the cause of his doom. The tradition was probably based on *2 Kings* xiv.26, which describes the great weight of Absalom's hair when he had it cut. In any case, Josephus described Absalom's death as follows (*The Famovs and Memorable Workes,* tr. Thomas Lodge [London, 1602], VII.ix, p. 178): "[Absalom] fearing to be surprised by his enemies, mounted vpon the royall mule, and fled in great haste. And for that by swift motion of his body, his lockes were scattered abroad, his bush of haire was entangled in a thicke and branchie tree, where he hung after a strange manner, and his mule ranne onward with great swiftness . . . but he hanging by the haire amidst the branches, sodainly fell into his enemies hands." That the tradition was current in the sixteenth century is obvious; note, for instance, Peter Martyr's statement (*In Dvos Libros Samuelis Prophetae . . . Commentarii* [Zurich, 1575], fol. 291*r*): "Quidam coma suspensum ad arborem dicunt: alij dicunt quod caput incusserit in acutum ramum, & ita pependerit. Quantum affaret galeam non habuit, forte detraxerat vt videret in fuga regiones, vel aestuabat. Forte etiam non habebant stapedes vt nunc."

Note that both these commentators felt compelled to explain how a man dressed for battle could get his hair tangled in the limbs of a tree. Watson too was sensitive to this difficulty, for as an apparent afterthought he added a line (V.3.108) explaining that Absalom lost his helmet in flight (see Textual Notes). The explanation is fairly ingenious and indicates the care which Watson was bestowing on Absalom's death. Although he took his hero off the Biblical mule and put him on a more heroic steed (V.3.106), he also wanted to emphasize his moral: Absalom's budding ambition in Act I led him to the grave in a kind of poetic justice reminiscent of Aristotle's statue of Mitys.

That the tradition of the hanging by the hair persisted is shown by its statement in W. Smith, *Concise Dictionary of the Bible* (abr. W. A. Wright [London, 1865], s.v. "Absalom"), and in Fallows *et al.;* see also "St. Swithin,"

"Absalom's Death," 8 *NQ*, I (1892), 91. One correspondent also observed the many old barbershop signs in England and on the Continent showing Absalom suspended by his hair and advising that a wig would have saved his life (T. R. G., "The Sign of Absalom Suspended by His Hair," 5 *NQ*, X [1878], 413).

H. THE DEATH OF CAIN

In I.2.33-36 of *Absalom*, Achitophel alludes to the death of Cain at the hands of Lamech, a descendant of Cain and Mathusael. The Biblical authority for the allusion is not very explicit: in *Genesis* iv.23-24, Lamech laments to his wives, "I have slain a man to the wounding of myself, and a stripling to my own bruising. Sevenfold vengeance shall be taken for Cain, but for Lamech seventy times sevenfold." The Douay commentators noted, "So hard and obscure is this place, that S. Hierom required by S. Damasus Pope to expound it, dareth not affirme anie one sense for certaine, but proposing diuers, which the text may seme to bear, wisheth the Pope . . . to examine al more at large" (*The Holie Bible* . . . [Doway, 1609-10], I, 16). The Geneva Version interpreted the speech as a boast that "there is none so lustie that were able to resist [Lamech], although he were alreadie wounded. Hee mocked at God's sufferance in Kain" (*The Bible* . . . [London, (1578)], fol. 2*v*). But the tradition which Watson was obviously using was the following one reported by the Douay commentators (*loc. cit.*): "The most probable exposition semeth to be gathered out of the Hebrewes Tradition, that this Lamech . . . much addicted to hunting, and his eyes decaying, vsed in that exercise the direction of a young man his nephew, the sonne of Tubalcain. VVho seing something moue in the bushes, supposing it to be a wild beast, willed his grandfather to shoote at the same: which he did, and stroke the marke with a deadlie wound, and . . . found it to be old Cain. VVhereupon sore amazed, afflicted, and moued with great passion, did so beate the young man, for his il direction, that he also died of the drie blows." God had promised, of course, that though Cain should wander "A fugitive and a vagabond . . . upon the earth" yet "whosoever shall kill Cain shall be punished sevenfold" (*Genesis* xiv.12-15). That the tradition quoted from the Douay Version was current in the sixteenth century is shown by its statement, on the authority of Philo, in Thomas Cooper's *Thesavrvs* ("Dictionarivm Historicum & Poeticum Propria Locorum & Personarum Vocabula," s.v. "Cain"): "Finally [Cain] was slaine by Lamech, when he was of the age of .730. yeares."

LIST OF WORKS USED

The following list includes a number of works not cited above, but it is not intended to be a complete reference bibliography for the various areas investigated. All works listed have been of some use, negative or positive, in my work. I have listed a few reference works, such as lexicons, which provided specific information to me; but I have not included such standard reference tools as *D.N.B.*, DuCange's *Glossarium, Harper's Latin Dictionary,* Martin's *Record Interpreter,* Graesse's *Orbis Latinus,* etc. I have not listed a number of manuscripts which I checked unavailingly for samples of the handwriting which appears in the *Absalom* manuscript. Although I checked nearly a hundred Bibles, old and new, for spellings and readings, I have listed only those which were most useful to me in my work.

The arrangement is basically alphabetical, all entries being in a single list by author or title. However, the works in three major categories are listed together under common headings, alphabetized by those headings: "Bible" (including Psalters and parts of Bibles); "Catalogues" (containing all catalogues and books about collectors and collections of books, manuscripts, and libraries); and "Commonplaces." Under these headings the arrangement is alphabetical. When more than one edition of a work is listed, the several editions are given in chronological order. Commentaries (on the Bible and on classical authors) are normally listed by the commentators' names.

I have shortened titles where feasible and have silently expanded old typographical abbreviations.

Adams, W. Davenport. *A Dictionary of the Drama.* London, 1904.

Allibone, S. Austin. *A Critical Dictionary of English Literature.* 3 vols. London, 1859-71.

Amerbachius, Vitius. *In Artem Poëticam Horatij Commentaria.* Strassburg, 1543.

Aphthonius. *Rhetorica Progymnasmata.* Paris, 1541.

Arber, Edward, ed. *A Transcript of the Registers of the Company of Stationers of London: 1554-1640 A.D.* 5 vols. London and (vol. V) Birmingham, 1875-94.

Aristotle. *On the Art of Fiction: An English Translation of Aristotle's* Poetics. By L. J. Potts. Cambridge, 1953.

———. *Francisci Robortelli Vtinensis in Librum Aristotelis De Arte Poetica Explicationes.* Florence, 1548.

Ascham, Roger. *Familiarum Epistolarum Libri Tres.* Edited by Edward Grant. London, [1576].

———. *Epistolarum, Libri Quatuor.* [Edited by William Elstob]. Oxford, 1703.

Ascham, Roger. *The Scholemaster.* London, 1570.

———. *The Schoolmaster.* Edited by James Upton. London, 1711.

———. *The Scholemaster.* Edited by James Upton. London, 1743.

———. *The Scholemaster.* Edited by John E. B. Mayor. London, 1863.

———. *The Whole Works.* Edited by J. A. Giles. 3 vols. London, 1864-65.

Baker, David Erskine, Isaac Reed, and Stephen Jones. *Biographia Dramatica; or, a Companion to the Playhouse.* 3 vols. London, 1812.

Baker, Thomas. *History of the College of St. John the Evangelist, Cambridge.* Edited by John E. B. Mayor. 2 vols. Cambridge, 1869.

Baldwin, Thomas Whitfield. *On the Literary Genetics of Shakspere's Plays 1592-1594.* Urbana, Ill., 1959.

———. Review of Gertrude Marian Sibley, *The Lost Plays and Masques 1500-1642. MLN,* XLIX (December, 1934), 552-553.

———. *William Shakspere's Five-Act Structure.* Urbana, Ill., 1947.

———. *William Shakspere's Small Latine and Lesse Greeke.* 2 vols. Urbana, Ill., 1944.

Bale, John. *The Dramatic Writings.* Edited by John S. Farmer. Early English Dramatists. London, 1907.

———. *Illustrium Maioris Britanniae Scriptorum . . . Summarium.* Wesel, 1548.

———. *Bales Kynge Johan nach der Handschrift in der Chatsworth Collection in Faksimile herausgegeben.* Edited by W. Bang. Materialen zur Kunde des älteren englischen Dramas, XXV. Louvain, 1909.

———. *King Johan.* Edited by J. H. P. Pafford. Malone Society Reprints. Oxford, 1931.

Bateson, Mary, ed. *Grace Book β Part II Containing the Accounts of the Proctors of the University of Cambridge, 1511-1544.* Cambridge Antiquarian Society. Luard Memorial Series, III. Cambridge, 1905.

Beazeley, Michael. *Tracings of Watermarks at Canterbury.* 2 vols. (MS). Additional MSS. 38,637-38 (B.M.).

The Bible. Translated According to the Ebrew and Greeke. [The Geneva Version]. London, [1578].

———. *Biblia Sacra iuxta Latinam Vulgatam Versionem.* Rome, 1953.

———. *Biblia Sacra Vulgatae Editionis.* Nova editio. By Gianfranco Nolli and A. Vaccari. 4 vols. Rome, 1955.

———. *S. Eusebii Hieronymi . . . Opera Omnia.* In *Patrologiae [Latinae] Cursus Completus,* XXII-XXX. Edited by J.-P. Migne. Paris, 1845-65.

———. *The Holie Bible Faithfvlly Translated into English, ovt of the Avthentical Latin.* [Douay Version]. 2 vols. Doway, 1609-10.

———. *Pentateuchus Moysi . . . Libri Regum IIII. . . .* 8 parts. Paris, 1532, 1531-35.

———. *Pentateuchus Moysi . . . Libri Regum IIII. . . .* 8 parts. Paris, 1539, 1531-40.

———. *Psalterium iuxta Hebraeos.* Edited by Dom Henri de Sainte-Marie. *Collectanea Biblica Latina,* XI. Rome, 1954.

———. *Le Psautier Romain et les Autres Anciens Psautiers Latins.* Edited by Dom. R. Weber. *Collectanea Biblica Latina,* X. Rome, 1953.

———. *Quincuplex Psalterium. Gallicum. Romanum. Hebraicum. Vetus. Conciliatum.* Paris, 1509.

Boas, Frederick S. *University Drama in the Tudor Age.* Oxford, 1914.
———. "University Plays Tudor and Early Stuart Periods." *Cambridge History of English Literature.* Edited by Sir A. W. Ward and A. R. Waller. Cambridge, 1910. VI, 330-369.
Bridgett, T. E., and T. F. Knox. *The True Story of the Catholic Hierarchy Deposed by Queen Elizabeth.* London, [1889].
Briquet, C. M. *Les Filigranes.* 4 vols. Paris, 1907.
Buchanan, George. *De Prosodia Libellvs.* Edinburgh, [?1595].
———. *Iephthes sive Votum, Tragoedia.* Paris, 1554.
———. *The Jephtha and Baptist.* Translated by Alexander Gibb. Edinburgh, 1870.
Calepinus, Ambrosius. *Dictionarivm.* Venice, 1548.
Canter, Howard Vernon. *Rhetorical Elements in the Tragedies of Seneca.* Illinois Studies in Language and Literature, X. Urbana, 1925.
Catalogues, etc. *The Ashburnham Library.* 3 vols. London, 1897-98.
———. [Bernard, Edward]. *Catalogi Librorum Manuscriptorum Angliae et Hiberniae in Unum Collecti.* Oxford, 1697.
———. [Bond, Edward A.]. *Description of the Ashburnham Manuscripts, and Account of Offers of Purchase.* [London, 1883].
———. *Calendar of the Manuscripts of the Most Hon. The Marquis of Salisbury.* Historical Manuscripts Commission [Ninth Report]. 18 vols. London, 1883-1940.
———. *Catalogue of Some Curiosities and Manuscripts Omitted in the Catalogue of the Library of Peter LeNeve.* [London, 1731].
———. *Catalogue of the Duplicates and a Considerable Portion of the Library of Sir John Sebright, Bart. . . . Also the Very Curious Collection of Manuscripts . . . Collected by Sir Roger Twysden and Mr. E. Lhwyd.* [London, 1807].
———. *Catalogue of the . . . Library of John Ives, jun. Esq. . . .* [and] *of Another Gentleman.* [London, 1777].
———. *Catalogue of the . . . Library . . . of . . . Richard Gough, Esq.* [London, 1810].
———. *Catalogue of the Manuscripts at Ashburnham Place.* London, 1853.
———. *Catalogue of the Manuscripts Preserved in the Library of the University of Cambridge.* 5 vols. Cambridge, 1856-67.
———. *Catalogue of the Valuable Library Collected by . . . Peter LeNeve.* [London, 1731].
———. *Catalogue of the Very Valuable Library . . . of the Late Andrew Coltee Ducarel.* [London, 1786].
———. Delisle, L. V. *Les Manuscrits du Comte d'Ashburnham.* Paris, 1883.
———. DeRicci, Seymour. *English Collectors of Books and Manuscripts (1530-1930) and Their Marks of Ownership.* Cambridge, 1930.
———. Dibdin, Thomas Frognall. *Bibliomania;* or *Book Madness.* London, 1811.
———. *Eighth Report of the Royal Commission on Historical Manuscripts.* London, 1881.
———. Haenel, Gustav. *Catalogi Librorum Manuscriptorum, Qui in Bibliothecis Galliae, Helvetiae, Belgii, Britanniae M., Hispaniae, Lusitaniae Asservantur.* Leipzig, 1830.

Catalogues, etc. Horwood, Alfred J. "The Manuscripts of the Right Honourable Lord De L'Isle and Dudley, at Penshurst, Co. Kent." *Third Report of the Royal Commission on Historical Manuscripts.* London, 1872. Appendix, pp. 227-233.

———. James, Montague R. *A Descriptive Catalogue of the Manuscripts in the Library of Corpus Christi College Cambridge.* 2 vols. Cambridge, 1912.

———. Kingsford, C. L., and William A. Shaw. *Report on the Manuscripts of Lord de L'Isle and Dudley Preserved at Penshurst Place, Kent.* Historical Manuscripts Commission Report No. 77. 4 vols. London, 1925-42.

———. [Mattingly, Harold, and I. A. K. Burnett]. *List of Catalogues of English Book Sales 1676-1900 Now in the British Museum.* Edited by A. F. Pollard. London, 1915.

———. *A Most Excellent and Curious Collection of Paintings, Drawings, and Prints, Marble Statues, and Heads.* [London, 1703].

———. *Musaeum Thoresbyanum. A Catalogue of the . . . Collection of . . . Ralph Thoresby.* [London, 1764].

———. O'Conor, Charles. *Bibliotheca MS. Stowensis. A Descriptive Catalogue of the Manuscripts in the Stowe Library.* 2 vols. Buckingham, 1818-19.

———. [Paoli, C.]. *I Codici Ashburnhamiani della R. Biblioteca Mediceo-Laurenziana de Firenze.* Ministero dell'Istruzione Pubblica Indici e Cataloghi, No. 8. Rome, 1887.

———. Quaritch, Bernard, *et al.*, eds. *Contributions Towards a Dictionary of English Book-Collectors, as Also of Some Foreign Collectors.* 14 parts (1 vol.). London, 1892-1921.

———. [Scott, Edward J. L., *et al.*]. *Catalogue of the Stowe Manuscripts in the British Museum.* 2 vols. London, 1895.

———. *Sixth Report of the Royal Commission on Historical Manuscripts.* London, 1877.

———. [Smith, William James]. *Catalogue of the Important Collection of Manuscripts, from Stowe.* [London, 1849].

Chambers, E. K. *The Elizabethan Stage.* 4 vols. Oxford, 1923.

———. *The Mediaeval Stage.* 2 vols. Oxford, 1903.

Churchill, George B., and Wolfgang Keller. "Die lateinischen Universitäts-Dramen Englands in der Zeit der Königin Elisabeth." *Sh.-Jbch.*, XXXIV (1898), 221-323.

Cicero. *Opera Omnia.* Edited by Jo. Augustus Ernest. 8 vols. Halle, 1819.

C[okayne], G[eorge] E[dward]. *The Complete Peerage.* New edition. By Vicary Gibbs *et al.* 12 vols. (and in progress). London, 1910-53.

Commonplaces. *Aristotelis, et Philosophorum Complurium Aliorum Sententiae Omnes Vndiquaque Selectissimae.* Antwerp, 1542.

———. *Auctoritates Aristotelis Senece Boetii Platonis Apulei Affricani Empedoclis Porphirii et Guilberti Porritani.* [?Paris, ?1520].

———. Barlandus, Adrianus. *Proverbialivm Versvvm ex Principe Poetarum Vergilio Collectanea.* Basel, [1535].

———. Erasmus, Desiderius. *Adagiorvm . . . Chiliades Qvatvor.* Geneva, 1612.

Commonplaces. Erasmus, Desiderius. *L. Annaei Senecae Philosophi Flores. . . . Item L. Annaei Senecae Tragici, Sententiae.* Amsterdam, 1642.

———. Haineccius, Martinus. *Ervctvs Terentiani.* Leipzig, 1614.

———. Langus Caesaremontanus, Josephus. *Novissima Polyanthea.* Venice, 1616.

———. Lycosthenes Rubeaquensis, Conradus. *Apophthegmatvm ex Optimis Vtrivsqve Lingvae Scriptoribvs.* Paris, 1567.

———. Otto, A. *Die Sprichwörter und sprichwörtlichen Redensarten der Römer.* Leipzig, 1890.

———. Pareus, Joh. Philippus. *Electa Plavtina.* Neustadt, 1617.

———. *Prouerbia Senece.* Daventrie, [1491].

———. [*Prouerbia Senecae Secundum Ordinem Alphabeti*]. Brescia, [1500].

———. Scutteputaeus, Hubertus. *L. Annaei Senecae Vtrivsqve, et Philosophi, et Poetae Sententiae.* Antwerp, 1576.

———. *Senece Prouerbia.* [Paris, ?1510].

———. *Sententiae Aliquot Memoratv Non Indignae.* Paris, 1543.

———. *Sententiae Ciceronis, Demosthenis, ac Terentii. Dogmata Philosophica. Item, Apophthegmata Quaedam Pia.* London, 1619.

———. *Sententiae et Proverbia ex Poetis Latinis. His adiecimus Leosthenis Colvandri Sententias Prophanas.* Venice, [?*ca.* 1550].

———. Smith, William George. *The Oxford Dictionary of English Proverbs.* Oxford, 1935.

———. Textor, Ioannes Ravisius. *Epitheta.* [Geneva], 1588.

———. ———. *Epithetorvm . . . Opus Absolutissimum.* Basel, 1592.

———. Tilley, Morris Palmer. *A Dictionary of the Proverbs in England in the Sixteenth and Seventeenth Centuries.* Ann Arbor, Mich., 1950.

Cooper, Charles Henry. *Annals of Cambridge.* 5 vols. Vol. V edited by John William Cooper. Cambridge, 1842-1908.

——— and Thompson Cooper. *Athenae Cantabrigienses.* 3 vols. Vol. III edited by Henry Bradshaw *et al.* Cambridge, 1858-1913.

Cooper, Thomas. *Thesavrvs Lingvae Romanae & Britannicae.* London, 1573.

Craig, Hardin. *English Religious Drama of the Middle Ages.* Oxford, 1955.

Creizenach, Wilhelm. *Geschichte des neueren Dramas.* 5 vols. Halle, 1893-1923.

Cunliffe, John W., ed. *Early English Classical Tragedies.* Oxford, 1912.

———. "Early English Tragedy." *Cambridge History of English Literature.* Edited by Sir A. W. Ward and A. R. Waller. Cambridge, 1910. V, 68-99, 438-445.

———. *The Influence of Seneca on Elizabethan Tragedy.* New York, 1893.

de Bofarull y Sans, Don Francisco. *Heraldic Watermarks or La Heráldica en la Filigrana del Papel.* Translated by A. J. Henschel. Hilversum, 1956.

Donno, Elizabeth Story, ed. *Sir John Harington's A New Discourse of a Stale Subject, Called the Metamorphosis of Ajax.* London, 1962.

Eckhardt, Eduard. *Das englische Drama im Zeitalter der Reformation und der Hochrenaissance.* Geschichte der englischen Literatur im Grundriss. Berlin, 1928.

[Egerton, John]. *Egerton's Theatrical Remembrancer.* London, 1788.

Erasmus, Desiderius. *Hecvba et Iphigenia in Avlide Evripidis Tragoediae in Latinum Tralatae Erasmo.* Vienna, 1511.

Erasmus, Desiderius. *Opera Omnia.* 10 vols. Utrecht, 1703-06.

Fallows, Samuel, *et al. The Popular and Critical Bible Encyclopaedia and Scriptural Dictionary.* 3 vols. Chicago, 1909.

Fischer, Rudolf. *Zur Kunstentwicklung der englischen Tragödie von ihren ersten Anfängen bis zu Shakespeare.* Strassburg, 1893.

Flaminius, M. Antonius. *In Librvm Psalmorvm Brevis Explanatio.* Venice, 1545.

Fleay, Frederick Gard. *A Biographical Chronicle of the English Drama 1559-1642.* 2 vols. London, 1891.

Foxe, John. *Actes and Monuments.* Edited by Stephen Reed Cattley. 8 vols. London, 1837-41.

———. *Christvs Trivmphans, Comoedia Apocalyptica.* Basel, 1556.

Fuller, Thomas. *The History of the University of Cambridge, from the Conquest to the Year 1634.* Edited by Marmaduke Prickett and Thomas Wright. Cambridge, 1840.

G., T. R. "The Sign of Absalom Suspended by His Hair." 5 *NQ*, X (1878), 413.

Gaisford, Thomas, ed. *Scriptores Latini Rei Metricae. Manuscriptorum Codicum Ope Subinde Refinxit.* Oxford, 1837.

Grande Encyclopédie Inventaire Raissoné des Sciences, des Lettres et des Arts. 31 vols. Paris, [1886-1902].

Greg, W. W., ed. *Henslowe's Diary.* 2 vols. London, 1904-08.

Grimald, Nicholas. *Archipropheta, Tragoedia Iam Recens in Lucem Edita.* Cologne, 1548.

———. *Christus Redivivus, Comoedia Tragica.* Cologne, 1543.

———. *The Life and Poems.* Edited by L. R. Merrill. Yale Studies in English, LXIX. New Haven, Conn., 1925.

Gualtherus, Rudolphus. *De Syllabarvm et Carminvm Ratione, Libri Dvo.* Zurich, 1549.

Halliwell, James O. *A Dictionary of Old English Plays.* London, 1860.

Harbage, Alfred. *Annals of English Drama 975-1700.* Philadelphia, 1940.

Hardie, William Ross. *Res Metrica: An Introduction to the Study of Greek and Roman Versification.* Oxford, 1920.

Harris, Jesse W. *John Bale: A Study in the Minor Literature of the Reformation.* Illinois Studies in Language and Literature, XXV. Urbana, 1940.

Hazlitt, William Carew. *A Manual for the Collector and Amateur of Old English Plays.* London, 1892.

Heawood, Edward. "Sources of Early English Paper-Supply." *Library,* 2nd ser., X (1929-30), 282-307, 427-454.

———. *Watermarks Mainly of the 17th and 18th Centuries.* Monumenta Chartae Papyraceae Historiam Illustrantia, I. Edited by E. J. Labarre. Hilversum, 1950.

Hephaestion. 'ΕΓΧΕΙΡΙΔΙΟΝ ΠΕΡΙ ΜΕΤΡΩΝ ΚΑΙ ΠΟΙΗΜΑΤΩΝ. *The Enkheiridion of Hehfaistiown Concerning Metres and Poems.* Translated by Thomas Foster Barham. Cambridge, 1843.

Herrick, Marvin T. *The Fusion of Horatian and Aristotelian Literary Criticism.* Illinois Studies in Language and Literature, XXXII. Urbana, 1946.

Hoche, Max. *Die Metra des Tragikers Seneca. Ein Beitrag zur lateinischen Metrik.* Halle, 1862.

Holyoke, Francis. *Dictionarivm Etymologicvm Latinvm.* [London, 1633].
Horace. *De Arte Poetica Opusculum Aureum ab Ascensio Familiariter Expositum. . . .* Paris, 1505.
———. *Ars Poetica, cum Trium Doctissimorum, A. Tani Parrhasii, Acronis, Porphyrionis.* Paris, 1533.
———. *De Arte Poetica Iacobi Grifoli Lucinianensis Interpretatione Explicatus.* Florence, 1550.
———. *Horativs.* [*Opera.* Edited by Benedictus Philologus.] Florence, 1503.
———. *Poemata.* Florence, 1514.
———. *Poemata Omnia.* [Venice, 1519].
———. *Satires, Epistles and Ars Poetica.* Edited and translated by H. Rushton Fairclough. Loeb Classical Library. London, 1939.
Josephus, Flavius. *The Famovs and Memorable Workes.* Translated by Thomas Lodge. London, 1602.
Kastner, L. E., and H. B. Charlton, eds. *The Poetical Works of Sir William Alexander Earl of Stirling.* The Scottish Text Society. 2 vols. Edinburgh, 1921-29.
Katterfeld, Alfred. *Roger Ascham. Sein Leben und seine Werke.* Strassburg, 1879.
Keil, Henrich, ed. *Grammatici Latini.* 7 vols. and supplement. Leipzig, 1857, 1855-80.
Kunitz, Stanley J., and Howard Haycraft. *British Authors Before 1800: A Biographical Dictionary.* New York, 1952.
LeClert, Louis. "Armorial Historique de l'Aube." *Memoires de la Société Académique d'Agriculture des Sciences, Arts et Belles-Lettres du Département de l'Aube,* LXXV (3rd ser., XLVIII) (1911), 65-421.
———. *Le Papier.* 2 vols. Paris, 1926.
[Lily, William]. *A Shorte Introdvction of Grammar Generally To Be Vsed.* [London], 1567. Facsimile edition. With an Introduction by Vincent J. Flynn. Scholars' Facsimiles & Reprints. New York, 1945.
Lucas, F. L. *Seneca and Elizabethan Tragedy.* Cambridge, 1922.
Martyr, Peter. *In Dvos Libros Samuelis Prophetae . . . Commentarii.* Zurich, 1575.
Mazzuchelli Bresciano, Conti Giammaria. *Gli Scrittori d'Italia cioe Notizie Storiche, e Critiche Intorno alle Vite, e agli Scritti dei Letterati Italiani.* 2 vols., 8 parts (discontinued). Brescia, 1753-63.
Mendell, Clarence W. *Our Seneca.* New Haven, Conn., 1941.
Meres, Francis. *Palladis Tamia. Wits Treasvry Being the Second Part of Wits Commonwealth.* London, 1598.
———. *Francis Meres's Treatise "Poetrie": A Critical Edition.* By Don Cameron Allen. Illinois Studies in Language and Literature, XVI. Urbana, 1933.
Moratín, D. Leandro Fernandez de. *Obras . . . Dadas á Luz por la Real Academia de Historia.* 2 vols. Madrid, 1830-31.
Mullinger, James Bass. *The University of Cambridge from the Earliest Times to the Royal Injunctions of 1535.* Cambridge, 1873.
———. *The University of Cambridge from the Royal Injunctions of 1535 to the Accession of Charles the First.* Cambridge, 1884.
Murer, Josias. *Absolom ein Spyl von einer jungen Burgerschafft. . . .* Zurich, 1565.

Murray, David. *George Buchanan.* Glasgow Quatercentenary Studies 1906. Glasgow, 1907.
Nashe, Thomas. *Works.* Edited by R. B. McKerrow. 5 vols. London, 1910.
Neale, C. M. *The Early Honours Lists (1498-9 to 1746-7) of the University of Cambridge.* Bury St. Edmunds, 1909.
Nichols, John Gough, ed. *Literary Remains of King Edward the Sixth.* 2 vols. London, 1857.
Niger, Franciscus. *Grammatica . . . cum Metrica Arte Eiusdem.* Basel, [1500].
Oldfather, William Abbott, *et al. Index Verborvm Qvae in Senecae Fabvlis Necnon in Octavia Praetexta Reperivntvr.* Illinois Studies in Language and Literature, IV. Urbana, 1918.
"Our Weekly Gossip." *The Athenaeum,* No. 1122 (April 28, 1849), p. 437; No. 1123 (May 5, 1849), p. 463.
Ovid. *Opera.* 5 vols. Oxford, 1825.
Pedimontius, Franciscus Philippus. *Ecphrasis in Horatii Flacci Artem Poeticam.* Venice, 1546.
Peele, George. *The Love of King David and Fair Bethsabe. With the Tragedie of Absalon 1599.* Edited by W. W. Greg. Malone Society Reprints. Oxford, 1912.
Peultier, Etienne, *et al. Concordantiarum Universae Scripturae Sacrae Thesaurus.* Cursus Sacrae Scripturae. Edited by R. Cornely *et al.* Pars Tertia, Textus V Concordantiae Latinae. [Paris, 1896].
Phillipps, Edward. *Theatrum Poetarum Anglicanorum.* Edited by S. E. Brydges. Canterbury, 1800.
"The Plays Acted Before the University of Cambridge." *The Retrospective Review,* XII (1825), 1-42.
Porson, Richard, ed. ΕΥΡΙΠΙΔΟΩ ΕΚΑΒΗ. *Euripidis Hecuba.* London, 1808.
Puteo, Franciscus de. *Cathena Avrea Svper Psalmos.* Paris, 1530.
Putschius, Helia, ed. *Grammaticae Latinae Avctores Antiqvi.* Hanover, 1605.
Quintilian. *The Institutio Oratoria.* Edited and translated by H. E. Butler. Loeb Classical Library. 4 vols. London, 1920-22.
Reynolds, E. E. *Saint John Fisher.* New York, 1955.
Robertson, William. *A Dictionary of Latin Phrases.* New edition. London, 1829.
Robinson, James Edward. "The Dramatic Unities in the Renaissance." Unpublished Ph.D. dissertation, University of Illinois. Urbana, 1959.
"St. Swithin." "Absalom's Death." 8 *NQ,* I (1892), 91.
Saintsbury, George. "Elizabethan Criticism." *Cambridge History of English Literature.* Edited by Sir A. W. Ward and A. R. Waller. Cambridge, 1909. III, 329-355.
Schoepperus, Iacobus. *Ectrachelistis, sive Ioannes Decollatus, Tragoedia Noua & Sacra.* Cologne, 1546.
———. *Tentatvs Abrahamvs Actio Sacra, Comice Recens Descripta.* Cologne, 1564.
Searle, William George, ed. *Grace Book* Γ *Containing the Records of the University of Cambridge for the Years 1501-1542.* Cambridge, 1908.

Seneca. *Sententiae.* Edited by Hubertus Scutteputaeus. Antwerp, 1576.
———. [*Tragoediae*]. "Lvcii Anaei Senecae Cordvbensis: Hercvles Fvrens Tragedia Prima Incipit." [Ferrara, ?1474].
———. *Tragoediae . . . cum Commento.* Lyons, 1491.
———. *Tragedie . . . cum Commento.* Venice, 1492.
———. [*Tragoediae cum Duobus Commentis*]. Venice, 1493.
———. *Tragoediae . . . cum Duobus Commentariis . . . Bernardini Marmitae & Danielis Gaietani.* [Venice, 1498].
———. *Tragoediae.* [Florence, 1506].
———. *Tragoediae.* [Florence, 1513].
———. *Tragoediae Pristinae Integritati Restitutae: Per Exactissimi Iudicii Viros Post Auantium & Philologum D. Erasmum Roterodamum. Gerardum Vercellanum. Aegidium Maserium . . . Explanatae . . . Tribus Commentariis. G. Bernardino Marmita . . . Daniele Gaietano . . . Iodoco Badio Ascensio.* [Paris, 1514].
———. *Tragoediae.* Edited by Hier. Avantius. [Venice, 1517].
———. *Opus Tragoediarum . . . cum Expositoribus . . . Bernardino Marmita: & Daniele Gaietano.* [Venice, 1522].
———. *Tragoediae X.* Basel, 1529.
———. *Tragoediae Septem.* Lyons, 1541.
———. *Tragoediae.* Lyons, 1554.
———. *Tragoediae X.* Basel, 1563.
———. *Tragoediae.* Edited by Georgius Fabricius Chemnicensis. Leipzig, 1566.
———. *In . . . Tragoedias Decem . . . Amplissima Aduersaria; Quae Loco Commentarii Esse Possunt. Ex Bibliotheca Martini Antonii Delrio.* Antwerp, 1576.
———. *Tragoediae.* Lyons, 1584.
———. *Tragoediae.* Antwerp, 1588.
———. *Tragoediae.* London, 1589.
———. *Decem Tragoediae . . . Opera Francisci Raphelengii Fr. F. Plantiniani, Ope V. Cl. Iusti Lipsi, Emendatiores.* Lyons, 1589.
———. *Tragoediae.* Edited by Rudolf Peiper and Gustav Richter. Bibliotheca Teubneriana. Leipzig, 1867.
———. *His Tenne Tragedies.* Translated by Thomas Newton, Jasper Heywood, *et al.* Edited by Thomas Newton. London, 1581. Tudor Translations, vols. XI-XII. With an Introduction by T. S. Eliot. London, 1927.
———. *Tragedies.* With an English Translation by Frank Justus Miller. Loeb Classical Library. 2 vols. Cambridge, Mass., 1953.
Setonus, Joannes. *Dialectica.* London, 1545.
Short Guide to Books on Watermarks Offered to Subscribers of Monumenta Chartae Papyraceae Historiam Illustrantia. Hilversum, 1955.
Sibley, Gertrude Marian. *The Lost Plays and Masques 1500-1642.* Cornell Studies in English, XIX. Ithaca, N.Y., 1933.
[Smith, G. C. Moore]. "The Academic Drama at Cambridge: Extracts from College Records." *Collections,* Vol. II, Part II. Malone Society Reprints. Oxford, 1923.
———. *College Plays Performed in the University of Cambridge.* Cambridge, 1923.

Smith, G. C. Moore. "Plays Performed in Cambridge Colleges Before 1585." *Fasciculus Ioanni Willis Clark Dicatus.* Cambridge, 1909, pp. 265-273.

Smith, William. *Concise Dictionary of the Bible.* Abridged by W. A. Wright. London, 1865.

———, ed. *Dictionary of Greek and Roman Biography and Mythology.* 3 vols. London, 1850-51.

Spenser, Edmund. *The Poetical Works.* Edited by J. C. Smith and E. de Selincourt. London, 1912.

———. *The Works.* Variorum edition. By Edwin Greenlaw *et al.* 10 vols. Baltimore, 1932-57.

Starnes, De Witt T. *Renaissance Dictionaries English-Latin and Latin-English.* Austin, Tex., 1954.

[Stephanus, Robertus]. *Dictionarivm, sev Latinae Linguae Thesaurus.* 2 vols. Paris, 1536.

Stirling, Brents. "Spenser and Thomas Watson, Bishop of Lincoln." *PQ,* X (1931), 321-328.

Stoppelaar, J. D. de. *Het Papier in de Nederlanden gedurende de Middeleeuwen, inzonderheid in Zeeland.* Middelburg, 1869.

"The Stowe Manuscripts." *The Athenaeum,* No. 1120 (April 14, 1849), pp. 380-381; No. 1121 (April 21, 1849), pp. 407-408.

Strype, John. *Annals of the Reformation.* 4 vols. Oxford, 1824.

———. *Eccesiastical Memorials.* 3 vols. Oxford, 1822.

———. *The History of the Life and Acts of . . . Edmund Grindal.* Oxford, 1821.

———. *Life of the Learned John Cheke.* Oxford, 1821.

———. *Memorials of . . . Thomas Cranmer.* 2 vols. Oxford, 1840.

Strzelecki, Ladislaus. *De Senecae Trimetro Iambico Quaestiones Selectae.* Polska Akademja Umiejętności Rozprawy Wydziału Filologicznego, LXV. Krakow, 1938.

Tannenbaum, Samuel A. *The Handwriting of the Renaissance.* New York, 1930.

Tanner, Thomas. *Bibliotheca Britannico-Hibernica.* London, 1748.

Terence. *Terentius in Sua Metra Restitvtvs.* Edited by Benedictus Philologus. Florence, 1505.

———. *Comoediae ex D. Erasmi et Io. Rivii Attendorientis Castigationibus Multo Absolutissimae.* Cologne, 1535.

———. *Comoediae.* Edited by Richard Bentley. Paris, 1846.

Terentianus, Maurus. *De Litteris, Syllabis et Metris Horatii.* Mailand, 1497.

———. *De Litteris, Syllabis, Pedibvs, et Metris. Item, Eiusdem Argumenti, Marii Victorini . . . de Orthographia, et Ratione Carminvm Libri IIII.* [Heidelberg], 1584.

Thomas, Joseph, ed. *Universal Pronouncing Dictionary of Biography and Mythology.* Fifth edition. Philadelphia, [1930].

Thylesius, Antonius. *Imber Aureus, Tragoedia Nova.* Antwerp, 1546.

Venn, John, ed. *Grace Book Δ Containing the Records of the University of Cambridge for the Years 1542-1589.* Cambridge, 1910.

——— and J. A. Venn. *Alumni Cantabrigienses.* Part I, 4 vols. Cambridge, 1922-27.

Vergil. [*Opera*] *Varietate Lectionis . . . a Christ. Gottl. Heyre.* Fourth edition. By G. P. E. Wagner. 5 vols. Leipzig, 1830.

Volkmann, Richard. *Rhetorik und Metrik der Griechen und Römer.* Third edition. By H. Gleditsch and Caspar Hammer. Handbuch der klassischen Altertumswissenschaft, II. Munich, 1901.

[Watson, Thomas]. *Certayne Experyments and Approved Medicines Good for ⟨Those That⟩ Be Any Wayes Diseased.* Sloane MS. 62, art. 1, fols. 1-15 (B.M.).

———. *Holsome and Catholyke Doctryne Concerninge the Seuen Sacramentes of Chrystes Church.* London, 1558.

———. *Sermons on the Sacraments.* Edited by T. E. Bridgett. London, 1876.

———. *Twoo Notable Sermons . . . Concerninge the Reall Presence of Christes Body and Bloude in the Blessed Sacrament: & Also the Masse, Which Is the Sacrifice of the Newe Testament.* London, 1554.

Watt, Robert. *Bibliotheca Britannica; or a General Index to British and Foreign Literature.* 4 vols. Edinburgh, 1824.

Way, Albertus, ed. *Promptorium Parvulorum sive Clericorum, Dictionarius Anglo-Latinus Princeps, Auctore Fratre Galfrido Grammatico Dicto . . . Northfolciensi, Circa A.D. M.CCCC.XL.* Camden Society, No. XXV (vol. I), LIV (vol. II), LXXXIX (vol. III). London, 1843-65.

Weller, Emil. *Das alte Volks-Theater der Schweiz.* Frauenfeld, 1863.

Whittinton, Robert. *De Syllabarum Quantitatibus Opusculum.* [London], 1519.

Willichius, Iodocus. *Commentaria in Artem Poeticam Horatii.* Strassburg, 1539.

Wood, Anthony à. *Athenae Oxonienses.* 2 vols. London, 1691-92.

Zovitius, Iacobus. *Didascalvs. Comoedia.* Cologne, 1541.